A Treasury of
ITALIAN FOLKLORE
AND HUMOR

A Treasury of
ITALIAN FOLKLORE
AND HUMOR

Henry D. Spalding

jɒ | JONATHAN DAVID PUBLISHERS, INC.
MIDDLE VILLAGE, NEW YORK 11379

A TREASURY OF
ITALIAN FOLKLORE AND HUMOR

Copyright ©1980
by
Henry D. Spalding

Address all inquiries to:

JONATHAN DAVID PUBLISHERS, INC.
68-22 Eliot Avenue
Middle Village, New York 11379

This is a reprint edition distributed by Bookthrift, New York.
Bookthrift is a registered trademark of Simon & Schuster, Inc.

ISBN 0-671-07481-4

Original title: *Joys of Italian Humor and Folklore*

The map on the jacket is used with permission of Simon & Schuster, Inc.

Library of Congress Cataloging in Publication Data

Main entry under title:

Joys of Italian humor and folklore.

    Includes indexes.
    1. Italian wit and humor. I. Spalding, Henry D.
PN6205.J6   857'.008   80-13750

Printed in the United States of America

To Robert L. Chianese, Ph.D., my good friend and neighbor, for his superb Italian-English translations which helped brighten and add flavor to this volume—my profound thanks.

CONTENTS

PREFACE

"Italian humor died with Ariosto,"* said the nineteenth-century historian, J. A. Symonds, noted authority on Italy. In the face of that dogmatic statement, any attempt to bring together a collection of examples, at least half of which belong to a later date, would appear to savor of presumption. But, at the risk of differing from such a recognized expert on Italian literature, I believe (and will demonstrate) that a mountain of humor has been produced since the age of Ariosto. There are, however, peculiar difficulties connected with its presentation in a foreign tongue.

It may as well be said at the outset that the professed humorist, that is, the writer who is comic and nothing else, or, at any rate, whose main scope is to be funny, was all but unknown in modern Italian literature until very recently. The jokes in Italian comic and other papers, prior to World War II, were not, as a rule, particularly amusing, and if we do come across an older book in Italy which sets itself forth as *umoristico*, the chances are it turns out to be very tragic mirth indeed. Yet, in novels and tales, even in essays and descriptions, none of which have an especially humorous intention, the reader will often be confronted with passages of pure and spontaneous humor, inimitable in its own kind.

Italian humor may be said to fall into two great divisions, or rather—for it is impossible to draw hard and fast lines—to present two main characteristics, which are sometimes present together, sometimes separately. The first of these is what we may call the humor of "ludicrous incident"—an elementary kind indeed, comprising what is usually known as "broad farce," and finding its most rudimentary expression in horseplay and practical jokes. The early stages of all humorous literatures afford abundant examples of this. There are, in fact, some stories which appear to be so universally pleasing to human nature that they reappear

---

*Lodovico Ariosto (1474-1533). Examples of his work are represented in this volume. Ariosto's career is briefly sketched in the Biographical Index of Authors, page 313.

in various forms all the world over, at times making their way into literature, at other times surviving in oral tradition as folk humor. Boccaccio and his predecessor, Franco Sacchetti, along with numerous other writers of the short story, which very early became a striking feature in Italian literature, afford plenty of examples.

The other characteristic is difficult to define, and its best examples are almost impossible to render into another language. It consists of a peculiar naive drollery—a drollery containing an element that reminds one of the Irish way of relating a story, only that it is quieter and more restrained. It has a simplicity that seems almost unconscious of the ludicrous side of what it is describing, till we are undeceived by a sly hit here and there. This, though far more developed in modern Italian writers, exists side by side with the broader comic element in the older literature. There is a certain childlike quality about the Italian of the age of Dante that lends itself admirably to the expression of this trait.

The French are said to possess wit, but not humor; the Italians have humor, but not wit—or, at any rate, more of the former than the latter. Broadly speaking, true humor is seldom divorced from pathos, and it is usually allied with the power of seeing the poetry in common things, as well as the ridiculous side. This was especially noticeable in such writers as Verga and Pratesi, whose works are full of humor, though not of a kind that appears to advantage in these selections. It is shown in delicate and elusive touches of description and narration, and provokes smiles— sometimes sad smiles—rather than earthy laughter. Verga's humor is often grim and bitter. The tragedy of the hard lives he wrote of has its farce too, but even that is a sad one. Something of this grimness comes out in his cynical sketch of the village priest who was also a farmer and money lender—hated by his flock in one capacity, reverenced in the other, and dreaded in both.

Italy is so intimately associated with music and drama that, in a book such as this, one might expect to find a large number of humorous quotations from comedies, light musicals, and opera. This, however, is not the case. With hundreds of comedies to choose from, for example, it is almost impossible to find anything adapted for quotation. It is quite true that quoting from a comedy, and especially from a drama, must always be more or less like handing round a brick as a sample of the house; but in Shakespeare, as an instance, we can find an abundance of single passages which will stand well enough by themselves to provide a taste of his humorous quality.

Had I been able to find in all the works I examined a passage comparable in nature to one of dozens readily available in, say, *Twelfth Night, Henry IV,* or *Much Ado About Nothing,* my task would have been much simpler. But in the best classical plays, such as Goldoni's, the interest is much more dependent on plot and situation than on character, and no short selection can either give an idea of the whole or be particularly amusing in itself. The liveliest bits of dialogue lose their point when taken out of context, and in any case are better adapted for acting than reading. The same might be said of any play worth the name, but it is perhaps peculiarly true of the eighteenth-century "comedy of intrigue."

The comedy of the late nineteenth and early twentieth centuries does not have the same drawback. The stereotyped characters are done away with, and there is more play than individuality. But it will be noticed that the selections appearing in this book consist of one or more whole scenes, sometimes of considerable length; that is, there is the same deficiency, or nearly so, of quotable parts. This, of course, is not a fault from the dramatic point of view, but it is an embarrassment for the editor who makes the selections.

Considering all these allowances, we find several of Torelli's and Ferrari's plays quite amusing; but we are forced to realize that some of them are lamentable comedies. It is not that they lack spirit and vivacity, but we are astonished at the subjects chosen. That any man should write a play called *The Duel*, in which the principle incident is in fact a duel, which really does come off, and in which a man is killed, and then call it a comedy, passes one's comprehension. Not that the subject is made light of; there are comic characters and situations—but these are subsidiary, and the main treatment is dignified and even pathetic; certainly not funny.

The fact that some plays are designated *commedia*, others *tragedia* or "drama" proves the distinction is observed, to some extent, in "modern" drama; that is, from the mid-1800s to the turn of the present century.

There was a peculiarly national development of entertainment in Italy called the Commedia dell'Arte. Briefly, this was a play in which the author furnished only the outline—the plot, the division into acts and scenes, and a few stage directions. The words were wholly or partly spoken extemporaneously by the actors. Today we might call this "improvisational theater." The dialogue of these plays consisted chiefly of gags, though the extent to which they were used appears to have varied. The author sometimes supplied hints for every speech, and even entire speeches. At other times he only indicated the general line to be taken during the scene. The Commedia dell'Arte was immensely popular during the first half of the eighteenth century, but then declined owing to the influence of Goldoni, who introduced the Comedy of Manners, in which he largely followed French models. It is curious that Moliere, who may have been instrumental in superseding the Commedia dell'Arte, should have received his first impulse from this very form of entertainment, as brought into France by Italian companies.

Most plays of that description were more in the nature of farce—what we would today term slapstick, rather than witty humor. The principal "players"—Harlequin, Columbine, Pantaloon, Coviello, Scaramouche, and others—had certain fixed traditional costumes and masks from which they never departed. The familiar figure of Punch, which has been so completely Anglicized as to appear one of the most English of all English institutions, was handed down through many generations of Italian players before he reached Great Britain's shores. As Pulcinella or Polecenella he is a typically Neapolitan figure, while Stenterello, another favorite mask, is typically Tuscan. The Tuscans, and more especially the Florentines, were famous throughout the Peninsula for their "economy" (to put it charitably). The "economy" of Stenterello, whose name is derived from "*stentare*" (to be in great want), was a prominent feature of his miserly character.

The Commedia dell'Arte was eminently suited to the Italian national character of the day, with its fluent eloquence and spontaneous drollery. The humor depended so much on facial and vocal expression, on ready repartee and apt illusion that it loses enormously on being written down, especially in English.

The scenario or outline of the acts and scenes, while it kept the action in a definite shape and prevented unnecessary diffusion, allowed the most unlimited scope for originality and creative fun, not only for conscious wit but for unconscious, or unwitting humor, too. The players were never loath to incorporate this unplanned humor into their later performances, often terming it a "carefully considered" joke. But there is nothing peculiar in that: today's comedians do it all the time.

Another development of the Italian theater which must not be passed over without notice is the comic opera which came into fashion during the latter half of the eighteenth century. Casti excelled in this form, producing, among others, *La Grotta di Trofonio* and *Il Re Teodoro*, which are somewhat similar to Gilbert and Sullivan's librettos in their lilting measures and rattling good fun. Other comic operas of the same period are *Il Paese di Cuccagna*, by Carlo Goldoni, and *L'Opera Seria* by Ramiere Calsabigi, a parody on the serious operas which were just then becoming fashionable. The poet and the composer are introduced respectively as Don Delirio and Don Sospiro (Master Delerious and Master Lamentation). The manager asks them in turn, "What the devil is the good of so many sentences just at the crisis of passion?" and "Who the hell can stand all those cadences in the midst of an aria full of action?" Later works of a more modern but similar kind were written by Pananti, Gherardini, Lorenzo del Ponte, and Angelo Anelli. Excerpts of their humor are included in this collection.

The Italians have always been good actors, entirely without self-consciousness and inflated affectation. Until the advent of Fascism, their life was public, out of doors, and gregarious, giving them confidence and a penchant for natural expression. The same absence of artificiality that marked their manner in life was visible on the stage, and to a great extent it remains so today.

However, one must understand the Italian nature and know their habits and peculiarities in order to fully relish their acting. It is as different from, let us say, French acting, as their character is different from that of the French. In character parts, comedy and farce, or slapstick and practical jokes, they are admirable. Out of Italy, the real *buffo* does not exist. Their impersonations, without overly exaggerating the truth of natural foolishness, exhibit a humor of character and a general susceptibility to the absurd which could hardly be excelled. Indeed, Italian humor is not dry, sarcastic and perhaps not even as witty as is the French, but rich, and with a drollery that evokes ready laughter.

In the nineteenth-century Italy's humor of the theater, the *primo comico,* who was always rushing from one predicament to another, was so full of chatter and blunder, ingenuity and good nature, that it was impossible not to laugh with him and wish him well. Yet, in the same play, the heavy father or irascible old uncle, in the midst of the most grotesque and absurdly natural mimicry, without altering his character in the least, would sometimes move the audience with sudden touches of pathos when least expected. A contemporary nineteenth-century American illustration of this technique is found in *Unce Tom's Cabin,* which caught the audiences unprepared and expecting laughter, and brought tears instead.

The use of dialect in comedies was widespread—not because it was inherently funny in itself, but because it imparted a sense of realism to the proceedings. That was the way people spoke in different areas of Italy, and the theater simply reflected that fact. But it sounded funny to those Italians who spoke their own dialects in the unswerving belief that theirs was the correct version of the language. In fact, dialect stories were just about as popular in Italy as they were in turn-of-the-century America.

The Neapolitan dialect, so closely connected with Pulcinella, became as much a stock property of the Italian writer and actor as the brogue of the stage Irishman was of the American. A comic journal, entirely in dialect, titled *Lo Cuorpo de Napole e lo Sebetto,* was published for several years during the 1860s, but its humor was exclusively political, and of a local and temporary character. The Sicilian dialect was brought into notice by Verga, Navarro della Miraglia, Capuana, and other writers. Goldoni used the Venetian throughout some of his best comedies (*Le Baruffe Chiozzote,* for instance). And D'Annunzio, in his *San Pantaleone,* and other stories, made very effective use of the dialect spoken along the Adriatic coast, about Pescara and Ortona, which is a kind of cross between the Venetian and Neapolitan. In Piedmont, there is (or rather, *was,* prior to World War II) a mass of widely read humorous literature in the—to outsiders—singularly unattractive *patois*, or dialect approaching gibberish, which was so dear to Cavour and Victor Emmanuel.

Among the cities of the Peninsula, Milan and Florence have always enjoyed a preeminent reputation for humor. The Florentines of the Middle Ages were famous for their biting wit and satirical speeches, their *motti* and *frizzi*. Franco Sacchetti and Luigi Pulce were Florentines, and Boccaccio was next door to one, being a native of Certaldo. Even Dante, though the last man in the world of whom we would expect anything in the way of humor, was not without a certain grim facetiousness of his own. We are reminded of the episodes, mentioned in this book, when he turned on the jeering courtiers at Verona with a bitter play on the name of *Can Grande,* or annihilated the harmless bore in Santa Maria Novella, with his *"Or bene, o lionfante, non mi dar noia."*

Giusti, whose poems were described by some of his contemporary critics as "rather satirical than humorous" (although, as satire is a department of humor, it is difficult to see the point of the definition), was, in many respects, a typical Florentine. He was not one by birth, however, he was born in Monsummano, in the Lucca district. His poems exhibit a singular union of caustic sarcasm and irony, fierce earnestness and merry *disinvoltura*—lighthearted Tuscan laughter. He wrote chiefly on political subjects, and never did a political poet have worthier themes for his verse. The times in which he lived were sufficient to call forth any amount of *saeva indignatio.* We have nothing quite like it in English-language literature, perhaps because the motivation for it did not arise.

But in spite of this earnestness, which is usually said to be fatal to a sense of humor, the Tuscan love of fun was always bubbling up in Giusti. His letters, in which he continually fell into the spicy idioms of his native hill-country, are full of it; and some of his poems are purely playful, without political or satiric intention—or, if satiric, only in a kindly spirit. Such is the poem *Love and a Quiet Life,* from which I have given an extract.

There seems to be no English version of the best of Giusti's works. I have not attempted a translation of the *Brindisi di Girella*—which, extracted from the main, could only result in spoiling that inimitable poem. I have, however, included the excellent renderings of *L'Amor Pacifico,* and some stanzas from *Gingillino,* contributed in the 1870s to the *Cornhill Magazine* of London by an anonymous writer.

Tuscan rural life was admirably portrayed by, among others, Mario Pratesi and Renato Ficini, both writers of considerable graphic power and a certain puckish humor, although they seemed to prefer tragedy to comedy. The latter's sketch of a day in a Tuscan country house has been included in the present collection.

So much for Florence and Tuscany. Milan is famous in Italy for various reasons: its Duomo and the singing at La Scala; for the gallant fight for liberty during the Five Days in 1848; for the delicacies known as *polpette* and *panettone*.* But, additionally, the Milanese are noted for a love of jokes and laughter, which they endeavored to suppress in the days of the Austrian dominion. They possess a dialect which seems as though it were intended for the comic stage, and one which is adaptable to classic wit. They produced a nineteenth-century dialect-poet of some note: Giacomo Porta, the friend of Grossi and Giusti. Giusti had a great sense of the humorous capabilities of the Milanese dialect and quoted verses in it (or more probably improvised quotations) in letters to his Milanese friends. Unfortunately Porta's poems are so strictly local, and lose so much by translation, that none of them have been found suitable for this book.

As a rule, the prose specimens of Italian humor have been more satisfactory as far as this present work is concerned, than the poetical, for two reasons: first, the latter are more difficult to translate with any degree of point and spirit; and secondly, whether from the choice of meter or other causes, they are apt to become long-winded, if not heavy. In any case, when exploring the humorous literature of Italy, we find a strong English and, to a lesser extent, Irish influence during the eighteenth century. Swift, Addison, and Sterne found not only eager readers but followers. Giuseppe Baretti, the friend of Johnson who, after a prolonged residence in London, returned to Italy for several years, helped popularize the language and literature of his adopted country. Count Gasparo Gozzi, elder brother of Carlo Gozzi, of the *Memorie* and the *Fiabe,* founded and published in Venice a journal called *L'Osservatore,* avowedly on the model of the *Spectator.* His writings were not servile imitations, but they did have an unmistakable Addisonian flavor.

Sterne's influence was perhaps more widely felt than any other. Ugo Foscolo probably came under it when writing *Didimo Chierico,* and the frequent allusions to the *Sentimental Journey* by Italian writers prove it to have been widely read. Leopardi's intensely original individuality owed little to any writer, yet I cannot help thinking that he may have found Swift, to whom he was in some respects similar, both suggestive and stimulating. Certainly, the masterly dialogues exhibit a biting saturnine humor very like Swift's misanthropic irony, though more subtle and refined, and made still more striking by that innocent-seeming naivete of expression which is so peculiarly Italian. The dialogue between the "First Hour and the Sun," translated in this volume, is one of the best examples.

Another feature of Italian humor which also appealed to the medieval

---

Polpette—meatballs. *Panettone* refers to fruitcake made of fine flour mixed with eggs, sugar, butter, and candied fruit peel.

imagination throughout Europe so strongly as to have survived far beyond those ancient times, was the constant insistence on the folly and. worthlessness of women. Apparently, it was the men who told the stories and made the sarcastic proverbs. But the tendency was more marked in Italy than in other countries, and in a collection such as this, which is intended to be representative, it seemed appropriate to give a sufficient number of specimens to illustrate the point. Many of those included in this book stem from the medieval and Renaissance eras, and well into modern times.

No survey of the humorous literature of Italy which did not take into account the blighting influence of censorship (abolished only in the late nineteenth century) would be complete. It was revived, of course, during Benito Mussolini's fascist regime. But he, at least, did not put offenders to the stake or have them tortured on the rack.

Dangerous, if not fatal, as the institution of censorship is to literature in general, the humorous genre feels its effects more than any other. It is surprising, considering the astonishing lengths to which the earlier and braver satirists, and even more modern writers were able to go in the direction of sexual explicitness, that they should have had anything to complain about in the way of restrictions. But we must remember that this was one of the few ways in which the writer could express a certain degree of literary freedom without bringing down upon his head a ferocious response from either the Church or the State. The animus of the political censorship seems to have been reserved for anything that savored of liberalism—a term which included the very mildest criticism of the Government or its actions. The Inquisition, meanwhile, was always inclined to regard the faintest suspicion of heretical dogma as a far worse offense. Thus, while he was restricted by both the Church and the political establishment, each of which was fairly tolerant of transgressions against the other's faction but strict to the point of near-insanity about deviations from its own edicts, the writer was comparatively free to create libidinous literature without too much fear of reprisal.

Let nothing that has been said here, however, be misinterpreted to mean that lascivious writings were a product of the Christian era. Pre-Christian Rome was a hedonistic society whose literature did not even possess the saving grace of classic Greek literature: that of tenderness in the expression of sexual conduct. And little of it was truly humorous, as, for example, *Requiem:**

---

*Publius Ovidius Naso (43 B.C.-17A.D.). From *Amores:* Book 2, Elegy 10.

Let soldiers steel their breasts and face the arrows
 and buy eternal glory with their blood;
Let misers hunt and lie for wealth—and perish,
 drinking waves which their own ship has plowed.
Just let me die abed with plump young maidens,
 And when I'm gone, inscribe upon my breast,
 "He died as he hath lived, this lucky fellow:
 what better way to go when go ye must?"

As I have mentioned in the introduction to Chapter 8 of this book, "The Italians Said It First," many restrictions still exist against the dissemination of anything that suggests "pornography." As a consequence, I have omitted a number of humorous gems in that vein. Nor have I quoted from the world's first novel and Rome's most riotous and ribald work, *The Satyricon of Petronius Arbiter*. Therefore, the selections do not include most of ancient Rome's outstanding poets, with the exception of a very few such as Ovid. The latter also wrote "pornographic" literature (the quotation marks must remain until someone gives to the world a precise definition), but his expressions were of sexual *love*, rather than undiluted passion or lust.

At any rate, this remains a "family" book, and, as such, the omissions are deliberate and conscious. There are a number of "naughty" anecdotes herein, and an occasional "naughty" word (again the quotes), translated into English as they were first written or recited. The inclusions were necessary in order to preserve the authentic flavor of the stories, and to avoid diminishing their impact. When Dante, as told in one of the tales, snaps that he was "up to his ass in water," the original Italian version did not use the polite form, "buttocks" or "behind." And while we are on the subject, we must emphasize that in no other culture have there been so many examples of folk humor devoted to affectionate references to the female posterior. From classic Rome to modern Italy's "fanny pinchers," this rather pleasant preoccupation seems to be a kind of national fetish. It begins at the birth of the infant. When family, friends and neighbors are gathered to view the new baby, it is dutifully turned over so that all who wish may "kiss it on the po-po," as the popular custom is expressed. Angelo Sicca, the nineteenth-century Italian-American journalist, derided the belief, however. "I never kissed a female behind until its owner was at least twenty," he wrote.

A word about the preparation of this book. The reader who is expecting the familiar (and often insulting) jokes about "valley wops and mountain guineas," organ grinders, "guinea stinkers" (cigars), "spaghetti benders," banana boats, and "dago red" (wine), will find no such representations in this volume. Many, if not most, of those so-called jokes had their origin in nineteenth- and early twentieth-century America, the barbs cloaking an anti-Italian bias and prejudice born of fear of an immigrant people competing for jobs. Moreover, the pejorative carica- tures were *about* Italians, not *by* them. In no sense did they reflect authentic Italian humor. Gone was the wit and wisdom of ancient Rome that glittered with intellectual diamonds; gone was the rich humor of the Renaissance that shone like spun gold—especially the tales told by that titan, Baldassare Castiglione. And gone, too, was the very flavor of the authentic Italian humor of modern times, sometimes caustic, at other times trenchant, but mostly good-natured; a humor that expressed the attitudes and characteristics of a people at their funny and sunny best. No, those caricatures were not included in this volume.

But what do we *mean* by Italian humor? In a pioneering work such as this, there were no guidelines which I could follow: no other book encompassing 2,500 years of Italian wit and humor had ever been attempted, in either the Italian or English language. For the purposes of this work, I defined Italian humor as that which revolves around a subject of interest to Italians everywhere, in Italy and in other countries; and which is told by Italians to other Italians. The definition is simplistic, to be sure, but at least it was a start.

Compiling the selections published in Italy took two years of intensive but pleasant research. The gathering of Italian-*American* humor, however, grew to be a chore. Of the more than 90 general magazines, some 200 newspapers dating to colonial times, and scores of other documents, I was able to salvage only a bare 38 jokes that did not savor of New York-style cooked chicken, but instead had the flavor of Milanese *pollo ai ferri*.[1] The bonanza was, in fact, mined from the Italian- American press of the past 70 years, beginning with the first decade of this century. Here I found not mere chicken, but *piccioncini con risotto*,[2] *anitra arrosto*,[3] and, yes, *fagiano*.[4] These were the morsels selected for that part of the book dealing with the Italian-American community.

It remains to say a few words about the translations included in this volume. When I could find existing versions I adopted them, always acknowledging their source. In other instances, I either translated them myself or had them translated for me (my knowledge of the Italian language being sadly lacking for this work). For that task I owe a debt of gratitude to my friend and neighbor, Dr. Robert L. Chianese, Director of the NEH Liberal Arts Project at California State University at North- ridge. Born in 1942, in Trenton, New Jersey, he received his B.A. in

---

[1]Broiled chicken.
[2]Squabs prepared on the spit and served with rice.
[3]Roast duck.
[4]Pheasant

English at Rutgers University, and his M.A. and Ph.D. from Washington University in St. Louis. He has been a professor of English at CSUN since 1969. He labored over the original manuscript, working out his Italian-English translations with good humor, except for an occasionally muttered *"Madonn'!"*

I have used the word "translation" several times, but perhaps I should have said "interpretation" instead. My purpose was to give a coherent picture of what the author had in mind, in a style that would at least give some idea of his tone and method of treatment, rather than rendering his exact words. Anyone having the curiosity to examine the Italian originals would often find considerable liberties taken with the text. I have expanded here and contracted there—sometimes paraphrased by giving corresponding English idioms or proverbs. And I have occasionally tried to preserve the spicy quaintness of the original by offering a mode of speech as it stands: "He said he would tie it to his finger till doomsday" (to indicate undying remembrance of a real or fancied injury); "It costs the very eyes out of one's head"; ". . . making a hole in the water" (for labor in vain); "As pleased as an Easter Day" *(contento come una pasqua)*—are vivid and picturesque locutions which it would be a pity to disguise under more commonplace terms.

The jokes, quips, witty anecdotes, short stories, plays, and proverbs selected for this volume were taken from all periods of Italian literature, from the era of ancient Rome, through the Middle Ages, the Renaissance and post-Renaissance centuries, and on through the years to today's United States.

As I have already pointed out, there are some rich and fruitful areas of Italy from which I was able to extract little or nothing. But that is not to say that those regions lack a written or oral humorous literature. Indeed, they remain a virtually untapped reservoir only awaiting the diligent researcher to yield their wealth of humorous folk tales.

In this work I have attempted to span some two-and-a-half millennia of Italian humor and wisdom. But it is comprehensive only in the sense that it is a representation, rather than an exhaustive portrayal of the subject. In any case, a collection of translations can never be other than an imperfect representative of an original literature, and I do hope that these pages will reveal the warm and fun-loving nature of a creative and very likable people.

HENRY D. SPALDING

June 1980
Northridge, California

1

Laughter in the Middle Ages

INTRODUCTION

When we speak of the Middle Ages we refer to that period which separates ancient and modern times in Western European history. The transitions came about gradually, however: there are no exact dates for the demarcation of the Middle Ages. It is generally agreed that the medieval world emerged from the disintegration of the West Roman Empire in the fourth and fifth centuries, and endured until the fifteenth century; that is, into the period of the Renaissance.

The Middle Ages have long been called the "Dark Ages," but medieval civilization is no longer thought to have been so dark as is often depicted, and the term "Dark Ages" is now more often applied to that period preceding the year 1000. But even in this evaluation, the time is not precise.

Little has been written of the humor of the Middle Ages. We do know that the classic wit of ancient Rome did not make its resurgence until the Renaissance. But it did not die out entirely: nearly all of it remained intact in the archives of the Roman Catholic Church. Its use, however, was confined to ecclesiasts who used the humorous sayings and anecdotes to illustrate their sermons. The humor was, however, only incidental to the sermon. The moral lesson was the one and only function of the stories or sermons, known as *"exempla."* Nevertheless, the witty and humorous inclusions served to hold the interest and attention of the listeners. It is a device used everywhere today by public speakers, both within and outside the clergy.

As Europe, and especially the Italian peninsula, entered the period known as the High Middle Ages, another type of humor gradually began to manifest itself: one that was independent of the exemplum, presaging the wit and humor that was soon to follow in the Renaissance. Not all of it can be said to be truly funny, and few of the anecdotes would be appreciated today. But it was there, ushering in the delights of jocular literature—oral as well as written—that have come down to us through the centuries.

1

The selections in this chapter owe their authorship to the poets and prose writers who were born prior to the year 1399. Admittedly. that period encompasses the dawn of the Renaissance, but the authors clearly represented much of the style of the Middle Ages, with flashes of the progressive drollery that would soon burgeon across the length and breadth of Western Europe. Indeed, it may be said that it was their influence that brought about the Renaissance in humor—an influence that inspired nearly all of the humorists of the following eight centuries.

Here, then, are the wits of the Middle Ages: Pucci, Boccaccio, Sacchetti, and Bracciolini—the latter undoubtedly the titan among the humorists of that period. Because of the physical confines of this volume, only brief selections of each writer could be included, and several others who perhaps should have been recognized have been omitted, either because of the length of their writings or because, when excerpted out of context, the anecdotes lose the spark the authors intended.

The following pages are representative of the humor that was popular in the closing decades of the Middle Ages: the high jinks, bon mots, and funny comments as appealing today as when they were first uttered.

—H.D.S.

A POET COMPLAINS OF UNREASONABLE FRIENDS

"Make me a sonnet or a canzonet,"
    Says one who's scant and short of memory.
It seems to him that, having given me
The theme, he's left me naught my soul should fret.

Alas! he knows not how I'm sorely let
    And hindered, nor what sleepless nights I see,
    Tossing from side to side most painfully
Ere from my heart I squeeze those rhymes—my debt.

At my own expense, three fair copies then
    I make. 'Tis well it were correct before
I send it forth among the sons of men;
    But one thing, 'bove all else, doth vex me sore—
No man had ever manners 'nough to say
"Here, friend, take this, and for the paper pay!"
    Sometimes, indeed, they may
    Treat me to half a pint of Malvoisie,
And think they've recompensed me royally.
                —Antonio Pucci (1312-75)

CALANDRINO FINDS
THE STONE HELIOTROPE

There lived in our city of Florence not too long ago, a painter named Calandrino. He was a man of simple mind, and much addicted to novelties. Most of his time was spent in the company of two brother painters, Bruno and Buffalmacco,* both men of humor and mirth. At the same time, and in the same city, there was a young man of very engaging manners, witty and agreeable, called Maso del Saggio. This fellow, Maso, having heard of Calandrino's extreme simplicity, resolved to derive some amusement from his love of the unique and marvelous, and to excite Calandrino's curiosity by some novel and wonderful tales.

One day, while Maso and a friend were in the Church of Saint John, he happened to see Calandrino attentively admiring the paintings and sculpture of the tabernacle which had been recently placed over the altar in that church. Here was the opportunity Maso had been awaiting to put his scheme to work. Acquainting his friend with his intentions, they walked to the spot where Calendrino was seated by himself and, seemingly unaware of his presence, began to discuss the qualities of certain precious stones, Maso speaking with all the confidence of an experienced and skillful lapidary.

Calandrino lent a ready ear to this discussion. Perceiving from their loud voices that their conversation was not of a private nature, he approached them, and asked where these stones were to be found.

"They mostly abound in Berlinzone, near a city of the Baschi, in a country called Bengodi," replied Maso, delighted that his strategy appeared to be working. "In that happy land the vines are tied with sausages, a goose is sold for a penny, and the goslings are given free into the bargain. There is also a high mountain made of Parmesan cheese, whereon dwell people whose sole occupation is to make macaroni and other dainties, boiling them with capon broth, and afterwards throwing them out to all who choose to catch them; and near to the mountain runs a river of white wine, the best that ever was drunk, and without one drop of water in it."

"Oh, what a delightful country to live in!" exclaimed Calandrino. "Have you ever been there?"

"A thousand times, at least," answered Maso.

"How far is this land from our city?"

---

*Buffalmacco and his practical jokes seem to have been the common property of the comic writers of the period, and a great many of the jokes which were considered exceptionally amusing were indiscriminately attributed to him. Boccaccio, the author of the above tale, made use of Buffalmacco, as did such other important Italian humorists as Castiglione and Poliziano, whose works are also represented in this volume.

"In truth," replied Maso, "the miles are scarcely to be numbered, but if you dream aright, as we do, you could be there in a short time; even in minutes."

Calandrino, noting that Maso spoke with an earnest and grave countenance, believed every word that had been said. "Believe me, sir," he ventured, trying to make his tone as honest as possible, "the journey is too far for me to undertake. I wish it were somewhat nearer. But as long as we are discussing it, allow me to ask you, sir, whether any of the precious stones you spoke of are to be found in that country."

"Yes, indeed," replied Maso. "There are two kind, both having eminent virtues. One kind are the sandstones of Settigniano and of Montisei. The other is a stone which most of our lapidaries call heliotropium, a stone of admirable virtue."

"What makes it so admirable?" asked Calandrino.

"Whoever carries the heliotropium about on his person is rendered invisible for as long as he pleases," explained Maso.

"Can these stones be found elsewhere?" asked Calandrino, trying hard to suppress the eagerness in his voice.

"Certainly," Maso assured him. "They are frequently found on the plains of our own Mugnone."

"Of what size and color are these stones?"

"They come in various sizes, some larger than others, but all are black."

Calandrino, treasuring all these things in his mind, pretended to have some urgent business on hand, took leave of Maso, secretly determined to find these stones. However, he decided to do nothing until he had first seen his friends, Bruno and Buffalmacco, to whom he was much attached. Having sought them out, and told them about the wonderful heliotropium, he proposed that they immediately go in search of it.

Bruno nodded his assent, but turning to Buffalmacco, he declared, "I fully agree with Calandrino, but this is not the proper time for our search. The sun is now high, and so hot that we will find the stones on Mugnone dried and parched, and the very blackest would seem the whitest. But in the morning, when the dew is on the ground, and before the sun has dried the earth, every stone will have its true color. Besides, there are many laborers now working in the plain, and were they to see us occupied in so serious a search, they might guess what we are looking for, and may find the stones before we do."

"Yes," agreed Buffalmacco, I think this enterprise should be started in early morning, when the black stones will be easily distinguished from the white, and a festival day would be best, as there will be no one about who might discover us."

It was then decided that the following Sunday would be the time for all to go in pursuit of the stones. Calandrino waited impatiently for Sunday morning, when he called upon his companions before break of day. All three then went out of the city at the gate of San Gallo, and did not halt until they came to the plain of Mugnone, where they immediately commenced their search for the marvelous stones. Calandrino went stealing on before the other two, persuading himself that he was born to find the heliotropium. Looking about on all sides, he rejected all other stones but the black, with which he filled his pockets. He then took off his large painting-apron, which he fastened with his girdle in the manner of a sack, and filled that also. Still not satisfied, he spread his cloak on the ground and loaded it up with the heliotropium stones, carefully tying the cloak together for fear of losing the very best of them.

Buffalmacco and Bruno had been attentively eyeing Calandrino during this time. Observing that he had completely loaded himself with the black stones, and that their dinner hour was drawing near, they proceeded with their plan.

"Buffalmacco," asked Bruno in a puzzled voice, pretending not to see Calandrino who was in plain sight, not more than five feet away, "whatever has become of Calandrino?"

"I saw him just a moment ago, standing right before us," said Buffalmacco, gazing about as though looking for him.

Calandrino, thoroughly convinced that, by virtue of the qualities of the stones, he was now invisible, grew ecstatic. Indeed, his joy was unbounded, and without saying a word, he decided to return home with all speed, leaving his friends to provide for themselves.

Buffalmacco, however, perceived his intent. "Bruno," he said loudly and clearly, "why should we remain here any longer? Let us return to the city."

"Yes, let us go," agreed Bruno, "but be sure that Calandrino will never again make a fool of me. In fact, if I were only as near to him now as I was a few minutes ago, I would give him such a remembrance on his heel with this flint stone that would give him a lasting lesson." He no sooner finished his threat when he struck Calandrino a violent blow on the heel with the stone. But though the blow was evidently very painful, Calandrino still preserved his silence, and only quickened his pace.

Buffalmacco then selected a large flint stone of his own. "See this pebble? If Calandrino were only here, he'd get a mighty knock on his behind." Then, taking aim, he threw it and struck Calandrino a violent blow on the lower back. Thereafter, all the way along the plains of Mugnone they did nothing but pelt him with stones, joking and laughing until they came to the gate of San Gallo. There they threw down the remainder of the stones they had gathered, and, hastening before Calandrino into the gateway, acquainted the guards with the whole matter. The guards, in turn, were delighted with the jest, and did not seem to see Calandrino as he passed by them, sweating and groaning under his burdensome load.

Without resting, Calandrino proceeded straight to his house, and was neither met nor seen by anyone, as everybody was then at dinner. When he entered his home, ready to sink under his burden, his wife—a handsome and discreet woman named Mona Tessa—happened to be standing at the head of the stairs. Disconcerted and impatient at his long absence, she angrily exclaimed, "I thought the devil would never let you come home! All the city has dined, and yet we are still without our dinner."

Calandrino, finding that he was not invisible to his wife, fell into a fit of rage. "Wretch! You have utterly ruined me! But I will reward you for it!" Ascending into a small room and ridding himself of the stones, he ran down again to his wife and beat her in a most unmerciful manner.

Buffalmacco and Bruno, after they had spent some time in laughter with the guards at the gate, followed Calandrino at their leisure, and, arriving at his house and hearing the disturbance upstairs, they called out to him. Calandrino, still in a furious rage, came to the window and begged them to come inside. They, pretending great surprise, ascended the stairs and found the chamber floor covered with stones and Calandrino's wife seated in a corner, severely bruised and disheveled. On the other side was Calandrino himself, weary and exhausted, flung on a chair.

"How now, Calandrino," exclaimed Buffalmacco, "are you building a house, that you have brought in so many loads of stones? And Mona Tessa—what happened to her? You surely have been beating her! What is the meaning of this?"

But Calandrino, exhausted with carrying the stones, and with his furious gust of passion, and moreover, with the misfortune he considered had befallen him, could not collect sufficient energy to speak a single word in reply.

"Calandrino," persisted Buffalmacco, "whether you have cause for anger in any other quarter is beside the point. You should not have made such a mockery of your friends as you have done today, carrying us out to the plains of Mugnone like a couple of fools, and leaving us there without so much as bidding us goodbye. But be assured, this is the last time you will ever serve us in that manner!"

"Alas, my friends, be not offended," replied Calandrino at last. "The case is very different from what you think. Unfortunate man that I am, I actually found the rare and precious stones. Here is the whole truth. When you asked each other the first time what had become of me, I was right near you, not more than two yards away. Perceiving that you could not see me, I started on my way home, smiling to myself to hear your rage against me." To further illustrate the truthfulness of his story, Calandrino then showed them where he had been struck on his backside and heel. After a pause he went on with his adventure. "As I passed through the gates, I saw you standing with the guards, but by virtue of the stones I was carrying, was undiscovered by all of you. But at length, arriving at my house, this fiend of a woman waiting on the stairhead happened to see me, although I was invisible to everyone else. You well know that women cause all things to lose their value, so here I am, Calandrino, who might have called myself the happiest man in Florence, am now the most miserable of all. Therefore did I justly beat her, and I know of no reason why I should not yet tear her in a thousand pieces, for well may I curse the day of our marriage and the hour she entered my house."

Bruno and Buffalmacco, feigning the greatest astonishment, though they were ready to burst with laughter, intervened when they saw that Calandrino might beat his wife again in his rage.

"She is in no way to be blamed," insisted Buffalmacco. "You alone are the cause of your misfortune. You knew beforehand that women cause all things to lose their value, and you should have commanded her not to be seen in your presence all that day, until you had satisfied yourself of the real qualities of the stones. Further, I have no doubt that Providence deprived you of your good fortune because, though we, your freinds, accompanied you and assisted in the search, you deceived us and did not allow us a share in the benefit of the discovery."

After much more conversation, and having reconciled Calandrino to his wife, Buffalmacco and Bruno took their departure, leaving him a wiser man, but still overwhelmed with grief for the loss of the heliotropium.

—Giovanni Boccaccio (1313-75)

DANTE AND THE SMITH

The great poet, Dante, having dined one evening, went out for a walk. Passing by the Porta S. Pietro, he happened to hear a blacksmith beating iron upon an anvil and singing some of his verses like a song. But the smith so jumbled the lines together, mutilating and confusing them, that Dante perceived himself as receiving a great injury. This was no way to treat his creations!

Dante strode into the blacksmith's shop, where there were many articles made of iron, and, saying nothing, he took up a hammer and pincers and scales and many other things, and threw them out into the road.

"What in hell are you doing?" cried the blacksmith, turning round upon him. "Are you mad?"

"What in hell are *you* doing?" demanded Dante.

"I am working at my proper business," said the blacksmith, "and you are ruining my work, throwing it out into the road."

"If you do not want me to spoil your things, then don't ruin mine," retorted Dante.

"What things of yours am I ruining?" asked the man.

"You are singing something of mine, but not as I wrote it," said Dante. "I have no other trade but this, and you are ruining it for me."

The blacksmith, too proud to acknowledge his fault, but not knowing how to reply, gathered up his things and returned to his work. But when he sang again, he sang "Tristram" and "Launcelot," and left Dante alone.

—Franco Sacchetti (1335-1400)

Messer Bernabo and the Miller

Messer Bernabo, Lord of Milan, was once outwitted by the clever reasoning of a miller and, as a reward, bestowed upon the miller a valuable benefice.* But let us go back to beginnings.

This lord, Bernabo, was in his time greatly feared beyond all other rulers, and though he was cruel, yet there was a measure of justice in his cruelty. It so happened that a rich abbot had neglected to properly feed two hounds belonging to the lord, and thereby had spoiled their tempers. For this act, he was fined 4,000 *scudi* by the said lord. At this, the abbot began to plead for mercy.

Lord Bernabo listened attentively and then said: "If you can answer four questions, I will remit everything. The four questions are these: How far is it from here to heaven? How much water is there in the sea? What are they doing in hell? What is the worth of my person?"

The abbot sighed, and thought himself in a worse plight than before; yet, for the sake of peace and to gain time, he begged Bernabo to grant him a term for the answering of such deep questions. The lord granted him the whole of the following day, and, as one impatient to hear the end of the matter, made him give security that he would return. Exceedingly sorrowful, the abbot returned to his abbey, full of thought, and puffing and blowing like a frightened horse. There, he met a miller, one of his tenants.

"My lord," asked the miller, seeing the abbot thus afflicted, "what is the matter, that you puff and blow like this?"

"I have good cause," replied the abbot. "His lordship will be the ruin of me if I do not answer four questions which neither Solomon nor Aristotle could do."

"What are these questions?" asked the miller.

---

*A position or post granted to an ecclesiastic which guarantees a fixed amount of property or income.

The abbot told him.

The miller thought for a while, and then said, "Sir. I can get you out of this predicament."

"Would to God it might be so!"

"I think both God and the saints will be willing."

"If you can do it, then take from me what you will. There is nothing I will not give you, if it is possible."

"Very well," said the miller. "I will put on your tunic and hood, shave my beard, and tomorrow morning, very early, I will meet with his lordship. I will say I am the abbot, and I will settle the four questions in such a way that I think he will be content."

The abbot could not wait a moment before he had substituted the miller in his own place, and so it was done.

Early in the morning the miller set out, and when he had reached the gate of Bernabo's house, he knocked and said that such and such an abbot wished to answer certain questions which the lord had put to him. The lord, interested to hear what the abbot had to say, and wondering that he had returned so quickly, had him admitted inside. The miller, coming into his presence in a room which was not very well lighted, made his obeisance, holding his hand as much as possible before his face.

"Are you able to answer the four questions?" asked Bernabo.

"I am, my lord," replied the miller.

"Very well, you may proceed."

"You asked how far it is from here to heaven," began the miller. "From this spot it is just thirty-six million, eight hundred and fifty-four thousand, seventy-two and a half miles, and twenty-two paces."

"You have given it very accurately," said Bernabo, "but how will you prove it?"

"Have the distance measured," said the miller promptly, "and if it is not exactly as I say, you may have me hanged by the neck."

"Well, what is your answer to the second question?"

"You asked how much water there is in the sea. This was very hard to find out, since it is a thing that is never still, and there is always more being added. But I have found out that there are in the sea 25 billion, 982 million hogsheads; seven barrels; 12 gallons; and 2 glasses."

"How do you know this?" asked Bernabo.

"I reckoned it as well as I could," answered the miller. "If you do not believe me, send for some barrels and have it measured. And if I am not correct, you may have me quartered."

"And the third question?"

"In the third place, your lordship asked what was being done in hell. In hell there is hanging, drawing, quartering, and cutting off of heads going on—neither less nor more than what your lordship is doing here."

"What reason do you give for this?" asked Bernabo.

"I have talked with a man who had been there," explained the miller. "It was from this man that Dante the Florentine heard what he wrote concerning the things of hell. But this man is dead, and if you do not believe me, send and ask him."

"What of the fourth question?"

"Fourthly, you would know the value of your lordship's person. I say that it is worth twenty-nine pence."

When Messer Bernabo heard this, he turned to him in a fury. "May the plague seize you!" he shouted. "Do you think I am worth no more than an earthen pipkin?"*

"My lord, listen to reason," replied the miller, not without great fear. "You know that our Lord was sold for thirty pence: surely I am right in supposing that you are worth one penny less than he."

Hearing the clever reply, Bernabo guessed that this man could not be the abbot. He looked at him fixedly, perceiving that he was a man of far more sense than the abbot. "You are not the abbot," said Bernabo at last.

The terror which the miller then had, everyone may imagine for himself. He knelt down, and with clasped hands asked for mercy, telling Bernabo that he was the tenant of the abbey mill. He told how and why he had appeared before him in this disguise, and that it was rather to please him than from any ill intention.

"Well, then," said Bernabo, "since he has made you abbot, I will confirm you in your new office. It is my decision that henceforth you will be the abbot, and he the miller, and that you will have all the revenue of the monastery, and he of the mill."

And thus Bernabo caused it to be, during all the rest of his life, that the miller should be an abbot, and the abbot a miller.

—Franco Sacchetti

IMMACULATE CONCEPTION No. 2

In the little fishing village of Gaeta, among the poorest of the poor, there lived a seafaring man named Paolo. Now this Paolo was a simple man, not very bright, and therefore often unable to find work in competition with the smarter men of Gaeta. So he said goodbye to Iolanda, his pretty wife, and departed for foreign places in search of employment. For seven years he traveled the ports of Europe, and finally managed to save a modest sum of money. He then decided to return to his wife and home.

But Iolanda, who had neither expected nor hoped for his return, especially after so many years, was now living with another man. She seated her long-missing husband at the table and poured him a glass of

---

*A small clay pot.

expensive, fine old wine. "Drink, Paolo," she urged, "and then you can tell me where you have been for these past seven years."

"I do not understand something," murmured Paolo slowly. "How were you able to buy this vintage wine? And the house itself has been enlarged, repaired and repainted," he added in bewilderment. "How could you afford to pay for all this?"

"Our blessed Saviour, who fed the multitude with a few fishes and some bread, fed and clothed and housed me," explained Iolanda, looking her husband straight in the eye.

"And all this beautiful new furniture?"

"The blessed Saviour took care of that, also."

"And all this clothing I see hanging on pegs, and the new gown you are wearing?"

"The Saviour, blessed be his generosity."

Completely overwhelmed by all this Divine liberality, Paolo was just about to ask how she had acquired the gold chain she was wearing around her neck, when a little boy rushed into the room and flung himself into Iolanda's lap.

"Iolanda," asked the stunned husband, "who's child is this?"

"He is yours, of course," said Iolanda.

A gnawing doubt grew within Paolo's simple mind. Mentally, he counted on his fingers: "A three-year-old son. Seven years absence from my wife's bed. Seven years, take-away three years, leaves four years. Four years, take-away nine months, leaves—hmmm. . . ."

"My dear wife," he said at length, having completed his arithmetic to the best of his ability, "how is it possible that I have a son when I did not participate in his conception?"

"For that, too, you can thank the blessed Saviour," replied Iolanda.

Paolo's indignation gave unexpected voice to his usually slow tongue. "Iolanda, I thank the Lord for taking such a keen interest in my personal affairs," he said, "but it seems to me that one immaculate conception should have been enough. *Goodbye!*"

—Poggio Bracciolini (1380-1459)

INCREDIBLE EDIBLES

In Milan, where now stands the City Hall, there used to be an ugly square house of stone with small barred windows. Inside this forbidding place were kept the feebleminded and the insane, whose families, if they had any, were unwilling or unable to keep them at home.

One day, as he was peering through the bars of a window, an inmate caught sight of an old farmer who was driving a horse and cart down the road. The cart was heavily laden with something, but the top was covered with straw, hiding the cargo from view.

"*Signore,*" called the inmate of the asylum, his curiosity aroused, "would you mind telling me what you are carrying in your wagon?"

"Not at all," replied the rustic. "It is a load of manure."

"*Manure!*" echoed the dumbfounded inmate. "What on earth and in heaven will you do with it?"

"I will spread it on my onions, my garlic, and other vegetables."

"*Dio mio!*"[1] cried the inmate. "And to think they locked me in here because I like to pour *miele*[2] on my *baccala!*[3]

—Poggio Bracciolini

Which of them was Crazy?

Angelo, a brilliant young student of mathematics and logic, won renown among the scientists of Milan for his success in complex calculations, his most famous being his precise count of the number of women who bathed naked in their private fountains. He accomplished this noble feat by peering through a crevice in the stone walls where the mortar had become loose. One day, he inadvertently blew some dust into his eye while looking through a crack. Subtracting one digit from his total number of eyes, he found he had only one left, and so brought an end to his research.

However, all this arduous mental labor took its toll upon the unfortunate young Angelo. Sad to relate, he suffered a collapse of his mental abilities. His memory fled his brain. He remembered very little of his own life or of worldly matters. This regrettable condition remained with him for two years.

During that period of forgetfulness, Angelo was sunning himself on a bench near the door of his little house when he beheld a sight that filled him with wonder and amazement. Approaching him was a man riding a horse, and on the man's leatherbound fist was a falcon. Trotting beside the horse were two hunting dogs. This was a new phenomenon for Angelo who, of course, could not recall anything that had occurred prior to the loss of his wits.

"Sir," he called out when the stranger pulled up alongside him, "what kind of animal is that you are sitting on?"

"It is a horse," replied the stranger.

"Why are you riding it?"

"I am going hunting."

"But what is that peculiar bird on your fist?"

---

[1]My God!
[2]Honey.
[3]Dried codfish.

"It is a falcon. It has been trained to hunt wild game, such as ducks and partridges."

"Those noisy animals following you—what are they?"

"They are hunting dogs. I use them to flush game from the underbrush. They are trained hunters and retrievers."

"Sir, it is clear you have gone to great trouble and expense for your hunting," observed Angelo. "But tell me, what is the value of all the wild ducks and partridges you catch in a year?"

"Oh, not very much," responded the hunter with an airy wave of his hand. "About seven ducats, I suppose. Certainly not more."

"And in a year, how much does it cost to maintain your horse, the falcon, and the two dogs?"

"Sixty ducats."

"What!" exclaimed mathematician Angelo, aghast at this display of foolish extravagance. "You spend sixty ducats for game worth only seven ducats? Sir, I can eat all the finest game I please for only five ducats, and it costs me nothing to hunt for them."

The stranger smiled. "Just what would you have me do?" he asked finally realizing that the younger man was ill.

"I would suggest, my dear sir, that you consult my doctor, and then join me where we can recover our senses together."

—Poggio Bracciolini

Lazy Logic

While attending the Council of Constance, in the year 1415,* Bonaccio de' Guasci, a young man of pleasant disposition, was invited to live at the home of Gianfranco, an old friend. Indeed, Gianfranco was delighted to have so agreeable a fellow for company. Bonaccio, however, had one minor fault, if one may call it that: he seldom arose early in the morning, being a late sleeper. His host soon took to teasing him, good-naturedly accusing him of being lazy.

"Bonaccio, it is eleven o'clock!" exclaimed Gianfranco one day. "Will you spend the rest of your life in bed? How can you be so lazy?"

"It is not laziness at all, I assure you," replied Bonaccio, smiling. "But the moment I open my eyes I always find two lovely women sitting on either side of my bed: *Signorina* Ambition and *Signorina* Laziness."

"How lucky!" sighed Gianfranco.

"No, it's not what you think," grinned Bonaccio. "First, *Signorina* Ambition urges me to throw off the covers and leap out of bed and be

---

*Poggio Bracciolini, the author of this anecdote, accompanied Pope John XXIII as apostolic secretary, to the Council of Constance, where John was denounced and deposed by the Council as an "illegitimate Pope."

about my business of the day. But then *Signorina* Laziness argues that the weather is cold and I will freeze if I remove my blankets. 'You will be nice and warm in your bed,' she tells me. Then she scolds me that too much work will send me to an early grave, and that my body needs plenty of rest. *Signorina* Ambition then raises her objections, and so it goes, with the debate raging furiously throughout the morning hours.

"Being a gentleman, I never take sides during an argument between two well-intentioned ladies. Therefore, I just listen to their dissension as an impartial witness until, finally, I get tired of all that bickering and I get up!"

—Poggio Bracciolini

Citrullo, the Fool

Umberto, a grain dealer in the province of Pesaro in central Italy, was having an affair with Francesca, the shrewd wife of a farmer who was called *Citrullo* (fool) by his neighbors. Even Francesca called him Citrullo. Yes, he was a foolish man indeed.

One afternoon, when Francesca and Umberto had just undressed and were preparing to go to bed, the wife looked out the window and happened to see her husband coming home unexpectedly early from the fields. But his unlooked-for arrival only sharpened her wits. She turned to the nervous Umberto and hissed, "Do exactly as I tell you! When you hear me say, 'There is a *poliziotto* (policeman) in the house!' you are to immediately stomp around and yell, 'Where is that scoundrel?' Then I will send him away."

"Do you think it will work?" asked Umberto doubtfully.

"Of course!" snapped Francesca. "He is the greatest fool in all Pesaro."

Francesca hastily threw a wrap around her shoulders and hastened to the door just as her husband was entering. "I came home early so I could do some extra work around the barn while there is still daylight." Citrullo explained, half apologetically.

"No, you must not come in," hissed Francesca. "Your creditors will wait no longer for you to repay your loans, and they sent a *poliziotto* to arrest you and throw you into debtor's prison. In fact," she concluded, raising her voice so that it could be heard in the bedroom, "there is a *poliziotto* in the house at this moment!"

In the bedroom, Umberto acted out his part well. He stomped about the floor, the old wooden boards creaking and groaning. He raised his voice in a roar of well-simulated authority: "Where is that *briccone* (rascal)? He is going to *prigione* (prison)!"

"Quick, run and hide in the fields!" urged Francesca. "I will come for you when he has left."

Poor Citrullo! His face turned white, like the belly or a fish. It turned green. It turned red, and then it started all over again with white. Heeding Francesca's advice, he raced toward the field on rubbery legs and hid himself amidst the full-grown wheat. Meanwhile, in the house, Francesca and Umberto leaped into bed and into each other's arms.

All night long, Citrullo watched his distant house, waiting for the "policeman" to leave. But, as dawn began to break, and he had not observed any departure in the bright moonlight, a small kernel of suspicion entered his simple mind. At last, when the sun came up over the horizon, he rose from his hiding place and purposefully strode toward his house. He threw open the door and burst into the bedroom. There, to his consternation, he found his wife and her lover in the very act of manufacturing a new Italian.

Fists clenched into hard knots, teeth set, his voice ice-cold with fury, he snarled, "What are you doing?"

Francesca turned to her lover. "See? Just as I told you—a fool!"

—Poggio Bracciolini

Gianozzo's Correspondence*

A long time ago, when Gianozzo Visconte was mayor of Vicenza, he would always call in his secretary to write letters for him—especially those intended for the old Duke of Milan which were required to be composed in an elegant style. Gianozzo was a decent man, very kind and truthful, except for one thing: he was illiterate, but pretended to be quite learned. However, it was probably the worst kept secret in all of Vicenza. Everyone, it seems, knew he could neither read nor write, and he would never have been appointed mayor had he not served the old Duke with distinction as a soldier. In fact, he had once saved the Duke's life.

The ritual for writing a letter never varied. "I would like to dictate a letter to the Duke," Gianozzo would say.

"I am ready," the secretary would reply.

The mayor would then dictate the salutation, explain briefly what he wished to convey, and then conclude, "I remain, Your Estimable, Gracious Highness, etcetera, etcetera."

When the secretary had composed the letter he would hand it to the mayor who "read" it carefully. His reaction was always the same. "I think the first paragraph needs strengthening, and the second paragraph needs a little more clarity. Correct it, please."

---

*This anecdote was related to Bracciolini by Antonio Loschi (1368-1441), a pamphleteer of Milan, also known as Antonius Luschus.

After an appropriate interval, the secretary would return with the very same letter, with not a single change whatsoever.

Gianozzo would "read" it again, nod, and then, in a satisfied tone, he would comment—

"Well, now, this is more like it!"

—Poggio Bracciolini

WHY THE CARDINAL REJECTED A FEAST IN PARADISE

What special attribute is required for a man to rise to the eminence of Cardinal? Piety and loyalty, to be sure, but two other qualities are important—a quick mind and a quicker tongue. As an example, when the Cardinal of Spain battled the enemies of the Pope, his mental agility was given a crucial test. His army was facing the formidable strength of the opposing legions at Agra Piceno, and the time had come for hand-to-hand combat.

"You need not fear death," the Cardinal exhorted his troops, "for I can promise you that he who dies in defense of God and the Church will be rewarded with remission of all sins. Now, I must retire to the rear lines to direct our grand strategy; and, to you who die on the battlefield, tonight you will feast at the banquet table with God and the angels."

"Your Excellency," shouted a corporal in the ranks, "why don't you stay with us so that you too can have supper with the Lord?"

"For two reasons," the Cardinal roared back. "First, I never eat in the evening; and, second, I am not that hungry!"

—Poggio Bracciolini

CHRISTIAN BURIAL FOR A DOG

Vittorio Brancaccio, a wealthy merchant of Tuscany, had a little dog which he dearly loved. When it finally died, he buried it in a cemetery. Now it so happened that the Bishop heard about the burial in consecrated ground. He summoned the local priest to explain why he had officiated at the grave-site services.

But the priest knew his Bishop better than most priests are supposed to know their Bishops. Before answering his superior's demand, he went to Vittorio Brancaccio's house, and, after explaining the problem, suggested that he hand over fifty ducats with which, the priest assured him, "all would be made well."

The priest then visted the Bishop, who met him with cold hostility.

"Do you realize that you have broken Church law by burying a dog in the holy ground of a Catholic cemetery?" grated the dignitary. "And do you know that you can be defrocked and thrown into jail for your crime?"

"Father," replied the shrewd priest calmly, "you would not be so upset if you knew that Vittorio's dog possessed human intelligence. In fact, Father, he was smarter than most humans and deserved burial with people."

"Deserved? Deserved, you say? What has his intelligence to do with the matter? He was still a dog."

"But not like the others, sir. Why, even in his last moments of life, and with his dying breaths, he dictated his last will. He knew you were a compassionate and understanding man, Father, so he bequeathed you these fifty ducats."

Astounded, the Bishop looked at the pile of money before him on the table.

"*Idiota!*" (Idiot) he finally grumbled. "Why didn't you say so in the first place, instead of wasting a whole hour of my valuable time!"

—Poggio Bracciolini

MY MONEY—YOUR MONEY

During a period of temporary public virtue in Terranova, a law was passed that prohibited gambling in that city. One of the inhabitants, Franco, an inveterate gambler, was soon arrested and brought before Mayor Pullini for judgment.

"I find you guilty of wagering," pronounced the mayor, after Franco had boldly confessed. "I hereby sentence you to jail for a period of two months from this date."

"Your Excellency, that is a harsh sentence," retorted the impenitant Franco. "After all, it was my own money that I wagered. I tremble to think what my sentence would have been if I had gambled *your* money!"

—Poggio Bracciolini

LUIGI'S OBSTINATE WIFE

In Tivoli, one day in August, a merchant whose name was Luigi learned that his wife had drowned in the fast-running river, and that her remains could not be found. He immediately set out to find her body. As he was walking upstream along the bank, he was met by another man in the searching party.

"Why on earth are you searching *up*stream?" asked the other man, amazed at such stupidity. "You should be going *down*stream if you expect to find your poor wife's body."

"No, you are wrong," countered Luigi with a certitude that brooked no argument. 'If you knew that obstinate, contradictory wife of mine as well as I, you'd know that, even now, she'd be floating against the current!"

—Poggio Bracciolini

A Friar Wins Approval

A friar who was well known for his habit of permitting his tongue to speed ahead of his mind, was preaching a stormy sermon to a congregation in Naples. On and on he thundered, inveighing against adultery. As his rage against that sin increased, so, too, did his rhetoric.

"I tell you this, you sinners: adultery is the most terrible sin of all. It is the loathsome destroyer of holy matrimony. I, myself, would rather sleep with ten virgins than one married woman!"

"I, too!" averred the sexton loudly.

"So would I!" agreed the organist.

"And I!" shouted each of the male members of the choir in one approving voice.

—Poggio Bracciolini

Please All—Please None*

Eugenius IV, who was elected Pope in 1431 and who reigned briefly until 1437, was discussing the matter of public opinion with his secretary.

"I assure you, dear Camillo, that the man who yields to public pressure makes a grievous mistake," asserted the pontiff. "It is simply impossible to please everyone. Let me illustrate with an old folk tale that supports my theory.

"One day, an old farmer and his young grandson were walking to town to sell their donkey which they were leading with a short length of rope. As they proceeded down the road, they met a group of peasants who were harvesting grain in the field.

"'Why do you make that poor little boy walk when you can let him ride on that lazy donkey?' one of the workers shouted. Soon the others joined in the cry: 'Let the tired little child ride!' So the grandfather, being a kind man, lifted his grandson to the donkey's back, and, with the old man walking behind, they trudged onward to the town.

"Before long they came upon another group of harvesters who voiced their displeasure with rude shouts: 'Just look at that strong boy, riding in comfort while that poor old man is forced to walk! Let the old man ride!'

---

* This fable is also found in the humorous folk literature of fifteenth century Russia and Poland, and in sixteenth-century Spain.

Shrugging, the grandfather asked the boy to dismount while he climbed onto the donkey's back.

"Soon, another group assailed the old man for forcing his grandson to walk behind like a lowly slave while he rode in grandeur. 'Why don't you *both* ride?' shouted one of the people, and, as usual, the cry was immediately taken up by the rest. '*Both* ride! *Both* ride!' they shouted. In his effort to be agreeable, the old man extended his hand to the youth and helped him up onto the donkey. Together, they rode on.

"But they had not traveled more than a few hundred feet when another crowd yelled at them: 'That poor little donkey! See how weary he is! Can't you see that you are too heavy for the poor animal? Why don't you both walk for a while, and carry *him*?' Once more, the old man, in his desire to appear reasonable, got off the donkey and also ordered his grandson to dismount. Then he tied the donkey's hooves together, and, putting a long, heavy stick between the bound hooves, he and the boy rested each end of the support on their shoulders, and started off again, carrying the innocent and bewildered animal between them.

"A half mile further down the road, the donkey, perhaps sensing the comedy of these episodes, gave vent to a loud and raucous *hee-haw*. Enraged at last, the old man dropped the mule to the ground, forcing the boy to do the same. Then, with a short length of sapling growing by the side of the road, he struck the mule. '*Hee-haw*, will you? I'll teach you to *hee-haw* at me, you brother of the devil!'

"But the donkey, now free, ran into the fields and made off for the distant woods, where it disappeared forever.

"And so you see," concluded Pope Eugenius, "because the old man tried to please everyone, he pleased no one, and lost his donkey as well!"

—Poggio Bracciolini

Dante and the Impudent Student

A young university student who was overblown with conceit for what he believed were his outstanding qualities—qualities which were not readily apparent to anyone else—somehow gained admittance to the home of Dante, the Florentine poet. For the next twenty minutes the brash youth recited examples of his brilliance, his charm, and his many talents, paying no attention to the great poet's glowering looks. At last the student put forth the question he had been most anxious to ask:

"Sir, I have a thousand florins. How can I best spend them so that I will become known?"

"Young fellow," replied Dante, making a manful effort to suppress his annoyance with the youth's rudeness and conceit, "it would be far better, for you and for mankind, if you spent your thousand florins to remain *un*known—and I shall be glad to inform anyone who is foolish enough to ask, that I never heard of you!"

—Poggio Bracciolini

A Full-Term Baby
in Six Months

A Florentine youth, clearly nervous and worried, was admitted to Father Berni's study.

"Good morning, Father," said the young man. "My name is Giorgio. You married me and Rosa six months ago."

"Yes, of course, my son," responded the priest. "I remember you well. Why do you look so upset?"

"Father, it's Rosa. She just had a baby."

"You should be happy, not downcast," reproved Father Berni.

"But it has only been six months since our wedding," protested Giorgio. "I have always heard that it takes nine months to make a baby."

Father Berni was not only a compassionate man but a quick-thinking one, as well. "How long did you know Rosa before you married her?" he asked.

"Three months," replied Giorgio. "We fell in love at first sight and were married right away."

"Aha! There you have your explanation!" cried Father Berni, seizing on this lone straw. "You knew her for three months before your marriage?"

"Yes, Father."

"And you have been married for six months?"

"That is so, Father."

"Then that explains everything," said the priest, his face beaming. Three months and six months are nine months . . . your full-term baby. It often happens that way in good Christian families, my son, but only with the first child!"

—Poggio Bracciolini

Father Galelli's Revenge

It so happened that Father Galelli, of Florence, while visiting in Hungary, was called upon by the local Bishop to say the Mass. After the services, he sprinkled holy water in the eyes of several people* and was ready to retire to his study when another group came forward, asking for his ministrations. It was apparent they were revelers: their eyes were

---

*In the old Kingdom of Hungary, it was the fourteenth-century custom for those with faulty vision to approach the altar after Mass, and request that the priest sprinkle their eyes with holy water from the chalice. The priest would do so, meanwhile uttering proper phrases from the holy books and asking God to relieve the afflicted petitioners.

bloodshot and watery, and their vision, according to their complaints, was blurry.

Father Galelli, his face stony with contempt, took the chalice and sprinkled them, meanwhile uttering the words they hoped would heal their vision. The Hungarians wondered why the Bishop found it necessary to rush from the room to suppress his laughter, for only he understood Italian. The Florentine priest had "blessed" them in his own language:

"*Andatevene che siate morti a ghiado.*" ["Get out of here—and drop dead!"]

—Poggio Bracciolini

How Tomaso's Sweet
Illusions Were Shattered

Tomaso, age nineteen, fell in love with Angela, a sixteen-year-old milkmaid. Her pretty face and figure was in his mind day and night—especially at night. But, because of her tender years, he manfully restrained his natural impulses. Angela, however, made no effort to restrain her fantasies, and her passions gave impetus to her impatience.

One day, when she had finished milking the cows, and she and her sweetheart were alone in the barn, she pressed close to him and murmured, "Tomaso, if you love me as much as you say you do, why is it that you never make love to me?"

"I have thought of it, Angela *mia*," he confessed, "but I hesitate to take advantage of you, young and innocent as you are."

"I am more mature than you think," she whispered in his ear.

Tomaso smiled indulgently at his darling, who reminded him of a kitten, but who fancied herself as so grown up.

"Not mature enough to know how babies are made," he observed, somewhat teasingly.

"Silly boy!" giggled the sweet *ragazza* (girl), her light laughter ringing pure and virginal in his ear. "I have a baby by Giuseppe; I have a baby by Marco; I have a baby by. . . ."*

—Poggio Bracciolini

---

*It is likely that author Bracciolini's humor was pivoted, in the original Italian, on the word "*da*," which would have appeared in both Tomaso's and Angela's utterances. "*Da*" carries multiple meanings: "of," "from," and "by." Thus, the Italian probably went something like:

Tomaso: "*Non abastanza matura per sapere* da che cosa *sono fatti i bambini. . . .*" [*Not mature enough to know from what* babies are made. . . .]

Angela: "*Sciocco! . . .Ho un bambino* da *Giuseppe; uno* da *Marco; uno* da. . . ." [Silly boy! . . . I have a baby *by* Giuseppe; one *by* Marco; one *by*. . . .]

Salvation in the Bedroom

In Sicily, according to my wife's father—a truthful man who seldom lied more than once or twice a week—there lived a lady called *Signora* Mona Torelli, known to all in the town as the *"vedova* [widow] of Vittoria."* She had lived alone for several years after the death of her husband, but now, still comparatively young, she decided to end her lonely existence by marrying again; provided, of course, that she could find a gentleman who was compatible with her delicate feelings and purity of thought.

To further her marital plan, she went to see old *Nonna* (Grandmother) Vecchia, who knew all the unmarried people in town, and charged a modest fee for arranging introductions that led to marriage.

"What kind of man do you prefer?" asked *Nonna* Vecchia, her toothless smile extending from one wrinkled cheek to the other.

"I seek only companionship and perhaps a little financial help," replied Mona thoughtfully. "But it is most important that he be a pious man who attends church regularly. Yes, a man of God, whose thoughts are on holy things, and not just on love-making."

"Why are you so concerned with his religious feelings, and against his natural urges?" asked *Nonna* Vecchia, her voice patient with the wisdom of her many years.

"Because I am more concerned about the salvation of my soul than the frivolities of the flesh."

"My dear Mona, salvation is one thing and joys of the flesh are another," said the old woman, choosing her words with infinite understanding. "All married people hope to live in harmony. But, being human, there are times when arguments arise and the husband and wife go to bed angry with each other. Now, my child, how can peace be restored after a quarrel when the husband is too saintly to use his peacemaker?"

—Poggio Bracciolini

Miracle of the Chicken*

Angelotto, the Cardinal of St. Mark, was jouneying from Rome to Reggio. Late in the afternoon of the second day, he became weary and hungry, so he stopped at an inn for a short rest and some nourishment. It being Friday, he asked the waiter to serve him fish for his supper.

---

*Bracciolini had little liking for the Cardinal of St. Mark, and delighted in making him the butt of his jokes. In this anecdote, for example, the cardinal is represented as hypocritical and impious. In the next tale, he is made to sound pompous and self-serving.

"A thousand pardons, Your Eminence," apologized the waiter, "but there is not a fish to be had anywhere. They were all bought early this morning by *le massaie* [the housewives] here in the village."

"Do you have anything else?"

"Yes, but it is chicken, cooked yesterday for Sunday dinner."

"Then bring me the chicken."

"B-b-but, Your Eminence," stammered the waiter, "it is forbidden to eat meat on Friday."

"Young man, do as I say!" ordered Cardinal Angelotto sternly.

The meat was brought to the table, and the Cardinal at once asked the perplexed waiter, "Do you believe in the miracle of changing bread into the body of Christ?"

"Yes, Eminence, of course!"

"Very well, then you shall now see another miracle," said the prelate, making the sign of the cross. "I hereby change this chicken into a fish!"

—Poggio Bracciolini

How a Boy Outwitted a Cardinal

In the year 1433, on a clear morning in October, Pope Eugenius, accompanied by the pompous Cardinal Angelotto, arrived in the city of Florence. There, the pontiff agreed to interview eleven-year-old Federico, a boy who had impressed many Florentines with his profound adult wisdom. For half an hour or more, the Pope conversed with the prodigy until he, too, was overwhelmed with the child's lofty intelligence. At last the Pope sent for Cardinal Angelotto and asked for his opinion. "If this boy possesses an intellect of such magnitude as it appears to me," observed the Pope, "he could go very far in the service of the Church."

The Cardinal, who found no pleasure in discovering a new person who might someday compete with him and perhaps challenge his authority, hesitated for a moment and then nodded his head. "I will question him," he muttered.

"Now, Federico," Angelotto began, turning to the boy, "I will put several questions to you in the areas of theology, logic, mathematics, astronomy, and history. You will answer each question within five seconds of the asking." He then launched into an intensive examination that he hoped would result in the boy's immediate dismissal. But the youth answered each of the difficult questions promptly and correctly. At length, Cardinal Angelotto surrendered, but not without attempting one more stratagem.

"Your Holiness, he said, once more addressing Pope Eugenius, "It may be true that young Federico here is a genius, but I have found that children of such great minds gradually lose their cleverness as they grow older, until, when they reach a mature age, they finally become stupid."

The Pope turned to the boy and asked, "Well, my dear Federico, what have you to say to that?"

"Your Eminence," replied the boy, "Cardinal Angelotto must have been much smarter than I when *he* was a boy!"

—Poggio Bracciolini

THE CARDINAL'S FOUR FEET

Although Cardinal Angelotto was admired and respected by many who did not know him intimately, he had very few close friends. Among those scarce few was Bernardo, the parish gardener, who had the mind of a child. Angelotto was quite fond of Bernardo and, on cold nights, he permitted the simpleton to sleep at the foot of his bed.

One bitterly cold night in January of 1435, the good Cardinal invited a woman to sleep with him, no doubt thinking the proximity would help keep him warm. Late at night, however, he awoke to find that Bernardo had crept into the bedroom and, as usual, crawled under the blankets at the foot of the bed.

Bernardo had just made himself comfortable when it slowly dawned on him that something was amiss. There seemed to be more feet in the bed than was customary. Gingerly, he touched one foot with a forefinger. "Is this your foot?" he asked, his voice puzzled.

"Of course," replied Cardinal Angelotto.

"And this one?" queried Bernardo, touching another foot. "Is this your foot, too?"

"Certainly."

Bernardo extended a shaking finger and touched a third foot. "Whose foot is this?"

"That, too, is mine."

A long pause followed. Then, summoning up what remained of his courage, Bernardo touched a fourth foot. "Your Eminence," he quavered, "can this foot also belong to you?"

"Yes, that one is also mine," affirmed the Cardinal.

Bewildered and frightened, poor Bernardo forced himself to peer out from under the covers, only to see a long tail of black tresses overhanging the side of the bed. And at that very moment, the woman, unable to contain her mirth, burst into peels of high-pitched laughter.

The four feet, the tail, the hee-haws—all these proved too much for simple Bernardo.

"Oh, Father in Heaven, save our Cardinal!" he screamed, leaping from the bed. "Satan has changed him into a jackass!"

—Poggio Bracciolini

Father Roselli Interprets the Gospels

Father Alonso Roselli was delivering a fiery sermon on the Gospels while the members of the congregation listened raptly in the packed church.

"You can accomplish anything with God's help," he declared, "just as our blessed Saviour fed five hundred people with seven loaves of bread."

"Father," whispered the altar boy, "you made a mistake. The Gospel says five *thousand*, not hundred."

"Hold your tongue!" snapped Father Roselli. "Those dolts are having enough difficulty believing five hundred!"

—Poggio Bracciolini

A Question of Breeding

A prince of the realm owned a stable of horses which were considered to be the finest in all of the Italian peninsula. One day, to his chagrin, he learned that a certain *condottiere,** Ridolfo di Varano, Lord of Camarino, had acquired a number of Arabian horses which surpassed his own. The proud prince, who could not abide second place, immediately dispatched a letter to Ridolfo, advising him that he would like to buy the noblest horse in his stable. He then listed all the attributes and qualities which he expected in a horse of that high caliber.

A fortnight later, the prince was taken aback to see a groom approaching his palace. He was on horseback, and leading a mare and a stallion behind him.

"Ridolfo of Camarino sends his respects," said the groom, after making himself known. "He regrets that he does not have a horse that meets with all the exceptional standards you listed in your letter. However, each of these horses has some of the high qualities you demanded, and his lordship suggests that you make your own!"

—Poggio Bracciolini

The Cunning Peasant and the Squire

A poor but very clever peasant, serf to Squire Maglione, learned one day that a distant relative whom he had not seen since childhood had died and left him a beautiful painting of the Madonna. Hanging it on a wall in his cottage, he gazed at it with rapture. Never in his life had he dared dream that he would ever own anything so valuable and so lovely.

*A military captain or mercenary leader.

Everyone was pleased with the peasant's good fortune; everyone, that is, except the squire, Maglione. He immediately set about devising a plan to confiscate the poor tenant farmer's new property. Finally, when he had conceived his scheme, the greedy old miser summoned the serf before him. So great was Maglione's authority that he now considered the painting as good as his own.

"I have a donkey in my stable—the most foolish beast in all of Italy," began the squire, his voice cold. "I want you to teach him how to talk. Moreover, I will expect him to carry on an intelligent conversation with me on any given subject!"

"But, sir, I will need enough time to teach the donkey so much," replied the clever peasant, reaching for any flimsy excuse.

"How much time will you need?" persisted Squire Maglione, inwardly congratulating himself for this easy victory.

"Ten years," said the peasant.

"Very well," agreed the squire. "But I warn you, if you are not successful, I will seize your painting and have you flogged within an inch of your life for wasting my time."

"Fool!" cried the peasant's wife when he returned to the cottage and explained the situation to her. "You have agreed to an impossible demand. Oh, what will become of us!"

"Have no fear," replied the peasant with a comforting smile. "I have good news for you. In the ten years given to us, either the donkey will die, or the squire will die, or, with good luck, *we* will die!"*

—Poggio Bracciolini

Yielding to Temptation

Bernabo, the Duke of Milan, a ladies' man of wide repute, was in the garden with a beautiful noblewoman when he was discovered in the very act of dalliance by a friar. What made it even worse, the friar was not only the duke's confessor, but also possessed great authority at the palace and could conceivably bring embarrassment to him as well as to the noblewoman.

"Sir," began the duke when his confusion had abated, "you have often said that you are no different from other men, and that you, too, might yield to temptation."

"Yes, I have said that," agreed the friar coldly.

"Then what would *you* have done if you found yourself under a bower of roses with a beautiful and willing woman?"

---

*Variants of this folk tale will be found in Hebrew, Arabic, and Turkish cultures, dating from the fifteenth to seventeenth centuries.

"I know what I might have *liked* to do," replied the friar, his eyes hard as iron, "but I also know what I ought *not* to do!"*

—Poggio Bracciolini

The Fable of the Ducks
and the Villager

A villager in Aiello, a mountain hamlet in the Apennines, kept a modest number of ducks behind his house. One afternoon, having decided to end his Lenten fast with a roast duck for supper, he selected a plump bird and, in full view of the flock, he chopped off its head. However, the farmer had been particularly fond of this particular duck. As he stooped to pick up the carcass, tender soul that he was, tears filled his eyes and coursed down his cheeks.

"Oh, see the tears of remorse in his eyes!" cried a young duckling. "I am sure he will never harm one of us again."

"Never mind his tears; observe his deeds," corrected an older and wiser duck. "You will notice that he did not throw away his axe, but carried it into the house with him!"

—Poggio Bracciolini

Vengeance Is Mine,
Sayeth Galenti

Vittorio Galenti, the Tuscan poet, although ugly as a toad, esteemed himself as being irresistible to women. This conceit may have resulted from the cleverness of his writings and his quick wit. Certainly, whatever amorous conquests he had experienced, they could not be attributed to his unattractive appearance.

One Sunday, as Vittorio was strolling homeward from a friend's house where he had imbibed his share of wine, he happened to meet the young but rather homely Maria Barlucchia. Nevertheless, although her face was plain, her figure could have inspired an elegy from the angels. Vittorio at once decided she would be his, no matter how temporarily. Taking a stand directly before her so that she could not pass without going around him, he executed an elaborate Florentine bow.

---

*Although this story's ending seems to be little more than a stern moral pronouncement by the friar on the conduct of one of his "pastoral lambs," it is probable that the original Italian-language version relied on the turning of a rhyme scheme to bring a smile to the lips of the reader:

"So quello che mi avrebbe piaciuto," *riprese il frate, occhi duri di ferro, "ma anche quello che non avrei* dovuto!"

"Signorina," he murmured in what he believed was his most dulcet tones, "never have I seen such a beautiful face."

Maria, annoyed with this display of impudence and patent falsehood, responded in a voice as chilly as the snows of winter: "I cannot say the same about you."

"Of course you could," retorted Vittorio, stung by the summary rejection, "if you were as great a liar as I!"

—Poggio Bracciolini

2

Jesters of the Renaissance

INTRODUCTION

The Renaissance, which marked the transition from medieval to modern times, first appeared in Italy in the early decades of the fourteenth century, reaching its height in the fifteenth and sixteenth centuries, about one-hundred years before it spread to the rest of Western Europe. This transition was a gradual one, with the values of the late Middle Ages not sharply distinct from those of the early Renaissance. Yet the Renaissance man, as he is termed, can be clearly distinguished from his medieval forefathers. For him, it was a time which stressed new importance to individual expression and worldly experience. Culturally, it was an age of new currents and brilliant accomplishments in scholarship, literature, and architecture. It was an era of emerging nation-states, of exploration and discoveries, of the incipient commercial and scientific revolutions.

Thus, as the early Renaissance emerged from the late manifestations of the Middle Ages, so too did Renaissance activity slowly blend with that of the Enlightenment; that is, the mainstream of eighteenth-century European thought. No one can deny that the Renaissance witnessed a soaring of man's spirit and a blossoming of his creative activities virtually unparalleled in historical annals. It was a period which produced that man of universal genius, Leonardo da Vinci, and those towering giants of Italian art, Michelangelo and Raphael.

The humanist emphasis on the individual was typified in the ideal of the Renaissance man, the most important of whom, undoubtedly, was Da Vinci. By the fifteenth century, society's emulation of this ideal produced a "courtier," the polished gentleman whose manners and deeds were codified by Baldassare Castiglione.

No comprehensive work devoted to Italian humor—or, indeed, to European humor—would be complete without mention of Castiglione, the author of *Il Cortigiano(The Courtier)*. This treatise, written in 1528, dealing with etiquette, social problems, and intellectual accomplishments, is one of the great books of its time. It gives an excellent picture of fifteenth- and sixteenth-century court life, describing all necessary qualifications for the perfect courtier. In his masterpiece Castiglione illustrates the various facets of wit and humor appropriate to the Italian court, a large number of which have been selected for this chapter. (Also see Biographical Index of Authors.)

In addition to Castiglione, who has been called with some justification the father of modern humor, this chapter includes a sampling of the humorous works of a dozen other authors, among them such notables as Leonardo da Vinci, Benvenuto Cellini, and Niccolo Machiavelli, not usually associated with humor. Some of this Renaissance collection is published here in English for the first time.

—H.D.S.

PRIEST ARLOTTO'S LIST OF FOOLS

In the year 1448, Priest Arlotto was aboard a Florentine galley, bound for Sicily, when he ran into a fairly heavy storm that resulted in some damage to the vessel. The captain of the ship decided to call at Naples for a few days so that repairs could be made.

Before many hours had passed, news of the famous priest's arrival was brought to Alfonso V of Aragon, King of Naples. "Bring him to me," he ordered one of his servants. "I have heard much of his humor, but I have never met him."

When Arlotto was ushered into the palace, King Alfonso greeted him warmly. Together they enjoyed some fine wine, and the good priest regaled the monarch with a number of droll stories that brought shouts of merriment from the king. At length, Alfonso posed the question he had been waiting to ask ever since the priest's arrival.

"I have heard that you carry a certain black book with you, everywhere you go," said the king. "And in the pages of that book you keep a list of all those whom you consider to be fools. Is that true?"

"Yes, it is true," replied Priest Arlotto.

"How long have you been here in Naples?"

"Three days, Sire."

"And during that time," persisted the king, "have you listed the names of any Neapolitans in your book of fools?"

"Only one."

"And whose name is that?"

"Yours, Your Majesty," answered Priest Arlotto calmly.

"*Mine!*" cried the king in amazement. "What could I have possibly done that was so foolish?"

Piovano Arlotto consulted his notes for a few moments before answering. "I see that you recently entrusted your servant, Teodorigo, a German, with five hundred gold ducats to buy cattle for you in Germany."

"My good Father, you have listed me unfairly," said Alfonso indignantly. "Teodorigo has been a member of my household since he was a small child, and he has been my most faithful servant for twenty years."

"Forgive me for saying this, Your Majesty," responded Arlotto, "but men have killed for far less than the five hundred ducats you gave him. Moreover, he is outside the Church, a German, and returning to his native land where you cannot reach him. He can now live comfortably for the rest of his life."

King Alfonso remained silent, in dark contemplation of his mistake. But suddenly his face brightened. "You may be right, Father; but then again, you may also be wrong. Now suppose Teodorigo *does* return with the cattle I ordered, or returns the gold. What will you do then with your precious book of fools?"

"In that case," replied the priest, "I will simply cross out your name and put his at the top of the list!"

—Anonymous*

No Saintly Help
for Omelets

As a young man, when his father, Cosimo, was yet alive, Giovanni de' Medici decided to spend a Friday evening in one of his palaces at Fiesole. With him went three of his friends: Piero de' Pazzi, Francesco Martelli, and Fruosino da Panzano, noblemen all. After some games to increase their appetites, and some wine to stimulate their spirits, Giovanni summoned the cook to the dining room and asked about dinner.

"I did not know you were coming," explained the cook apologetically. "This being Friday, I cannot, of course, serve meat, and there is no fish available."

"Then prepare some eggs for us," ordered Giovanni, "Prepare them as plain omelets and also a few stuffed omelets."

But, unfortunately, the omelets turned out very poorly, as sometimes happens even for a fine *cuoco* (chef) such as he. Shrugging, he brought the food to the noblemen. They stared aghast at the mess.

"Have you lost your culinary talents?" asked Giovanni in a wintery voice.

---

*The above anecdote, and the eleven which follow, all alluding to Priest Arlotto (1396-1484), were compiled in the book, *Motti e facezie del Piovano Arlotto (Witticisms and Pleasantries of Priest Arlotto)*, published in 1514. The book's author remains anonymous. For details about the principal character, see Arlotto Mainardi (Priest Arlotto) in the Biographical Index of Authors.

"I am sorry, my lord. I was in a hurry to serve you."

"Well, try again. And this time I want you to make a vow to Saint Cresci. If he grants you your petition that the eggs are well cooked, I will give you a *grosso* * so that you can buy a fine candle to place at his shrine."

The cook, anxious to regain his hitherto unblemished reputation, and also because the *grosso* was from the Medici purse rather than his own, made his vow with unusual fervor and earnestness. He then set about preparing the omelets again, but this time the eggs stuck to the pan. He scraped up the dried chunks, and sighed, knowing that this second attempt was even worse than his first. Giovanni and his friends, now famished, had to eat the eggs as they were, meanwhile averting their eyes so that they would not have to look at their dinner.

On the following Monday, they returned to Florence where, as it happened, Giovanni met Priest Arlotto. Still indignant at the treatment he had endured, Giovanni related the story of the omelets and the cook's prayers, complaining sullenly that the priest's Saint Cresci had refused to grant the small favor asked.

"Just a moment, young man!" snapped Arlotto. "How dare you demean Saint Cresci with such a frivolous request? Is he a saint for omelets? But just break a leg, or crack your skull, and *then* you will see the miracles he can work for you!"

CONFESSION AND PENANCE

Piovano Arlotto was alone in his church one Holy Wednesday when a rustic, about thirty years of age, furtively entered his study. "Father," said the visitor in contrite tones, "I would like to confess my sins."

"Kneel, my son," said the kindly priest, "and tell me what you have done."

"I have robbed hundreds of people," the penitent began.

"*Hundreds?*" gasped Priest Arlotto.

"Yes, Father. And I stole from the poor as well as the rich."

"Hmmm!"

"And I might as well tell you, I broke into your own house one night last year, and I stole a bushel of wheat."

"I must say, that was indeed sinful. I needed that wheat."

The rustic continued his long recitation of dreadful crimes when, all of a sudden, he fell silent.

"Are you finished?" asked Arlotto hopefully.

"I have one more sin to confess," the kneeling man groaned, "but the very thought of it fills me with shame."

---

*An ancient Italian coin.

Priest Arlotto, convinced that he was about to hear an act of depravity that might shock even the Lord, intoned, "Remember, whoever is willing to confess, to repent, and to do humble penance, will be forgiven. Confess, my son."

"It hurts me to say this, Father, but when I was sixteen I met a beautiful girl, and Satan spoke to my 'little boy,' causing me to surrender to the temptations of the flesh. So great was the devil's influence that my 'little boy' found it a most pleasant experience. Oh, Father, I am so ashamed!"

For a moment Piovano Arlotto was too astonished to reply. Did this peasant really believe that his youthful escapade was a more heinous sin than his countless crimes? Then his sense of humor asserted itself. Trying manfully not to laugh, he gave his absolution:

"You are forgiven your sexual transgression, my son. And remember that your 'little boy' is a domestic animal, so see to it, in the future, that he stays at home where he belongs. Moreover, do not steal again or, I assure you, you will suffer for it. But, most important, and this is your penance, give me back my wheat!"

On Going to the Seat of Authority

One Sunday morning in June, Priest Arlotto was at the church of Santo Spirito in the city of Florence, when he noticed a woman in deep and emotional prayer before the image of Saint Nicholas of Tolentino. Interested in her wide gestures, her weeping, and her fervent supplications, he watched her for some time. At length, he approached the devout woman and touched her arm.

"*Signora,*" he said gently, pointing to another, more imposing image of the crucified Christ, "if you are so much in need of help, may I suggest that you direct your prayers to the Teacher rather than His pupil?"

Purity—Before, During, and After

Priest Arlotto was invited to dinner at the home of his friend, Francesco Dini. When they were seated at the table, Francesco asked, "Father, will you have your wine before dinner or after?"

"I would prefer it before, during, and after," replied Arlotto.

Francesco stared at him as though his guest had suddenly become a drunkard.

"Do not be alarmed; I have not changed," chuckled the priest. "In fact, I have it on the holiest authority: the blessed Mary was a virgin before delivery, during delivery, and after delivery."

Francesco, still perplexed, poured the wine. But after a few minutes of deep thought, he asked, "Father, would you mind repeating that?"

HEAVEN IS NOT FOR WOLVES

A number of Catalan noblemen were aboard a galley, sailing from Naples to Catalonia. One of them, Don Lupo ("Mr. Wolf"), became ill and a few days later passed away. Dropping anchor, the captain of the vessel asked Priest Arlotto to deliver the eulogy in honor of the departed stranger.

"Gentlmen," began the priest when he had entered the pulpit, "it is our custom, in Florence, to recite a few words of praise when a good man or woman departs this life. Among those in the animal kingdom there are four which apply to my sermon of goodness and life. First, there is the donkey, which is good alive but not dead. The next is the hog, which is good dead but not alive. Another is the ox, which is good both dead and alive. The fourth, however, is neither good dead nor alive, and that is the wolf. Any man who would deliberately choose a name such as Don Lupo will undoubtedly be refused admittance to heaven, and will spend eternity with the rest of the wolves down below!"

HOW TEMPTATION MADE FAUSTO COLOR-BLIND

Fausto the tailor, a longtime neighbor of Priest Arlotto, was a master craftsman, but a thoroughly dishonest man. Refusing to change his ways, he simply shrugged off the priest's reprimands. One night, however, Fausto had a particularly horrifying dream. In his nightmare, he found himself naked in a dark and forbidding cave. All at once, from the blackest corner, there arose a mighty fire, and from the flames which danced like insane demons, there emerged an evil-looking figure who held a flag in his hand. The flag was like no other he had ever seen in his life. It was sewn with almost every color on earth. Slowly, the sinister apparition approached him, as though to engulf and smother him with the gaudy flag, when, at the last moment, he awoke, his body wet with cold perspiration.

In the morning, still trembling with fear of the unknown, Fausto sought out Priest Arlotto and related the entire dream. "What does it mean?" he asked.

"It means that your sins are about to catch up with you," replied Arlotto. "You are a wicked man who has never forsaken your thieving ways, much less made your peace with the Lord. However, if you will now confess your sins and return to the Church I shall explain the full meaning of your dream."

Fausto, weeping, knelt at Arlotto's feet and made his long list of confessions. "I have been stealing cloth and selling it to others all my working life," he concluded at last. "I have never cut one piece of cloth, however small, that I did not steal some of it."

"You are to stop stealing from this very moment on," ordered the priest sternly.

"I would like to, but how?" wailed Fausto. "I have become so accustomed to cutting off a piece of the customer's cloth for myself that I don't even realize I am doing it."

"If you are that deeply steeped in evil," counseled Priest Arlotto, "then you must always have an apprentice or other workman by your side whenever you cut cloth. You can protect your reputation by giving him no reason, but simply tell him that the moment you lay your hand on the scissors he is to say, 'Remember that flag!'"

Fausto dutifully hired an apprentice, and for the next six months all dealings in his shop were impeccably honest. Every time Fausto picked up the scissors, the apprentice would, as ordered, warn him: "Remember that flag!" And Fausto, thus reminded, would bring his shears back to the proper line.

One day, however, a nobleman came to Florence and bought a very expensive fabric of gold brocade, to be made into a fine robe. Upon the advice of his old friend, Piovano Arlotto, he brought the fabric to the shop of Fausto the tailor.

At his cutting table, Fausto laid out the beautiful material and picked up his scissors. But as he was about to cut the brocade, the magnificence of the cloth overcame him and he reached out as far as his arm would extend.

"Remember that flag!" cried the apprentice.

"To hell with the flag!" snapped the tailor. "This color wasn't on it!"

Fausto Loses His Temper

One evening at vespers, Priest Arlotto and his friend, old Fausto the reformed tailor, were passing through Borgo Santo Apostolo when they came upon a group of women sewing in a courtyard. It was customary in those days for Florentine women to escape the indoor heat of summer by gathering together outside their houses, sewing, knitting, and gossiping.

As Priest Arlotto and his aged companion strolled by, one of the gossips cried out, "Ha, Fausto, so your young wife has had a fine baby! And you seventy years old!" The other women joined her in laughter.

"Pay no attention to them, my friend," urged the priest.

"Hoo, Fausto," yelled another, "the father of that baby must be a strong man to produce such a healthy son."

Again there was derisive laughter. Fausto's face turned purple with rage, and he would have screamed a series of curses at them, had it not been for Arlotto's calming advice. "They do not really believe what they say," he murmured gently. "They only seek entertainment by making you angry."

"Does your wife have a handsome young lover?" one brazen woman called out.

"Gently, Fausto; gently," cautioned Arlotto when he saw that the old man could no longer restrain his fury.

"I do not believe that my wife has a secret lover, young or otherwise," retorted Fausto in a voice like the cold north wind, "although there is always that remote possibility. After all, you are not the only whores in Florence!"

FAUSTO LEARNS ABOUT
DIVINE PROTECTION

In his study one day, Priest Arlotto was poring over some church records when Fausto, the pious tailor, entered the sanctum.

"Father," he asked. What prayer would be best to say every morning to help me lead a more worthwhile life? On my word of honor, I wish to do the will of God."

"The first thing you must do when you awaken, my dear Fausto," replied the priest, "is to make the sign of the cross and, with deep reverence, say an Our Father and a Hail Mary. Then conclude your devotions with this prayer: 'My Lord Jesus Christ, protect me from the conscience of priests. Protect me from the prescriptions of doctors. Protect me from the deviousness of lawyers. Protect me from the man who says two Masses every morning. And above all, protect me from the man who always says, 'On my word of honor!'"

THE FABLE OF THE CATS
AND THE MICE*

At dinner, one evening, Priest Arlotto and his friend, Salvatore, a merchant of Genoa, were discussing their travel experiences when the

---

*This fable also appears in Jewish folklore, but, instead of cats and mice, deals with onions and garlic. See Henry D. Spalding, *Encyclopedia of Jewish Humor*, pp. 1-2. New York: Jonathan David Publishers, Inc.

priest happened to mention an exotic, distant land, almost unknown to the Christian world.

"It is a very rich kingdom," said Arlotto, "and ruled by a wise and generous monarch. But they have one great problem: the country is overrun with mice. They are everywhere, like a plague."

"But where are all the cats?" asked the merchant.

"My dear Salvatore, they have no cats. There is not a single cat in all the land. In fact, they never heard of them."

"What? No cats?" exclaimed the merchant, his eyes gleaming. "Why, if I were to go there with a few cats I could make a fortune!"

"Yes, you undoubtedly could," agreed Arlotto, "but it may not be necessary to engage in trade. The king would probably reward you handsomely. It would be best if you presented them as a gift."

Salvatore spent the next day gathering up all the homeless cats he could find. Then he set sail for the faraway kingdom with his precious cargo. After a long voyage over strange and uncharted seas, he finally reached his destination and was quickly ushered into the royal presence of the king.

"Sire, I bring you a valuable gift," began Salvatore, bowing low. He then produced two cats from a box. "These animals are known as cats," he explained. "It is their nature to catch and kill mice."

"If that is true, you will indeed have proven yourself to be a friend," said the king. "Tonight we shall have a banquet in your honor, and your cats shall be put to the test."

The banquet was a formal one. All the ministers of state, nobles, and the high panjandrums and potentates of the mighty realm were there. Then a procession of Nubian porters, carrying gold and silver platters of food, came to the table and placed the bountiful repast before them. But before the assemblage could taste one morsel, a loud squeaking was heard on all sides and suddenly hundreds upon hundreds of mice leaped out, as if from nowhere. They came in a deluge, like a gray tide, jumping upon the table, snatching food from the plates, and eating everything that was not tightly covered.

"Now, Your Majesty, I shall demonstrate the value of my cats," said the merchant. This time he opened two boxes, and out leaped four famished cats. In a frenzy they threw themselves upon the mice, killing them everywhere and frightening off the others, until the immense room was free of the creatures.

"Now, sire, I give you these two pairs of cats, and eight more pairs which I brought with me. They are yours as a token of my esteem and friendship," declared Salvatore. "With proper care and breeding you will have enough cats within just a few years to rid your entire kingdom of mice."

So elated was the king that he presented Salvatore with six boxes of gold and silver, diamonds, rubies, and other precious stones. Jubilantly, the merchant set sail for his homeland, where Priest Arlotto and a committee of prominent citizens were on hand to greet and congratulate the daring adventurer. For three whole days he was occupied with telling and retelling of the splendors he had witnessed in that distant and mysterious country where jewels and gold were cheaper than cats.

Fired by these wondrous tales, one enterprising individual, Alberti by name, went to see Priest Arlotto and asked the exact location of the fabulous kingdom. "I, too, will trade them cats for whatever wealth they wish to exchange."

"But they already have ten pairs of cats," objected Arlotto. "Their value will surely have decreased."

"True, but only ten pairs in such a vast and rich land can make but little difference."

So, despite the priest's warnings, Alberti set sail according to the directions given him. In due course he reached the kingdom and was brought before the king and queen.

"Sire," he began without wasting a moment of time, "I have brought ten pairs of cats such as you have never dreamed. They are called Angoras, and are beautiful to look at as well as superior catchers of mice." He then opened one of the boxes which held the cats, and out came the lovely, snow-white Angoras.

"Oh, how exquisite!" gasped the queen. "They are truly gorgeous!"

"Do these beautiful animals catch mice as well as our other cats?" asked the king.

"Better," replied Alberti, glad that Priest Arlotto was not there to correct the exaggeration.

Once more, as he had with Salvatore's cats, the king tested Alberti's Angoras at a banquet. Again the cats scrambled to catch the mice, although there were only a few left in the king's palace. As before, the monarch was highly pleased.

"You are right, these Angora cats are excellent hunters, in addition to their beauty," said the king with much enthusiasm. "You must have very few mice left in your country, with so many cats of your own."

"None, noble sire," murmured Alberti, crossing his fingers. "We have no mice at all."

"I can readily understand the reason," said the king with an admiring glance at the Angoras which were now purring contentedly. "You shall be amply rewarded.

The monarch then summoned his ministers for a consultation to determine the form of recompense to be offered the generous visitor. Jewels and gold and silver, they decided, would not be adequate for such exquisite cats. Therefore, in their wisdom, they decided to present him with a gift that would be most precious in his own country where there were no mice at all, as the visitor himself had testified.

So it was that Alberti, the clever trader, returned home with two thousand mice.

LUCKY SONG OF THE CUCKOO

Ercole and Camillo, two farmers, were in the fields when suddenly they heard the loud sweet call of a cuckoo. As is well known, the song of the cuckoo bird is considered a sign of good luck. Immediately, they fell into a dispute as to which of them the bird had addressed his call.

"He sang for me," declared Ercole. "Each morning I have scattered food for him in the garden. He is grateful, so he wishes to bring me good fortune."

"You are mistaken," argued Camillo. "I built a fine little house for him in my fig tree. Now he shows his appreciation by singing his song of luck to me."

"I will wager you a donkey worth two ducats that you are wrong," said Ercole heatedly.

"Very well, I will match your bet with two ducats in money," agreed Camillo. "But only on the condition that Priest Arlotto be the final judge."

Truth to tell, Arlotto was not pleased with this trivial and non-pious waste of his time. Nonetheless, after hearing all the details of the event, he agreed to think it over and give them his decision in a few days.

That night, Ercole called on Priest Arlotto and presented him with a basket of fresh eggs. It was obvious, of course, that he was seeking to sway the priest's judgment in his direction.

The next morning, Camillo visited Arlotto and gave him two fine cheeses, and again the priest accepted the bribe.

Twice a day, for the next three days, the two farmers brought gifts: plump young hens, capons, fruits and vegetables, and each time the offerings were silently accepted. On the fifth day, Arlotto summoned Ercole and Camillo to his house.

"Which of us did the cuckoo sing for?" they asked eagerly.

"It is my considered judgment that you are both mistaken about the bird, so save your bets," asserted Priest Arlotto. "Having given much thought to all the fine gifts you have so generously bestowed upon me, I have reached the conclusion that the cuckoo did not sing for either of you—he sang for *me!*"

CONFORMING IN AN INSANE WORLD

A number of self-appointed protectors of the public virtue were enjoying a pleasant afternoon in the outskirts of Florence when, in a large clearing within a grove of olive trees, they were astounded to find Priest

Arlotto and several companions jousting on horseback, using sticks with which to dismount each other. It was nothing more than a game, of course, but this pleasurable form of outdoor exercise apparently did not meet with the onlookers' approval.

"A priest, jousting!" cried the leader of the honorable ones. "Have you no shame, Father?"

"Not in this instance," replied Arlotto. "We had some wine with our lunch today, and perhaps imbibed a trifle too much. But let me explain the situation with a parable.

"There were ten learned scholars whose knowledge of science and astrology was so vast that they could predict natural occurrences in advance of their happening. Based on their deep studies they foretold that the town would be inundated by a great rainstorm, and that the spoiled earth and vegetation would produce a horrible stench. Moreover, anyone who was exposed to that effluvium—man, woman, or child—would become completely mad.

"But the population did not believe them, and heaped ridicule and insults upon their noble brows. Nevertheless, the ten scientists were far from resentful for this rejection by the people. 'When they have once inhaled the stench they will all be insane,' they told each other. 'If we take the proper precautions, we alone will be normal, and therefore we will become the new rulers of the city.'

"On the morning of the predicted rainstorm, they sealed the windows and doors of their houses and covered the chimneys tightly. As they foretold, the rains poured down in a deluge, and from the earth, long parched by drought, there arose the most abominable stench imaginable. But not a breath of the awful smell penetrated the sealed houses of the ten scholars. Outside, however, as they peered through their windows, they could see that the entire population had indeed gone mad. They gesticulated wildly, their arms flailing about; they danced like demons from hell—grimacing, screeching, laughing, snarling, and roaring.

"After the torrential rains had stopped and the stench dissipated, the scientists and astrologers left their houses and went into the streets. 'Now,' they proclaimed triumphantly, 'we are the masters!'

"But they were quickly brought to the facts of human nature. As soon as the people noticed the 'peculiar' behavior of the scholars, they rushed toward them as though to tear them to pieces. And so, in order to save their lives, they were compelled to act the role of lunatics and conform to the behavior of everybody else.

"Now, my friends, I, Priest Arlotto, and my companions here, are much in the same position as those scientists and astrologers. I beg of you, therefore, to overlook our game of jousting, and we, in turn, shall try to conform to *your* standards!"

Piovano Arlotto Earns a Place by the Fire

Piovano Arlotto, returning from Casentino one terribly rainy Sunday, was exhausted and soaking wet. He dismounted at the inn, at Pontassieve, and entered to dry himself by the fire.

But, as it happened, there were thirty or more villagers present, drinking and playing cards, and they were crowded so closely about the fire that he could not get near it. Nor would they make room for him, even though he politely asked. At last, the innkeeper, who knew Arlotto as a man of high humor, approached him.

"Father, why are you so sad this evening? It is so unlike you. If there is anything troubling you, just tell us. You know I would do anything for you."

"Truly, I am in a bad state," sighed Arlotto. "I have just lost fourteen *lire* in small change, and eighteen gold florins."

"Where did you lose the money," asked the innkeeper eagerly, as the villagers gathered round.

"Only within the last three miles, I am sure. I must have dropped them right in the middle of the road. But the weather is so bad, no one else will be traveling that road tonight, so the money will certainly be there tomorrow morning. If it stops raining by then, perhaps you can come with me, or send a man back along the road with me to find it."

The innkeeper was thinking about the best means of finding the priest's lost money when Arlotto interrupted his thoughts.

"Aha, everyone seems to have left—and so suddenly," he smiled. "Now where do you suppose they are going in all this foul weather? Well, no matter. Bring me some wine, while I warm myself by the fire. There now seems to be plenty of room."

—Anonymous
(See footnote, page 31)

If One Cup of Wine is Good, Two Must be Better

Giuliano Davanzati, who served as *Gonfaloniere* (Minister) of Justice, and represented the Florentine State on several diplomatic missions, was once appointed ambassador of the Florentines to King Alfonso of Naples. By sheer chance, the distinguished statesman, accompanied by a lesser diplomat who was also to be received by the Neapolitan emperor, arrived on the very morning that the first hearing was scheduled. Ambassador Davanzati ordered a modest breakfast and, to his colleague's evident distress, also ordered a large cup of malmsy wine to "wash down" the morning repast.

"Giuliano, your mission is far too important to drink so heavily," protested the companion. "You should be absolutely sober when you meet the king."

"Have no fear," replied Davanzati, taking a huge drink and smacking his lips with audible pleasure. "One cup of wine, big as this cup may be, will have no effect on me at all."

He indeed spoke the truth. Under his colleague's worried eye, Davanzati comported himself extremely well, successfully accomplished his mission, and was, in fact, commended by King Alfonso and the members of his court.

When they returned to their lodgings, the companion joyously clapped the ambassador on the back. "Giuliano, you were superb!" he enthused. "Congratulations!"

"I thank you," responded Davanzati with a merry twinkle in his eye. "But think how much more superb I would have been if I'd had *two* cups of wine!"

—Niccolo Angeli dal Bucine (*c*.1430-99)

LADY LUCRETIA'S BLEMISHES

Not long after Florentine Ambassador Giuliano Davanzati was received at the court of King Alfonso of Naples, it was strongly rumored that the emperor had fallen madly in love with Lady Lucretia, a Neapolitan noblewoman. Of course, it was commonly assumed that he was sleeping with her. Giuliano, who had become quite friendly with the king, was consumed with curiosity as to whether or not the gossip was fact or fiction (although he was the first to admit that it was none of his business).

One balmy spring morning, Giuliano accepted an invitation from King Alfonso to ride with him and enjoy the lovely weather. As they rode together, they happened to meet Lady Lucretia—she of the raven hair, flashing eyes, and breasts that made men moan *mama mia!* She smiled and deferentially inclined her head in a most charming manner.

Here was the opportunity Giuliano had been waiting for. When he and the emperor had exchanged greetings with the beauteous noblewoman, and had passed each other, the impudent ambassador commented, with studied casualness, "Lady Lucretia is truly one of the loveliest women I have ever seen. Isn't it unfortunate that she has those two ugly blemishes on her body?"

"Ugly blemishes!" the king fairly exploded. "What in hell are you talking about?"

"I have heard rumors, Your Majesty, that she has two large moles—one on her left buttock and the other on her right thigh."

"*Per cap de Dieu* ["By God"], that's a damn lie!"

"Per cap de Dieu, I believe you!" grinned Giuliano. "I was only exploring a rumor."

—Niccolo Angeli dal Bucine

LAW OF DIMINISHING RETURNS

Messer Diomede Caraffa, Count of Matalona, was a close friend of King Ferrando of Naples. Besides acting as the king's confidant, he also served as prime minister of the state, and frequently took on additional duties, as well. He was a busy man indeed. His only form of relaxation was draughts,* which he played slowly and very poorly. Truth to tell, he seldom won a game.

One evening, as he was playing draughts with a Florentine citizen named Albizi, and deliberating even longer than usual over each move, the visitor finally gave voice to his exasperation.

"*Signor* Caraffa, why do you take so long to make simple moves? *Must* you play so slowly?"

"My dear Albizi," explained Caraffa with a patient smile, "experience has taught me that the slower I play during the course of an evening, the less I lose!"

—Niccolo Angeli dal Bucine

HEART'S DESIRE

The famous preacher, Brother Roberto from Lecce, was to deliver a sermon in Perugia. Now Brother Roberto was an observant friar of the Order of Saint Francis, and though his piety was blameless, he was not above adding a few dramatics to his exhortations to heighten the interest of his listeners.

On this occasion the topic of his sermon was "Love for the Church." He selected four of the prettiest girls in the congregation, bade them dress in snow-white robes and adorn their long black tresses with white and pink flowers. And when they had complied with his demand, they did indeed look like four beautiful angels, as Brother Roberto had intended. He then approached a simple-minded young fellow named Marcone, and explained the role that the backward youth was to play in the forthcoming drama.

"I will discuss the love everyone should have for the Church," explained the friar, "and, finally, I will point to you and ask that you, too, affirm your love. Do you understand?"

---

*The game of checkers.

"I—I think so," replied simple Marcone uncertainly.

That Sunday, the entire congregation filled the church to hear the famed preacher. Brother Roberto, surrounded on the podium by the four lovely "angels," and well-satisfied with his prearrangements, launched into his sermon:

"Ask any king where lies his greatest love, and he will answer, 'The Church!' Ask any prince, count, or duke the same question and he will say, 'The Church!' Yes, you can even ask any simpleton, and he will say, 'The Church!'"

Brother Roberto now fixed a holy eye on Marcone who was conveniently seated in the first row.

"And you," thundered the preacher, pointing to Marcone, "with your mouth open and drooling down your chin, you are the perfect example. Stand up, young man, and tell us what you most love."

Marcone rose from his seat, cleared his throat, and announced in tones loud enough for the entire congregation to hear:

"I would most love to have one of those four girls!"

—Niccolo Angeli dal Bucine

Young Men are Durable

We are informed by Tomaso Betti who, in turn, was told by his wife that on the hot summer day of July 10th, in 1481, a group of Florentine housewives were gathered together in the courtyard outside their homes to catch any wayward breeze that might arise. As they gossiped, their conversation turned into a spirited argument as to whether it was preferable for a young woman to marry a fellow in his twenties or an older man of forty or more.

"A woman would be wiser to marry a man in his forties, or even fifties," insisted one. "At that age he has settled down. He is less likely to chase other women. He gives his love to his wife. And he is always home at night, as he should be."

"Well, older men may be more mature and give more attention to their wives," admitted another of the women, "but a younger man in his twenties, being more passionate by nature, is therefore a better lover. Wives should just overlook his absences on those evenings when he does not come home."

Neither side in the debate was able to convince the other, and the argument was becoming heated, when Monna Bartolomea, highly respected wife of Tomaso Betti, passed by.

"She will settle the dispute," cried one of the group. "Let us ask her opinion."

The good woman listened carefully to both sides, and then stated her view.

"A woman should marry a young man," she asserted. "True enough, he might occasionally stay out late at night, but no matter what time he returns home—he's still young!"

—Niccolo Angeli dal Bucine

OWNERSHIP IMPROVES THE VIEW

Although the hills of Fiesole were rocky and steep, Giovanni, son of Cosimo de' Medici, decided that this would be the ideal place on which to build a magnificent palace. The rugged terrain made the construction more difficult and expensive than he had first thought, but now that it was completed, he was well pleased.

Several weeks later, Giovanni's father, Cosimo, came to visit his son and to inspect the new palace. The older man was quite impressed with the structure, but disappointed with the bleak location.

"Giovanni," he said when he had finished his inspection, "your palace is undeniably beautiful, but why did you select such a bare, stony hillside, instead of building on our own land in Cafaggiuolo?"

"I chose this place because of its high elevation," explained Giovanni. "The view from here is very pleasing."

"Pleasing!" snorted Cosimo. "You would have found the view far more pleasing in Cafaggiuolo."

"But that's in the valley!" protested Giovanni.

"Yes, it is," agreed Cosimo. "But the view from here in Fiesole looks out over the lands of strangers, while in Cafaggiuolo, everything that meets your eye belongs to you. My son, no view in the world is more pleasing than that!"

—Niccolo Angeli dal Bucine

CREATIVITY BY INSTINCT

Among the many painters in fifteenth-century Florence, there was one known as Gherardo, a fine painter, perhaps, but not one to be numbered among the masters. One day, a prospective customer called on Gherardo and introduced himself as Simone. The customer had brought with him a sketch from which he wanted a painting made.

But it soon became evident that Simone had some misgivings about Gherardo's ability. He inspected the progress of the picture repeatedly, a worried look on his face, voicing his concern that it might be less than satisfactory when finished.

The constant annoyance proved too much for Gherardo. "Simone," he snapped, turning to point at his comely young son who was standing nearby, "would you agree that this boy is handsome?"

"I would indeed," responded Simone, surprised at the question.

"Then you will be interested to know that I created him in the dark of night," Gherardo said through clenched teeth, "so just imagine what I can create in the light of day!"

—Niccolo Angeli dal Bucine

How a Lawyer Got His Money's Worth

In our city of Bologna there flourished a learned advocate, a member of the great Castello family, Messer Dionisio by name. On the occasion of which I now speak, Messer Dionisio was retained as counsel to *Signor* Giovanni de' Bentivogli. I do not recollect the name of the opposing attorney just now, but the case was tried before our worthy magistrate, Messer Nicoluzzo de' Piccoluomini, of Siena.

As it often happens to lawyers when deeply engaged in the interests of their clients, they became so abusively personal that at length the other lawyer—unable to bear the bitter taunts that were being flung at him—called Messer Dionisio, in open court, "a rogue without honor" and "a God-damned liar"; whereupon Messer Dionisio, who found no enjoyment in the insults, doubled up his fist and smashed the other advocate in the mouth.

The presiding magistrate, greatly scandalized at this new method of emphasizing an argument, vigorously scolded Dionisio, and threatened to enforce the full penalty of the law for this act of contempt of court, adding that he was being very lenient in not committing him to jail on the spot. He would have carried out the threat, had not the thought of Messer Dionisio's high connections restrained him. But the impertinent lawyer seemed well able to defend himself.

"Most noble sir," Dionisio said with perfect composure, "according to our civil law, I believe you will only be able to fine me about ten pieces." He put his hand in his pocket and withdrew ten gold ducats. "Here, take these twenty pieces, and if the fine be only ten, as I surmised, just return the remainder."

The judge, however, in a rage, seized the entire twenty. "The fine is ten ducats for striking the other attorney, and ten ducats for offending the principles of law," he snarled. "You will have to look elsewhere for the other ten pieces. I'll not be returning it."

Turning quickly around, Dionisio suddenly hit the other lawyer again, a blow of the fist that was even more forceful than the first one. Once more he turned to the bar of justice and addressed the judge.

"My lord, I have paid ten ducats for enforcing my arguments against a disreputable advocate, and I have paid another ten pieces for contempt. However, I did hit him again, for which I now pay an additional ten gold ducats. I believe, sir, we are now equally satisfied." Dionisio then turned his back on the court and left.

The judge, though incensed at Dionisio's audacity, and remembering again the lawyer's important connections, finally came to his just and impartial decision:

"The party who received the injury sustained all the loss."

—Sabadino degli Arienti (c. 1450-1500)

PIRRINICOLO AND THE ARROGANT SPANIARD

Messer Pirrinicolo, a Gascon, was a tolerant man, but his tolerance did not include Spaniards. Neither could he abide arrogance—in anyone, whether Spanish or not. Woe betide the man, however, who was both Spanish *and* arrogant.

One evening, while on a journey, and finding himself hungry, he stopped at an inn where he was served a plump and juicy duckling. Messer Pirrinicolo had scarcely tasted the first morsel when suddenly a shadow fell across his table. He looked up to see a bearded stranger, resplendent in colorful Spanish garb, standing haughtily before him, gazing at the roasted duck.

"Have we met, sir?" asked Pirrinicolo curtly.

"Perhaps not," replied the stranger in Spanish-accented Italian, "but surely you will invite an important traveler to your table."

"What is your name?" snapped Pirrinicolo, wishing to confirm his suspicions before answering the man's impertinent suggestion.

"I'll have you know," said the man in a lofty manner, "you are addressing Don Carlos Aloponzio Castenada Gonzales de Castile."

"Oh, my, you don't say!" retorted Messer Pirrinicolo, his voice dripping sarcasm. "That's very impressive! But I am afraid, your Godship, that this little duck would hardly be enough to satisfy four such important men as you. However," he concluded in a low but deadly voice, "please feel free to invite yourself to my table again when you have changed both your nationality and your manners!"

—Leonardo da Vinci (1452-1519)

DOUBLE STANDARD

Antonio da Palermo, a sensitive and witty man of gentle birth, was discussing the institution of marriage with a friend. The friend insisted that, because of the many arguments that arose between husband and wife, the possibility of an ideal marriage was very remote.

"Not as remote as you think," countered Antonio. "When all is considered, there are only two requirements for an ideal marriage."

"Two requirements? What are they?" demanded the friend.

"First, the husband should be deaf as a stone, and second, the wife should be blind as an oyster," explained Antonio with a wide grin. "In those happy circumstances, the wife would not see her husband's escapades, and he would not hear her constant nagging."

"Oh, so that's the way the maxim goes!" exclaimed the friend. "I heard it some time ago and it almost ruined my marriage. It was first told to me in reverse!"

—Leonardo da Vinci

PROCESS OF ELIMINATION

In celebration of a recent military victory, Federigo, king of Naples, invited his general of the army, Prospero Colonna, to dine with him. Also present at the dinner was Vito Pisanello, the emperor's chief adviser, a man with kinky hair usually seen on Africans. The fact that both guests held a deep dislike for each other only served to amuse the king, who felt that their mutual hostility would help enliven the evening.

When they had finished their repast, and the wine had been flowing for some time, the king, in an expansive mood, was struck with a humorous thought. Smiling, he turned to his general.

"Prospero," he began, making an effort to appear serious, "have you ever noticed how a man's physical characteristics are often held to be an indication of his nature? For instance, a man with a receding chin is thought to be weak; one with small eyes and thin lips is believed to be mean and miserly; a man with kinky hair, such as Vito's here, is said to be either poetic or evil."

"Your majesty," declared Prospero, as the kinky-haired adviser maintained a sullen silence, "surely Vito is not poetic!"

—Leonardo da Vinci

BLESSINGS FROM ABOVE

Seated by a window in his second-floor studio, Marco Vitelli, the painter, was adding a touch of color to an oil he had almost completed, when all at once the door opened and Priest Satrielli entered the room. Immediately he began to sprinkle water on the floor, the walls, and then on Marco's treasured masterpiece. The water spots on his new landscape almost caused the painter to faint.

"What are you doing?" he screamed.

"I am doing what I am supposed to do," replied Priest Satrielli in a calm voice. "This is Holy Saturday. You certainly know that every priest visits the homes in his parish on this day, to bless them with holy water."

"But *why*?" Marco wailed, almost hysterical with anger at the sight of his splattered painting.

"Because it is good in the sight of our Lord," explained the priest. "Remember, God has told us that every good deed we perform will be returned to us a hundredfold from above."

As soon as the departing priest closed the door behind him, Marco, with a despairing look at his water-marked landscape, rushed into an adjoining bedroom and seized his night bucket, which was filled to the brim. He then raced to the open window and emptied the contents of the bucket down upon the head of Priest Satrielli as the good Father emerged from the house.

"Here is the hundredfold you expected from above!" yelled the raging Marco. "And don't forget to come back next Saturday, for an even greater good return!"

—Leonardo da Vinci

Reincarnation of an Ass

Bardella from Mantua, the same whose life was to end on the gallows, had become interested in the doctrine preached by the ancient Greek philosopher, Pythagoras, relating to the transmigration of souls. So firmly did Bardella come to believe in the Pythagorean theory that he was at last convinced of his own former incarnations.

But not all his friends shared his opinions. On his thirty-fifth birthday, while chatting with his friend, the outspoken senator Queraldo of Aragon, Bardella made the rather startling observation that he clearly remembered a previous life in which he had been a miller.

"That is pure nonsense!" declared Queraldo with his customary rudeness. "I fear, my friend, that you are losing your God-given good sense!"

Bardello's temper flared. It was one thing to disagree, but quite another to suggest that he was insane.

"I haven't the slightest doubt about the humble role I played in my previous life," he hissed through his teeth. "My vision was quite clear. In fact, at the same time I saw myself as a miller, I noticed that you were the ass that carried the flour!"

—Leonardo da Vinci

Abbondio's Unpriestly Candle

No doubt you will recall Father Abbondio, the priest who was defrocked last year [1497] in Florence. It pains me, as a gentleman, to relate this story, but the truth must be told.

Father Abbondio, returning from a mission in the countryside, happened to pass by a comely young woman whose name was Maria. At once, he noticed that her feet, which were bare, were also very red.

"My good woman," exclaimed the priest, "why are you not wearing shoes on this chilly day? Your feet are red with cold!"

"I need no shoes," laughed Maria with a wanton toss of her head. "My feet are red because of the fire burning in my love nest."

The woman's answer aroused that part of Father Abbondio which was responsible for his being a priest instead of a nun. "Madam," he crooned, "would you be kind enough to light my candle?"

—Leonardo da Vinci

A Priest's Hidden Assets

At dinner with a group of friends one winter evening, Lorenzo de' Medici and the others got around to discussing some church fathers of their acquaintance.

"It seems that we lesser mortals are unable to protect ourselves from priests," laughed one of the diners.

"And no wonder, considering the long cassocks they wear," agreed Lorenzo, grinning. "When you are not facing them they can kick your ass without your seeing them; and when you are turned toward them they can kick you in the balls before you can see their leg move!"

—Angelo Poliziano (1454-94)

Greetings to an old Friend

It so happened that Martino dello Scarfa, who weighed almost as much as a full-grown cow, and whose belly hung halfway to his knees, felt an urgent desire to pass his water. As he was in the countryside and thought no one was near, he relieved himself by the side of the road. But as he was completing the activity, he noticed that a small wide-eyed farm boy had been staring at him. Martino, however, was anything but embarrassed.

"If you should happen to see him, say hello for me," said fat Martino, grinning. "I haven't seen him in years!"

—Angelo Poliziano

Powerful Neighbors Require Caution

Sandro Botticelli, the eminent Florentine painter, was escorting his friend, Palla Strozzi, through his new house.

"I do like my home," remarked Botticelli, "except for one thing: the view from this front window is blocked by that large tree over there. Can you suggest anything I might do about it?"

"Who owns the property where that tree grows?" asked Strozzi.

"Nannina de' Medici."

"Then my suggestion is that you brick up your window!"*

—Angelo Poliziano

No Pears for a Pig

At an inn, Cosimo de' Medici noticed that a farmer was eating his meal without fruit. Being a compassionate man, Cosimo ordered the waiter to serve a big Anjou pear to the rustic.

"What is this?" exclaimed the peasant in surprise when the large fruit was placed before him.

"It is called an Anjou," explained Cosimo.

"Sir, you probably expect me to thank you," said the farmer crossly, "but I only eat the little pears that grow wild. We feed pears like this to the pigs."

"Well," snapped the irate Cosimo, snatching the pear from the table, "I do not!"

—Angelo Poliziano

Not Ashamed of Wearing Silk

Dante Alighieri, the great Florentine poet, was walking to his home on

---

*The de' Medici family directed the destinies of Florence from the fifteenth century until 1737. Of obscure origin, they rose to immense wealth as merchants and bankers, became affiliated through marriage with the major houses of Europe, and, in 1569, acquired the title grand dukes of Tuscany. The family also produced three popes (Leo X, Clement VII, and Leo XI), two queens of France (Catherine de' Medici and Marie de' Medici), and several cardinals. From 1516 to 1521 they also ruled the duchy of Urbino.

Until 1532 the democratic constitution of Florence was outwardly upheld, but the de' Medici exerted actual control over the government without holding any permanent official position. They were driven from power and expelled from Florence several times, but the attempts (such as the Pazzi conspiracy of 1478) of the Florentine republicans to restore the former liberties failed ultimately because of the de' Medici's wealth and powerful connections.

The rule of the de' Medici, though denounced by their enemies as tyrannical, was at first generally tolerant and wise, but became stultifying and bigoted in the seventeenth and eighteenth centuries. However, under them, early Florence experienced a great cultural flowering, accompanied by tremendous economic prosperity and territorial expansion. Florence as it is today is largely the accomplishment of the de' Medici.

a Sunday afternoon when he met a poor man wearing a threadbare patched coat. Stopping to give him a few coins, Dante asked, in a kindly manner, "Aren't you embarrassed to go about with a big silk patch in your coat?"

"Not at all," replied the man. "I wish the rest of the coat were exactly like it!"

—Angelo Poliziano

Tall Tales—Italian Style

Two seafaring traders, Antonio, a Roman, and Luigi, a Venetian, met at a hostelry in Florence, and decided to spend a pleasant evening together over some good malmsy wine. As they drank, they entertained each other with stories of the unusual events and sights they had witnessed in their travels. The more they imbibed of the heady wine, the more imaginative grew their tales.

"None of the things you ever saw can equal a sight that met my eyes in Tuscany," declared Antonio solemnly. "I was riding past a farm one day in the latter part of autumn, when I perceived what I thought to be a large hill in the center of the field. But as my horse brought me closer, I now saw that it was a gigantic cabbage that took me a full hour to ride around it."

"That was indeed a sight," agreed Luigi, "but not equal to the cauldron I once saw in Venice. That pot was so big that it required an army of workmen to construct it. It was so large that the workers on opposite sides of the cauldron could not even see each other. When they needed to communicate, they sent messengers on horseback, so they might have a reply on the following day."

"My goodness!" exclaimed Antonio, clearly impressed. "Why in the world would anyone build such a huge cauldron?"

"Reason enough," grinned Luigi. "To cook that cabbage!"

—Angelo Poliziano

A Peasant Gives
Antonio His Due

There is no doubt that Messer Antonio da Cercina was a gentleman of high birth, but he was also an arrogant man who prided himself on his quick, biting wit. After a lengthy absence, he was returning to his home in Florence when he met a peasant who worked for a neighboring prince.

"Ho, there, Bernardo," called Antonio, drawing in the reigns of his horse. "What is the news in Florence? Start with your best lie."

"Sir," responded peasant Bernardo promptly, "the news is that you are a decent and modest man!"

—Angelo Poliziano

Lorenzo de' Medici Meets a Cross-eyed Genius

Returning from Pisa with a group of friends, Lorenzo de' Medici noticed a cross-eyed student emerging from a university door.

"Who is that young fellow?" asked Lorenzo.

"I know his father well," answered one of the group. "That young man is Federico, son of Giovantomaso Galeotto, my neighbor. Why do you ask?"

"I predict that he will be a genius," asserted Lorenzo, and I would like to employ him someday to keep my accounts."

"What impresses you so much about the boy?"

"With those crossed eyes," explained Lorenzo, "he should be able to read both pages of a book at the same time!"

—Angelo Poliziano

Rinaldo Enjoyed His Own Happy World

It is said, on very good authority, that after Rinaldo degli Abizzi was exiled from Florence, he lost his mind for a period of two years. Hearing of this rumor, a simple peasant woman whose only son had suffered a mental collapse, went to see the gentleman.

"Messer Rinaldo, please help me," implored the woman. "My son went crazy six months ago, and no one knows a remedy that will heal his brain. They tell me there is no cure for insanity, but I have heard that you yourself were cured. I beg you, Messer Rinaldo, tell me how I can help my son."

"My dear lady," replied Rinaldo sympathetically, "don't worry about cures. Believe me, your son is happy. Why, when I was crazy, I enjoyed two of the happiest years of my life!"

—Angelo Poliziano

Bartolomeo Chooses Between a Wise and a Stupid Woman

Long after he became famous as one of the most skilled physicians in Pistoia, Bartolomeo let it be known to a matchmaker that he wished to marry. The matchmaker, eager to please this important client, searched far and wide for suitable brides, and finally settled on two young women from whom Bartolomeo could make his selection.

"Messer Bartolomeo," declared the marriage broker, "I have found the most outstanding ladies for you, and either one would make a fine wife. Angela is the wisest woman in all the provinces of Italy, but she brings a dowry of only two hundred ducats. Louisa, the other young lady, is said to be rather stupid, but she comes with a dowry of six hundred ducats. Both are pretty and have nice figures."

"Very well, I'll see them both," said Bartolomeo. "Bring Angela, the wise one with the small dowry, this evening. Tomorrow night you may bring Louisa, the stupid one with the larger dowry. On the third day I will tell you my choice."

Dutifully, the matchmaker complied with the noted physician's demands. On the third day he returned. "Which one did you choose?" he asked.

Messer Bartolomeo leaned back in his chair and offered a bit of Italian philosophy before making known his decision.

"I enjoyed meeting both women," he said. "They reinforced my long held opinion that there is not a grain of difference between the wisest of women and the most stupid. So I chose Louisa, the stupid one. I see no advantage in losing four hundred ducats for that non-existent grain!"

—Angelo Poliziano

The Long and Short of Choosing a Wife

Signora Bartolomeo was a small, slight young woman, at least two inches short of five feet. At a social gathering one evening, *Dottore* Bartolomeo introduced his bride to some guests who had traveled a long distance to view the physician's new wife. Later, one of the guests asked why he had taken such a tiny woman in marriage.

"Because," replied the wise doctor, "the less wife a man takes, the better off he is!"

—Angelo Poliziano

Fools and High Office

The Florentine ambassador to Rome, Piero, son of Cosimo de' Medici, was journeying homeward one hot day in July, when he was met by a group of officials of Perugia. They invited Piero to spend the cool of the evening and a restful night in their city. Gratefully, the weary Piero accepted, and they enjoyed each other's company until midnight. But, as in all groups, there was one official whose foolish statements and asinine questions almost drove the visiting ambassador to distraction. One of the hosts, noting Piero's mounting irritation, took him aside.

"Don't be too hard on him, Piero," counseled the man. "I am sure that you, too, must have fools just like him in Florence."

"Yes, we do," snapped Piero. "But we don't appoint them as officials!"

—Angelo Poliziano

Puccio Takes No Chances with Astrological Signs

For more than a week, the Florentine ambassador, Puccio di Antonio Pucci, waited impatiently, and with growing anger, for an audience with Duke Filippo in Milan. Puccio soon learned that Filippo conducted all his activities according to the conjunction of the stars. Precisely fourteen days after his arrival in Milan, the ambassador was visited by an official messenger of the court.

"His lordship, Duke Filippo, will see you within the hour," said the messenger. "The astrologer advises that this is the most propitious time for the duke."

"Young fellow," snapped Puccio, outraged, "you may inform Lord Filippo that I will call on him at another time. If this exact hour is most propitious for *him*, it certainly can't be for me!"

—Angelo Poliziano

Deep Thoughts on Intelligence—and the Lack of It

Giovanni de' Bicci, father of Cosimo de' Medici, once found himself in lively conversation with a traveler from Siena. Apparently the Sienese visitor had gained a negative impression of the inhabitants of Florence. Sourly, he remarked, "Florentines seem to have lost their common sense."

"That is not possible," retorted Giovanni defensively. "No one can lose the intelligence he was born with." Then, an impish afterthought brought a smile to his face. "However, looking at it more objectively," he added, "neither can anyone lose something he never had!"

—Angelo Poliziano

He Smiled at Me,
I Smiled at Him

The great *scultore* [sculptor], Donatello,* and his most talented apprentice, Ernesto, were quite fond of each other. One day, due to a relatively minor disagreement, Ernesto left his master.

Donatello, usually a mild and gentle man, flew into a rage. Ernesto had not only defied the law of the land, for he was legally bound in service, but he had brushed aside as of no consequence all the acts of kindness and patient hours of training he had received. To make matters worse, Donatello had boasted of Ernesto's loyalty to all who would listen. And now the sculptor had been publicly shamed. In a fury, he went to see his mentor, Cosimo de' Medici.

"Sir, will you tell me where I can find Ernesto?" he pleaded. "I am sure you know where he is."

"I know why you ask," replied Cosimo. "I have already heard that your apprentice left your service without your permission. But why do you seek him? Is it not beneath your dignity to forcibly return an unwilling servant?"

"*Return* him?" exclaimed the angry sculptor. "I intend to *kill* him!"

Cosimo, knowing Donatello's gentle nature, smiled inwardly, certain that the man's anger would quickly subside. "Very well, I'll tell you where you can find him. He has sought out the protection of my friend, the Marquis of Ferrara. But you can't just break in upon him: you would be beaten by his soldiers. I will write a letter of introduction for you."

Donatello accepted the letter with thanks, and made his departure. But Cosimo immediately wrote another letter in which he informed the Marquis of the sculptor's mild temperament, assuring him that it was very unlikely that harm would befall the wayward Ernesto. Cosimo then dispatched the letter by messenger astride his fastest horse.

In due time, Donatello appeared at the Marquis of Ferrara's palace. The Marquis, after listening with grave countenance to the complaints, gave Donatello his permission to kill Ernesto on sight.

An hour later, Donatello, calm and smiling, returned to the palace. "Did you find your apprentice?" asked the Marquis.

"Yes, we met in your olive grove," replied Donatello.

"Is he dead?"

"No, of course not! I was unable to take his life."

"Why not?"

---

*Donatello (Donato di Niccolo di Betto Bardi), a major innovator in Renaissance art, was born in Florence, in 1386. He created such classics as the bronze *David*, *Saint George and the Dragon, Magdalen,* and other noble works. Donatello died in 1466.

"Well, when we met I—er—you see—well, he smiled at me, and I smiled at him!"*

—Angelo Poliziano

Pope John's Worst Mistake

In the year 1415, events were clearly moving against Pope John at the Council of Constance where he was on trial.** Charge after serious charge was hurled against him, but to each one he would only respond with a muttered, "I have done worse."

At last, when a particularly harsh accusation was leveled at the impenitent Pope, and he again answered with the same enigmatic reply, the chief inquisitor rose up in unchurchly wrath.

"What could you have possibly done that was worse than the misdeeds we have uncovered?" thundered the inquisitor.

"The worst error I ever committed," explained the Pope mildly, "was in allowing myself to attend this trial!"

—Angelo Poliziano

What the Holy Mother Was Doing at the Time of the Annunciation

Father Bianchi of Castellina, a little town in the Chianti region of Tuscany, was a dedicated priest and, of course, a very devout man. But he had one regrettable fault: a foolish mouth. Whenever he spoke, his tongue ceased to be the servant of his mind and became its master. There was, for example, the unfortunate incident when Father Bianchi was delivering a sermon on the Annunciation. Apparently the congregation, nearly all women, were not as attentive as the good priest would have preferred.

"Ladies," he finally snapped, "try to put yourself in the Virgin Mary's place at the time of the Annunciation. Do you think, for one moment, she was dying her hair blonde? Was she knitting, or carrying on a conversation with her neighbor? No!" Father Bianchi paused for a second or two to heighten the dramatic effect, and then made his point:

"I'll tell you what the Blessed Mother was doing. She was holding a crucifix before her, and she was reading the Book of Hours of Our Lady!"

—Angelo Poliziano

---

*Donatello's comment, "I smiled at him, he smiled at me," has endured as a popular Italian saying, these past 500 years. Its meaning is akin to "A soft answer turneth away wrath."

**See footnote, page 13.

Little Carlo and His Hoped-for Inheritance

A fond father was teaching his small son, Carlo, the technique of safe horsemanship. Holding himself properly erect in his magnificent saddle of burnished leather and handsome brass fittings, he gave instructions to the boy who was astride a saddle blanket on a gentle mare. But the child was more interested in spectacular riding than in safe horsemanship.

"I want to gallop at full speed and jump over fences the way you do," protested Carlo.

"My son, you will need more experience to ride like that," explained the father kindly. "The slightest mishap could cause you great injury, perhaps death. Why, even with all my experience, every time I put my horse into a gallop and fly over a fence, I face death."

Little Carlo gave this possibility his serious consideration. "Papa," he said at last, "if you get killed, can I have your saddle?"

—Angelo Poliziano

The Fast Learner

In a small village near Arezzo, there lived an *avvocato* (lawyer) who had a wide reputation for his ability to win cases in the Court of Justice. A "simple" *contadino* (peasant) came to him, seeking information. It happened that the *contadino* was as "simple" as the foxes that killed his chickens but always managed to elude capture.

"Sir," asked the *contadino*, "will you teach me how I, too, can always win a legal dispute?"

"Yes, I will tell you my secret," agreed the *avvocato*, "but only on the condition that you pay me five ducats for my advice."

"Very well, I promise," affirmed the *contadino*. "I have been saving my money for years, hoping for this opportunity."

"The secret is to deny everything. Deny, deny, deny, and you will never lose. *Questo e tutto* (that is all)."

"*Grazie tanto*" ("Thanks very much"), said the *contadino*, rising to leave.

"*Aspetti un momento!*" ("Wait a moment!") snapped the *avvocato*. "You just promised me five ducats for my secret."

"Sir," came the quick reply, "I deny any such promise!"

—Angelo Poliziano

Beards and Wisdom

The *Signoria* (lordship) of Venice, seeking friendlier relations and more trade with Corsica, sent two brilliant but quite young ambassadors to that nation. To their chagrin, however, the Corsican ruler refused to grant them an audience. They demanded to know the reason.

"It is not only our custom," explained the king's messenger, "but also a matter of respect, that ambassadors who expect to conduct official business be older men, not mere youths."

"Please," they begged, "convey to his majesty our promise that if he will see us for only a few minutes, we will not speak of any official matters."

The king, informed of that promise, agreed to receive them. "What can you beardless boys possibly say that would interest me?" he rasped.

"Your Highness," declared one of the young Venetians, "we respectfully advise that if our *Signoria* had only known of the importance you attach to beards, we would not be here. Instead, he would have sent a couple of goats!"

—Angelo Poliziano

Botticelli Scolds a Vulgar Nursing Mother

Although it was not uncommon for peasant women to nurse their infants in public, such a display was always an affront to the moral and aesthetic sensibilities of Sandro Botticelli.*

On one occasion, while journeying through the countryside near the village of Maciuoli, he came upon a fat, unkempt farm woman who was nursing her child in full view by the side of the road. He was about to turn his head in annoyance when the woman suddenly perceived the distaste in his face. Apparently it angered her. With a quick and bold move, she contemptuously dropped her shoulder-cloth altogether, exposing both her breasts that hung like sacks of grain on either side of her navel. She then thumbed her nose at the appalled spectator.

But when Botticelli could finally speak, his comment came as a surprise to the impudent female.

"*Signora*," he said in what was almost a courteous tone, "Nature has indeed been kind to you."

Completely astonished, the woman could only stammer, "I—I—thank you, *Signor*, b-but how has Nature been kind to me?"

"It occurred to me," spat Botticelli, his voice undergoing a remarkable change from warm to cold, "if Nature had placed your breasts between your thighs, as she has with all other animals, you would scarcely be more unattractive when you nurse than you are now!"

—Angelo Poliziano

---

*Distinguished Florentine painter of the Renaissance (1440-1510), whose real name was Alessandro di Mariano Filipepi.

Ode to a Fool

> How happy is he, as all may see
>> Who has the good fortune a fool to be,
> And what you tell him will always believe!
> No ambition can grieve,
>> No fear can affright him
> Which are wont to be seeds
>> Of pain and annoy.
> This doctor of ours,
>> 'Tis not hard to delight him—
> If you tell him 'twill gain him
>> His heart's wish and joy,
> He'll believe in good faith that an ass can fly,
> Or that black is white, and the truth a lie;
> All things in the world he may well forget,
> Save the one whereon his whole heart is set.

—Niccolo Machiavelli (1469-1527)
Chorus from "La Mandragola"

Fra* Timoteo's Monologue

I have not been able to get a wink of sleep tonight, for wondering how Callimaco and the rest have been getting on. I have been trying to pass the time, while waiting, by attending to various matters. I said the morning prayers, read a chapter of the *Lives of the Holy Fathers*, went into church and lit a lamp which had gone out, and changed the veil of a statue of the Madonna which works miracles. How many times have I told the monks to keep that image clean? And then they wonder why there is a lack of devotion!

I remember the time when there were five hundred images here, and now there are not twenty. This is all our own fault; we have not been able to keep up the reputation of the place. We used to go in procession after service every evening, and have the Lauds sung every Saturday. We always made vows here, so as to get fresh images, and we used to encourage the men and women who came to confession to make vows likewise. Nowadays none of these things are done, and we are astonished that there is so little enthusiasm.

What an amazingly small quantity of brains these monks of mine have among them!

—Niccolo Machiavelli

---

*In the Roman Catholic Church, a title of address for a friar or brother. In Italian, a shortened form of *frate* (brother).

A Roman Prelate of 1519

His hungry congregation waits in vain,
Wishing he'd come the Gospels to explain,
Begin, or rather end, his dull though noisy strain.

At last he comes, deep-crimsoned o'er his face,
A certain token of unlettered grace;
He mounts, the pulpit crackles with his weight,
His awful eyebrows the most distant threat;
Against his brethren he exclaims aloud
That they are too luxurious in their food,
In taverns more than churches take delight,
Feast on fat capons; quaff the livelong night;
While, could you rummage his own private cell,
No noble larder e'er was stuffed so well.

Let me have books those moments to beguile
When the rich prelate, in his haughty style,
Roars to his porter, "Here let who will come,
But be sure you tell them I am not at home."
So monks, carousing at their favorite meals,
Silence the interrupting sound of bells.

"Sir," should I say (for *Sir*'s the proper word
Even at a cobbler's stall or tailor's board),
"Good sir," though to a tattered Swiss, "I pray,
May I not see His Eminence today?"
"*No sproka to my Maister bater goud,
You go your lodgee, come as when you coud.*"*
"Sir, be so kind at least to let him know
That Lewis Ariosto is below."
He answers that his Rev'rence would not see
Saint Paul himself, though on an embassy. . . .
                              —Lodovico Ariosto (1474-1533)

---

*In the original, these lines are a barbarous mixture of Spanish, German, and Italian.

Astolfo in the Valley of Lost Wits*

. . . Now Astolfo was conducted by his guide into a narrow valley between two steep mountains. And in this place there was miraculously collected together everything which gets lost on earth, either through some failing of our own, or by the fault of time or fortune. I mean not only riches and power, but also those things which fortune alone can neither give nor take away. Many a reputation lies up there, which time, like a moth, has long been gnawing at here below, and also numberless vows and good resolutions made by sinners. There we will find the tears and sighs of lovers, the time lost in gaming, all the wasted leisure of ignorant men, and all vain intentions which have never been put into action. Of fruitless desires there are so many that they clutter up most of the place. In short, whatever you have lost here below you will find again if you go up there.

Astolfo, as he passed along, now and again asking questions of his guide, saw a mountain of blown-up bladders which seemed to be full of noise inside. And he knew that these were the ancient crowns of the Assyrians, and of Lydia, and of the Persians and Greeks, which once were famous, while now their very names are almost forgotten. Close by he saw great masses of gold and silver piled up in heaps, which were the gifts that people made to kings and princes, in hopes of getting a reward. He saw wreaths of flowers with traps hidden among them, and heard, in asking, that they were flatteries. Verses that men made in praise of their patrons are seen there, under the form of grasshoppers who have hurt themselves with silly chirping.

He saw many broken bottles of different kinds, and found that they stand for the service men pay to courts, and the thanks they get for it. Then he came to a great pool of spilled broth, and asking what it was, his guide told him that it represented the alms people direct to be given after their deaths. Then he passed by a great heap of various flowers which once were sweet scented, but now have a foul odor; this was a gift (if we may be permitted to say so) that Constantine bestowed on the good Pope Sylvester.

He saw a great quantity of twigs covered with bird-lime: there, O fair ladies, are your beauty! He saw . . . but it would be an endless task to count up the things which were shown him there. The only thing he did

---

*An account of Astolfo's journeys to the moon, on the winged steed Hippogrif, to recover the wits which Orlando lost for love of Princess Angelica. Orlando, whose true name was Roland, was the great French hero of medieval times, who served as Charlemagne's army commander, and who was killed in battle in the year 778. Italian Renaissance poets transformed the Oliver epics into poems of Orlando. Ariosto's epics are the most famous.

not find was folly: that remains here on earth, for no one ever parts with it.

At last Astolfo came to that which we are all so firmly persuaded we possess that no one has ever prayed to have it given to him—I mean common sense. There was a huge heap of it, as big as all the other things put together. It was like a clear, soft liquid which easily evaporates if it is not kept rightly corked, and was contained in bottles of various shapes and sizes, each labeled with the name of its owner. Astolfo noticed one which was much larger than the rest, and read on the label, *"Orlando's Wits."* He also saw a great part of his own; but what made him marvel more than anything was the fact that many people whom he had believed to have plenty of sense were now shown to have little or none, the bottles marked with their names being nearly full.

Some lose it through love, others in striving after honors; yet others, in seeking for riches by land and sea, or by putting their trust in great lords and princes, or in pursuing after follies of magic and sorcery, or gems or pictures, or anything else which a man values above others. There was a great quantity of the wits of philosophers and astrologers stored there, and also of the wits of poets.

Astolfo took up his own, having received permission to do so, and put the flask to his nose; and it appeared that his wits returned to their place right enough, for Astolfo thenceforth lived very wisely indeed for a long time. But afterward, it is true, he made one mistake which once more deprived him of his brains. Then he took up the large flask which contained Orlando's, which was no light weight, and turned to depart— pining with love for Princess Angelica, dead these many centuries.

—Lodovico Ariosto

An Independent Prisoner Asserts His Rights

Although Duke Ercole of Ferrara could be a stern disciplinarian when the occasion warranted, he was also noted for his broad streak of compassion—even for criminals. For example, should a lawbreaker commit such a grave act as to justify a flogging, Duke Ercole would assign a doctor to remain in attendance during the punishment.

On one such occasion, a man who had stoutly maintained his innocence was nevertheless sentenced to be flogged as he walked around the public square. To the attending doctor's amazement, the culprit, instead of walking as quickly as possible to bring the whipping to a speedy end, simply bowed his head and very slowly made his way around the square.

The doctor, who had been walking abreast of the prisoner, turned to him. "Look here, my good fellow, you are taking more punishment than the duke intended. Why don't you walk faster and get it over with?"

The man lifted his head until his eyes were level with the doctor's. It was a proud face, the doctor noted, full of anger and fierce independence.

"Don't tell me how to live my life!" the victim snarled. "As long as I'm the one being flogged, I'll walk as fast or as slow as I damn well please! When your turn comes for a flogging, you can choose your own pace!"

—Baldassare Castiglione (1478-1529)

THE PRIEST WHO WAS AN ENGINEERING GENIUS

In the palace of Duke Guidubaldo of Montefeltro, Messer Bernardo* was explaining the various facets of humor. Having discussed the sophisticated forms, he next turned to the subject of simple jokes.

"Before this palace was built," he said by way of introduction, "Guidubaldo's father, Federico, ordered that a huge pit be dug for the foundation. When the hole had been excavated, Federico was left with a hugh mound of earth from the pit. But where was he to put it? A priest from another city, visiting one day, gave the problem his serious thought, and was struck with a novel idea.

"'My lord, why not dig another hole,' suggested the priest, 'and put the earth from the first hole into it?'

"Federico, not wishing to embarrass the priest, restrained his impulse to laugh aloud. 'But where would I put the earth from the second hole?' he asked in a strained voice.

"'You need only dig a third hole,' explained the priest. 'But this time be sure to make the hole twice as large, so that it can hold the earth from both holes!'"**

—Baldassare Castiglione

FREE CHICKENS— SICILIAN STYLE

There was once at Padua a Sicilian scholar named Pontius. Now it so happened that he met a countryman who was carrying a pair of fat hens. Pontius, pretending that he wanted to buy them, made a generous offer to the rustic:

---

*Bernardo Dovizi da Bibbiena (1470-1520), a friend of the Medici; appointed cardinal by Pope Leo X.
**Eighteenth-century variants of this anecdote appear in the folk humor of Ireland and Eastern Europe (see Henry D. Spalding, *Encyclopedia of Jewish Humor* (1969), and *The Lilt of the Irish* (1978)(New York: Jonathan David Publishers, Inc.)

"Come home with me, and I will not only pay for the hens, but I will also give you a fine breakfast."

"Agreed," said the rustic. "Lead the way."

But instead of going directly to his home, Pontius led the simple man to a church tower. The structure was separated from the church, so that one could walk all around it. And opposite one of the four sides of this campanile,* in the rear, was the end of a little street. Here Pontius, who had already conceived a scheme to relieve the man of his chickens without payment, put his plan into action.

"Aren't you curious as to why I wish to buy your hens?" he asked.

"To eat them, of course," said the surprised rustic.

"No, I do not eat chicken," replied Pontius. "The fact is that I made a wager with one of my friends who insists that this tower has a forty-foot perimeter; and I say it doesn't. The loser must pay the winner two fat hens, exactly like yours. So, just a moment or two before I met you I bought this string to measure the base of the tower."

"What has that to do with me?" asked the countryman.

"Before we go home," explained Pontius, "I want to ascertain which of us won the bet." He then handed one end of the long string to the man. "Here, I'll hold the hens for you. You stand here while I measure the campanile." Now, holding the other end of the string in one hand, and the two hens cradled in his other arm, he slowly and carefully made his way around the tower, as if measuring it. Soon he disappeared around the corner of the building.

The countryman waited patiently for Pontius to complete his measuring, but finally, when he had waited long enough for Pontius to have measured three towers or more, he grew nervous. Following up the length of string, he turned the corner, then another corner to the rear of the tower. There, he found, not Pontius, but the other end of the string tied to a nail in the wall.

"The thieving bastard!" fumed the rustic. "He had no right to treat a fellow Sicilian like this. And to think I stole those two fat hens only this morning!"

—Baldassare Castiglione

Music from the Inner Man

"A man need not be a simple peasant to be awed by the uniqueness of

---

*An Italian form of bell tower, constructed chiefly during the Middle Ages. Built in connection with a church, but as a detached unit, it served as a belfry and watchtower. The first campaniles, built in the sixth century, were circular in shape. In the eighth century, the square plan was adopted. It is this latter type to which author Castiglione refers in this anecdote.

new experiences," remarked Cesare Gonzaga.* "I recall the time, earlier this year, when a friend of mine, a Brescian, journeyed to Venice for the Feast of the Ascension. He marveled at the abundance of beauty he found there, especially the glorious music. On board a ceremonial galley, the music was so beautiful it made him gasp with pleasure.

"'What did you like best about it?' I asked.

"'The perfection,' replied the Brescian. 'But what intrigued me most of all was one musician who played the strangest instrument I had ever seen. It was fashioned something like a trumpet, and I believe he called it a trombone. First he would slide it way down his throat. Then he would pull it all the way out; then he would slide it down into his throat again: in and out, out and in. I swear to you, Cesare, if it weren't for all that gorgeous music he was making, it would have made me sick just to watch!'"

—Baldassare Castiglione

Delayed Communications

At a gathering of intellectual friends, one evening, someone remarked that the Greeks are the world's most delightfully entertaining liars. Giuliano** quickly rose to the defense of his countrymen.

"One of the more outrageous stories in Greek mythology," began Giuliano, "is that of Daedalus and his son, Icarus, who attempted to fly from Crete on wings of wax and feathers. Such folk tales have earned the Greeks an unmerited reputation for fanciful prevarication. I say 'unmerited' because we Italians are really the indisputable champions. Permit me to offer one modest example.

"Vittorio, a merchant of Lucca, usually spent several weeks each year traveling through Europe, searching out those products he could buy cheaply and bring back to Italy for sale at a substantial profit. One bitterly cold day in January, Vittorio found himself in Poland, where he learned that a quantity of sable furs was being offered for sale. Unfor-

---

*Cesare (1475-1512) was the cousin of author Castiglione, and related to the Duchess Elisabetta Gonzaga (1471-1526), wife of Guidubaldo of Montefeltro, Duke of Urbino (1472-1508).

**Giuliano de' Medici (1479-1516) was the third son of Lorenzo de' Medici (known as *Il Magnifico*) and Clarice Orsini, and brother of Pope Leo X. He entered Florence in 1512 when the Holy League restored his family to rule the city. Having married a princess of the Nemours branch of the house of Savoy, he was invested with the duchy by Francis I of France, who also intended to place him on the throne of Naples. Giuliano was a patron of the arts and letters. His statue, by Michelangelo, together with the statues of Day and Night, adorns his tomb in the Church of San Lorenzo, Florence.

tunately, the owners of the furs were on the opposite side of the Dnieper River, in Muscovy,* an area he could not enter because of the war then being fought between the King of Poland and the Duke of Muscovy. But Vittorio was a resourceful man. Through the intervention of several Polish merchants whose trust he had won, Vittorio arranged to transact his business on the Polish frontier. The Muscovites were to stand on the bank of the Dnieper, on their side, while he was to take his place on the Polish side.

"The following Monday morning, Vittorio and a group of his newly-acquired Polish friends arrived at the riverbank, as expected. The weather had turned colder than anyone could remember in his lifetime. Indeed, it was so cold that the Dnieper was frozen as hard as iron, to its full depth.

"On the opposite bank, the Muscovite traders were ready. Time after time they called out the selling price of their furs, but their shouts could not be heard, for the cold was so intense that their words were frozen halfway across the Dnieper. There, in the middle of the frozen river, the words hung suspended in the air like droplets of ice.

"'I have a solution to this problem,' offered one of Vittorio's companions. 'We can build a fire halfway across the river. That should thaw out the words so they can continue across to our side and within hearing distance.'

"It was a good idea, they all agreed. Vittorio and each of his friends gathered up heavy loads of thick branches and built a huge fire in the middle of the river, knowing that the ice was too thick and rock-hard to melt. They then retired to their own side and waited for the words to thaw. But the Muscovites, unable to comprehend what Vittorio and his companions were doing, angrily departed.

"Several hours later, exactly as anticipated, the words that the now absent Muscovites had shouted began to thaw, gradually becoming loud and distinct enough so that the prospective buyer could at last hear the selling price of the furs.

"'Why, you dishonest sons of bitches!' roared Vittorio, infuriated at the high price. '*Prendetevi 'sti peli e ficcateveli in culo!*'"**

—Baldassare Castiglione

Golpino's Lucky Day

You say you never heard the singular adventure that befell old Gol-

---

* The Grand Duchy of Moscow, one of the major principalities of what was later to become Russia.
** "Take your furs and shove them up your. . . !"

pino? Well, in the interest of truth, as it is sometimes told, here is the incredible story.

Golpino, servant of Mario da Volteria, had grown so old and emaciated that he weighed scarcely more than a feather. One windy morning in March, about six years ago, Golpino was having some difficulty starting the fire for the day. To help kindle the sparks, the old man leaned forward and blew his breath on the dry sticks. He was successful far beyond his wishes. Suddenly the flames leaped out and skinny old Golpino was abruptly swept up the chimney by the draft.

But this was Golpino's lucky day, for he was caught crosswise at the very top of the chimney and became stuck there. I say he was lucky because, in another moment he would have been caught up by the wind and blown away to who knows where: possibly to some God-forsaken island where he would undoubtedly have starved to death or been eaten by cannibals.

—Baldassare Castiglione

AMBITION THWARTED

The Bishop of Corvia was an ambitious man who hoped that, by some stroke of good fortune, he would be appointed governor. Not one to wait idly for the whims of chance, he decided to increase his opportunities by prompting the Pope with a calculated hint.

"Holy Father," began the bishop when he was at last alone with him, "it is commonly reported in all Rome, and even in the palace, that your holiness is about to make me governor."

"Pay no attention to those silly rumors," snapped the Pope, annoyed with the poorly-disguised hint. "Those lies are being spread by rascals who do not have a word of truth in them.

—Baldassare Castiglione

DOG OR LAWYER?

A lawyer of Milan was pleading his client's case with such eloquence, and for so long a time, that his adversary at law, Antonio Roveni by name, called out in irritation, "What are you barking for?"

"Because," answered the talkative lawyer, "I see a thief!"

—Baldassare Castiglione

Physician, Lawyer, Theologian—Heal Thyselves

Messer Bernardo and *Magnifico* Giuliano were exchanging humorous philosophies, each adding a whimsical detail or two to the other's stories.

"I recall the time," said Bernardo, at his turn to reminisce, "when the Archbishop of Florence told Cardinal Alessandrino that a man has nothing but his goods, his body, and his soul. But his goods are ruined for him by lawyers, his body by doctors, and his soul by theologians."

"There is some truth in the observation," agreed Giuliano, laughing. "Nicoletto wasn't joking when he said that it was rare to find a lawyer who would go to court for a lawsuit of his own, a doctor who would take a physic, or a theologian who was a good Christian."

—Baldassare Castiglione

Gratitude

A miser, who had refused to sell his corn while prices were high, hoping they would go still higher, awoke one morning to find that the price had gone down. In his despair, he hanged himself to one of the beams in his chamber.

Pietro, one of his servants, hearing the noise, ran into the room and, appalled at finding his master hanging from the ceiling, he forthwith cut the rope and saved his life.

When the miser was refreshed with a cup of water and was himself again, he insisted that Pietro pay for the rope he had cut.

—Baldassare Castiglione

It's a Wise Horse That Knows It's Master

Although Giovantomaso Galeotto was widely known as a courageous soldier, utterly without fear, he could not fool Emilio, his old and faithful servant who had known the military officer since his boyhood.

Not long ago, when Giovantomaso's horse died, he asked Emilio where he might buy a fine young horse—one suited to warfare, and at a reasonable price. The servant promptly suggested his brother-in-law, a dealer in horses. A few hours later, Giovantomaso returned, fuming with outrage.

"That brother-in-law of yours is a damned thief!" he snarled.

"How strange," replied Emilio calmly. "He has been honest enough these past forty years. Why do you call him a thief?"

"Because he had the audacity to demand 150 ducats for a horse that was not worth a single ducat—not one!"

"What was the matter with the horse?"

"Physically the horse was all right," Giovantomaso admitted reluctantly, "but its temperament was absolutely unsuitable for a soldier. It was so shy that, at the mere sight of a weapon, it reared up on its hind legs, whinnied in fear, and ran off."

"My dear Giovantomaso," replied Emilio with all the impudence of a very old family retainer, "if my brother-in-law knew you as well as I, he would have demanded a *thousand* ducats for a horse that retreats at the very sight of a weapon!"

—Baldassare Castiglione

A PRIEST'S CONFESSION

A young priest of Bari, a town in the Po Valley, was saying Mass to his flock with all the earnestness of his pure and devout heart. He then launched into the general confession in the name of the congregation: "I have sinned in doing evil; I have sinned in saying evil; I have sinned in thinking evil." He then went on to name all the mortal sins, preceding each with "I have sinned."

One of the congregants, a righteous woman new to the town, was horrified at this public "confession" by a man of the cloth.

"Did you hear what that priest has done?" she whispered to her neighbor in the adjacent seat. "I will certainly report him to the bishop."

"Don't waste your time," cautioned the neighbor. "He is the bishop's favorite pupil!"

—Baldassare Castiglione

LORENZO HECKLES A JESTER

"Among the most devastating and cutting remarks that ever came to my attention," claimed Cardinal Bernardo Dovizi Bibbiena, "was the one made by Lorenzo de' Medici.

"For the better part of an hour, Lorenzo had been bored to the point of anger by a jester whose quips and jokes were as stale as last week's bread. At last, unable to endure even one more of the tired old jests, Lorenzo stood up and interrupted his tormentor.

"'Sir,' he said in a wintry voice, 'you couldn't even make me smile if you tickled me with the waving tail of a laughing hyena!'"

—Baldassare Castiglione

A Prostitute's Privilege

There is a custom in Spain that when a condemned man stands at the gallows, he may be saved from hanging only if a known prostitute requests that he marry her. The custom, unusual as it is, evokes many witticisms.

On one occasion, in our own time, the King of Spain became annoyed at some trifling breach of court etiquette committed by a novice Italian diplomat, and sentenced the offender to spend the night in jail.

The next day, upon his release, the Italian returned to the king's court so that he might continue his official and social duties. There, in the main hall, he joined a number of other diplomats, cavaliers and highborn ladies. Among them was *Signora* Boadilla, a malicious noblewoman who had gained the Italian's enmity from the moment they met.

"Aha," she exclaimed by way of greeting, "so you are still among the living! I was afraid you might be hanged."

"Thank you for your concern," he replied, bowing gravely. "I, too, was afraid—but only of the possibility you would not request to marry me!"

—Baldassare Castiglione

Short Cuts in Long Masses

A chaplain was conversing with the Duke of Calabria one Good Friday afternoon, when, in the course of their conversation, the cleric remarked that he could say the Mass faster than the Cardinal.

"You are taking liberties," smiled the duke. "I myself was present one Sunday when the Cardinal finished more quickly than any other priest I ever heard."

"He could not possibly say the Mass faster than I," insisted the chaplain heatedly. "I don't recite even half the silent prayers!"

—Baldassare Castiglione

Buffalmacco and His Demon Cockroaches

Buonamico Di Cristofano, the painter, nicknamed Buffalmacco,* was a pupil of Andrea Tafi, and has been celebrated as a practical joker by Boccaccio and Franco Sacchetti. From Sacchetti's notes, we glean this story:

When Buffalmacco was still a youth, studying under Andrea, his master had the habit, when the nights were long, of getting up before

---

*See footnote, page 3.

daylight, and calling his apprentices to work. This was displeasing to Buffalmacco, who had to rise in the middle of his best sleep. He gave serious thought as to how he might prevent Andrea from starting work before dawn. This is what occurred.

Buffalmacco searched out thirty great cockroaches in an ill-kept cellar, and fastened a little candle on each of their backs. At the hour when Andrea was accustomed to rise, he put them one by one through a hole in the door into Andrea's bedroom, having first lighted the candles. His master, awakening at the usual hour for calling Buffalmacco, and seeing the eerie lights moving about in the dark, was seized with terror. He began to tremble like the fearful old man he was, and to say his prayers and repeat the psalms until, at last, he put his head under the covers and thought no more of calling Buffalmacco, but lay shaking with fear till daybreak

In the morning, Andrea asked Buffalmacco if, like him, he had seen more than a thousand devils during the night.

"No, I saw nothing," replied Buffalmacco. "It is my custom to sleep with my eyes closed."

The next night, although Buffalmacco put only three cockroaches into Andrea's bedroom, the old man, still filled with the last night's terror and the fear of those few devils, could get no sleep at all. As soon as day came, he left the house determined never to return. It took a great deal of strong counsel to make him change his mind.

At last Buffalmacco brought the priest to his master, in an effort to console the distraught man. With the priest nodding in agreement at every word, Buffalmacco launched into an explanation of the nocturnal devils:

"I have always heard it said that demons are the greatest enemies of God. Consequently they can be reasonably expected to be the chief adversaries of painters because we not only make them hideous, but we also never cease making saints on all the walls, thus causing men to become more devout. So these devils, being enraged against us, and having greater power by night than by day, come during the dark hours, playing their tricks."

"Yes," affirmed the priest, and I can assure you that things will get worse if this custom of getting up early is not given up."

So it was that Buffalmacco, with the help of the priest, dissuaded Andrea from getting up so early, and the devils no longer went about the house at night with candles. But not many months after, Andrea, drawn by greed, began afresh to get up early and to call Buffalmacco; whereon the cockroaches began again to appear with their unholy lights. This final time, however, he was not only forced to give it up entirely by his own fears, but by the stern orders of the priest.

The matter was soon noised throughout the city, and that is why neither Andrea nor any other painter has since ventured to get up at night to work.

—Giorgio Vasari (1511-74)

VANITY

A certain painter completed a picture of a rural landscape in which several farm animals were shown. Among them was a jackass which looked better than all the other animals.

Michelangelo Buonarotti and another painter were studying the picture one day at a studio, when the other painter asked, "Have you noticed that the jackass is more lifelike than the rest? I wonder why."

"The reason is simple," declared Michelangelo. "Every painter succeeds best in a portrait of himself!"

—Giorgio Vasari

LIMITED ETERNITY

An obscure painter had executed a historical picture in which every figure was copied from some other artist, so that no part of the picture was actually his own. It was shown to Michelangelo by an intimate friend, who asked what he thought of it.

"The artist has done very well," observed Michelangelo, "but at the Day of Judgment, when all bodies will resume their own limbs again, I don't know what will become of that historical picture. God will be looking at a blank piece of canvas!"

—Giorgio Vasari

BENVENUTO CELLINI
OFFENDS THE POPE

When I had my little disagreement with the emissary of Cardinal Santa Fiore, my every word was forthwith taken to the Pope by the Cardinal. The Pope remained swelling with rage, but said nothing.

Now I do not wish to fail in stating my reasons in a just and righteous manner. That emissary of Santa Fiore's came to me one day and brought me a little ring all tarnished with quicksilver. "Burnish this ring for me," he commanded, "and be quick about it!"

I had a great many pieces of goldsmith's work on hand, with most valuable jewels waiting to be set; but hearing myself, moreover, ordered about with so much assurance by a man whom I had never seen or spoken to before, I answered him rather curtly: "I do not have a burnisher available at this time. I suggest you go elsewhere."

"You are an ass," he said to me, without any reason in the world.

"And you, sir, are a stinking liar," I said quietly, not wishing to overly offend an emissary of so important a man as the cardinal. "I am not an ass, but a man, and on every account a better man than you, and if you continue to bother me I will certainly kick harder than any ass in memory."

The emissary went straight to the Cardinal and made out that I had all but murdered him. And the Cardinal went to the Pope.

Two days after that incident, I was shooting behind the palace at a wild pigeon which had its nest in a hole, very high up. I had seen that same pigeon shot at by a goldsmith named Francesco della Tacca, a Milanese, who had never hit it. On the day when I was shooting, it had become shy, scarcely showing its head, and because this Giovan Francesco and I were rival marksmen, certain gentlemen and friends of mine pointed to the bird and said, "That is Tacca's pigeon; he often shoots at it. See how suspicious the poor bird has grown—it scarcely shows its head."

I looked up. "It shows quite enough for me to hit it, if only I had time to take aim first."

Those gentlemen then said that the man himself who invented the firelock could never hit it.

"I'm willing to bet a pitcher of the best Greek wine that I can bring that pigeon down," I told them. Then, taking aim, I did what I had promised.

Now I want it known that I accomplished this feat of luck without a single thought of the Cardinal or anybody else. Thus may the world see what diverse ways Fortune chooses, even when she initially takes what appears to be the ruination of a man.

To return to the Pope: he remained all swollen and sulky, brooding over what the Cardinal had told him about me . . . but that didn't impair my lucky shooting, either.

—Benvenuto Cellini (1500-70)

A Churchly Contribution
for Ser Nastagio

Faustino, of Bologna, was in love with the beautiful Eugenia, but was unable to meet her because of the hostility of her parents, who kept a very strict watch over her, and prevented him from seeing her as much as they possibly could.

The girl's mother, being of a religious turn of mind, was unwilling that her daughter relinquish her usual attendance at church, so she, herself, accompanied Eugenia every morning to hear Mass. They participated in the divine services at a very early hour so that not even the artisans of the city, much less the young men of the place, were stirring. And there Eugenia heard the service performed by a priest expressly for her, though several other persons might happen to be present, who were in the habit of rising early. But Faustino, a late sleeper, was not one of them.

Now among those who did attend divine worship at that early hour was a certain corn merchant named Ser Nastagio de' Rodiotti. This fellow was a man who had driven many a hard bargain and who had thrived wonderfully in his trade. But he was so devout that he would not for the world have made a usurious contract, or even speculated to any extent, without first having attended Mass. He never lost a single opportunity of showing himself at church among the earliest of the congregation, and was ready for business before a great portion of his fellow citizens were awake.

Now in a short time it also reached the ears of Faustino, through the good graces, it is supposed, of his sweetheart, that the High Mass was being heard at a certain church, with details about the worshipers who attended, and the shortest way to that certain church. Rejoicing at this news, he resolved to rise somewhat earlier than he had been accustomed to do, so that he might avail himself of the same spiritual advantage that the girl enjoyed; namely, starting the day with religious observances. For this purpose he wore different clothing, to deceive her careful mother, being perfectly aware that she only made her appearance at such an early hour with her daughter to keep the lovers apart. So it was that the young lady "brought" Faustino to church, where they gazed at each other with the utmost devotion.

But, alas, their gazing was often interrupted. With growing frequency, the aforementioned Ser Nastagio, the corn merchant, would accidentally place himself exactly in their way, so as to blot out the silent communion of souls. And this he did in so vexatious a manner that they could hardly observe each other for a moment without exposing themselves to his searching eye and keen observation. Greatly displeased at this kind of inquisition, however unwitting it may have been, the lover frequently wished the devout corn dealer in Purgatory, or that he would at least offer up his prayers in another church. Such an antipathy did he at length conceive to Ser Nastagio, that he resolved to employ his utmost efforts to prevail upon him to withdraw from that house of worship.

At last, Faustino hit upon a plan which he thought sure to succeed, and in a manner equally safe and amusing. He hastened without delay to the officiating priest.

"It has always been considered a laudable act to devote ourselves to the relief of our poorer brethren," Faustino began virtuously. "That fact, Messer Pastore, you doubtless know far better than I. But there are many who, however destitute, feel ashamed to come forward for the purpose of begging alms. I have, of late, observed one of them who frequents your church. His name is Ser Nastagio, a man whose exemplary life and conduct make him in all respects worthy of being called a Christian."

"You say this good man is very poor?" asked the sympathetic priest.

"There is not a more destitute being on the face of the earth. Yet, such is his modesty, I assure you I had the utmost difficulty in persuading him to accept alms. It would really be a meritorious act, Father, were you to touch some morning on his cruel misfortunes, and tell of his singular modesty with which he attempts to conceal his needs. If you would plead in his behalf, good Father, it would probably procure for him a handsome contribution. Indeed, if you would only be so kind as to suggest the day, I will bring a number of my friends along with me to help the poor fellow."

Our kindhearted priest cheerfully complied with the wily lover's request. He proposed the next Sunday morning, when a large number of people would be present, regretting that he had not sooner been informed of the affair. Faustino next gave an exact description of the corn merchant, observing that the poor man always appeared neat and clean, so that he could not possibly mistake him. Then, taking leave of the good friar, he hastened to communicate this piece of mischief to some of his young friends.

Punctually next Sunday they were at the church, even early enough to hear the first Mass—and there, already seated at his usual post, surrounded by a crowd of people, was Messer Nastagio. After going through the Evangelists and the Creed, and muttering a few *Aves*, the good priest paused and looked about him. Then, wiping his forehead and taking a few breaths, he again addressed the congregation:

"Dearly beloved brethren, you must be aware that the most pleasing thing you can do in the eyes of the Lord is to show your charity toward poorer Christians. As I know you are not lacking in charity, but rather abounding in good works, I am not afraid to inform you that there is a most deserving yet destitute man in our midst, who, though too modest to urge compassion, is in every way worthy of it. Pray take pity on him. Behold him!" he cried, pointing straight at Ser Nastagio: "Lo, thou art the man!"

"Yes," he continued, while the corn merchant stared at him in the utmost astonishment, "thou art the man! Thy modesty shall no longer conceal thee from the eyes of the people which are now fixed upon thee."

The priest continued to address Ser Nastagio, yet the bewildered and embarrassed merchant could not persuade himself against the evidence of his own reason that he was the person pointed out. Without stirring, therefore, he somewhat reluctantly put his hand into his pocket, preparing to bestow his alms in the same manner as the rest of the congregation. The first person to present his contribution was the author of the trick, who approached Ser Nastagio and, despite the merchant's strenuous objections, dropped some coins into his hat.

"I have a longer purse than you have ears," howled the incensed tradesman.

But his protests availed him nothing. The good priest pursued his theme and dismissed Ser Nastagio's remark with another impassioned plea.

"Give no credit to his words, dear people, but give him alms, give him alms," cried the priest. "It is his modest nature which prevents him from accepting your charity. Yes, go thrust your gifts into the good man's pockets; fill his hat, his shoes, his clothes with them, and make him take away with him the good fruits of your charity."

The priest once more directed his attention to the confused and angry merchant. "Do not look thus ashamed, but take them, take them. Believe me, good friend, many greater and better men have been reduced to the same piteous plight. You should consider it an honor, and not as otherwise, inasmuch as your poverty has not been the consequence of your own misconduct, but that you, as I have been told, were formerly an Israelite, and having converted to the one true religion, you lost your possessions only because you embraced the light of truth."

In his seat, Faustino sighed with relief. He had feared that the priest might have forgotten that little added touch.

The priest had no sooner ended than there was a general rush of the whole congregation toward the place where the merchant stood, endeavoring who should be first to deposit their donations in his hands, while he in vain attempted to resist the tide of charitable contributions which now poured in on every side. He had likewise to struggle against his own avarice, for he would willingly had received the money, though he did all in his power to repulse the gifts.

When the tumult had subsided, Ser Nastagio began to attack the priest in the most virulent terms, until the preacher was inclined to suspect that in some way he had been misinformed. He thus began to make his excuses, as well as he could, for his error. But Faustino's purpose was accomplished and the deed could not be recalled. For the story of the lover's prank was quickly circulated through the whole city, and Ser Nastagio was never known to enter that church again.

A joyous time occurred when the girl's mother later relented. Faustino and his beautiful Eugenia were finally joined in the bonds of holy wedlock, and they lived happily ever after—or until the honeymoon was over, which is all that decent people should ask or expect of the good Lord.

—Girolamo Parabosco (1507?-57)

WRONG DIRECTION

The Duke of Milan, an ill-tempered, often cruel man, finally met his match when he married Bianca, the worst, vile-mouthed shrew in all of Turino. When they were not exchanging obscenities, they were hitting each other. The duke often thought of putting her to death, but so great was his fear of her eight stalwart brothers that he restrained his daily impulse to end her existence. But the day finally arrived when she passed away—all by herself, with no assistance, evil or otherwise, from him. And two years later, the duke himself died. His ghost soon appeared at the gates of the Hereafter.

"Enter, and enjoy your eternal reward," said the gatekeeper. "You may now join your wife."

"*Enjoy my reward!*" screamed the outraged Duke. "Is this all I can expect in Heaven?"

"Heaven?" asked the gatekeeper, his voice puzzled. "Who said this was Heaven?"

—Ludovico Domenichi (1515-64)

Vows Must be Observed

It so happened that in the month of August, 1541, a young nun, whose age was twenty years, grew perceptibly round in the abdomen. The abbess finally noticed the young sister's condition and summoned her to appear forthwith before the chapter of nuns.

"You have slept with a man and brought disgrace on our convent," accused the angry abbess. "What have you to say for yourself?"

"You accuse me unjustly," replied the nun in self-defense. "I was in my room, preparing to retire for the night, when a handsome, very strong young man forced his way into my room and assaulted me. It would have been futile for me to have fought off such a powerful intruder. Surely, a woman who has been attacked cannot be accused of engaging in a sinful act."

"I still do not understand, sister," the abbess said, but in a more sympathetic voice. "Why did you not scream, so that we could all have run to your assistance?"

"I thought of that," admitted the nun, "but fortunately I remembered that I must not break our holy vow of silence!"

—Ludovico Domenichi

Desire and Old Age

Alberto, a simple fisherman, fell in love with the flirtatious Sofia, an orphan girl whose only living relative was an old grandmother. The young couple were duly married, but Alberto's wedded bliss was shattered within a year when he discovered that Sofia had been visiting the bedrooms of at least a half dozen other men on the wharves. Deeply hurt and angered, he made his complaints to his errant wife's grandmother, a scrawny, toothless, withered old crone whose incredible ugliness made her look more like a witch than a woman. She peered at him through her one faded, watering eye, cupping her hand to her ear so that she might hear him better.

"*Nonna,*" snapped Alberto after he had enumerated Sofia's many adulteries, "I have no choice but to send her back to you. I cannot have a wife who sleeps with every fisherman in town."

"Do not be hasty," cautioned Sofia's grandmother in a cracked voice. "Just be patient, and let nature take its course. She is young and filled with healthy animal spirits. But she will undoubtedly settle down with age. Why, when I was young, I myself had more affairs than I can remember, but when I grew old I reformed. I assure you, my dear Alberto," concluded the shriveled grandmother, wagging a bony finger in his face, "Sofia will someday be just like me—the most virtuous woman in all Italy!"

—Ludovico Domenichi

Rewarding a Robber

Perino, the old soldier, was awakened one night by a stealthy sound in his room. Seizing a sword he had worn during his younger days, he leaped out of bed and confronted a badly frightened robber.

"Sir," quavered the thief, "are you going to send me to prison?"

"No," replied Perino. "In fact, if you can find anything of value while searching in the dark, when I myself can't find anything worthwhile in broad daylight—I'll share it with you!"

—Ludovico Domenichi

Elena Knows Her Nose

On a lovely summer's day, not long ago, a young fellow named Pietro was lying under a bower of roses with Elena, the milkmaid. Elena was quite pretty, except for her nose, which, it must be said, was of majestic Roman proportions. Nevertheless, the fragrance of the flowers, the cool shade of the leaves which hid them from view, and Elena's apparent willingness to cooperate, made it all very romantic.

But Pietro, who considered himself to be a great wit, could not resist an urge to make a little joke.

"My dear Elena," he said in a serious tone, "I would love to kiss you, but that nose of yours prevents my lips from reaching yours."

"Pietro," she whispered, putting her arms around his neck and drawing his mouth close, "kiss me where I haven't got a nose!"

—Ludovico Domenichi

Whore or Queen—Always Respect the Elderly

One evening, as Cardinal Vespi of Rome was enjoying his usual after-supper repast of cheese and wine, the shocking news was brought to him that Brother Ventura, of his own court, had been seen in the company of Angela del Moro, the eighty-year-old madam of most of Rome's prostitutes. The outraged Cardinal immediately summoned the Brother to his chambers.

"Is it true that you have publicly honored the notorious Angela del Moro?" demanded the Cardinal.

"Yes, My Lord," admitted Brother Ventura without a trace of embarrassment. "I happen to be fond of her."

The brazen admission caused Cardinal Vespi's face to grow red with anger. "Have you taken leave of your mind?" he shouted. "How could you, a man of holy orders, lower your sense of dignity by honoring an old whore with your affection, and for all to see?"

"My Lord," explained Brother Ventura calmly, "I simply followed a precept which you yourself taught me when I first came to Rome: *Semper veneranda senectus!*"*

—Ludovico Domenichi

Following God's Example

Marco Cadamosto had a young son, a sociable youth of fifteen who was totally unlike his strong-willed, surly father. One day, the son, whose name was Vito, removed a prize fat hen from his father's flock of chickens to enjoy a clandestine feast with his companions. . . . This despite the older man's warning that the youth was forbidden to touch that particular hen. Now any other father would have admonished—perhaps punished—a son for the act of disobedience, but Marco Cadamosto was an unforgiving man. So great was his fury that he drove Vito from the house, ordering that he never return.

When the news of this expulsion reached the ears of the parish priest, that worthy and pious man quickly voiced his protest to the elder Cadamosto.

"Marco, how could you drive your own son—your own flesh and blood—from his home?" demanded the priest. "It is an offense in the eyes of God."

"I must respectfully disagree with you," countered Marco.

"On what grounds?" snapped the priest.

"I have two reasons," explained Marco. "First, we all know that God,

---

*Old age must always be honored.

the perfect Father, drove Adam from the Garden of Eden for eating the forbidden apple, while I, the imperfect human father, cast out my son for eating a much more valuable commodity—a chicken. Second, God created Adam of His own free will, in broad daylight, knowing exactly what He was doing. I, on the other hand, created my son, not in daylight, but in the dark, and certainly not aware that I was producing an offspring . . . and you have the audacity to ask how dare I cast Vito from his home? You may be a priest, but in this instance, Father, shame on you!"

—Ludovico Domenichi

DON CASTANEDA'S YOUNG BEARD

Of the many jests that Pope Paul III* loved to relate, the story of the black-bearded Spaniard was among his favorites. The incident, according to His Holiness, occurred during his visit to Siena, where he met a distinguished-looking traveler from Castile whose name was Don Castaneda. The stranger proved to be such a witty and altogether charming fellow that the Pope was quite taken with him. In the course of their conversation, he asked the Spaniard his age.

"I am sixty years old," said Don Castaneda.

"What! Sixty, you say?" exclaimed Pope Paul.

"You appear to doubt me," grinned the Spaniard. He removed his cap to reveal a shock of snow-white hair.

The Pope stared in astonishment. "My dear Don Castaneda, I did not mean to question your truthfulness," he said when he could finally speak. "I did not know, of course, that your hair was white. I only judged your age by your black beard. It makes you look like a man of forty."

"And why not, Your Holiness?" replied the Spaniard with a broad smile. "My beard is twenty years younger than the hair on my head!"**

—Ludovico Domenichi

---

*Paul III (1468-1549) was born Alessandro Farnese, in Rome. One of the most astute diplomats in the Church, he directed his efforts to the Catholic Reformation, attempting to reconcile the Protestants and reform the Church. After elaborate preparations and countless intrigues, the Council of Trent convened in 1545. Paul also patronized the newly founded Jesuits, the great agents of the Catholic Reformation. An art lover, he commissioned Michelangelo to decorate the Sistine Chapel and rebuilt and repaved many streets in Rome. He is often called the last Pope of the Renaissance because of his nepotism and his enthusiasm for art.

**This five hundred-year-old anecdote also appears in the humorous folk literature of other cultures; among them the Jewish people of Eastern Europe, the peasantry of Ireland, and in the orally transmitted folk tales of the mountain people of Appalachia in the eastern part of the United States, many of them descendants of early Irish settlers.

MICHELANGELO'S REVENGE

When Michelangelo Buonarroti had almost completed his painting of the *Last Judgment* in the Sistine Chapel, loud protests against the nude figures were raised by Biagio da Cesena, social director for Pope Paul III. The Pope, who was fond of Michelangelo, brushed the objections aside, but Michelangelo, upon hearing of the protests, grew furious with anger—not only because of the complaints, but also because Biagio had dared criticize his exquisite painting before it was finished. Michelangelo's revenge was swift and devastating. He added a nude figure in Biagio's image, portraying him beset and tormented by the devils of hell.

Once again, Biagio returned to Pope Paul to voice his outrage.

"I have never been so insulted in my life," he stormed. "Michelangelo is completely immoral. How dare he paint me naked, and present me as suffering in hell!"

"Just what would you have me do about it; ask him to paint a figleaf over your private place?" inquired the Pope, suppressing an urge to laugh aloud. "You would indeed look peculiar as the only modest figure in hell."

"But, surely, Your Holiness," persisted Biagio, you can at least use your influence to see that I am taken out of that place entirely."

"My dear Biagio, I am sorry to say that your request is beyond my power," observed the Pope calmly. "My authority is limited to Heaven and Earth. I have no jurisdiction in Hell!"

—Ludovico Domenichi

FRANCESCO'S PRECIOUS ANTIQUE

On an April afternoon in 1521, in the city of Florence, Francesco Berni* and a secretary of the Cardinal of San Giorgio were sipping wine in a tavern and chatting amiably. Their rambling conversation at length wandered to the subject of antiques—a hobby which the secretary followed with great passion.

"Do you happen to have any truly ancient antiques?" asked the secretary.

"Yes, I do have one," replied Francesco. "The only one in existence."

"The only one?" gasped the secretary. "I would love to see it."

"Very well, but you must give me your solemn promise that you will not ask to buy it. I simply cannot part with my treasure."

---

*Francesco Berni (1497-1535) served as a canon in the cathedral of Santa Liberata, and was a leading satirical poet of sixteenth-century Italy.

"Oh, I promise! I promise! Where is this remarkable antique?"

"At home," grinned Francesco. "She's my wife!"

—Ludovico Domenichi

Age of a Fool

Nicolo Fabiano, a wise and courtly gentlemen of sixty years, whose wife had passed away four years earlier, fell in love with Verda, a beautiful young woman. Now it happened that Verda was also being wooed by Salvatore, a youth of twenty-three. Salvatore, unlike his older rival, was a swaggering braggart and a practical joker who had never entertained a serious thought in his empty head: in short, a fool.

One evening, upon learning that the young lady had invited Nicolo to her home for supper—under the watchful eye of her mother, of course—Salvatore also presented himself at her door. There was nothing Verda could do but admit him. As they sat around the table, Salvatore, with a wicked smirk on his face, turned to the older man.

"Messer Fabiano," he asked abruptly, "how old are you?"

"Young man," replied Nicolo, well aware that the impertinent question was meant to embarrass him, "my age is not a matter of importance, but I can tell you this: a jackass of twenty-three is older than a human being of sixty!"

—Ludovico Domenichi

Acts of Friendship

Agostino, a one-eyed soldier from Parma, and his lovely bride, Giulia, awoke late on the afternoon following their wedding. Giulia at once perceived that her new husband seemed to be depressed.

"*Prediletto,*" [Darling] she crooned, "what is troubling you?"

"Giulia, it appears that you have misled me," he replied curtly. "I took it for granted that you were a virgin. Now, of course, I know better."

"You never asked me, and I did not think it proper for a lady to mention the subject," she said in her own defense. "But, really, what difference does it make?"

"You are not whole," he muttered sadly.

"Now see here, Agostino," snapped Giulia, unhappy that their first wedding day should be marred by an argument, "you are not whole, either. After all, you did lose an eye."

"Yes," admitted Agostino, "but my enemies caused my loss."

"Well," retorted Giulia, "my friends caused mine!"

—Ludovico Domenichi

The Brave Peasant

A simple Sicilian farmer and his wife were bringing their produce to the marketplace when a burly stranger leaped out of the bushes beside the dusty road. The brigand drew his sword and marked a circle in the dust at the peasant's feet. He then ordered the quaking farmer to get inside the circle.

"If you take so much as one step outside the circle, I'll cut your head off," the stranger warned grimly. He then took the peasant's wife into the woods where he had his way with her. When she returned, she found her husband still standing within the circle.

"Coward! Rabbit!" she yelled at him. "How could you stand there, doing nothing, while that animal raped me?"

"Doing nothing?" retorted the peasant, offended at the accusation. "I'll have you know I put my left foot outside the circle four times!"*

—Ludovico Domenichi

Quality of Life

A young fellow of twenty was caught in the very act of committing an especially vile criminal act, and was sentenced to thirty years at Le Stinche, a jail in Florence. Upon his release, the prison priest asked the now gray-haired man his age.

"I am twenty years old," was the prompt answer.

"But that's ridiculous!" exclaimed the priest. "You've been living right here at the Stinche for the past thirty years!"

"I do not count those years," snapped the man. "Do you call that living?"**

—Ludovico Domenichi

Dante Squelches
Three Hecklers

If ever there existed the slightest doubt as to Dante Alighieri's nimble

---

*A similar version of this tale is found in fifteenth-century Greek folk humor. Other variants appear in eighteenth- and nineteenth-century humor of Jugoslavia (Croatian), and in Russian folk literature.

**This ancient joke is found in the oral and written folk humor of all Mediterranean cultures. An eighteenth-century variant of this anecdote, in which a divorced wife refuses to count the years in which she was married to her former husband, replies, "Do you call that living?" appears in the folk humor of Northern Ireland, England, and the Jewish people of nineteenth-century America.

wit, the following confrontation between the great poet and several of his detractors should dispel all such doubt.

Three Florentine writers, none sufficiently gifted to attain prominence, were discussing Dante, jealousy plainly evident in their every jeering word. Particularly irritating to them, aside from his superior literary talent, was Dante's reputation for clever, instant retorts. As they strolled through Borgo Santo Apostolo, exchanging their sarcasms, whom should they see but Dante himself, approaching on horseback.

"Ahah!" exclaimed one, "here is our chance to deflate Messer Dante. Let us each, in quick turn, ask him a question or make a comment that requires an immediate answer. We will then see just how glib he really is."

"Yes, yes!" agreed the other two, eager to embarrass the poet.

As Dante drew near, they hailed him in quick succession, giving him no time to reply to each. "*Buon giorno*, Messer Dante," the first man called out. "Where have you been?" immediately asked the second. "Was the river high?" asked the third man rapidly.

Making no attempt to slow down his horse, Dante grinned, waved cheerily at them, and replied to each of the three without pausing for a single breath:

"*Bon giorno!* Rome! Up to your ass!"

—Ludovico Domenichi

FORGIVE FRIENDS, PUNISH ENEMIES

Perversions of humor wear many masks, as this example indicates.

Castruccio, the cruel monarch of Lucca who died in the year 1328,* learned of a plot to drive him from the throne. Acting swiftly, he sent a contingent of soldiers to arrest several members of the prominent Quartigiani family, and immediately had them put to death.

A few evenings after the executions, Castruccio was enjoying a pleasant conversation and sipping wine with Francesco Dolce, one of his very few intimate friends.

"My Lord," said Dolce after some time, "I was surprised to hear of the drastic punishment you dealt the Quartigianis. After all, they were your old friends."

"I did not execute my old friends," retorted Castruccio, "but rather my new enemies!"

—Ludovico Domenichi

---

*Castruccio was admired by Machiavelli, who wrote a romanticized biography about the tyrant.

Blessed Is the Peacemaker, For He Shall Suffer the Injury

Two peasants, Tesetto and Gelsomini, became so enraged during a heated argument, that they sprang at each other with fists and knives. At this point, Paolo, the village peacemaker, stepped between them and received an accidental knife-blow to his head. The injury was superficial, only the point of the blade penetrating his scalp, but the flow of blood was frightening, nonetheless.

Forgetting their differences, Tesetto and Gelsomini took him to the local barber for treatment.*

"What happened to him?" asked the barber as he dressed the wound in the peacemaker's scalp.

"Paolo tried to stop our fighting," confessed Tesetto ruefully, "and caught the knife-blade by accident."

"Yes," agreed Gelsomini, "and now we are afraid the wound might be deep enough to damage his brain."

"Have no fear of that," snapped the barber crossly. "If Paolo had any brains he would never have interfered in the first place!"

—Ludovico Domenichi

In the Eating Lies the Test

It was King Alfonso's pleasure to enjoy an occasional nap during the lazy summer afternoons.** On those occasions, he demanded quiet from all in the vicinity of his chambers and in the courtyard below. One day, however, the king was awakened by a loud disturbance emanating from the palace grounds near his window. He summoned his servant and ordered that the miscreants be brought before him forthwith. A few minutes later, two bloody figures stood before him.

---

*Barbers were legally allowed to perform minor surgery and prescribe remedies, although they did not practice medicine as did the qualified physicians and surgeons of Renaissance Italy. The barber pole, with its red and white spiral stripes signifying arteries, was the emblem of the barber-surgeon.

**The several anecdotes recounted by author Ludovico Domenichi concerning King Alfonso of Naples, refer to Alfonso V (Alfonso the Magnanimous), 1396-1458, King of Aragon and Sicily (1416-58) and of Naples (1443-58). He was the son of Ferdinand I, whom he succeeded in Aragon and Sicily. In 1420, Queen Joanna II of Naples sought his aid against Louis III, rival king of Naples, and adopted him (Alfonso) as her heir. However, they quarreled in 1423, and at her death in 1435 Joanna left her throne to Rene of Anjou. In 1442 Alfonso conquered Naples, and a year later was recognized as king by the Pope. Considered a "good" king, Alfonso was a patron of the arts and letters, and did much to beautify the city.

"What is the meaning of this?" demanded Alfonso.

"Your Majesty," explained one of the Neapolitans, "this fellow called me a name that insulted my ancestry, so I drew my knife. He then had the temerity to draw *his* knife. Then we went at each other."

The king turned to the other man, whose face was so badly slashed that his cheek and jaw had been cut open. "It would seem," he remarked drily, "that you received the worst of the fight."

"Sire, I demand that you punish my attacker," snarled the wounded man. "He started the fight on palace grounds. Therefore, according to your own law, this inury to my mouth and jaw was really inflicted upon yourself, if you will forgive me for mentioning it, Sire."

"Yes, that is the law, and your reasoning is logical," agreed King Alfonso after a thoughtful pause to consider the facts, "but let us withhold final judgment as to which of us is really the injured party, until the next time we try to eat!"

—Ludovico Domenichi

A QUESTION OF DUTY VERSUS PLEASURE

Guido, the dullard Tuscan farmer, had been to the marketplace to sell his produce. Completing his business sooner than usual, he returned home much earlier than his wife had expected. There, in his bedroom, he surprised his wife and a handsome young miller in the very act of creating a new citizen. Outraged, Guido drew his knife and advanced toward the violated family bed. But he stopped abruptly at his wife's shrill command.

"Wait!" she cried. "I can explain everything. This man is only obeying God's command to go forth and mulitply, and I am letting him only because he paid us for the three bushels of wheat he bought last month."

"Oh, that's different," said Guido, sheathing his knife. "I thought you were both enjoying it!"

—Ludovico Domenichi

HOW A SICILIAN FARMER OUTWITTED A CLEVER VENETIAN

"Trust a Venetian, but beware of Sicilians," cautions an ancient, though misleading Italian adage. The falsity of the maxim is well expressed in the following tale.

Leopoldo Capuana, a Sicilian farmer who could neither read nor write, was walking along a riverbank one Sunday afternoon when he heard feeble cries for help. Looking around, he saw a man flailing about in the deepest part of the river. It was clear that the man had reached the limits of his endurance and that he would drown within moments. Leopoldo, without a second thought, leaped into the water and rescued the exhausted stranger.

When the man had thanked his benefactor, he introduced himself:

"I am Count Girolamo, of Forli. I was returning home to my city when my horse stumbled in the river, and then ran off. You have saved my life, and I wish to reward you. Here are one thousand ducats. When I return home I shall immediately send you another *two* thousand."

Poor Leopoldo, who had never possessed a fraction as much money in his life, accepted the reward with effusive thanks. Upon returning to his own home, he counted the thousand ducats over and over again, meanwhile wondering where he could hide the money from the robbers in the area. At last he had an inspired idea. He would bury it at the far edge of the field behind his little dwelling. Confiding in no one except his best friend and neighbor, a Venetian named Enrico Gozzi, he went into the field and, under an olive tree, he dug a hole and buried his treasure.

A short time later, Leopoldo received the other two thousand ducats from the grateful Count Girolamo. Taking his shovel with him, he joyously set out for the olive tree, to add the remainder of his reward to the first payment. But he had only to dig a few inches into the earth to realize that his initial thousand ducats had been stolen. Now Leopoldo Capuana was not the smartest man in Sicily, but neither was he the most stupid. Suspicion inexorably pointed to the one man he had confided in; namely Enrico Gozzi. Still, he could not prove his suspicion to a magistrate, should Enrico deny his guilt. Slowly, a plan evolved in his mind. He visited his neighbor's house the next day.

"Enrico, I want to confide in you again," began Leopoldo. "I have just received the other two thousand ducats that were promised to me by the count. Tomorrow night I will add them to the first thousand I buried under the olive tree."

"An excellent idea," agreed Enrico heartily—too heartily!

Just as Leopoldo had expected, Enrico returned immediately to the hiding place and replaced the money he had stolen. "I'll soon have the full three thousand ducats," he said to himself, "as long as that fool, Leopoldo, suspects nothing."

But when Enrico Gozzi returned, early the next morning, he was greeted by nothing more than an empty hole. The Sicilian farmer had outwitted the dishonest Venetian.

And that is why, to this very day, the people of Venice will not trust the people of Sicily, who leave respectable friends and neighbors with nothing but empty holes.

—Ludovico Domenichi

CATERINA'S CONVENIENT MOURNING MANNER

In the city of Forli, Countess Caterina* had just put her children to bed for their afternoon nap, and was enjoying a quiet moment in the castle, when suddenly a group of musicians struck up a merry tune outside the children's bedroom window.** Furious, she summoned her maidservant.

"Tell those musicians to leave immediately," she ordered. "My uncle died and I am in no mood for music."

The servant quickly completed her errand and returned to offer her condolences.

"When did your uncle die, Your Ladyship?" she asked in a properly subdued voice.

Replied the countess: "Twenty years ago!"

—Ludovico Domenichi

"ITALIAN 'MOULDS' ARE FOR LOVING, NOT FIGHTING"

In 1488 the soldiers of King Louis XII of France attacked the city of Forli. During the hostilities, Count Girolamo, lord of the little realm, was assassinated by a group of traitors, and his widow, Countess Caterina, and her children, were captured by the renegades. The city was now occupied by the French invaders, but the castle itself, and its fortress, continued to resist. The French knew very well that their cause would be lost if they failed to conquer the castle with its vast quantity of weapons, many skilled fighters, and ample food supplies.

It was then that Countess Caterina offered her captors, the French and their local conspirators, a solution to the problem.

"With your permission I will go inside the castle and order the soldiers to lay down their arms," she promised. "You will still have my children as your prisoners, should I fail to keep my word."

The enemy agreed, confident that no mother would forfeit her own flesh-and-blood children. Caterina soon entered the castle, but instead of pleading with her soldiers to surrender, she went forthwith to the battlements where, in plain view and hearing of the enemy, she shouted

---

*Caterina was the daughter of Count Galeazzo Maria Sforza of Milan, and wife of Count Girolamo Riario, who was killed in 1488. Six years later, she fought off the French who attempted to seize the city of Forli and, in 1494, she again defended her rule over the city against Caesar Borgia.

**It was the custom of the day for wandering bands of musicians to earn their livelihood by playing music on the grounds of wealthy families.

her defiance, vowing that the murderers of her husband would be put to death and the French driven from the city.

Surprised and chagrined, the would-be conquerors threatened to kill her children before her very eyes if she did not immediately surrender the castle as she had promised.

For a few moments Caterina made no answer, and then, to their utter astonishment, she raised her skirt so that her thighs were exposed for all to see.

"Look well, you fools," she shouted. "I still have the mould to make many more children!"

The French, unable to argue this fact of life, applauded the brave countess and began their withdrawal from the city. The renegade conspirators slunk away in disgrace to await their punishment.

Said King Louis XII of France, when he heard the news: "My officers retreated as the gentlemen they are. An Italian mould is for loving, not fighting!"

—Ludovico Domenichi

Praises of the Wine
of Montepulciano*

> Oh, how widely wandereth he
> Who, in search of verity,
> Keeps aloof from glorious wine!
> Lo! the knowledge it bringeth to me.
> For Barbarossa,** this wine so bright,
> With its rich red look and its
>   strawberry light,
> So invites me
> And so delights me,
> I would infallibly quench my inside
>   with it,
> Had not Hippocrates
> And old Andromachus
> Strictly forbidden it
> And loudly chidden it,
> So many stomachs have sickened
>   and died with it.

---

*A city in north-central Italy, famous in the sixteenth century as the source of especially fine wines.

**In Italian, *barbarossa* translates to "red beard." Also the surname of the fifteenth-century corsair who ravaged the coasts of Greece, Spain, and Italy.

Yet, discordant as it is,
Two good biggins* will not come amiss;
Because I know, while I'm drinking them down,
What is the finish and what is the crown.
A cup of good Corsican
Does it at once;
Or a cup of old Spanish
Is next for the nonce;
Quackish resources are things for a dunce.

Cups of chocolate,
Ay, or tea,
Are not medicines
Made for me.
I would sooner take to poison,
Than a single cup set eyes on
Of that bitter and guilty stuff ye
Talk of by the name of coffee.
Let the Arabs and the Turks
Count it 'mongst their cruel works:
Foe of mankind black and turbid,
Let the throats of slaves absorb it.
Down in Tartarus,
Down in Erebus,
'Twas the detestable Fifty invented it;
The Furies then took it,
To grind and to cook it,
And to Prosperpine all these presented it.
If Musselman** in Asia
Dotes on a beverage so unseemly,
I differ with the man extremely.
There's a squalid thing called beer:
The man whose lips that thing comes near
Swiftly dies, or falling foolish,
Grows, at forty, old and owlish.
She that in the ground would hide her,
Let her take to English cider:
He who'd have his death come quicker,
Any other Northern liquor.

---

*An archaic term meaning close-fitting caps usually worn by children; also refers to soft caps worn while sleeping; a nightcap.
**Mohammedan.

Those Norwegians and those Laps
Have extraordinary taps:
Those Laps especially have strange fancies:
To see them drink,
I verily think
Would make me lose my senses.

But a truce to such vile subjects
With their impious, shocking objects.
Let me purify my mouth
In a holy cup o' the south:
In a golden pitcher let me
Head and ears for comfort get me,
And drink of the vine of the wine benign
That sparkles warm in Sansovine;*
Or that vermillion charmer
And heart-warmer,
Which brought up in Tregonzano
And on stony Giggiano,**
Blooms so bright and lifts the head so
Of the toasters of Arezzo.

       —Francesco Redi (1626-96)

ADVANTAGES OF USING WHITE
WINE TO TEMPER COLORS

(From a letter to the painter, Pier Maria Baldi)

Buffalmacco was a famous painter in his day. In my judgment (and I am not altogether a fool in these matters), he still deserves to be preferred to Titian and the divine Michelangelo—and no one can go further than that.

If you wish, *Signor* Baldi, to know the reasons and motives of this

---

*A reference to Jacopo Sansovino (1486-1570), famous Italian sculptor and architect of the Renaissance. His surname was taken in place of his own, Tatti, as homage to the Florentine sculptor Andrea Sansovino, under whom he was apprenticed. Both Sansovinos liked their wine.

**This line is printed in the 1825 edition (the present editor is not aware of any other) as "An old stony Giggiano," which does not make sense, since there appears to be no such word as "Giggiano" in Italian, except as a proper name, applied to a district in Tuscany. The change as now shown gives the author's sense correctly. Leigh Hunt seems to have sent the manuscript of his translation from Florence in January 1825, to London, where it was published for him by his brother; so that it is probable the proofs were not revised by the author.

judgment of mine, do not expect me to say that Buffalmacco was so skilled and perfect a master as to be able to teach the art of painting to an ape which the Bishop of Arezzo kept for his pastime; but I shall certainly tell you that it was Buffalmacco who discovered that noble and ever-to-be-praised invention of tempering colors, not with water from the well, but with the most brilliant white wine that could ever be produced by the best shoots of the most renowned vines on the Florentine hills.

Before Buffalmacco had made this discovery, he used to execute paintings which—you may rely on it—were exactly like your own face; that is to say, pale, washed-out, and mouldy-looking. Yes, and in many of them I fancy I recognize my own portrait, with a face like a mummy, thin, dry, hollow-cheeked, worn to a shadow, and colored with a certain hue like that of bread crust or a quince baked in the oven, and so melancholy as to make people weep who were quite ready to laugh.

But when this great master of all masters began to use wine with his colors—

> "He painted saints on the wall he discloses
> With fresh, blooming faces, all milk and roses!"

and they were all the right sort of folks—jovial, cheerful, wholesome, and good-tempered, so that people talked about them even as far as the gates of Paris. The ladies of Faenza—certain knowing nuns whose convent stood where the lower fort is now—had more faith in Buffalmacco than in all the Appelleses and Protogenes who were in credit with the ancient Greeks.

Now, what do I mean by all this screed of nonsense? I mean to draw the conclusion that, since you are so kind as to draw the illustrations to that book of mine, you will most assuredly come to grief unless you mix your colors with *Vernaccia* or some other good wine, and you will do no work that is worth looking at. And since it is not right that you should be at any expense in consequence of this work of mine, I send you a sample of white wine of Syracuse, with other samples of wine given me by his Serene Highness the Grand Duke; with which, if you mix your colors, you will not only give a good appearance to your pictures, but also get back to your former healthy looks, in spite of those disgusting messes which you are made to swallow every morning by those two physicians, your friends.

Try this new precription and you will soon be well.

—Francesco Redi

3

Modern Times—
Classics of the Funny Short Story

INTRODUCTION

Some of the most entertaining short stories in the history of Italian literature were written during the period of the Enlightenment of the eighteenth and nineteenth centuries. Gone was the exemplum with its touches of humor only incidental to the moral or lesson to be learned. In its place was the funny anecdote whose sole function was to amuse, rather than to educate or inspire. As with nearly all works of art, the stories were products of their times, illuminating for future generations, no matter how unwittingly, the customs and attitudes of the people.

The earliest works of Italian vernacular literature, as distinct from those written in Latin, are twelfth-century interpretations of the songs of Provencal troubadours, developed chiefly at the court of Frederick II of Sicily. Also included, it is interesting to note, were the comic poems of Rustico di Filippo, in the Tuscan language. In the late thirteenth century a group of poets originated the "sweet new style" (*dolce stil nuovo*); among them Dante Alighieri, whose *Vita Nuova* is one of the high achievements of all poetry. Dante's *Divine Comedy*, a masterpiece of world literature, established Tuscan as the Italian language. Acceptance of the language was furthered by Petrarch, whose sonnets are still a model to poets, and by Boccaccio, who invented the modern short story.

For a century after the plague known as the Black Death of 1348, Italian literature was sterile. The rise of humanism ushered in a period of fruitfulness, the Renaissance. Although Latin was still regarded as the language of formal communication, the literary use of the vernacular was encouraged in Florence by the circle of humanists around Lorenzo de' Medici. Vernacular- or modern Italian, prose was still in its infancy, but the Renaissance vitality continued into the sixteenth century, when Italy produced her third great poet, Ariosto. The century also boasted the lyricists Michelangelo and Gaspara Stampa; the historian Guicciardini, and the biographer Vasari. Great single works of the period are *The Prince* by Machiavelli, who also wrote a comedy in verse, *La Mandragola; The Courtier* by Baldassare Castiglione; and Cellini's *Auto-*

biography. The climactic expression of the Renaissance creativity that made Italian letters the envy and model of the rest of Europe was Torquato Tasso's *Jerusalem Delivered,* written in 1581.

But the artistic heights achieved during the Renaissance came to a shameful end. By the mid-sixteenth century the political and economic decay of the country, and the pressures imposed by the Church, again stultified the arts. The philosopher Bruno was burned at the stake. Campanella and Galileo were punished for their unorthodox views. The development of the Commedia dell' Arte (see Preface, page xi) and the opera declined. A whole century was to pass before the natural creativity of the Italian people was to again assert itself.

The growth of national consciousness in the eighteenth century brought with it a revival of literature. With the Enlightenment for inspiration, the theater was revived with the comedies of Goldoni and Gozzi. But the giants of the early nineteenth century were Leopardi, an intense, pessimistic poet, and Manzoni, a novelist, author of the classic *I Promessi Sposi (The Betrothed).* It was Manzoni who provided a model for subsequent novels and helped established modern Italian prose style. After the unification of Italy in 1870, and the decline of Romanticism, Capuana, Verga, De Amicis, and others introduced naturalism into fiction.

None of the aforementioned writers were comics, in the sense that they devoted all or even a substantial part of their literary work to humor. But they did have their moments, and they were often at their best when they chose to be funny.

The selections which appear in this chapter represent some of the outstanding authors of the era, prior to the reign of Benito Mussolini. The collection, it is hoped, will prove a point long held by the present writer: when it comes to mirthful tales, the Italians have captured the joys of laughter as have few other peoples anywhere on earth.

—H.D.S.

THE GOOD-HEARTED, UPSIDE-DOWN BERGAMASC

A certain Bergamasc,* an honest fellow, and ignorant as a log, came up here some years ago, with five or six thousand *scudi*** in cash. He at once encountered a group of astute rustics who, making him believe that black was white, and dazzling him with the most extraordinary promises, soon

---

*A native of Bergamo, city of Lombardy, in northern Italy.

**Various gold or silver coins, of various Italian states, issued from the late sixteenth through the early nineteenth centuries.

succeeded in borrowing the greater part of his money. Now, alleging as excuses to avoid repayment, sometimes storms, sometimes drought, and then again thunder and lightning, they have managed to postpone an accounting so that the poor fellow cannot get back a farthing of his money to this day.

Do not imagine, however, that this difficulty causes him any sorrow; on the contrary, it gives him the greatest delight in the world, for it has opened up to him the possibility of unlimited lawsuits—a prospect as dear to his heart as sugar to flies. And, not content with civil suits, he worried his debtors for so long that, at last, one of them—better at paying up than the rest—attempted to pay his whole debt at once, which he did with a scythe, on top of the creditor's head. It was well for the Bergamasc that the blow did not reach his neck, at which it was aimed, and which it would have cut through like a stalk of clover, but glanced off on the forehead, only wounding the skin.

You never saw such greater joy than he experienced when he felt the blood running down his face. I think he would have died of sheer satisfaction had his delight not been tempered by the disappointed reflection that, after all, his skull was not broken. He went off at once to find me—and nearly frightened me out of my wits with his gory countenance.

"I am going!" he shouted. "I am off to Venice this minute! Give me an introduction to an honest lawyer!"

Seeing the state he was in, I thought his mind had gone astray, and that, instead of an attorney, he meant to ask for a surgeon. But when I had heard what happened and understood what his intention was, I promised to do what he asked. He was pacified so far that he even allowed the steward's wife to dress his head with a little white-of-egg and bandage it with a piece of rag. Then he insisted on telling me his story all over again, and how fortunate he was in having another plea to enter in court. He would not, he said, part with his broken head for several ducats. In fact, he was quite ready to pay his debtor a dozen ducats or so for the favor done to him.

Now, having gotten together all his documents, and further, written out on a sheet of paper, in the Bergamasc dialect, the whole history of the quarrel—a curious and valuable manuscript—he is coming to Venice to get legal advice about it and be directed how to get back his money, by means of his broken head. Here he is, then, with his spurs on, like a fighting cock, and I have given him this present letter to you. So please send him to some man with a conscience: one who will try and help him get back what is truly owed him, and also persuade him that he will do well to leave this part of the country—for it is not a good idea to jest with our farmers, and if he tries it he will soon find himself skinned.

I recommend him to you most earnestly because he is in the right;

because he is a good fellow by nature—and, I suppose, because of his shocking ignorance. Before sending him to the lawyer, get him to tell you a little about his litigations. I promise you that you will hear words which all the commentators of the Pandects* would never have discovered. Besides this, he begins to speak in a big bass voice which gradually rises and ends in a falsetto, so that his conversation is a species of music. His eloquence and arrangement of facts are something marvelous; he will begin by telling you of his broken head, and his disputes with the farmers; he will then go on to say that he has lent them money, and end up by telling you that he was from Bergamo.

In short, he begins with death, and goes backward till he gets to the christening. When you find a lawyer, be sure, in the first place, to choose one who understands stories told upside-down. Help him all you can, and let me know what you think of him. Goodbye.

—Gasparo Gozzi (1713-86)

How to Succeed
in Literature

In those old-fashioned times when people lived haphazardly, so to speak, and when, if a man wished to gain a reputation for learning, he forgot himself and all he had and stuck to his books day and night, the ways of acquiring an honored and illustrious name were very different than what they are now. But in those days the business was a long one, and the path to be trodden was steep and rugged. Few were those who reached the top of the mountain, where learning sheds abroad her gifts and graces.

In our own day, however, we have shortened the journey and opened a level and easy road wherein you may walk, as it were, on cotton, with no other trouble than that of elbowing back those rival competitors who are pressing forward too boldly, or firing off sarcastic or satirical critiques at those who are spreading their wings too rapidly.

If any young writer wishes to get on quickly, and to be greatly honored, let him lay up a good store of quips and jokes against his rivals, and have his head so full of them that they may fall from his tongue in showers like hailstones. And let him utter them on every possible occasion, whether in or out of season does not matter. Let him remem-

---

*The Pandects, or Digest, are the most important parts of the comprehensive Code of Roman law and the basic document of all modern civil law. Compiled by order of Justinian I, the first three parts appeared between 529 and 535 and were the work of a commission of 17 jurists presided over by the eminent jurist Tribonian. The *Corpus Juris Civilis,* as the entire Code is called, was an attempt to systematize Roman law after 1,000 years of development.

ber, moreover, that it is not enough to speak ill of others, but that he must also speak well of himself; and remember that Horace and Ovid, both of them, said that neither time, nor fire, nor any other calamity could destroy their works out of the world. If he cannot imitate Horace and Ovid in any other respect, let him do so in this.

The modern writer should not spend much time and labor in composition, but dash off everything in hot haste, for the file and the foot-rule will spoil all the fire of his writing. Once upon a time the great art was to use art and yet conceal it, but nowadays, in order to make no mistake in the using of it, it is considered the safest thing to have no art at all.

Those who are considered good authors should be left alone, otherwise they may be accused of plagiarism. Let him make capital of himself and his own brain, and fly wherever the latter is disposed to carry him.

These are the general principles which, if followed, I promise eternal fame to the young writer. It is true that in this way a man does not leave a great literary reputation behind him after his death, but what matters this last vanity, or the glory of an epitaph either?

—Gasparo Gozzi

Fable of the Spectacles

Jove, having one day drunk more nectar than usual, and being in a pleasant humor, his fancy took him to make some present to mankind. He called Momus and gave him what he had decided upon, and which he had packed in a large suitcase. "Take this down to earth," he commanded.

"Oh, truly blessed generation!" cried Momus when he arrived in a chariot. "Oh, fortunate human race! Behold how Jove, liberal with his benefits to you, opens his generous hand! Come, hasten, receive! Never again complain that he has made you short-sighted. His gift now compensates you for that defect."

Momus then unfastened the suitcase, and emptied out of it an enormous heap of eyeglasses. Behold, all mankind was busy picking them up, so that every man had a pair. All were content, thanking Jove for having acquired so excellent an aid to their eyesight.

But the spectacles caused them to see things under a deceitful appearance. To one man a thing seemed blue, while another saw it yellow; one thought it white, and another black, so that to everyone it appeared different. But what of that? Every individual was delighted with his pair, and insisted that it was the best.

My dear friends, we are the heirs of those people, and the spectacles have been passed on to us. Some see things one way, and some another, and everyone thinks he is right.

—Gasparo Gozzi

The Poet Laments the Good Old Days, Previous to the Existence of Duns, Bailiffs, Writs and I.O.U.'s

Oh, blissful days, what time Queen Bertha* spun!
    Most fortunate and highly favored season!
That age called anciently the golden one,
    No doubt because so happy was the reason;
No I.O.U.'s were then, nor writs to dun,
    Nor frequent lawsuits, such as now, with fees on;
Nor people then were summoned, should they run
    In debt, nor lost their liberty in prison.

But times have changed—not now what once they were;
    And woe to that poor devil who gets in debt!
For he must go to jail and perish there!
    And though his dun be not so long due, yet
    He plagues him night and day, wherever met,
As thou dost me—pursuing me everywhere!
                —Giovanni Battista Casti (1721-1803)

The Poet Complains That His Creditor Is Worse than a Pirate

Algiers and Tunis, Tripoli, Sale,
    Places that lie where are the days most hot,
    So brute a race of men perhaps are not
As brutal as my creditor with me.

This man not born like other men could be,
    But in an ill-will and rancorousness begot
By one that ne'er sucked mercy's milk, I wot,
    And daily set him bad examples see.

The Barbary pirate, when he makes a slave,
    Robs him of cash that he may find on one,
    But does not want his money when he has none;

---

*An Italian expression for the Golden Age.

But using me more cruelly than a pirate,
>My dun cares not whether or no I have it—
When I've no money, still he doth require it.

—Giovanni Battista Casti

THE DAY THE SUN REFUSED TO MOVE—AND WHY THE EARTH NOW REVOLVES AROUND THE SUN*

FIRST HOUR: Good morning, Your Excellency.

SUN: Yes, or rather good night.

FIRST HOUR: The horses are ready.

SUN: Very good.

FIRST HOUR: The morning star has been out some time.

SUN: Fine! Let her come or go as it suits her.

FIRST HOUR: What does Your Excellency mean?

SUN: I mean that I want you to leave me alone.

FIRST HOUR: But, Your Excellency, the night has already lasted so long that it cannot last any longer. If we were to wait, you see, Your Excellency, it might give rise to some disorder.

SUN: Let come of it what will: I shall not move.

FIRST HOUR: Oh! Your Excellency, what is this? Don't you feel well?

SUN: No, no, no! I don't feel anything, except that I don't want to move, so you may go about your business.

FIRST HOUR: But how can I go if you do not come? I am the first hour of the day. And how can there be any day at all if Your Excellency does not deign to come out as usual?

SUN: If you are not the first hour of the day, you can be the first hour of the night; or else the night hours can go on double duty, and you and your companions may take it easy. Because—I'll tell you what it is—I am tired of this continual going round and round in order to give light to a few little animals living on a handful of mud, so small that I, though I have pretty good sight, cannot manage to see it. So this

---

*This dialogue was supposed to have taken place at the date of Galileo's discovery of the relationship between the sun and the solar system. Galileo Galilei (1564-1642), astronomer, mathematician, and physicist, published a work in 1632, titled *Dialogo—sopra i due massimi sistemi del mondo (Dialogue on the two chief systems of the world)*. He was summoned to Rome and tried (1633) by the Inquisition where he was forced to recant all beliefs and writings that held the sun to be the central body and the earth a moving body revolving with the other planets about it. Since 1761, accounts of the trial have concluded with the legendary statement that Galileo, as he arose from his knees uttered *sotto voce,* *"E pur' si muove"* ("Nevertheless it does move").

night I have made up my mind that I can't be bothered any more. If men want light, let them keep their fires burning, or provide it in some other way.

FIRST HOUR: But how does Your Excellency expect the poor wretches to manage it? It will be an enormous expense for them to keep up their lamps and provide candles enough to burn all day long. If they had already discovered the kind of air that will burn, and could use it to light up their streets and rooms and shops and cellars, and everything else—and all at small expense—why, then I might say the thing was not so bad. But the fact is, that it will be three hundred years, more or less, till men find out that expedient. In the meantime they will get to the end of all the oil and wax and pitch and tallow, and have nothing more to burn.

SUN: Let them go and catch fireflies, or those little worms that shine in the dark.

FIRST HOUR: And how will they provide against the cold? Without the help they have had from you the wood of all the forests will never be enough to warm them. Besides which, they will also die of hunger, for the earth will no longer yield its fruits. And so, at the end of a few years, the entire race of these poor animals will be lost. They will crawl about for a time, groping in the dark after something to eat and to warm themselves. And in the end, when the last spark of fire has died out, and they have eaten everything that a human being could possibly swallow, they will all die in the dark, frozen hard like bits of rock crystal.

SUN: And if they do, what business is that of mine? Am I the nurse of the human race? Or perhaps their cook, who has to provide and prepare their food for them? What is it to me that a certain small quantity of invisible animalcules, thousands of miles distant from me, cannot see, or bear the cold, without my light? Besides, even though it were my duty to serve as a stove or hearth, so to speak, to this human family, it is surely reasonable that, if the family want to warm themselves, they should come and stand around the stove—not that the stove should walk round the house. And so, if the Earth has need of my presence, let her bestir herself and see that she gets it; for, as far as I am concerned, I want nothing of her, and there is no reason why I should go after her.

FIRST HOUR: Your Excellency means, if I understood aright, that what you did formerly is now to be done by earth?

SUN: Yes, now and henceforward—forever.

—Giacomo Leopardi (1798-1837)

SISTERS FASHION AND DEATH*
REACH AN UNDERSTANDING

FASHION: Madam Death! Madam Death!

DEATH: Wait till the time comes and I'll come without your calling.

FASHION: Madam Death!

DEATH: Go—and the Devil go with you! I shall come fast enough when you don't want me.

FASHION: As if I were not immortal!

DEATH: Immortal? It is a thousand years past since the days of the immortals were ended.

FASHION: Why, madam, you are talking in the manner of Petrarch, as though you were a lyric poet of the sixteenth—or the nineteenth century.

DEATH: I am very fond of Petrarch's rhymes, because there is my *Triumph* among them, and the rest of them are nearly all about me, too. But, anyway, get out of my sight at once.

FASHION: Come—for the love you bear to the seven deadly sins, stop a little and look at me.

DEATH: I *am* looking at you.

FASHION: Don't you know me?

DEATH: You ought to know that my sight is not good, and that I cannot use spectacles because the English do not make any that would serve me—and even though they made them, I have no nose to put them on.

FASHION: I am Fashion, your sister.

DEATH: My sister?

FASHION: Yes—don't you remember that we are both daughters of Decadence?

DEATH: What should *I* remember, whose business it is to destroy all memory?

FASHION: But I do, and I know that we are both equally busy, continually undoing and changing the things of this world, although you set about this task in one way, and I in another.

DEATH: If you are not talking to your own thoughts, or to some person whom you have inside your throat, then do raise your voice a little, and pronounce your words more clearly; for if you go on mumbling between your teeth with that thin cobweb of a voice of yours, I shall need until tomorrow to hear you. My hearing, as you know, is no better than my sight.

FASHION: Although it is not exactly usual—in France, you will be inter-

---

*This is one of the few instances in Italian literature in which Death is depicted as a woman.

ested to know, people do not speak in order to be heard—yet, as we are sisters, and can drop ceremony between ourselves, I will speak as you wish. I say that the nature and custom of both of us is continually to ruin the world. But you, from the beginning, have thrown yourself on the person and the blood, whereas I mostly content myself with beards, hair, clothes, furniture, palaces, and suchlike.

It is true that I have not failed to carry on certain games which may well be compared to yours; as, for instance, piercing holes in ears, lips, or noses; burning flesh of men with red-hot irons, with which I make them mark themselves for the sake of beauty; forming the heads of babies by means of bandages and other contrivances, so that all the people in a country may have heads of a same shape; laming people with narrow shoes; choking the breath out of them, and making their eyes start out of their heads with the tightness of their corsets and collars; and a hundred other things of the same kind.

Not only so, but, generally speaking, I persuade and force all people of any position to bear unending fatigue and discomfort everyday of their lives—oftentimes pain and torture; and some of them will even die gloriously for the love they bear to me. I say nothing of the headaches, chills, colds of every kind, and daily fevers, all of which men get through obeying me; submitting to shiver with cold and be suffocated with heat, as I please; to cover their bodies with woollen stuff and their chests with linen, and do everything in the way I tell them, even though it be to their own hurt.

DEATH: Well, I am quite willing to believe that you are my sister, and, if you wish to have it so, I will consider it more certain than death—and you need not prove it out of the parish register. But if I stand still in this way I turn faint; yet, if you have the courage to run alongside of me, take care not to kill yourself, as I go at a fast pace. If you can run you can tell me all you have to say as we go along. If not, I must leave you with a salutation, and promise you, in consideration of our relationship, to leave you all my property when I die.

FASHION: If we had to run a race together, I don't know which of us would win. If you run, I do more than gallop. So then, let us run together and, as you say, speak of our affairs as we go.

DEATH: Let it be so. Since, then, you are my sister, it would be the right thing if you could help me somehow or other in my business.

FASHION: I have already done so, more than you think. In the first place, though I am continually destroying or changing all other customs, I have never in any place induced people to leave off dying; and for that reason, you see, the practice has universally remained in force from the beginning of the world up to the present day.

DEATH: It is a mighty miracle that you should not have done what you cannot do.

FASHION: What I cannot do? You do not seem to know the power of fashion.

DEATH: Well, it will be time enough to talk about this when the fashion of not dying has come in. But meanwhile, I would like you, as a good sister, to help me obtain the opposite, more easily and quickly than I have been doing.

FASHION: I have already told you of some of my work which is very profitable to you. But that is a trifle in comparison with what I am going to tell you. For your sake I have gradually—especially in these later times—caused people to disuse and forget the exercises which are beneficial to health, and brought in other customs which weaken the body and shorten life. Besides which, I have introduced into the world such rules and customs that life itself, both the body and soul, is more dead than alive, so that this century may truly be called the Age of Death.

Moreover, whereas formerly you used to be hated and abused, nowadays, thanks to me, things have reached such a pass that whoever has any intellect at all values and praises you, preferring you above life, and turns his eyes to you as his greatest hope. Finally, seeing that many had made their boast of living after death, in the memories of their fellow men, . . . I have abolished this habit of seeking after immortality, and of conferring it in case there should be any who deserve it.

These things, which are neither few nor small, I have, up to now, accomplished for the love of you, wishing to increase your state and power on earth, as has, in fact, been the case. I am disposed to do as much as this, and more, everyday, and it was with this intention I set out to seek you. I think it would be well that, for the future, we should remain together. Thus we could lay our plans better than formerly, and also carry them out more effectually.

DEATH: You speak truly. I am quite willing we should do so.

—Giacomo Leopardi

DON ABBONDIO AND THE BRAVOS* (FROM I PROMESI SPOSI)

(Don Abbondio, a village priest, walking by himself in a lonely place, sees two bravos waiting for him in a narrow lane.)

---

*The "bravos" were daring bandits and assassins, usually in the pay of others, who stole, intimidated or murdered for their employers, much as did the "hired gun" of America's frontier West, or the "hit" man of today's underworld.

. . . He quickened his pace, recited a verse in a louder tone, composed his countenance to all the calm and cheerfulness he could summon up for the moment, made every effort to prepare a smile, and when he found himself right in front of the two swashbucklers, he exclaimed, mentally, "Now I'm in for it!" and stopped short.

"Your Reverence," said one of the two, looking him full in the face.

"Who wants me?" replied Don Abbondio, raising his eyes from his book, and holding it open in both hands.

"Sir," intoned the other bravo with the cold, threatening, and angry look of a man who has caught his inferior in the commission of a crime, "you intend to perform the ceremony of marriage tomorrow between Renzo Tramaglino and Lucia Mondella?"

"Well, ah—er, that is . . ." began Don Abbondio in a quavering voice, ". . . gentlemen, you are men of the world, and you know how these matters take place. The poor priest has nothing whatever to say in the business. They arrange everything between themselves, and then . . . then they come to us, as you would come to a bank to draw out your money, and we—well, we are the servants of the congregation."

"Well, then," said the bravo in an undertone, but with an impressive air of command, "this marriage is not to take place, either tomorrow, or at any other time."

"But, gentlemen," protested Don Abbondio in the meek and gentle voice of a man trying to persuade an impatient listener, "do be good enough to put yourself in my place. If the thing depended on me, now . . . you can see perfectly well that it matters nothing to me, one way or the other."

"Come, come!" interrupted the bravo. "'If this business had to be settled by talk, you would have us all in a moment. We know nothing more about it than we have told, or warned, you—and we don't want to. A man warned . . . you understand?"

"Gentlemen, you are too just, too reasonable . . ."

"But," interjected the second bravo, who now spoke for the first time, "either the marriage will not take place or—or the man who performs it will not repent of doing so because he will not have time," he concluded with a menacing hiss.

"Be quiet!" returned the first bravo. "His Reverence knows the ways of the world. We are gentlemen, and do not want to do him any harm, if he will only show a little common sense. Your Reverence, the most illustrious *Signor* Don Rodrigo, our master, sends you his most respectful regards."

This name was like a flash of light in the darkness and confusion of Don Abbondio's mind. But it only served to increase his terror. He instinctively made a low bow, and said, "If you could suggest to me . . ."

"Oho! Suggest to *you* who knows *Latin?*" again interrupted the first bravo with a laugh that was half ferocious and half foolish. "Suggestions are *your* business. And above all, never let a word escape you about this little hint we have given you, for your own good; otherwise—ahem!—it would be the same thing as if you were to perform the marriage. Come, what message do you wish us to give to the illustrious Don Rodrigo?"

"My respects."

"Explain yourself, Your Reverence."

"Er—ah—umm—disposed . . . always disposed to obedience. . . . "

Even while uttering the words, he did not quite know, himself, whether he was giving a promise or merely bestowing a commonplace compliment, such as "obediently yours" at the ending of a letter. The bravos took it—or appeared to do so—in the more serious sense.

"Very good. Good night, Your Reverence," said one of them, turning with his comrade to depart.

But Don Abbondio, who a few minutes earlier would have given one of the eyes out of his head to get rid of them, now would have liked to prolong the conversation.

"Gentlemen," he began, shutting his book with both hands; but, without listening to him, they took to the road by which they had come, singing, meanwhile, a ditty better not transcribed, and were soon out of sight.

Poor Don Abbondio remained for a moment with his mouth wide open, as if spellbound. Then he turned up the lane leading to his house, walking slowly, and seeming scarcely able to drag one leg after the other.

—Alessandro Manzoni (1784-1873)

THE INTERRUPTED WEDDING

(A Sequel to *Don Abbondio and the Bravos*)

> *(Don Abbondio, by finding one excuse after another for deferring the marriage of Renzo Tramaglino and Lucia Mondella, has driven Renzo nearly to despair. At last, having discovered the reason for the priest's hesitation, in Don Rodrigo's hostility, he eagerly adopts a suggestion of Lucia's mother, Agnese, to the effect that a perfectly legal, though irregular, marriage may be performed by the parties severally pronouncing, before a priest, "This is my wife," and "This is my husband." Renzo easily secures two witnesses, his friend Tonio and the latter's half-witted brother. Tonio owes Don Abbondio twenty-five lire, for which the priest holds his wife's necklace in pledge, and Renzo secures his cooperation by giving him the amount of the debt. The five start at dusk for Don Abbondio's house. Agnese engages the priest's housekeeper in conversation outside the front door,*

and the others slip upstairs unnoticed—the bride and bride-
groom waiting on the landing while Tonio knocks at the door of
Don Abbondio's sitting room.)

"*Deo gratias!*" said Tonio in a loud voice.

"Tonio, eh? Come in," replied a voice from within.

Tonio opened the door just wide enough to admit himself and his brother, one at a time, of course, and then closed it after him, while Renzo and Lucia remained silent and motionless in the dark.

Don Abbondio was sitting in an old armchair, wrapped in a dilapi-dated dressing gown, with an ancient cap on his head, which made a frame all round his face. By the faint light of a small lamp the two thick white tufts of hair which projected from under the cap, his bushy white eyebrows, moustache, and pointed beard all seemed, on the brown and wrinkled face, like bushes covered with snow on a rocky hillside seen by moonlight.

"Aha!" was his greeting as he took off his spectacles and put them on the book he was reading.

"Your Reverence will say we are late in coming," said Tonio, bowing, as did his brother, Gervaso, but more awkwardly.

"Well, it certainly *is* late—late in every way. Did you know that I am ill?"

"Oh, I am very sorry, sir!"

"You surely must have heard that I am ill, and don't know when I can see anyone. But why have you brought that—that fellow with you?"

"Just for company, sort of, sir."

"I see. Now, shall we proceed?"

"Here are twenty-five nice new *lire*, sir," declared Tonio, drawing a folded paper from his pocket.

"Let's see, now," said Abbondio, taking the paper. He put on his spectacles, unfolded the paper and shook out the twenty-five *lire*, counted them, and found the sum to be correct.

"Now, Your Reverence, will you kindly give me my Tecla's necklace?"

"Yes, of course," replied Don Abbondio. Going to a cupboard, he unlocked it and, having first looked round as if to keep away any spectators, he opened one side, stood in front of the open door so that no one could see in, put in his head to look for the pledge, and extracted it. He then locked the cupboard, unwrapped the paper, said inter-rogatively, "All right?" wrapped it up again, and handed it over to Tonio.

"Now," said Tonio, "would you please let me have something in black and white, sir?"

"That, too!" exclaimed Don Abbondio. "Do you think I am about to play some trick? How suspicious the world has grown! Can't you trust me?"

"How could I not trust you, Your Reverence? You do me an injustice! But as my name is down on your book, on the debtor side, in case anything were to happen—you know. . . . "

"All right, all right," grumbled Don Abbondio. He opened the table drawer, took out pen, paper, and inkstand, and began to write, repeating the words out loud as he set them down.

Meanwhile, Tonio, and at a sign from his brother, Gervaso, placed themselves in front of the table so as to prevent the writer from seeing the door, and, as if in mere idleness, began to move their feet about noisily on the floor in order to serve as a signal to those outside, and at the same time, to deaden the sound of their footsteps.

Don Abbondio, intent on his work, noticed nothing. Renzo and Lucia hearing the signal, entered on tiptoe, holding their breath, and stood close behind the two brothers. During all this time, priest Abbondio had been busily scratching away with his pen. Now, with the writing finished, he read over the document attentively without raising his eyes from the paper, folded it, and at last said, "Are you satisfied now?" He took off his spectacles with one hand and held out the sheet to Tonio with the other.

Tonio, while stretching out his hand to take the paper, stepped back on one side, and Gervaso, at a sign from him, on the other, and between the two appeared Renzo and Lucia.

Don Abbondio started, was dumbfounded, became furious, thought it over, and came to a resolution, all in the time that Renzo took to utter the words: "Your Reverence, in the presence of these two witnesses, this is my wife!"

His lips had not yet ceased moving when Don Abbondio let fall the receipt which he was still holding in his left hand, raised the lamp, and seizing the tablecloth with his right hand, pulled it violently toward him, throwing book, papers and inkstand to the floor. Springing between the chair and table, he approached Lucia. The poor girl, with her sweet voice all trembling, had only just been able to say, "This is . . . " when Don Abbondio rudely flung the tablecloth over her head, and immediately dropping the lamp which he held in his other hand, used the tablecloth to wrap it tightly round her face, nearly suffocating her. And all the while he kept roaring at the top of his voice, "Help! Help! Treason!"

When the light went out, the priest released his hold of the girl and groped for the door leading into an inner room. He entered, still shouting, "Perpetua! Treason! Help! Get out of my house! Out! Get out!"

In the other room all was confusion. Renzo, trying to catch the priest, was waving his hands about as though he had been playing blindman's buff. He reached the door and pounded on it, crying out, "Open this damn door! Open it, do you hear!"

Lucia called to Renzo in a feeble voice, "Please, we must go!"

Renzo, still banging away on the door, realizing the consequences of his rash plan, was yelling "Don Abbondio! Don Abbondio! Don't make so much noise! You'll bring the police!"

Tonio, down on the floor upon his hands and knees, was feeling about blindly, searching for his receipt, while Gervaso jumped about like a man possessed, trying to get out by the door leading to the stairs.

In the midst of this confusion, we cannot refrain from a momentary reflection. Renzo, raising a hullabaloo by night in another man's house, which he had surreptitiously entered, and keeping its owner besieged in an inner room, had every appearance of being an oppressor; yet, after all, when you come to think of it, he was the oppressed. Don Abbondio, surprised, put to flight, frightened out of his wits while attending to his own business, would seem to be the victim; and yet, in reality, it was he who did the wrong.

But that's the way of the world: at least that's the way it used to be in seventeenth-century Italy.

—Alessandro Manzoni

Love and a Quiet Life
(from L'Amor Pacifico)

O blessed peace! O close and sacred tie!
    Long life to Veneranda and her dove!
But I must need inform you how and why
    This faithful pair first told their tender love.
At a friend's house they'd dined, and when upstairs
Found themselves side by side in two armchairs.

When half an hour had mutely passed away,
    Taddeo plucked up heart and broke the ice.
"Pray, madam, did you like the cream today?"
    "Delicious!" "I'm so glad you thought it nice.
The ham too?" "Exquisite." "And then the birds?"
"Perfection!" "And the fish?" "Beyond all words!

'Tis true that we had hardly room to sit."
    "Nay, 'twas a pleasure, when one sat by *you*;
But if, dear ma'm, I jogged your arm a bit,
    Trust me, 'twas what I could not choose but do."
"Don't mention it. *You* suffered, I suspect?
I'm stout, you see!" "An excellent defect!"

"Indeed?" "Indeed! That face now, in my eyes,
    Blooms like Mayday. Long may it glow!"

"I'm healthy!" "Healthy! Fresn as Paradise!"
        "Come, come! I'm somewhat stout" "And better so!
For my part, if I might, I'd very fain
Have leave to call upon you now and then."

"Oh, you'd be bored!" "I bored! What words are these?
        'Twould rather be my best and primest pleasure."
"Fie! Now you're flattering! Well, come when you please."
        "I think, dear madam, in no common measure,
Our characters are fitted to unite,
What do *you* say?"

        "La!—Well—perhaps they might!"
                                    —Giuseppe Giusti (1809-50)

Instructions to a Young Aspirant for Public Office

That you must cut all liberals whatever,
        All men of genius, all the "dangerous" crew,
Not prate of books or papers, but endeavor
        To prove that they are all High Dutch to you;
That you must bolt your heart and hold your tongue,
You've known, yourself, I'm well aware, for long.

Now, first and foremost, learn to bend your back:
        Be Veneration's self personified.
Dress ill; your clothes should fit you like a sack,
        And always take some bigwig for your guide.
The cowl does make the monk in such a case,
And the wall's valued by its plaster face.

Get introduced, and every blessed night
        Visit some lout they've made a minister.
There choose your time, and change your stops aright,
According as his tastes or whims prefer.
And if tomfoolery's the thing for winning,
Play the tomfool, and set the folks a-grinning.

Keep him supplied with news, and ferret out
        Fresh scandal, gossip, all that folks will tell you;
And, so to speak, what the whole town's about,
Down from His Highness even to Stenterello.*

---

*A favorite Florentine comic character of the day. (See Preface, vii.)

Say there arise a scandal, a dispute,
   A hurly-burly in your patron's house;
"Know-naught knew much, who knew when to be mute,"
   Says the old saw. Be mute, then, as a mouse!
Great men wil sometimes act like fools, 'tis certain,
In their own homes. Be ours to—drop the curtain!

Jump at all hints. Keep begging every way.
   Take all they give you, so they let you serve;
But—beg! *"The toad refused to beg,"* they say,
   "And therefore got no tail." Besides, observe
That, if not propped and fostered by our need,
Great men's authority's a dream indeed.

Remember to ignore and overpass
   Each rude rebuff, each peevish look and tone,
And, like Pope Sixtus, write yourself an ass
   If you're resolved to reach *your* papal throne.
After the bitters, sweets will come at length,
And sturdy begging beat close-fisted strength.

With profit Gingillino did attend
To the sage preaching of his vulpine friend.
He went; he knuckled down; he bared his crown;
He crept, crawled, coaxed, and cringed to sword and gown;
And when they'd dried him, tried him, sifted him, drifted him,
From Dan to Beersheba, at last they lifted him—
When the whole process they'd gone through and through,
With rites baptismal and with chrismal too—
Their heaven of three-piled roguedom to ascend,
Took him within the fold—and that's the end!
                       —Guiseppe Giusti

COLLODI—ON LITTLE BOYS

Nowadays, things are not what they were.

There are no more little boys. Instead we have a swarm of miniature politicians as yet unchristened: a crowd of Machiavellis seen through the wrong end of an opera glass, who, if they do go to school everyday, only do so for the sake of teaching their masters something: the latter being sorely in need of instruction.

What is it that has exterminated our boys from the face of the earth? The reading of political newspapers!

Fathers of families, of course, are perfectly at liberty to buy a daily paper—or two, or five, or ten; for newspapers, even if taken to excess, are like tamarind* jelly: if they do no good, at least they can't do much harm. Newspapers are quite safe, if you know how to use them.

But the mischief is this: fathers of families, when they have glanced over the paper, usually leave it on the table, or the sofa, or in one of many places that are within sight and reach of small boys. This is imprudent to the extreme, because we must remember that our boys are victims of a gluttonous, eager, devouring passion for the reading of political papers. Perhaps this is an outcome of that inborn instinct which shows itself at a very early age in the love of fables and fairy tales.

Then begin the troubles in the family.

A small boy comes with the newspaper in his hand and asks his mother:

"Tell me, Mama, what is the difference between 'authentic news' and 'various news'?"

"'Authentic' is what really happens," replies the mother at random, "and 'various' is what the journalists invent to fill up the paper."

"Oh, what storytellers!"

"Well, then, you should be very careful to always tell the truth. If you don't, you will go to Purgatory for seventy years, and in this world everyone will take you for a journalist!"

Amid the infinitely varied ranks of youth there are many who, through innate depravity and a fatally precocious hankering after political life, carry their reckless temerity so far as to read all the Parliamentary reports, from the first line to the last!

Let us say it once and for all. When a boy gives himself up without restraint and without shame, to the reading of the Parliamentary debates, it is all over for him! Goodbye to candor; goodbye to innocence and the simple language of the age of infancy.

One day little Cecco receives a maternal reprimand because, with his customary negligence, he has omitted to wash his hands.

I repudiate the malignant insinuation," replies the culprit, immediately hiding the two inconvenient "documents" in the pockets of his pants.

Another day, Gigino refuses to go to school unless his mother gives him the money to buy a cardboard Punch.**

---

*The sweet and acid fruit of the tamarind tree. Seeds and juicy pulp contained in the pods are used for jellies and beverages.
**Principal figure in a slapstick comedy or tragicomic misadventures with a conventional plot. The main actor, "Punch," or with other names attributed to him (see Preface, xii), wore the colormask of a grotesque, hook-nosed hunchback, as in the much later English Punch and Judy shows. Judy was Punch's wife. Italian children loved to wear these Punch masks, just as children today enjoy comic masks.

"All right, dear," says his mother, "but first go to school, and when you come home I will buy you the Punch."

"No, I want it now! And if I don't get it, I'll make it a Cabinet question!"

The poor mother finds her understanding failing her, and remains openmouthed and silent. Then enters Raffaello, the elder brother, who says to the younger:

"Instead of thinking about Punches, you would do better to study your grammar. Remember how yesterday the master called you a donkey three times?"

Gigino was about to reply with an impertinence, but unwilling to scandalize his mother's ears with what he had in mind, he contented himself with making faces at his brother.

Mama, who has at last again found her voice, admonishes: "Is that the way you treat your brother? He is older than you: you ought to respect him."

Gigino (raising his voice): "I have all possible esteem and respect for the honorable member who has just preceded me"—the Debates again—"but on the other hand, as far as I am concerned, he will always be a liar and a spy!"

Now take Beppino, as another example. Beppino is made of quick-silver. While carrying out one trick he is already thinking of a new one, so that neither in school nor at home is there any peace to be had because of him.

At last his father, unable to stand it any longer, called him into his study for a parental lecture.

During the first division of the lecture, Beppino was surrepitiously gnawing a dried plum. At the opening of the second division, he removed the pit and shot it at the nose of a plaster Dante on the writing desk. At the third division, Beppino lost all patience and began to yell:

"Enough! Enough! Cloture!"

"Cloture or no cloture!" cried the infuriated parent. "If you interrupt me again with your impudence—you rascal, you street-boy, you chatter-box, you . . ."

"Order! Order!" cried Beppino, pulling at the bell-rope.

"I'll order you . . ."

But just as his father was about to rise, Beppino snatched the cap from his head and, putting it on himself, remarked in a nasal voice:

"Gentlemen, the President has put on his hat and the discussion is adjourned."

The violent ringing of the bell summons the mother, two aunts, the housemaid, and the lady's little dog. These, having heard the narrative of Beppino's unparalleled insolence, are seized with such indignation that they begin to laugh like mad.

The little dog, unable to laugh like the rest, barks, and evidences his share in the family's joys and sorrows by gnawing on his dear master's embroidered slippers.

—Carlo Collodi (1826-1890)

STRAY THOUGHTS ON
AN IDLE AFTERNOON

All professions can yield a man enough to live on—except professions of faith.

————

When attending the performance of some modern operas, it has struck me that the conductor was only beating time because he could not beat the composer.

————

If in the sight of the law all men are equal, Heaven save us from getting into its sight.

————

A hospital full of sick people is called a *Casa di Salute* (House of Health); and the place where they ruin people's voices and throw aside all canons of art is called the *Conservatoire*.

————

How many old phrases are required to make a new election campaign!

————

All musical notes may express cheerful ideas, but the notes of creditors arouse only melancholy reflections.

—Antonio Ghislanzoni (1824-91)

MEN AND
MUSICAL INSTRUMENTS

We have been told over and over again that "the style is the man."
I would substitute for this, "The instrument is the man."
And whereas the proverb runs, "Tell me who your friends are, and I will tell you who you are; I would amend it thus, "Tell me what you blow into or scrape upon, and I will tell your fortune."
Having made those statements, I must now request all professional gentlemen who may be employed in orchestras or otherwise, not to suspect any malicious intent in my remarks, which are principally aimed at amateurs—those who murder some instrument or other out of pure conviction—all who began to twang the guitar when they were studying

medicine, or to practice on the cornet after a year's experience with matrimony.

THE CLARINET

This instrument consists of a severe cold in the head, contained in a tube of yellow wood.

The clarinet was not invented by the *Conservatoire*, but by Fate.

A chiropodist may be produced by study and hard work; but the clarinet player is born, not made.

The citizen predestined to the clarinet has an intelligence which is almost obtuse up to the age of eighteen—an epoch of incubation, when he begins to feel in his nose the first thrills of his fatal vocation.

Then his intellect—limited even then—ceases its development altogether; but his nasal organ, in revenge, assumes colossal dimensions.

At twenty he buys his first clarinet for fourteen francs; and three months later his landlord gives him notice. At twenty-five he is admitted into the band of the National Guard.

He dies of a broken heart on finding that not one of his three sons shows the slightest inclination for the instrument with which he has blown out all his wits.

THE TROMBONE

The man who plays this instrument is always one who seeks oblivion in its society—oblivion of domestic troubles or consolation for love betrayed.

The man who has held a metal tube in his mouth for six months finds himself impervious to every disillusion.

At the age of fifty he finds that, of all human passions and feelings, nothing is left him but an insatiable thirst.

Later on, if he wants to obtain the position of janitor in a building, or aspires to the hand of a woman with a delicate ear, he tries to lay aside his instrument, but the taste for loud notes and strong liquor leaves him only when life itself leaves.

Finally, after a harmonious career of seventy-eight years, he is apt to die of grief because the local tavernkeeper will not let him have a glass of wine on credit.

THE ACCORDION

This is the first instrument of youth and innocent hearts.

The individual begins playing it in the back room of his father's shop—the latter, as a rule, is a chemist by profession—and continues it up to the age of fifteen. At this period, if he does not die, he deserts the accordion for—

THE OBOE

This instrument, because of the nature of its monotonous sounds and tremendous plaintiveness, acts on the nerves of those who hear, and predisposes to melancholy those who play it.

The oboe player is usually tender and lymphatic of constitution, with blue eyes, and eats only white meat and farinaceous food.

If a man, he is called Oscar; those of the other sex are named Adelaide.

At home, he or she is in the habit of bringing out the instrument at dessert time, and dinner being over and the spirits of the family, therefore, more or less cheerfully disposed, will entertain the company with the *Miserere* in *Il Trovatore,* or some similar melody.

The practitioner of the oboe weeps easily. After practicing on the instrument for fifteen years or so, he or she dissolves altogether and turns into a brook.

THE ORGAN

This complicated and majestic instrument is of a clerical character and destined, by its great volume of sound, to drown out the flat singing of clergy and congregation in church.

The organist is usually a person sent into the world with the vocation of making a great noise without undue expenditure of strength; one who wants to blow harder than others without wearing out his own bellows.

At forty, he becomes the intimate friend of the parish priest, and the most influential person connected with the church. By dint of repeating the same refrains everyday at matins and vespers, he aquires a knowledge of Latin, and knows all the anthems, hymns, and masses by heart. At fifty he marries a devout spinster recommended by the priest.

He makes a kind and good-natured husband, his only defect in that capacity being his habit of dreaming out loud on the eve of every ecclesiastical solemnity. On Easter Eve, for instance, he nearly always awakens his wife by intoning with the full force of his lungs, *"Resurrexit!"* The good woman, thus abruptly aroused, never fails to answer him with the orthodox, *"Alleluia!"*

At the age of sixty he becomes deaf, and then begins to think his own playing perfection. At seventy he usually dies of a broken heart because the new priest, who knows not Joseph, instead of asking him to dine at the principal table with the ecclesiastics and other church authorities, has relegated him to an inferior place, and to the society of the sacristan and the gravedigger.

THE FLUTE

The unhappy man who succumbs to the fascinations of this instrument is never one who has attained the full development of his intellectual faculties. He always has a pointed nose, marries a shortsighted woman, and dies when run over by a bus.

The flute is the most fatal of all instruments. It requires a peculiar conformation and special culture of the thumbnail, with a view to those holes which have to be only half closed.

The man who plays the flute frequently adds to his other infirmities a mania for keeping tame weasels, turtle doves, or guinea pigs.

THE VIOLONCELLO

To play the 'cello you are required to have long, thin fingers, but it is still more indispensable to have very long hair falling over a greasy coat collar.

In case of fire, the 'cellist who sees his wife and his 'cello in danger will save the instrument first.

His greatest satisfaction, generally, is that of "making the strings weep." Sometimes, indeed, he succeeds in making his wife and family do the same thing as a consequence of his regimen of excessive frugality. Sometimes, too, it happens that he makes people laugh and yawn, but this, according to him, is the result of atmospheric influences.

Through his loftily attuned strings, he can express all possible griefs and sorrows, except those of his audience and his creditors.

THE DRUM

An immense apparatus of wood and sheepskin, it is full of air and sinister presages. In melodrama the roll of the drum serves to announce the arrival of a fatal personage, an agent of Destiny; in most cases an ill-used husband. Sometimes this funeral rumbling serves to describe silence—sometimes to indicate the depths of the prima donna's despair.

The drummer is a serious man, possessed with the sense of his high dramatic mission. He is able, however, to conceal his conscious pride, and sleep on his instrument when the rest of the orchestra is making all the noise it can. In such cases he commissions the nearest of his colleagues to awaken him at the proper moment.

On awakening, he seizes the two drumsticks and begins to beat, but should his neighbor forget to rouse him, he prolongs his slumbers till the fall of the curtain. Then he shakes himself, perceives that the opera is over, and rubs his eyes. If it happens that the conductor reprimands him for being remiss at the *attack,* he shrugs his shoulders and replies:

"So what? The tenor died just the same. A roll of the drum more or less, what does it signify?"

THE BASS DRUM

Of this it is quite unnecessary to speak. It is the instrument of the age. Ministers, deputies, men of science, poets, hairdressers, and dentists have all learned to perform on it to perfection.

The multitude will always answer the summons of its *boom-boom—* and whoever thumps it the hardest will always be in the right.

—Antonio Ghislanzoni

THE GREEKS HAD A WORD FOR IT—AND STILL DO!

It is said among businessmen that it requires twelve Scotsmen to cheat a Genoese, but twelve Genoese are not enough to cheat a Greek. Only one person that I ever heard of, enjoys the not very enviable distinction of having cheated—not merely one Greek—but two.

He was a Bari man.

He was returning to Italy, but had no boots—or rather, the things he wore were no longer boots. He carefully counted up his money, found that he did not have enough to buy a new pair, and so quieted his conscience. Then he went to a shoemaker's in the Street of Hermes.*

"I want a pair of shoes by Monday morning, to fit me exactly, with round toes and medium heels," and so forth, giving the fullest directions.

"Certainly, sir. You will have them without fail. They will be sent to your home on Monday morning, at ten o'clock."

---

*Athens.

The Bari man left his address and departed.

In the street of Aeolus he entered another shoemaker's shop and ordered a precisely similar pair of shoes on the the same terms.

"Have I made myself understood?"

"Perfectly. Let me have the address, and on Monday at ten . . ."

"I won't be in at ten. Send them after eleven."

"At eleven you can count on having them, without fail."

On Monday at ten the first victim appeared. The gentleman tried on the shoes. The right one was a perfect fit, but the left was fearfully tight over the instep. It needed stretching a little.

"All right," said the obliging tradesman, "I'll take it away, and bring it back to you tomorrow."

"Very well; and I'll pay for the pair when you return the other shoe."

The shoemaker bowed himself out with the left shoe.

At eleven, punctual as a creditor, the second predestined victim arrived. The same scene was repeated, but this time it was the right shoe that did not fit.

"You will have to stretch it a little, my friend."

"We'll soon set that right, sir." But the shoemaker, more knowledgeable than the other, was about to take both shoes away with him.

"Leave the other," said the Bari man. "It's a notion ôf mine. If you take them both, someone may come in and find that they fit him, and you'll sell them to him, leaving me to wait another week."

"But I assure you, sir . . ."

"No, my friend; I know how things go. I want this pair of shoes and no other. I insist on keeping one."

The shoemaker nodded his head with a sigh, and went away to stretch the right shoe.

An hour later, the Bari man and his shoes were already on board the Piraeus steamer.

On the following day, the two victims met on his doorstep, each with a shoe in his hand, and looked into each other's rapidly lengthening faces.

—Napoleone Corazzini (1840-1909)

Spalletti—the Famous Tenor

About a week after my arrival in Athens I was enjoying a tête-à-tête at the Samos Restaurant with a lamb cutlet of the most unexampled toughness, when there entered a stout gentleman, somewhere on the wrong side of fifty. He was dressed with great care, and sporting a gold chain of such length and massiveness that it might have served to fasten up a mastiff. His hands were covered with rings, and, upon entering, he made enough noise for ten.

"*Giuraddio!*" he roared when he had accosted a waiter who could speak Italian. "What has become of my usual place?"

"This way—this way, sir. There are four places at this table."

It was the one where I was sitting.

The stout gentleman contorted his features with disgust, uttered language which would have been enough for any Sicilian, and sat down beside me.

"*Giuraddio,*" he began, "I hate to have my place taken!"

Everyone present was looking at him, and smiling compassionately. Before he had finished unfolding his napkin he was already asking me—

"Are you Italian, sir?"

"Yes"

"Been in Athens long?"

"A few days."

"I've been here three months. Everyone knows me."

"I should think so, if you always make as much noise as that."

"You see how they are all looking at me?"

"How could I help but notice?"

"Apparently you don't know who I am."

"I do not have that honor."

"I am the celebrated Spalletti. Er—umm—you know?"

"No, I confess my ignorance."

"*Giuraddio!* Half the newspapers in the world have noticed me."

"I read very few newspapers."

"Why?"

"Because I am a journalist."

"I am here, in person! I have already given six performances of *Le Prophète.*"

"And you are. . . ?"

"The celebrated tenor, Spalletti."

"Blessed be modesty."

"Eh! What?"

"Nothing: only a remark on my part. A fine opera, *Le Prophète.*"

"Yes, so they say."

"*So they say!* Haven't you heard it?"

"I—well—I have other things to do. I get through my scenes and that's enough."

"But surely you must have read the words!"

"I've read my part—and even that's too much. However, I plan to read it over one evening before going to bed: I want to know who on earth this Prophet is."

Yet it was this very part of the Prophet which he had just enacted for the sixth time!

He then told me that he had been engaged to sing in Thomas' *Omeleto*—I would not have been surprised had he said *omelette*—and left, after telling me to come and see him there.

At the door, he turned and said:

"You must come and hear me at the theater tonight. I assure you, I will make you shed tears."

I went—and found that the worthy man was right. His performance was such that it would have drawn tears from a stone.

I later heard that the same gentleman had been asked to sing at a charity concert. On being told that he would be performing "an act of philanthropy," he replied that he was sorry but he was not acquainted with the play of that name, and therefore could not sing in it.

—Napoleone Corazzini

Deadly Rivals

There was a long-standing rivalry between the telegraph clerks of the towns of Pietranera and Golastretta. It is said to have begun at the Technical College, when the former carried off a silver medal hotly contested by the other; but this is not quite certain.

What is indeed certain is that Pippo Corradi could not undertake the smallest thing but that Nino d'Arco immediately proceeded to do likewise. Thus, when Pippo took a fancy to become an amateur magician, Nino at once went in search of the necessary apparatus with which to amuse his friends with the miracles of white magic.

He was not a success. He raised many a laugh by his lack of skill. But this did not prevent him from wasting still more money on boxes with false bottoms, pistols to shoot playing cards instead of bullets, wonderful balls which multiply and grow larger in your hands, and the like. Cost what it might, he was determined to astonish his Golastretta friends, who extolled him to his face about the same tricks they had seen accomplished, to a far better degree, by Corradi, in Pietranera, and derided him by way of contrast.

Then, when the fickle Pippo Corradi gave up his white magic in order to devote himself to music, and the study of the clarinet in particular, Nino d'Arco suddenly laid aside the magic toys, which had already wearied him, and took music lessons from the parish organist. He bought a brand new ebony clarinet, and rode over on a donkey to call on Corradi, under the pretext of consulting him on his choice, but really with the sole intention of humiliating him.

It was the only time he ever succeeded. He found him blowing into the mouthpiece of a boxwood instrument which he had bought secondhand for a few francs from an old clarinet player in the town band. Nino swelled visibly with satisfaction at seeing the admiration and envy in his rival's eyes when he opened his leather case and showed him the polished keys of white metal, shining even more than the freshly varnished wood.

Nino put the instrument together delicately, and set it to his mouth, thinking to astonish Pippo with a scale in halftones. Unluckily for him, however, he broke down in the middle of the recital.

Then Corradi was able to take his revenge. He played scales in all tones, major, minor, diatonic, and chromatic; and not content with that, and without warning to Nino who kept staring at his rival's flying fingers maneuvering over the holes and keys, he dashed point-blank into his *pièce de résistance—La Donna è Mobile,* tootling away quite divinely until checked by the imperative need of taking a breath. His eyes were nearly starting out of his head; his face was purple—but what did he care? That was nothing! He chuckled inwardly at Nino's crestfallen look. The latter, disassembling his instrument, put it back in the case, thus declaring himself vanquished.

Nino, returning to Golastretta, vented his anger and frustration on his donkey. as though it had been she who taught Corradi to play *La Donna è Mobile.* So true is it that passion renders man unjust! He rushed at once to his music teacher to learn *La Donna è Mobile* for himself, so that he might, in a short time, play it before his hated rival.

But Corradi, however, had another great advantage, besides being able to murder *Rigoletto:* he was the local postmaster. In this point it was useless trying to rival him, however much Nino might dream of a spacious office like the one in Pietranera. There, Corradi, between the sale of one stamp and the next, between registering a letter and administering a reprimand to a postman, could divert himself by blowing into his clarinet to his heart's content. But Nino was forced to escape from his house if he wished to practice and remain at peace with his family. Corradi, in his post office, disturbed no one; or so he thought.

What Nino did not know, of course, was that his rival's clarinet could be clearly heard outside the post office, tormenting the neighborhood with its shrilling from morning to night. The shopkeeper across the street, poor wretch, swore all day long, worse than a Turk, and did not know whether he was standing on his head or his feet every time that Pippo began to repeat *La Donna è Mobile;* that is to say, he swore seven or eight times a day. He made mistakes in his weights, he counted his change wrong; though it is only fair to state that these errors were more often in his own favor than in that of his customers. And if by any chance the shopkeeper saw Corradi at the window, he raised his hands toward him with a supplicating gesture, pretending to be humorous.

"Do you want me to die of a fit?" he would call out. "Good Lord!"

Of all this, Nino d'Arco was quite ignorant when he started for Pietranera a month later. It was his mission, this time, to surprise Corradi with *Mira Norma* which he had learned, in addition to *La Donna etcetera*. He found Pippo adding up his monthly accounts, and not inclined to talk about music or anything else. The fact was that the shopkeeper on the opposite side of the street had indeed fallen down dead in a fit at the third or fourth rendering of *La Donna e Mobile*, as he had said, just as though he had a presentiment of what was to happen. The occurrence had such an effect on Pippo that he felt as if he had killed the man, and could not bear to touch the clarinet again. He would not even mention the subject.

Nino bit his lips and returned home, without having so much as opened his clarinet case. Once more it was the donkey who paid the penalty. He had to relieve his feelings on someone or something.

If there were any need of an instance to prove that emulation is the most powerful agent in the development of the human faculties, this one would suffice. Seeing that Corradi had renounced the clarinet and all its delights, Nino no longer felt the slightest inclination to go on wasting his breath on his instrument, even though it was of ebony, and had keys of white metal. As a faithful historian, I ought to add that, for a moment or two, he was tempted by the idea of trying to attain the glory of causing someone's death by a fit. But whether the Golastretta people had harder tympanums than those of Pietranera, or whether he himself was not possessed of the necessary strength and perseverance, no victim fell to Nino d'Arco's clarinet.

And the fact of having no death on his conscience made him feel degraded in his own eyes for some time.

—Luigi Capuana (1839-1915)

RIVAL EARTHQUAKES

Golastretta was situated between the central office of the province and the rival telegraph station of Pietranera. It was telegrapher Nino d'Arco's duty to signal to his hated rival in Golastretta the mean time by which he was to regulate his clock—a supremacy which Pippo Corradi could never take from him.

Having very little to do, Nino was accustomed to reading the *Gazette* or the last paper-covered novel, and then taking a nap in the office. One morning, when he least expected it, the telegraph machine began clicking, and would not stop. It was his "dear friend" at Pietranera, sending dispatches after dispatches, and would not let him drop off to sleep comfortably.

Listening attentively, he soon made out what was the matter. On the previous evening, the village of Pietranera had begun to dance like a man bitten by a tarantula, set in motion by earthquake shocks. The 'quakes were being repeated from hour to hour. Messages were flowing almost continually from the Syndic* to the Prefect and the Meteorological Office of the province in the name of the terrified population. And Corradi, too, was telegraphing his own account, signaling the shocks as fast as they occurred, and indicating their length or the nature of the movement. But this, according to Nino d'Arco, was only Pippo's sneaky way of gaining credit with his superiors. Yes, Nino was vexed, as might be expected, that his own town of Golastretta did not have its half dozen earthquakes as well.

How cruelly partial was Nature! Scarcely twenty kilometers away she was rendering Corradi an immense service with eight, ten, twenty shocks, day and night, within a week; but, for him, not even the smallest vestige of any shock whatever. He could get no peace, and kept his ear to the telegraph machine.

One day, behold! there passed the announcement of a scientific commission on its way to Pietranera in order to study these persistent seismic phenomena. A few days later, Nino became aware of the transit of another dispatch appointing the Pietranera telegraph agent as director of the Meteorological-Seismic station, which the commission thought it advisable to establish at that place. In a month from that time the speedy arrival of a large number of scientific instruments was wired down from headquarters.

Nino d'Arco could stand it no longer. Nothing would do but that he go and see with his own eyes what the new "director" was doing under the canopy of the Meteorological-Seismic Observatory which would not let him live in peace.

He could not recover from his astonishment at the sight of all the machines already set up in position, whose strange names Pippo Corradi reeled off with the greatest ease, as he explained the working of each. Rain gauge, wind gauge, barometers, maximum and minimum thermometers, hygrometers, and besides that a tromometer, and all sorts of deviltries for marking the very slightest earthquake shocks, indicating their nature and recording the very hour at which they occurred, by means of stopwatches.

Nino was very far from understanding it all, but made believe he did.

---

*A person representing a university or corporation; also, a civil magistrate, having different powers in their respective countries. In modern day Italy, the *Sindaco* is considered to be the mayor.

At last he came to a pendulum which was constructed to register the movements of the earthquakes by marking them with a sharp point on a sheet of smoked glass placed beneath it. He remained for a long time, gazing at the pendulum through a magnifying glass.

The contraption was that moment moving, sometimes from right to left, sometimes backward and forward, but so imperceptibly that it could not be discerned by the naked eye.

Suddenly—*drrrnnn! drrrnnn!* There was a ringing of bells; the pendulum quivered.

"A shock!" cried Pippo triumphantly, rushing to his telegraph machine to announce it.

"I didn't feel anything," said Nino d'Arco, white with terror.

Nino hastened to leave. But he was simply flabbergasted by all those machines and the satisfied air of his colleague. Pippo Corradi already signed his dispatches, "Director of the Meteorological-Seismic Observatory at Pietranera," as though he were a very important person, and he seemed to be—reflected Nino—even to him, who knew very well that he was nothing more than a telegraph clerk just like himself.

All along the homeward road, when he had finished settling accounts with the donkey, he ruminated over the money which all that apparatus must have cost. The seismographic pendulum, however, was only worth about eighteen francs. He would like to have at least a pendulum. What would he do with it if he had it? He didn't know, but the pendulum kept vibrating in nis brain all week, backward and forward, right and left, scratching the smoked glass at every stroke. Nino constantly saw himself peering through the magnifying glass as he had done at Pietranera. It was a diabolical persecution!

He had to humble himself before his detested colleague in order to get information, explanations and instruments; but after all, in the end, a pendulum was finally in his possession, near his office window. It had cost him nearly half his month's salary. But what did that matter? Now, he too could telegraph the most beautiful earthquakes.

—Luigi Capuana

SEQUEL TO RIVAL EARTHQUAKES

Nino d'Arco did not figure on the pervisity of machinery. That infamous pendulum he had bought to record earthquakes and thus make him equal to or better than Pippo Corradi, remained perfectly motionless—as if on purpose to spite him—even when he peered at it through the magnifying glass. He passed whole days ruining his eyes with that glass, anxious to observe the first trace of movement, so that he might signal the occurrence to all Italy, and thus begin his competition with Pippo's observatory in Pietranera. He ground his teeth in rage, especially on the days when his fortunate rival seemed to be mocking him with the ticking of the messages which announced to the Provincial Office some little shock his instruments had recorded.

For an earthquake—a real earthquake!—Nino would have given anything; perhaps his very soul. Meanwhile, he dreamed of earthquakes, often awakening terrified in the night, uncertain whether it were a dream or if the shock had really taken place. But the pendulum remained stern and unmoving. It was enough to drive a saint to desperation.

Ahah! Was that the game? Did the earthquakes obstinately refuse to manifest themselves? Well, then, in that case he would *invent* them! After all, who could contradict him? And so, that unlucky parish, which had been for centuries quietly anchored to the rocky mountainside, began to perform an intricate dance of shocks, slight shocks, and approaches to shocks, in the reports to the Meteorological Office in Rome.

There was no means of keeping it still any longer. Nino could not forego the glory of showing his friends the sheet where his name appeared in print beside those of several famous men of science, and the report spread through the country that the mountain was moving imperceptibly, threatening to come down in a landslide.

"Is it really true?" the most timid came to ask.

"True, indeed!" replied Nino solemnly, pointing to the pendulum. But he would allow no one to examine it at close quarters.

Just as though Nature had done it on purpose, the Pietranera observatory no longer signaled any disturbances since Golastretta had begun to amuse itself by frequent vibrations. Pippo Corradi, suspecting the trick of his colleague, was gnawing away at his own heart because of all the false indications that were quietly being foisted in among his genuine ones of the official report to Rome, making a mockery of science.

Pippo, for his own part, did his work seriously and scrupulously, even leaving his dinner when the hour for observation came. His reports were models of scientific accuracy. Should he take it upon himself to denounce his colleague? He could not make up his mind. Nino, as bold as brass, went on making the village quake and tremble, as though it were nothing at all.

This time, the proverb that "lies have short legs" did not hold good, for the lies in question reached Tacchini in Rome, and Father Denza in Moncalieri. Even those two eminent scientists, like all the others, were very far from suspecting, in the remotest degree, the wickedness of Nino.

But one day, all of a sudden, the Golastretta pendulum awoke from its torpor and began to move behind the magnifying glass, although to the naked eye its motion was scarcely discernible.

Nino gave a howl of joy. "At last! At last!"

He greeted the first person who happened to come into his telegraph with a majestic sweep of his arm. "Look here!"

"What does it mean?"

"We will have a big earthquake," explained Nino gleefully, rubbing his hands.

"Mercy!"

Now, the exultant Nino rushed at once to spread the terrible news in streets, shops and cafes. In an hour the telegraph office was invaded—besieged. Everybody wished to see with his or her own eyes, so as to be certain. And when they had indeed seen, they frightened the others with their accounts, giving explanations more terrifying than those they had received and half understood, and so increasing the panic which now began to seize the most skeptical individuals.

It was an extraordinary success for Nino d'Arco. He seemed to see before him the image of his colleague, Pippo Corradi, jaundiced with envy. Again he rubbed his hands with delight.

Outside, the street was full of people discussing the affair. Some women were crying, boys shouting, men calling, "Is it still moving?" "Worse than before." "Oh, blessed Madonna!" The parish priest hastened to the spot, frightened as badly as the rest by the news which had been carried to him by the sacristan. He had scarcely looked through the glass than he sprang from his chair as if he had felt the ground rocking under his feet.

"It is the judgment of God, gentlemen! On account of our sins, gentlemen!"

Then the people began to get away as fast as they could.

There was a banging of shutters, a hurried closing of doors, a rushing about, a shouting of each other's names. "Is it still moving?" "Worse than ever! The whole mountain is about to slide down on us!" It got so bad that, at last, Nino himself no longer felt easy. From time to time he turned back to look once more at the pendulum, which continued to vibrate. It was the first time that Nino found himself actually, as it were, face to face with a distant indication of an earthquake, after the hundred or so shocks of all sorts, strengths and sizes he had invented and caused to be published in the Report to Rome. And now it was not exactly amusing—that dumb menace to which his ignorance gave a false significance. Pendulum of the devil! Would it never be still? A beautiful invention of science, calculated to kill a peaceful citizen with anticipatory fear! Who ever heard of the earth being shaken without people becoming aware of it?

It seemed to him that the vibrations increased from hour to hour, and that the danger of a general fall of buildings became more imminent every minute. He was alone in the office—there was not a soul to be seen in the street—everyone had left the village to seek safety in the open plains; and his duty, as telegraph operator, forbade him to move.

Toward evening he closed the office and went out to the plains himself. The people were standing about in groups, telling their beads and chanting litanies. When they saw him they came near to falling upon him, as the cause of the mischief. Was it not he who had turned the whole village upside down with that accursed pendulum of his? The whole scene had a depressing effect on him, however he might try to keep up his courage and convince his fellow townsmen of the great benefit of his warning. For all they knew, he reasoned, it might have saved many lives.

But at noon on the following day nothing had yet happened.

Every quarter of an hour one of the bravest came in from the countryside to the telegraph office, to find out how things were going. The pendulum still vibrated, but there was no news of the predicted earthquake.

The evening came, with not the ghost of an earthquake. A few, here and there, began to ridicule the whole idea. The Syndic, who had a head on his shoulders, sent a messenger to Pietranera. He soon returned with Pippo Corradi's answer:

"It's all nonsense! Let your minds rest easy; there will be no earthquake."

Cries of indignation arose, and those who had been most frightened and convinced that they had been made to seem like fools, began to yell, "Imbecile! Blockhead! Idiot!"

They rushed in a tumultuous noisy crowd to the telegraph office, and had they not met the lieutenant of the *Carabinieri** who had also hastened to the office after receiving a coded telegram from the chief constable—Lord knows how the matter might have ended for Nino d'Arco.

"What in hell have you been doing here?" demanded the lieutenant. "You've been disturbing the public peace."

Nino was petrified for a moment. Then, seeking to excuse himself by proof positive, he pointed to the pendulum.

"Well, what about it," asked the lieutenant.

"Look—it moves."

"You must be seeing things. There's nothing moving here."

"Look carefully."

"I am. There's not a damn thing moving!"

The pendulum had, in fact, stopped.

"I confiscate it, for the present," announced the lieutenant. And, raising the glass top of the case, he took out the tube in which the pendulum was fixed. "When one is as ignorant as you, sir. . . ." The rest of his statement

*Soldiers, usually equipped with carbine rifles.

was drowned out by everyone present who applauded vigorously. "And I will report this matter to headquarters," the officer concluded.

To Nino, it meant nothing that the crowd applauded and hissed, or that the lieutenant of the *Carabinieri* would report him to headquarters. He was thinking only of Pippo Corradi, and how he would laugh behind his back when he heard about it. Tears stood in his eyes.

And, as though all this had not been enough, behold! on the following day, another message from Corradi clicked along the wires:

"Today, 2:00 P.M., upward shock of first degree lasting three seconds; followed, after interval of seven seconds, by undulatory shock, south-north, also first degree, lasting five seconds. No damage."

"Infamous fate!" groaned Nino d'Arco. He shut off the current to escape from the clicks that seemed to deride him.

—Luigi Capuana

THE WAR OF THE SAINTS

All of a sudden, while San Rocco was quietly proceeding on his way, under the baldachin,[1] with a number of wax candles lit all around him, and with the band and the procession and the crowd of devout people, there arose a mighty tumult, confusion, and general helter-skelter. There were priests running in all directions, with the skirts of their cassocks flying wildly, drummers and fifers with agitation distorting their faces, women screaming, blood flowing in streams, and clubs wielded under the very nose of the blessed San Rocco.

The praetor,[2] the syndic, the *carabinieri* all hastened to the spot. Those with broken bones were carted off to the hospital. A few of the more riotous members of the community were marched off to spend the night in jail. And the saint returned to his church at a run rather than a processional step. Thus, the festival ended like the comedies of Pulcinella.[3]

And all this through the spite of the people in the parish of San Pasquale. That year, the pious souls of San Rocco had been spending the very eyes out of their heads in order to do things in grand style. They had sent for the band from town; they had discharged more than two hundred scribes and clerks; and they had now obtained a new banner, all embroidered with gold which, it was said, weighed over a quintal.[4] They

---

[1] A portable canopy carried in religious processions.

[2] One of a number of elected magistrates charged mainly with the administration of civil justice, especially in the ancient Roman republic.

[3] Another name for Punch, used by Neapolitans. (See Preface for detailed discussion.)

[4] A metric unit of weight equivalent to 100 kilograms, or 220.462 pounds.

tossed the banner up and down in the midst of the crowd, like a wave crested with golden foam.

It was that selfsame banner which, by sheer contrivance of the Evil One, was a thorn in the sides of the followers of San Pasquale; so much so that one of them at last lost patience and, pale as death, began to yell at the top of his voice, *"Viva San Pasquale!"*

It was then that the cudgels began to fly.

After all, let it be borne in mind, to go and cry *"Viva San Pasquale"* in the very face of San Rocco is really a good, sound, indisputable provocation: it is just like going into a man's house and spitting on the floor, or amusing yourself by pinching the girl's behind while she is walking arm-in-arm with him. In such a case there is no longer any sense of right and wrong, and that slight amount of respect which people still have for the other saints—who, actually, are all related to each other—is trampled underfoot. If it happens in church, seats are flung into the air; if it happens during a procession, there are showers of torch stumps like swarms of bats; and at the table, the dishes fly.

"Santo diavolone!" (Great holy Devil!) cried *Compare** Nino, panting, heated and disheveled. "I'd like to know who has the courage to cry *Viva Pasquale* again!"

"I!" yelled Turi, the tanner, who looked forward to being his brother-in-law, now quite beside himself with rage and nearly blinded by a chance blow received in the melee. *"Viva San Pasquale* till death!"

"For the love of heaven!" shrieked his sister Saridda, throwing herself between her brother and her betrothed. All three had been taking a walk in all love and good fellowship until that moment.

Compare Nino, the expectant bridegroom, kept crying in derision, "Long live my ass! *Viva San Stivale!"*

"Take that!" howled Turi, swinging his fist. He was foaming at the mouth, his eyes pinched and his face like a tomato. "Take that for San Rocco, you *and* your ass!"

They exchanged blows which would have felled an ox, till their friends succeeded in separating them by dint of cuffs and kicks. Saridda, who by this time, had grown excited on her own account, now cried *Viva San Pasquale,* and was close to striking her lover, just as if they were already husband and wife.

At times such as those, parents quarrel most desperately with their sons and daughters, and wives separate from their husbands, especially if, by some misfortune, a woman of the parish of San Pasquale has married a man from San Rocco.

"I don't want to hear another word about that detestable man!" cried Saridda, standing with her hands on her hips.

---

*Pronounced kohm-pah-reh.

"But what about your intended marriage?" asked one of the neighbors who surrounded her.

"I wouldn't have him if they gave him to me dressed in gold and silver from head to foot! Do you hear?"

"Saridda can stay as she is until her hymen turns moldy, for all I care!" snapped *Compare* Nino, in his turn, as he was washing the blood from his face at the public bathhouse. "A bunch of beggars and cowards in the tanner's section of town! I must have been drunk when I went to look for a sweetheart there!"

"Since this is the kind of conduct we can expect," concluded the syndic, frustrated and angered by the general rioting, "and they can't carry a saint into the square without all that fighting, so that it's perfectly beastly, I will not permit any more festivals, nor processions, nor outdoor services. If they bring out so much as a single candle—under whatever name they want to call it—I'll have every one of them in jail."

In time, the matter became important. The bishop of the diocese had granted to the priests of San Pasquale the privilege of wearing copes.* The parishioners of San Rocco, whose priests had no copes, had even gone to Rome to raise an outcry at the foot of the Holy Father, carrying with them documents on stamped papers, and everything else. But all had been in vain. Their adversaries, who, as everyone remembered, had once been without shoes for their feet, had now grown as rich as Turkish rug merchants, through this new industry of leather tanning. And, in this world, one knows that justice is bought and sold like the soul of Judas.

At San Pasquale they were awaiting Monsignor's delegate, a man of importance, with silver buckles on his shoes weighing half a pound apiece—and a fine sight they were to see. He was to bring the copes to the local church dignitaries. For this reason, they, in their turn, had sent for the band, with everyone prepared to meet Monsignor's delegate three miles outside the town. It was said that in the evening there were to be fireworks in the square, with *Viva San Pasquale* over and over again, in letters as big as those on a store front.

The inhabitants of the upper town were therefore in a great ferment. Some, more excited than others, were trimming certain staves of pear and cherry wood, as big as cavemen's clubs, and muttering, "If there is to be music, we'll want to beat time!"

The bishop's delegate ran a great risk of emerging from his triumphal entry with broken bones. But the reverend gentleman was cunning enough to leave the band waiting for him outside the town, while he took a short cut, quietly walking to the parish priest's home. From there he summoned the principal men of both factions.

---

*A long mantle or cloak of silk or other material worn by ecclesiastics in processions and on other occasions.

When the opposing parties at last found themselves face to face, for the first time since the feud had started, each man glared into the whites of his neighbor's eyes as if he could scarcely keep his nails out of them. In fact, it required all the authority of His Reverence—who had donned his new cloth soutane* for the occasion—to get the ices and other refreshments served without accidents.

"That's right," said the syndic approvingly, with his nose in a glass. "When you want me for the cause of peace, you'll always find me on the spot. That's why I came."

The delegate then affirmed that he had come for the sake of conciliation, with the olive branch in his mouth, like Noah's dove. He finished his exhortation, distributing smiles and handclasps all around. "Gentlemen," he concluded, "will you do me the favor of coming into the sacristy to take a cup of chocolate on the day of the festival?"

"Please, I urge you, leave the festival alone," cautioned the vice-praetor, "or more mischief will surely come of it."

"Mischief will come of it only if we allow this tyranny to continue!" exclaimed Bruno, the carter. "If a man cannot amuse himself as he likes, and pay for it with his own money, he is not free."

"I wash my hands of the matter," said the vice-praetor stubbornly. "The orders of the government are explicit. If you celebrate the festival I will send for the *carabinieri*. I'm for order."

"I'll answer for order!" interjected the syndic, tapping the ground for emphasis with his umbrella.

"Bravo!" retorted the vice-praetor sarcastically. "As if we didn't know that it's your brother-in-law Bruno who blows the bellows for you in the town council!"

"Gentlemen, gentlemen!" entreated the delegate. "We'll get nothing accomplished if we go on this way."

"We'll have a revolution, that's what we'll have" shouted Bruno, gesticulating with his hands in the air.

Fortunately, the parish priest had quietly put away the cups and glasses, and the sacristan had rushed off at top speed to dismiss the band.

The delegate was just about worried to death by the thought that the harvest was already ripe for cutting in his own village, while he was wasting his time here talking to *Compare* Bruno and the vice-praetor, who hated each other because of an old grudge and were ready to tear the souls out of each other.

The delegate, in order to conciliate the local mind, would sit boxed up in his confessional, like an owl in its nest, from morning till evening, and

---

*Cassock: a long, close-fitting garment worn by clergymen or laymen participating in church services.

all the women were eager to confess to the bishop's representative, who had the powers of plenary absolution for all sorts of sins, just as though he had been the Monsignor in person.

"Your Reverence," said Saridda, with her nose at the grating, "*Compare* Nino makes me commit sin every Sunday in church."

"In what way, my daughter?"

"He was to have married me, but now that the wedding is broken off, he stands near the high altar and stares at me, and laughs with his friends, all the time holy mass is going on."

"No, it's she who turns her back on me," said Nino, when His Eminence tried to touch his heart. "She ignores me whenever we happen to meet, just as if I were a beggar."

But Nino, on the other hand, gave himself airs as if he were a brigadier or some other great personage, whenever Saridda passed across the square on Sundays. He did not even seem to see her. Saridda was exceedingly busy preparing little colored paper lanterns, on one occasion, and put them out in a row on the windowsill, in his very face, under the pretext of hanging them out to dry. At another time, they found themselves together in church, at a christening, and took no notice of each other, just as though they had never met before. In fact, Saridda even went so far as to flirt with the godfather.

"A poor sort of godfather," sneered Nino.

Saridda turned away, pretending to talk to the baby's mother: "What's bad does not always come to do harm. Sometimes, when you think you've lost a treasure, you ought to thank God and San Pasquale; you can never say you know a person till you've eaten seven measures of salt. After all, one must take troubles as they come, and the worst possible way is to worry about things which are not worth the trouble. When one Pope dies they make another. It's foreordained what sort of nature children will be born with, and it's the same with marriages. It's far better to marry a man who really cares for you and has no other ends to serve, even though he has no money or fields or mules or anything."

On the square the drum was beating to give notice of the festival.

"The syndic says we will definitely have the festival," was the murmur that ran through the crowd.

"Dammit all!" cried Nino. "I'll go to the law if it leaves me as poor as Job, with nothing left but the shirt on my back, but I won't pay a fine. No, not if I have to leave directions about it in my will."

Since March not a drop of rain had fallen, and the yellow corn, which crackled like tinder, was dying of thirst. Bruno, the carter, however, proclaimed that when San Pasquale was carried out in procession it would rain for certain: God would be pleased. And so they carried San Pasquale in procession to the east and to the west, and set him upon a hill to bless the country: this, on a stifling May day when the sky was covered with clouds, one of those days when the farmers are ready to tear out their hair before the scorched fields, and the stalks of corn droop as if they are dying.

"A curse on San Pasquale!" exclaimed Nino, spitting in the air and rushing about among his crops like a madman. "You've ruined me, San Pasquale; you've left me nothing but the reaping hook to cut my throat with!"

The upper town was a desolate place enough. It was one of those long years when the hunger begins in June, and the women stand at their doors with their hair hanging about their shoulders; doing nothing; staring with fixed eyes. Saridda, hearing that *Compare* Nino's mule was to be sold in the public square to pay the rent on his farm, felt her anger melt away in an instant, and sent her brother Turi in hot haste, with a few *soldi** they had put aside, to help him.

Nino was in one corner of the square, with his eyes averted and his hands in his pockets, while they were selling his mule, with all its ornaments and the new bridle.

"I don't want anything," he replied sullenly. "My arms are still left to me, thank God. A fine saint that San Pasquale of yours, eh?"

Turi turned his back on him to avoid unpleasantness, and went on his way. But the truth is that the people were exasperated, now that they had carried San Pasquale in procession to east and west, with no more result than that. The worst of it was that many from the parish of San Rocco had been induced to walk with the procession too, thrashing themselves like asses, and with crowns of thorns on their heads—all for the sake of their crops. Now they relieved their feelings in exceedingly bad language. The bishop's delegate was obliged to leave town as he had entered it: on foot, and without the band.

The vice-praetor, by way of retaliation on his opponent, telegraphed that the people were getting out of hand and the public peace compromised, so that one fine day a report went through the town that the soldiers had arrived and everyone could go and see them.

"They've come because of the cholera," others declared, however. "Down in the city, they say, the people are dying like flies."

The chemist locked the door of his shop, and the doctor left the place as speedily as possible to escape being knocked on the head.**

"Have no fear, it won't come to anything," said the few who had remained in the place; especially those who were unable to fly into the country like the rest. "The blessed San Rocco will watch over his own town."

---

*Pennies.

**This is what usually happened at the outbreak of cholera in nineteenth century southern Italy.

Even the lower town folks had begun to go barefoot to San Rocco's church. But not long after that, deaths began to come thick and fast. They said of one man that he was a glutton, and died of eating too many prickly pears, and of another that he had come in from the country after nightfall.* But, in short, there *was* the cholera: it could not be disguised, in spite of the soldiers, and in the very teeth of San Rocco—notwithstanding the fact that an old woman in the aura of sanctity had dreamed that the saint himself had said to her:

"Let your minds be at ease—the cholera will not touch you: I am taking care of that. I am not like that useless old ass of a San Pasquale."

Nino and Turi had not met since the mule was sold, but scarcely had Nino heard that the brother and sister were ill, than he hastened to their house where he found Saridda, black in the face and her features all distorted, in a corner of the room. Her brother was recovering, but he did not know what to do for her, and was nearly beside himself with despair.

"Ah, thief of a San Rocco!" groaned Nino. "I never expected this. Saridda, don't you know me anymore? It's Nino: your own Nino."

Saridda looked at him with eyes so sunken that it was necessary to hold a lantern to her face to see them. Nino felt his own eyes running over.

"Ah, San Rocco!" he said again. "This is a worse trick than the one San Pasquale played on me."

However, in time Saridda grew better, and as she was standing at the door with her head tied up in a handkerchief, she managed a smile, even though her face was still yellow as new wax.

"San Rocco has worked a miracle for me," she said, "and you ought to come too, and carry a candle at his festival."

Nino's heart was too full to speak. He just nodded assent. But before the festival came around, he too was taken with the plague and lay at the point of death. Saridda tore her face with her nails, and said that she wanted to die with him; that she would cut off her hair and have it buried with him, and no one would ever look her in the face again as long as she lived.

"No, no!" protested Nino, his face all drawn with agony. "Your hair will grow again, but I'm the one who will never see you again—I'll be dead."

"A fine miracle that San Rocco has worked for you!" said Turi, by way of comforting him.

Both of them slowly recovered. But when they sat sunning themselves, with their backs to the wall and with very long faces, they kept throwing San Rocco and San Pasquale in each other's teeth.

One day, Bruno, the carter, coming back from the country after the cholera was over, passed by.

---

*A euphemism meaning that he had really died of malarial fever.

"We're going to have a grand festival to thank San Pasquale for having saved us from the cholera," he informed them. "We'll have no more demagogues and no more opposition, now that the vice-praetor is dead."

"That's just fine!" sneered Nino. "A festival for the dead."

"Now just a moment! Do you think it was San Rocco that kept you alive?"

"Stop it! Stop it, right now!" cried Saridda, outraged. "Must we have another cholera to make peace between you?"

—Giovanni Verga (1840-1922

PEPPE'S PURLOINED PIG

Mastro[1] Peppe La Bravetta was a fat, stupid, good-natured man of Pescara, who sold pots and pans. He was terribly in awe of his wife, the severe and miserly *Donna* Pelagia, who ruled him with a rod of iron. In addition to the income he derived from his business, he owned a piece of land on the other side of the river which produced enough to keep a pig. Every January, the couple would go to this property to preside over the butchering and salting of the pig which had been fattening through the year.

It so happened that, one year, Pelagia was not very well, and La Bravetta went to attend the butchering alone. During the course of the afternoon he was visited by two of his friends, graceless vagabonds, Matteo Puriello, nicknamed Ciavola,[2] who was a poacher, and Biagio Quaglia, better known as Il Ristabilito,[3] whose most serious occupation was that of playing the guitar at weddings and on other festive occasions.

When he saw the two approaching he welcomed them enthusiastically, and led them into the shed where the recently demised pig was laid out on the table, in all its grandeur: truly a wonderful sight.

"Isn't he a beauty?" asked the proud owner.

The two friends contemplated the pig in silent wonder, and Ristabilito clicked his tongue appreciatively against his palate.

"What are you going to do with it?" asked Ciavola.

"Salt it down," replied La Bravetta, in a voice that trembled with greedy delight of future banquets.

"*Salt it?* Is that what you said?" cried Ristabilito suddenly. "Cia, did you ever see another man as stupid as this one? To let such a chance slip by!"

---

[1]Master

[2]A loafer; also a rumormonger; a malicious gossip.

[3]The re-maker, or re-doer; loosely, a conniver who is always changing something to his own advantage.

La Bravetta, quite dumbfounded, stared first at one and then at the other.

"*Donna* Pelagia has always kept you under her thumb," continued Ristabilito. "But this time she can't see you. So why not sell the pig and then we can feast on the money."

"B-b-but Pelagia! How would I explain it?" stammered La Bravetta, who was filled with an immense consternation by the image of his wrathful wife in his mind's eye.

"Tell her that the pig was stolen," suggested Ciavola, impatience in his voice.

La Bravetta shuddered.

"I don't dare go home and tell her that. Pelagia won't believe me. She'll drive me—she'll. . . . You don't know what Pelagia is!"

"Pelagia! *Donna* Pelagia!" jeered Ristabilito, imitating Peppe La Bravetta's whining voice.

"Come on, let's go!" interrupted Ciavola.

"You can stay for supper, if you wish," suggested *Mastro* Peppe in a constrained voice.

"No, thanks," replied Ciavola. "Just do as your Pelagia tells you, and salt the pig."

As the two friends walked along the road, Ristabilito remarked in a too-casual tone: "*Compare,** we could steal that pig tonight."

"How?" asked Ciavola promptly.

"Believe me, I know how, if it's still in the same place when we get there."

"Then let's do it," agreed Ciavola. "But then what?"

"Never you mind—I have something in mind," he said enigmatically.

As they strolled homeward they saw Don Bergamino Camplone approaching in the moonlight—a black figure between the rows of leafless poplars with their silvery trunks. They immediately quickened their pace to meet him.

The jolly priest noted their festive looks. "What's up, this time?" he asked with a smile.

The friends briefly communicated their project to the playful Don Bergamino, who assented with much cheerfulness.

"We'll have to manage things cleverly," warned Ristabilito. "You know that Peppe has become very stingy ever since he took up with that ugly old hag of a *Donna* Pelagia, and that he is also quite fond of wine. You, *Don* Bergamino, must treat us all around. Peppe will drink as much as he can, as long as it costs him nothing, and you can rely on it that he'll get drunk as a lord. Then. . . ."

---

*Properly, *Compadre:* friend, pal. In Neapolitan dialect, *Cumpa'*.

The others agreed, and they went to Peppe's house which was not more than two rifle-shots distant. When they were near enough, Ciavola lifted his voice:

"Ohe-e-e! Yooo-hooo! La Bravetta-a-a! Are you coming to Assau's? The priest is here, and he's going to pay for a bottle of wine for us. Ohe-e-e!!"

La Bravetta was not long in descending, and all four set off in a row, joking and laughing in the moonlight. In the stillness the caterwauling of a distant cat was heard at intervals.

"Oh, Pe!" called out Ristabilito, laughing at his own sarcasm. "Don't you hear Pelagia calling you back?"

They crossed the ferry, reached the tavern, and sat till late over Assau's wine. Peppe found it so good, in fact, that he became incapable of walking home. His companions kindly assisted him back to his house and permitted him to stagger upstairs alone, which he finally managed with some difficulty. His three friends grinned as they heard him talking disconnectedly as he climbed the stairs, mumbling about Lepruccio the butcher and the quantity of salt needed for the pig, completely unaware that, in his befuddled state, he had left the house door unlocked.

They waited a short while and then entered quietly. As expected, there was the pig, still on the table. Shaking with suppressed laughter, they carried it off between them. It was very heavy, and they were quite out of breath when they reached the priest's house.

In the morning, having finally slept off the wine, *Mastro* Peppe awoke. He lay still on his bed for a few minutes, stretching his limbs and listening to the bells as they rang for the Eve of Saint Anthony. Even in the confusion of his first awakening he felt a contented sense of possession steal through his mind, and tasted, in anticipation, the delight of seeing Lepruccio cutting up the plump joints of pork and covering them with salt.

Now motivated, he rose from the bed and hurried downstairs. But nothing was to be seen on the table but a bloodstain.

"The pig! Where is my pig?" screamed the bereaved one hoarsely. He then noticed the open door, struck his forehead with his fists, and burst into the open air yelling aloud—calling all his farm laborers round him, asking if they had seen the pig—if they had taken it. He multiplied his complaints, raising his voice even more stridently, until at last the doleful sound, echoing along the riverbank, reached the ears of Ciavola and Il Ristabilito.

The two culprits strolled over to the scene at their ease, fully prepared to enjoy the sight and maintain the joke. When they came in sight, *Mastro* Peppe rushed to them, nearly hysterical and in tears. "Oh, poor me! They've stolen my pig! What shall I do? Oh, poor me!"

Biagio Quaglia, otherwise known as Il Ristabilito, contemplated this most unhappy victim out of his half-shut eyes, his expression midway between derision and admiration, and his head inclined toward one shoulder as if critically judging some dramatic effort.

"Ah, yes, it can't be denied: you play your part very well."

Peppe, not understanding, lifted his face all furrowed with the tracks of tears.

"To tell the truth, I never thought you had such dramatic talent," Ristabilito went on. "Well done! Bravo! I'm delighted!"

"What are you talking about?" asked La Bravetta between sobs. "Oh, poor me! How can I ever go home again?"

"Bravo! That's right!" insisted Ristabilito. "Go on! Yell harder! Cry! Tear your hair! Make them hear! That's it! You're making them believe!"

"But they really stole my pig," said Peppe, still weeping.

"That's it! Don't stop. Say it again, only louder!"

Peppe, quite beside himself with exasperation and grief, doubled his protests.

"I'm telling the truth. May I drop dead right now, on the spot, if they haven't stolen that pig from me."

"Oh, you poor innocent victim!" jeered Ciavola. "How can we believe you when we ourselves saw the pig here yesterday evening? Has Saint Anthony given him wings to fly?"

"I swear to blessed Saint Anthony, it's just as I say!"

"It's not so!"

"It is!"

"It is not!"

"But it is - it is! I'm a dead man! I don't know how in the world I can go home and face my wife. Pelagia won't believe me, and even if she does I'll never hear the end of it. Oh, I'm dead!"

At last they pretended to be convinced, and proposed a remedy for his misfortune.

"Listen here," said Ristabilito, "it must have been one of the people hereabouts. Certainly no one would have come from India to steal your pig, would they?"

"I agree," said Peppe.

"Well then," continued Ristabilito, delighted with the devout attention he was receiving, "if no one from India came here to rob you, then there can be no question that one of our local people must have been the thief. Don't you think so?"

"Yes, yes!"

"Well, there is no use in calling the police. Most of them couldn't find their own behinds with both hands and a lantern. What we must do is to get all these laborers together and try some sort of magic charm to discover the thief. And if we find the thief we've found the pig. Right?"

"Right," agreed *Mastro* Peppe, his eyes brightening with eagerness. He drew closer, for the idea of a charm had kindled all his innate superstitions.

"As you may be aware, there are three kinds of magic: the black, the red, and the white," explained Ristabilito. And as you may also know, there are three women in the village who are skilled in the art: Rosa Schiavona, Rosaria Pajara, and Ciniscia. Just choose any one of them."

Peppe remained in thought for no more than a moment or two. He then decided on Rosaria Pajara who enjoyed great fame as a sorceress, and had in past time performed several marvelous feats.

"Very well," concluded Ristabilito, "There is no time to lose. Now, just for your sake, and only to do you a favor, I'll go into town and talk to Rosaria. I will also get her to give me everything we will need and come back before noon. Give me the money."

Peppe took three *carlini**from his pocket and, after a second's hesitation, held them out.

"Three *carlini!*" shouted Risabilito indignantly, pulling back his hand. *"Three carlini!* She'll want ten at least!"

"What? Ten *carlini* for a charm?" stammered Peppe, almost struck dumb. He felt in his pocket with trembling fingers. "Here are eight. I have no more."

"We'll see what we can do," said Ristabilito dryly. "Are you coming along, Cia?"

The two conspirators set off for the town of Pescara where they entered the shop of a certain Don Daniele Pacentro, a chemist of their acquaintance. Here they purchased certain drugs and spices, and had him make them up into little balls the size of walnuts. These were finally coated with sugar and baked. Ristabilito, who had disappeared during the baking process, then returned with a bag full of dirt swept up in the road. He insisted on having two pills made of the dirt, exactly the same as the others in appearance, but mixed with bitter aloes and only slightly coated with sugar. The chemist made them as instructed, putting a mark on the two bitter pills, also as ordered.

The two jokers now returned to Peppe's farm, reaching it about noon. Peppe La Bravetta was awaiting them with great anxiety. "Well?" he called out as soon as he saw them.

"Everything is in order," replied Ristabilito triumphantly, showing the little box of magic confectionery. "Now, seeing that today is the Eve of Saint Anthony and the peasants are all taking a holiday, I want you to call them all together, out here in the open, and give them a drink. I know you have some casks of Montepulciano—you might as well put some of that out for once. When they are all assembled it will be up to me to do and say all that has to be said and done."

---

*Small Neapolitan silver coins. (Sing. *carlino.*)

La Bravetta spread the report, and two hours later on that warm, bright afternoon, all the farmers of the neighborhood and their laborers came in response to the invitation. A great flock of geese went waddling about among the heaps of straw in the yard; the smell of the stable came in puffs on the air. They stood there, quietly laughing and joking with each other as they waited for the wine—these rustics, with their bowlegs bent by heavy toil, some with faces wrinkled and ruddy as old apples, and eyes that had been made gentle by long patience, or quick with years of cunning; others young and limber, with beards just beginning, and home care evidenced in their patched and mended clothes.

Ciavola and Ristabilito did not keep them waiting long. The latter, holding the box in his hand, directed them to form a circle around him, and then, standing in the center, gravely addressed his audience.

"Neighbors," he began, "none of you, I am sure, knows the real reason why *Mastro* Peppe de' Sieri has summoned you here. . . . "

A wave of nervousness at this strange preamble passed round the circle, the joy at the promised wine giving place to uneasy expectations of various kinds. The orator continued:

"But, as something disagreeable might happen which could give you cause for complaint, I will tell you what it is all about before we conduct the experiment."

The puzzled listeners looked at each other uncertainly and cast curious glances at the little box which the speaker held in plain view. One of them exclaimed impatiently, "Well?"

"Presently, neighbors, presently," responded Ristabilito with maddening slowness. "Last night there was stolen from *Mastro* Peppe a fine pig which was to be salted down. No one knows who the thief is. But it is quite certain that no one would come from India to steal Peppe La Bravetta's pig. Now, to find out the thief, *Mastro* Peppe intends to give some good *confetti** to eat, and you will drink certain old Montepulciano, which he has tapped today for this very purpose. But I must tell you one thing first. The thief, as soon as he puts the sweets into his mouth, will find them bitter—so bitter that he will be forced to spit them out. Now, are you willing to try? Or perhaps the thief would rather go and confess to the priest, rather than be found out in this way? Answer, neighbors."

"We are willing to eat and drink," replied the assembly, almost with one voice. A wave of suppressed emotion passed through all these guileless folk. Each one looked at his neighbor with a point of interrogation in his eyes, and each naturally tried to put a certain ostentatious spontaneity into his laughter.

---

*Confections.

Said Ciavola: "You must all stand in single file, in a row, so that no one can hide himself."

When they had all complied, he took the bottle and glasses, preparing to pour the wine. Ristabilito went to one end of the line and began quietly to distribute the *confetti*, which crunched and disappeared in a moment under the splendid teeth of the rustics. When he reached *Mastro* Peppe he handed him one of the pills prepared with aloes, and passed on down the row without giving any sign.

Mastro Peppe, who till that moment had been standing there staring with his eyes wide open, intent on surprising the culprit, put the pill into his mouth almost with gluttonous eagerness, and began to chew. Suddenly his cheeks rose with a sudden movement toward his eyes, the corners of his mouth and his temples filled with wrinkles, the skin of his nose was drawn up into folds, his lower jaw was twisted awry: all his features formed a pantomime of horror. A visible shudder ran down the back of his neck and over his shoulders. Then, suddenly, since his tongue could not endure the bitterness of the aloes, and his constricted throat made it simply impossible for him to swallow, the miserable man was forced to spit.

"Oho, *Mastro* Pe, what are you doing?" exclaimed the sharp, harsh voice of Tulespre dei Passeri, an old goatherd, greenish and shaggy as a swamp tortoise.

The sound of the old man's voice reached Ristabilito, who had not yet finished distributing the *confetti* pills. He turned around, to behold La Bravetta contorting his features, his limbs in agony. With an air of the greatest benevolence he again reached into his little box.

"I'm sure there must have been a mistake," said Ristabilito comfortingly. "Here is another. Swallow it, Peppe." With his finger and thumb he rammed the second aloe "confection" into Peppe's mouth.

The poor man took it, and feeling the goatherd's sharp, malignant eyes fixed on him made a supreme effort to overcome his disgust. He neither chewed nor swallowed the concoction, but kept his tongue motionless against his palate. But when the aloes began to dissolve, he could bear it no longer. His lips began to writhe as before, his eyes filled with tears which soon overflowed and ran down his cheeks. At last he had to spit the nasty thing out.

"Ohe, *Mastro* Pe! What are you doing *now*?" cried the goatherd again, with a grin that showed his toothless, whitish gums. "Surely you can tell us what this means!"

All the peasants broke from their ranks and surrounded La Bravetta, some with laughing derision, others with angry words. The sudden and brutal eruption of pride to which the sense of honor of the rustic Italian is subject—the implacable rigidity of superstition—now exploded all at once in a tempest of abuse.

"Why did you make us come here? To blame *us*? Thief! Liar! Son of a bitch! Were you about to cheat us, you scoundrel? We'll break all your pots and dishes, you bastard!" etcetera, etcetera, *da capo*.*

Having smashed the bottle and glasses, they went their ways, shouting back their imprecations from among the poplars.

There remained on the threshing floor Ciavola, Ristabilito, the geese, and La Bravetta. The latter, filled with shame, rage, and confusion, and with his mouth still sore from the bitterness of the aloes, could not utter a word. Ristabilito, with a refinement of cruelty, stood looking at him, shaking his head ironically, and tapping the ground with his foot. Ciavola, with an indescribable mockery in his voice, turned to the humiliated and bewildered Peppe:

"Well, well, well!" he crowed. "So that's the way it is! Bravo, La Bravetta! Tell us—how much did you get for that pig? Ten ducats?"

—Gabriele d'Annunzio (1863-1938)

Thorny Thoughts on the Theorem of Pythagoras

"The forty-seventh proposition!" said Professor Roveni in a tone of mild sarcasm as he unfolded a paper which I had extracted from a box on his desk. Then he showed it to the Government Inspector for Education who stood beside him and whispered something into his ear. Finally, he handed me the document so that I might read the question with my own eyes.

"Go up to the blackboard," added the professor, rubbing his hands.

It was a stifling day in August. The great sun-blinds of blue canvas were a feeble defense against the glass, so that the Venetian shutters had been closed as well. The little light that remained was concentrated on the schoolmaster's desk. The blackboard, however, was sufficiently illuminated to illuminate my defeat.

"Are you going to move or not?" snapped Professor Roveni. "I asked you to go to the blackboard and draw the figure."

Tracing the figure was the only thing I knew how to do. I took a piece of chalk and conscientiously went to work. I was in no hurry—the more time I used in this graphic part, the less remained for oral explanation.

But the professor was not the man to lend himself to my artifice.

"Make haste," he said. "You are not drawing one of Raphael's Madonnas."

I had to come to an end.

"Now write the letters in. Quickly! You are not giving specimens of handwriting. Why did you erase that *G*?"

---

* "and over again."

"Because it is too much like the C I already made. I was going to put in an H instead of the G."

"Oh my! What a subtle idea!" observed Roveni with his usual irony. "Have you finished?"

"Yes, sir," said I, adding under my breath, "more's the pity!"

"Well, then why are you standing there moonstruck? Enunciate the theorem!"

Then began my sorrows. My memory was a blank.

"In a triangle . . ." I stammered.

"Yes, yes. Go on."

I took courage and said all I knew:

"In a triangle, er—uh—the square of the hypotenuse is equal to the squares of the other two sides."

"In any triangle?"

"No, no!" suggested a compassionate soul behind me.

"No, sir," said I.

"Explain yourself. In what sort of a triangle?"

"A right-angled triangle," whispered the prompting voice.

"A right-angled triangle," I repeated like a parrot.

"Silence there, behind!" roared the professor. He again turned to me and continued: "Then, according to you, the big square is equal to each of the smaller ones?"

Good gracious! The question was absurd. But I had a happy inspiration.

"No, sir, to both of them added together."

"To the sum then: say to the sum. And you should say *equivalent*, not equal. Now demonstrate."

I was in a cold perspiration—icy cold—despite the tropical temperature. I looked stupidly at the right-angled triangle, the square of the hypotenuse, and its two subsidiary squares. I passed the chalk from one hand to the other and back again, and said nothing, for the very good reason that I had nothing to say.

No one prompted me any more. It was so still you might have heard my diploma drop. The professor fixed his gray eyes on me, bright with a malignant joy. The Government Inspector was making notes on a piece of paper. Suddenly the Inspector impatiently cleared his throat, and Professor Roveni said in his most insinuating manner, "Well?"

I did not reply.

Instead of sending me about my business at once, the professor chose to imitate the cat which plays with the mouse before tearing it to pieces.

"Young man, perhaps you are seeking a new solution. I do not say that a brand new solution may not be found, but we will be quite satisfied with one of the old ones. Go on. Have you forgotten that you ought to produce the two sides, *DE, MF,* till they meet? Produce them, please. Go on!"

I obeyed mechanically. The figure seemed to attain a gigantic size, and weighed on my chest like a block of stone.

"Put a letter at the point where they meet—an N. So. And now?"

I remained silent.

"Don't you think it necessary to draw a line down from N through A to the base of the square, $BHIC$?"

I thought nothing of the kind, but I obeyed.

"Now you will have to produce the two sides, BH and IC."

I could endure no more. I was sure he sensed it.

"Now," the professor went on, "a child of two could do the demonstration. Have you nothing to observe with reference to the two triangles, BAC and NAE?"

As silence only prolonged my torture, I replied laconically, "Nothing."

"In other words, you know nothing at all?"

"I think you should have seen that some time ago," I replied, with a calm worthy of Socrates.

"Well, well! Is that the tone you take? And don't you even know that the theorem of Pythagoras is also called the Asses' Bridge, because it is only the asses who cannot get past it? You can go. I hope you understand that you have not passed this examination. That will teach you to read *Don Quixote* and draw cats during my lessons!"

The Government Inspector took a pinch of snuff. I laid down the chalk and walked majestically out of the room, amid the stifled laughter of my classmates.

Outside, three or four comrades who had already undergone the ordeal with no very brilliant results were waiting for me.

"You've been ploughed under?" they asked.

"Ploughed," I acknowledged, throwing myself into an attitude of heroic defiance. "I always said that mathematics were only made for dunces."

"Of course," agreed one of my rivals.

"What question did you have?" asked another.

"The forty-seventh proposition. What can it matter to me whether the square of the hypotenuse is or is not equal to the sum of the squares of the two sides?"

"Of course it can't matter to you—nor to me—nor to anyone in the world," chimed in a third with all the petulant ignorance of fourteen. "If it is equal, why do they want to have it repeated so often? And if it isn't, why do they bother us with it?"

"Believe me, fellows," I said, resuming the discussion with the air of a person of long experience, "you may be quite certain of it—the whole system of education is wrong. And as long as the Germans are in this country, it will remain so."

Thus, being fully persuaded that our failure was a protest against the

Austrian dominion, and a proof of our vivid and original genius, we went home. Once there, however, I confess that my first enthusiasm quickly evaporated.

My ignominious failure in that examination had a great influence on my future. Since it was absolutely impossible for me to understand mathematics, it was decided that very day that I was to leave school, especially as the family finances made it necessary for me to begin earning something as soon as possible.

It was the most sensible solution that could have been arrived at, and I had no right to oppose it. Yet, I again confess, I was deeply saddened by it. My aversion to mathematics did no extend to other branches of learning, in which I had made quite a respectable showing. Besides, I loved the school. I loved those sacred cloisters which we boys filled with life and noise; and I loved the benches carved with our names: even the blackboard which had been the witness of my irreparable defeat.

I blamed Pythagoras' theorem for it all. With some other question—who knows?—I might just have scraped through by the skin of my teeth, as I had done in past years. But, as Fate would have it, it was just that one!

I dreamed about it all night. I saw it before me—the fatal square with its triangle atop, and the two smaller squares, one sloping to the right and the other to the left. There was a tangle of lines, a great confusion of letters which I heard beating through my head like the strokes of a hammer: $BAC=NAF$; $RNAB=DEAB$.

It was some time before I was free from that nightmare and could forget Pythagoras and his three squares. In the long run, however, Time, who wipes out so many things from the book of memory with his sponge, had nearly effaced this; when, a few weeks ago, the ill-omened figure appeared before me in one of my son's textbooks.

"Has this curse been transmitted to my descendants?" I exclaimed. "Poor boy! What if the theorem of Pythagoras should be as fatal to him as it was to me?"

I thought I would question him about it when he returned from school.

"So," I began gravely, "you have already reached the forty-seventh proposition of Euclid in your geometry?"

"Yes, father," he replied simply.

"A difficult theorem," I added, shaking my head.

"Do you think so?" he asked with a smile.

"Oho, you want to boast and make me think you find it easy!"

"But I do find it easy."

"I would like to see you try it"—the words slipped out almost involuntarily.

"At once," said my son quickly. Action following words, he took a piece of paper and a pencil, and rapidly traced the cabalistic figure.

"As for demonstrations," he began, "there are plenty to choose from. Is it all the same to you which I take?"

"Yes," I replied mechanically. In fact it *had* to be all the same to me. If there had been a hundred demonstrations I would not have known one from the other.

"Then we'll take the most usual one," my mathematician went on. He proceeded to produce the lines which Professor Roveni, of respected memory, had made me produce twenty-seven years before, and, with sincerest conviction in his accents, he began to prove that the triangle *BAC* was equal to the triangle *NAF*, and so on.

"And now," said my son when he had finished, "if you wish, we can arrive at the same conclusion in another way."

"For pity's sake!" I exclaimed in terror. "We've reached the journey's end. Let it rest."

"But I'm not tired."

Not even tired! Was the boy an embryo Newton? And yet people talk about the principle of heredity!

"I suppose you are at the top of your class in mathematics," I said, my voice revealing a touch of reverential awe.

"No, no" he replied. "There are two better than I. Besides, you know very well that everybody—except downright asses—understands the forty-seventh proposition."

"Except downright asses!" I blurted out before I could think. After twenty-seven years I heard, from the lips of my own son, almost the very identical words which Professor Roveni had used on the memorable day of the examination. And this time they were heightened by the savage irony of the added *"You know very well!"*

"Of course I know that," I added hastily, wishing to save appearances. I was only joking. I just hope you won't be overly proud of trivial accomplishments."

Meanwhile, however, my Newton had repented of his too sweeping assertion.

"After all," he went on, with some embarrassment, "there are some who never attend to their lessons, and then—even if they are not asses . . ."

It seemed to me that he was offering me a loophole of escape. I seized the opportunity.

"That must be the way it is," I said with a sudden impulse of candor. "I suppose I never paid attention."

"What? *You?*" exclaimed my boy, reddening to the roots of his hair. Yet, I had an uneasy feeling that, at the bottom of his heart, he was longing to laugh.

I flung up my palm to halt all further discussion. "That will be enough," I said, trying to sound stern. "We will not pursue this into detail."

Well, the Theorem of Pythagoras has, as you now see, cost me a new and very serious humiliation. In spite of this, I no longer hold the old grudge. There will never be any confidence between us, but I consider it as a family friend whom we must not treat with rudeness, even though he may not be personally congenial to ourselves.

—Enrico Castelnuovo (1839-1909)

An Eccentric Orderly

There is a great variety of originals under the canopy of heaven, and I have enjoyed the acquaintance of several, but among them all I never met his match.

He was a Sardinian peasant, twenty years old, unable to read or write, and a private in an infantry regiment.

The first time I saw him, in the office of a military journal in Florence, he aroused a certain sympathy within me. I soon understood, however, from his looks and some of his answers, that he was a character. His very appearance was paradoxical. Seen in front, he was one man; looked at in profile, he was another. Of his full face there was nothing to remark about—it was a countenance like any other. But it seemed as though, in the act of turning his head, he became a different man, the profile having something irresistably ludicrous about it. The point of his chin and the tip of his nose seemed to be trying to meet, but were hindered by an enormous thick-lipped mouth which was always open, showing two rows of teeth, uneven as a file of national guards. His eyes were scarcely larger than pinheads, and disappeared altogether among the wrinkles into which his face was puckered when he laughed. His eyebrows were shaped like two circumflex accents, and his forehead was scarcely high enough to keep his hair out of his eyes.

A friend of mine remarked that he seemed to be one of Nature's practical jokes. Nevertheless, his face expressed intelligence and good nature, but an intelligence that was, so to speak, sporadic, and a good nature that was entirely *sui generis;* that is, one-of-a-kind, or unique.

He spoke in a harsh, hoarse voice, enunciating a kind of Italian for which he had every right to apply for an inventor's patent.

"How do you like Florence?" I asked, seeing that he had arrived in that city the day before.

"It's not bad," he replied.

Not bad! Coming from a man who had previously only seen Cagliari and one or two small towns in northern Italy, the answer appeared to be rather austere.

"Do you like Florence or Bergamo best?"

"I couldn't say—I only arrived yesterday."

The following day he made his entry into my quarters, as my orderly.

During the first week I was more than once within an ace of losing all patience, and sending him back to the regiment. If he had contented himself with understanding nothing, I could have let that pass. But the misfortune was that, partly through the difficulty he had in understanding my Italian, and partly through the unaccustomed nature of his tasks, he understood about half, and did everything the wrong way. Were I to relate how he carried my razors to the publisher, and my manuscripts ready for the press to the razor grinder; how he left a French novel with the shoemaker, and a pair of boots to be mended at a lady's house, no one who had not seen him would believe me. But I cannot refrain from relating one or two of his more interesting exploits.

At eleven in the forenoon—about the time when the morning papers were hawked in the streets—it was my custom to send him out for some ham for my breakfast. One morning, knowing that there was an item in the newspaper that I wanted to see, I said to him hurriedly, "Quick! The ham and the *Corriere Italiano*." He could never take in two distinct ideas at once. He went out and returned shortly afterward with the ham wrapped in the *Corriere*.

One morning he was present when I was showing one of my friends a splendid military atlas which I had borrowed from the library. Unknown to me at the time, he heard me remark to my friend: "The trouble with this book, indeed with any atlas, is that we can't see all the maps at a glance. Each one has to be studied separately. To follow the whole course of a battle, they would have to be pinned up alongside each other, so as to form a single diagram."

That evening, when I returned home—I still shudder to think of it—all the maps in that atlas had been cut out and were neatly nailed to the wall. To add to my sufferings, he appeared before me the next morning with the modestly complacent smile of the man who expects a compliment.

But all this is nothing to what I went through before I succeeded in teaching him to put my rooms in order—not, I must say, as I wanted them, but in a manner remotely suggesting the presence of a rational being. For him, the supreme art of putting things aright consisted of piling them one on top of the other, and his great ambition was to build them up into structures of the highest possible altitude. During the first few days of his tenure, my books formed a semicircle of towers that trembled at the slightest breath. The washbasin, turned upside down, sustained a daring pyramid of plates, cups and saucers, at the top of which my shaving brush was planted. My hats, both new and old, rose to a dizzy height in the form of a triumphal pillar.

As a consequence, there occurred—usually in the dead of night—ruinous collapses which made a noise like a small earthquake, scattering my property to such an extent that no one knows where it would have finally landed if it had not been for the walls of the room. To make him understand that my toothbrush did not belong to the genus hair brush, and that the shoe-polish jar was not the same as the one that contained bowel medicine, required the eloquence of Cicero and the patience of Job.

I have never been able to understand whether my attempts to treat him kindly met with any response on his part. Only once did he show a certain solicitude for my personal welfare. I had been ill in bed for about two weeks, and neither got worse nor better. One evening he stopped the doctor—an exceedingly touchy man—and said abruptly, "I suppose you know what you are doing, *dottore,* but once and for all, are you going to cure him or not?" The doctor lost his temper and fairly blew up. My orderly's only response was a mild, "I think you ought to rub some oil of *pesce*[1] on his chest."

It is difficult to give any idea of the language he spoke—a mixture of Sardinian, Lombard, and Italian, with idioms all his own; eliptical sentences, mutilated and contracted words, verbs in the infinitive flung about haphazard. The whole was like the talk of a man in delirium. At the end of five or six months, by dint of attending the regimental schools, he learned, to my misfortune, to read and write after a fashion. While I was out of the house he would practice writing at my desk, and would write the same word a couple of hundred times over. Usually it was a word he had heard me pronounce when reading aloud, and which, for some reason or other, had made an impression on him. One day, for instance, he was struck by the name *Vercingetorix.*[2] When I came home in the evening, I found *Vercingetorix* written on the margins of the news-papers, on the backs of my manuscript proofs, on the wrappers of my books, on my letters, on the scraps in the wastepaper basket—in every place where he could find room for the thirteen letters beloved of his heart. Another day the word *Ostrogoths*[3] touched his soul, and on the next my rooms were invaded by Ostrogoths. In like manner, a little later, the place was full of *rhinoceroses.*

On the other hand, I was so far a gainer by this extension of knowledge on his part, that I was no longer obliged to mark with crosses, in different colored crayons, the notes I gave him to deliver to various people. There was no way of making him remember the names, but he got to know my correspondents as the blue lady, the green journalist, the orange pub-lisher, the yellow government official, and so on.

Speaking of writing, I discovered a habit of his, much more curious than the one I have mentioned. He had bought himself a notebook into which he copied, from every book that fell into his hands, the author's dedication to his parents or relatives. But he always took care to sub-

---

[1]Fish.

[2]Gallic leader of the great revolt against the Romans in 52 B.C. He was put to death by Julius Caesar in 46 B.C.

[3]Members of the easterly division of the Goths, maintaining a monarchy in Italy, from 493 to 555 A.D.

stitute the names of his own father, his mother, and his brothers, to whom he imagined he was thus giving a brilliant proof of affection and gratitude.

One day I opened his notebook and read, among others, the following:

"Pietro Tranci (the Sardinian peasant, his father), born in poverty, acquired, by study and perseverance, a distinguished place among men of learning, assisted his parents and brothers, and worthily educated his children. To the memory of his excellent father this book is dedicated by the author, Antonio Tranci"— Instead of Michele Lessona.

On another page he had copied the dedication of Giovanni Prati's poems, beginning:

"To Pietro Tranci, my father, who, announcing to the Subalpine Parliament the disaster of Novara, fell fainting to the ground and died within a few days, I consecrate this song. . . ."

What astonished me most in one who had seen so little was an absolute lack of the feeling of wonder. During the time he was in Florence he saw the festivities at Prince Humbert's[1] marriage, the opera and the dancing at the Pergola (he had never been inside a theater in his life), the great Florentine Carnival, and the fantastic illumination of Celli Avenue. He saw a hundred other things which were quite new to him, and which, one would think, should have surprised or amused him, or at least made him talk. Nothing of the sort. His admiration never went beyond the terse response, "Not bad!" Santa Maria del Fiore[2]—not bad! Giotto's tower[3]— not bad! The Pitti Palace[4]—not bad! I really believe that if the Creator in person had asked what he thought of the universe, he would have replied that it was not bad.

---

[1]Humbert I (1844-1900). Assuming the throne in 1878, he helped consolidate the new kingdom. His tolerance and generosity won him the nickname Humbert the Good. Escaping two attempts on his life, he fell victim to the third, at Monza. His son, Victor Emmanuel III, succeeded him.

[2]The church of Saint Mary of the Flowers, in Florence.

[3]Refers to the campanile (see footnote, p. 65) designed by the great Florentine painter and architect, Giotto di Bondone (c.1266-c.1337), but known simply as Giotto. His biography may be found in most standard encyclopedias. His campanile was built next to the cathedral in Florence.

[4]A massive Florentine palace of the early Renaissance period. Designed about 1435, it was built for Luca Pitti, head of the Florentine Republic at that time. It has been an art museum since 1922.

From the first day of his stay to the last, his mood never changed. He continually preserved a kind of cheerful seriousness: always obedient, always muddle-headed, always most conscientious in understanding things the wrong way, always with the same extravagance of eccentricity. On the day when his term of service expired, he scribbled away for several hours in his notebook with the same calm as on other days. Before leaving, he came to say goodbye to me. There was not much tenderness in our parting.

"Are you sorry to leave Florence?" I asked.

"Why not?" he replied.

"Did you like this city?"

"Not bad."

And so he left the house, after being with me for over two years, without the slightest sign either of regret or pleasure. In parting, however, he did murmur, "If you ever want anything, sir, write to me and I will be happy to do anything I can for you."

I watched as he descended the stairs.

Suddenly he turned around.

Ah, now we shall see! I thought. His heart has been awakened. He is coming back to take leave in a different sort of way!

Instead of which—

"Lieutenant," he said, "your razor and shaving supplies are in the wine cabinet, sir, where they're supposed to be!"

With that he disappeared.

—Edmondo de Amicis (1846-1908)

The Year Diego Brought Culture to Town

The newly-married couple, whose name was Diego, settled in our small country town, where they were not long in gaining the hearts of all the inhabitants. The more sensible and influential people in the place thought the advent of such wealthy residents a great piece of good fortune. "They will be of so much advantage to our little community," was the remark made in the chemist shop one evening.

It soon began to rain advantages: dinner parties, picnics, gifts, patronage, entertainments for charitable purposes—hospitalities of all sorts; and then the grand balls they held to celebrate holidays! A dash of gaiety, a profusion that no one could either believe or imagine. The Diegos created a kind of splendor, the memory of which, as all the journals in the area put it, "would flourish with perennial vigor in the hearts of a grateful populace."

We thought we had returned to the very flower of the golden age of Arcadia. It was two talents, more than any of his others, which won golden opinions for *Signor* Diego among the worthy citizens of our little town—his magnificient expenditures and his humor. He possessed enough Attic salt* to pickle the whole place within a very short space of time. The town soon became one of the wittiest in the world.

I do not say that the inhabitants did not possess a great deal of wit before he arrived; nor do I wish to hint that the conversation of the educated persons who visited the house of Diego was mere insipid triviality colored with a little presumption and that touch of perfidy which is, so to speak, the *sauce piquante* of empty gossip. No indeed! They, too, took their share of public life and talked politics, speaking highly of themselves and of the party in power, and exceedingly ill of those who were not present to hear them. But what I mean is that *Signor* Diego, profiting by all that he had learned in his travels, showed them a more excellent—that is to say, a more Parisian—way, and taught them the great mystery of *chic*.

He instructed them in all the arts of gilding and veneering, by means of which the most contemptible trifles may be made to appear noble and graceful. He taught them to laugh at serious matters, but to take the most religious care of their hair, their clothes, and the dignity of their attitudes and movements, practicing the worship of themselves with unheard-of austerity and entire self-devotion.

And he knew they were finally civilized when he taught them to pronounce the most severe sentences on the unfortunate who transgressed the least important of the rules established by social etiquette.

—Mario Pratesi (1842-*c*.1915)

THOSE SUPERIOR TUSCANS— LORDS OF CREATION**

Men, as well as women, speak ill of their neighbors: there is no denying that fact. But they can never do it as efficiently. In any case, they do not do it for the same reason. Men nearly always speak ill of others because they believe themselves greatly superior to them. But if there is a race in the world in which every individual believes that the phrase "man is the lord of creation" was made for his own personal use, that race is the Tuscan.

Yesterday evening I was listening attentively to a dialogue between a Livornese and a Florentine seated at a table in the Giardino Meyeri. The conversation turned on the English nation.

"The English," said the Livornese, "are a selfish, heartless nation who,

---

*Dry, delicate wit.

**Excerpted from *Cronache dei Bagni di Mare (Seaside Chronicles)*.

if the world were on fire, would think that Providence had done it on purpose to heat the boilers of their steam engines without expense."

"That is true," replied the other. "The French . . . "

"Worse than ever!" interrupted the first. "They are a nation of barbers, of Robert Macaires who took Nice and Savoy out of our pockets. Yes, sir, out of our pockets, as a pickpocket does a handkerchief. The Spaniards—boastful, proud, vain, ignorant, bigoted talkers. Come now, admit it! Speaking quite frankly and honestly, the Italians are the first people in the world, after all. It's true that the Piedmontese are a little hard, the Genoese too keen after money, the Neapolitans superstitious, the Sicilians ferocious, and that the proverb says: 'Beware of a red-haired Venetian, a black-haired Lombard, and any kind of a *Romagnole!*° Everyone with the least bit of intelligence must agree that Tuscany is the garden of Italy, as Italy is the garden of the world, and that the Tuscans, speaking without conceit, are the pearls of mankind.

"The home of civilization is in Tuscany," he went on. "I have heard that said since my childhood, and always by Tuscans, who surely ought to know. Not that I would not admit that the Pistojans are all voice and pen, that the Aretines are excessively devout, not to say hypocrites; that the Siennese are vain, and that the Pisans—why, Dante called them 'the scorn of nations'; and the Florentines—well, excuse me, but they are a little given to loud talking and short of action. . . .

"But the Livornese—ah! the Livornese are really the flower of the Tuscans. And you may say what you please, but the finest street in Livorno is Via Vittorio Emmanuele, where I live. You will pardon me for saying so, I am sure, but I don't know how anyone can stay in Livorno and not have a house on that street. It is good living there; at least, that is to say, on the left-hand side, because the sun never shines on the right, the houses are damp, and anyone who takes one on that side is certainly an idiot.

"On the left side, however, one can live like a prince; and among all the houses on that side there is not one like mine. I do not say that the other tenants are all first-rate people—oh dear no! On the fifth floor, there is an idiot whose wife—well, never mind! On the fourth is a nobleman with plenty of pride but no money; on the third a family all show and pretension, who spend their money right and left in order to look more than they really are, and who will assuredly come to ruin. On the ground floor there is a wretch—that turncoat, that crawling insect who has made money—the hell with him! On the second floor, I live with my family.

"My home, I may say, is a real paradise. My father is dead—he was a gentleman! A little hot-tempered if you like, a little obstinate, but no

---

°A native of the province of Romagna.

human being is without fault. Then there's my mother, who is old and, well, you know how it is, inclined to be querulous and tiresome. My sister lives there, too. She would be the best girl in Livorno if it were not for a touch of ambition and a slight tendency to flirting. And then—there is myself. There! It is not for me to say—but you know me. I am quiet, peaceable, well-educated, and sincere. I know how to keep within my means. I am—well, in short, I am what I am."

He might as well have said at once—"I am the lord of creation!"

—F. P. L. C. Ferrigni* (1836-1907?)

Getting Along
with the Sun**

I don't say that the sun and I are great friends. I have too much respect for my courteous readers (including those who get their reading for nothing by borrowing this book instead of buying it) to permit myself the slightest and most harmless of falsehoods where they are concerned.

I am not a friend of the sun's because I do not esteem him. That way he has of shining indiscriminately on all, of working in partnership with everybody, from the photographer who forges banknotes to the laundress and the plasterer, seems to me to show a lamentable want of dignity in the Prime Minister of Nature. Besides, I remember that, many years ago, he was kept under arrest for twelve hours by a gendarme of antiquity, Captain Joshua, who must have had his reasons for taking so momentous a step.

Perhaps he was set at liberty again because no grounds could be discovered for taking proceedings. But, at the same time, entirely respectable people do not, as a rule, get arrested for nothing!

However, the sun and I live so very far apart from one another that I cannot say I see the necessity of breaking with him altogether. Every year, about the middle of spring, I take a run down to the Ardenza, stop at the seashore, pass respectfully in front of the villas and palaces of the neighborhood, and return home with an easy conscience and the feeling of having left my card at summer's door. Thus, later in the season, when I meet the July sun, a sun which is quite Livornese, a municipal sun (the city authorities are extremely proud of it), we greet each other like old acquaintances.

The July sun is a great benefactor to the Livornese. If gratitude were still fashionable, he would be made mayor, and his painted image would

---

*Ferrigni used the pen name, "Yorick," and was well known under his *nom-de-plume*. (See the Biographical Index of Authors.)

**Translated from *Cronache dei Bagni di Mare.*

figure on the municipal shield, instead of the present device of the two-towered fortress in the middle of the sea.

—P.F.L.C. Ferrigni

RAIN IS NOT NECESSARY[*]

Suppose for a moment—and note, when a man says "suppose" he is perfectly sure of his ground, and woe be to any who contradicts him—suppose, then, for one moment that man is really a rational animal.

The bizarre originality of being rational, which constitutes the *first* term of the definition, does not prejudice the wisely general character of the *last* term, which is: Man is an animal.

Now, I ask, what use is reason to a man if it does not make him take an umbrella when it rains? It is all very well for you to think yourself superior to all other created beasts, to be proud of your learning, your science, your experience, your laws, your noble blood, or your income, but if you find yourself out in the rain without an umbrella, you will always be the most contemptible figure in creation.

Let us be just. Humanity is not lovely when seen through falling drops of rain, by the cold, dull light of a sunless day, under a dreary, leaden, low, foggy sky, resting like a cover on the circle of horizon. All men wear faces of portentous length: one can see that they bear an undying grudge against meteorologic science as a result of that phenomenon of aqueous infiltration which is so deadly to new hats and old shoes. They go their ways dripping along the rows of houses, under the deluges from the water pipes, picking their way between the puddles, with countenances cloudier than the skies, muttering the devil's litanies between their teeth with a muffled murmur like the gurgling of a boiling saucepan.

At every corner, such accidents as making too close an acquaintance with the ribs of an umbrella coming the other way, getting splashed with liquid mud by a passing coach, or spoiling the freshness of a new pair of trousers by means of an overflowing gutter, provoke a glance which, if looks could kill, would be downright murder. That killing glance is achieved by a contraction of the facial muscles which recalls the grin of the ancestral ape in a bad temper, and is invariably accompanied by an explosion of *sotto voce* ejaculations expressing a pious desire to see one's neighbors in general attached to the muzzle of a breech-loading *mitrailleuse*[**] in full activity.

Now, to orthodox minds there cannot be the slightest doubt on the subject: rain is by no means a fitting and necessary part of the order of

---

[*]Adapted from *Su e giu per Firenze (Up and Around Florence)*.

[**]Machine gun (French).

things, but rather in the nature of a judgment. The Scriptures make no mention of bad weather before the time of the Flood. Rainwater was in no way needed for the development of germs or the ripening of the harvest. Adam had been condemned to water the earth with the sweat of his brow, and this irrigation would have been quite sufficient to raise corn and beans over the whole surface of the globe.

From the preceding considerations it seems to me that one can draw two principle conclusions:

1. That rain is not a necessity of Nature, but rather what is commonly called a judgment of Providence.

2. That human beings, when it rains, are exceedingly ugly.

Take these two conclusions and carefully file them for future reference. You may want to consult them later as a source of comfort the next time excessive moisture in the atmosphere results in the curious and obnoxious conduct of humanity in general and Italians in particular.

—P.F.L.C. Ferrigni

4

The Play's the Thing

INTRODUCTION

Although they are technically designated "plays," the selections offered in this chapter might be more properly termed "situation comedies." The humor, it will be seen, lies in the unfolding of the entire story. Nearly all of the longer plays—this editor had more than 150 at his disposal—were simply unsuitable for inclusion here; not only for their length, but because passages could not be excerpted from the main text without destroying their humor and indeed, their very meaning.

As stated in the Preface of this volume, it is almost impossible to find plays suitable for comic excerpting since the liveliest bits of dialogue lose their point apart from their context, and in any case are better adapted for acting than reading. This is especially true of the longer plays. To enjoy their full essence, they must be read in their entirety: extracted passages offer little or no resemblance to the meaning of the whole— certainly the broad humor is completely lost.

In the short plays presented in the following pages, the authors' intentions have not been altered; their humor remains intact. All were men of the nineteenth century with the exception of Francesco Cerlone, a writer of eighteenth-century Naples. To the best of this editor's knowledge, their inclusion in this volume marks the first time these humorous works have been published in the United States.

—H.D.S.

THE ADAPTABLE SONNET*

GIANNI: I have three systems for making money, but the principle one is that of poet. Suppose, for example, there is a wedding, or a young man who has just earned his degree, or a dancer who has been a great

_____
*From *Il Signor Lorenzo.*

success, or a celebrated preacher, or a new member of the Chamber of Deputies—I have a sonnet that will do for any of them. It only needs the last three lines varied to suit the occasion.

I have six alternative versions of those three last lines. It is a revolver-sonnet: you can fire six shots with it. Do you see? The two quartets consist of philosophical observations on the joys and sorrows of life. They will do for everyone. But in the first tercet I descend from the general to the particular. "O thou!" I say without further appellation. That *thou* has neither sex nor age; it is equally suitable for man or woman, old or young, noble or bourgeois.

(Gianni begins to recite, gesticulating):

> And thou, into whose heart high Heaven all pure
>   Virtues did gather, and a noble need
> Did grant of soothing woes that men endure.

You see that it is adapted to all, and the point of the whole thing is the idea of *soothing the woes that men endure.* Now the last tercet is, so to speak, the loaded cartridge in the revolver. Suppose I am addressing a bride:

> Enjoy, O gentle bride, the crown
>   Due to all generous souls elect indeed;
> May Heaven today send thee this guerdon* down!

Or else, for a graduate:

> Enjoy, O gentle scholar, thou the crown
>   Due to all generous souls elect indeed;
> May Science send today this guerdon down!

Or, "Enjoy, O gentle artist"; or, again, "Enjoy, O offspring of a royal race"; or, "O industrious plebein"—according to circumstances.

GERTRUDE: Yes, but supposing there were a death in the family?"
GIANNI: In that case I would say, "Enjoy, O gentle heir!"
                                        —Paolo Ferrari (1822-1901?)

---

*Reward; compensation.

Love by Proxy

(Virginia has succeeded in urging Petronio to court her, in order to make Carlo jealous. Petronio, now regretting the decision, confronts Carlo.)

PETRONIO: I tell you I'm tired of it! And it is you I complain of—you and your apathy, which Virginia thinks she can cure by using me to stimulate your jealousy. And I, of all people, am supposed to act the part of the stimulus! Well, it's a part I don't at all relish because, when you come to think about it, the stimulus is acting on me instead of you. In other words, I am falling in love—do you understand that?

Yes, Carlo, I am falling in love with your Virginia. I am becoming your rival, my good friend—and a neglected rival, at that! Because I truly am your friend I speak of nothing but you when I am with her. She accuses, and I defend you—you idiot! She doubts you, and I keep on swearing that you adore her—blind fool! And all this is very dangerous to my virtue. For, while it is quite true that I speak on your account, I feel my ears burning on my own. It is indeed a fact that Virginia is touched by my words because, liar that I am, I keep telling her that they are yours. But I know well enough that they are my own words. Therefore, as she listens to them, is the look that flashes from those expressive eyes of hers, mine or yours?

Ah, there's the problem! I can't tell, and the effort to find out causes such a confusion of emotions that my head spins round faster than Angiolina's reel. Is that look of surrender mine, thine, his, ours, yours, everybody's. . . ?

—Paolo Ferrari

Wet Night and a Party

(Luisa and Lauretta, her maid, packing trunks.)

LAURETTA: Here—this trunk is locked. We're all ready.

LUISA: Oh, I hear my husband's voice!

GUILIANO *(behind the scene):* Yes, yes—don't worry. I'll be punctual.

ANOTHER OFF-STAGE VOICE: Fine! And your wife, too. Don't forget!

GIULIANO: Then it's understood. Goodbye for now. *(Enter Giuliano.)* Good evening, dear. *(Lays aside his hunting gun.)* Here I am back again. *(Looking around.)* Oh, good—the trunks are all ready; even the smaller boxes are packed. Everything is in order—law and order forever!

LUISA *(smiling):* And you're as mad as ever! Are you tired?

GIULIANO: According to you, I never get tired. A good thing, too. There's to be dancing this evening.

LUISA AND LAURETTA (*astonished*): Dancing this evening?

GIULIANO: Dancing. You know, with the feet.

LUISA: But don't you think . . .

GIULIANO: I never think—another of your own judgments. Yes, I repeat, there will be dancing, and what is better, you will dance too.

LUISA: I'll do no such thing!

GIULIANO: Oh, yes you will, dear. You will come to the party with your husband. We thought it up on the spur of the moment, and I know you'll be lovely—adorable! Don't say no—I beg you—I entreat you. That is; as a friend I entreat you. As a husband, I command you.

LUISA (*laughing in spite of herself*): You make me laugh, but don't think I'm going to change my mind. I'm not going. How did this party notion come about?

GIULIANO: Ah, so you want a story, do you? Well, listen. This is how it happened. Coming back from our hunt, as we drew near the village, we began to debate how we might spend the evening most agreeably. We stopped in a meadow to form a club, and, of course, once a club is formed, matters must be discussed. Many absurd measures were proposed until, at last, someone suggested that we get up a dance. The motion was vetoed by the mayor and his secretary, whose figures are obviously incompatible with any kind of gymnastic exercise, except, perhaps, whatever workout can be gotten on a seesaw. It was then that I carried my coup d'etat. We were all seated, so I took in the situation at a glance, and exclaimed, "The motion is put to a vote. Those against it will kindly rise; those in favor will remain seated." Our two fat friends exchanged a look full of anguish, and seeing that they could not record a negative vote without the frightful exertion of rising from the ground, preferred to affirm by remaining as they were. The resolution was therefore passed by acclamation, and the dance is to begin immediately in the drawing room of the Manfredi Palace, not far from here.

LUISA: But think of the consequences! *We* are going to this dance? *We*, who have to start at daybreak? Just think about it—it's just impossible!

GIULIANO: Why?

LUISA: Can't you see? All my dresses are already packed in this trunk. The tulle, the ribbons and flowers in that box, the jewelry locked up in my jewel case. I would have to open everything upside down; and the coachman may be here any minute. No, no—it's impossible.

GIULIANO: Hmm! Well, if there's no way out—if it will cause so much inconvenience—well, sometimes it's just as well to be reasonable.

LUISA: Now, that's better.

GIULIANO: All right, I'll make this sacrifice.

LUISA: Yes, for my sake. Well done!

GIULIANO: Yes, for your sake I'll try to put up with it. I'll go alone.

LAURETTA *(aside, laughing):* Oh, I didn't expect *that!*

LUISA *(astonished):* What! You're going?

GIULIANO: Why, certainly!

LUISA: But, my gracious, your clothes are all packed!

GIULIANO: They can be unpacked, I suppose.

LUISA: But the trunks are all locked.

GIULIANO: They can be opened.

LUISA: But do you or don't you understand that the cabman may call for them any moment?

GIULIANO: Send him to the devil! I'll take care of that matter myself.

LUISA: Now you listen to me, Giuliano. This is mere childishness, and I am not going to be the victim of all your whims and fancies. Here I've nearly killed myself getting things straight, packing and getting ready and all, and you're asking me to upset everything again. I tell you I just won't do it! I don't feel up to it, and I'm telling you I won't open a single trunk—so there! *(Walks up and down.)*

GIULIANO: You're not going to unpack anything?

LUISA: No, I'm not.

GIULIANO: You're sure?

LUISA: Absolutely.

GIULIANO: Then I will. *(Opens a trunk.)*

LAURETTA *(aside):* It's all up now!

LUISA *(quickly):* Don't—don't! You're turning everything upside down.

GIULIANO: Either you or I. I never was much good at this sort of thing.

LUISA: Stop! Good heavens, what can anyone do with a lunatic? Get out of the way, *please!* What is it you want?

GIULIANO: Not much: shirt, socks, white waistcoat, black necktie, dress coat, gloves, hat, handkerchief, breastpin, eau de cologne—nothing else!

LUISA: Mercy on us! Oh, poor me!

GIULIANO: And don't forget my boots. You wouldn't want your loving husband going to a party in his socks—like an American.

LUISA *(resignedly):* Anything else? Lauretta, where are the boots? Do come and help me here.

LAURETTA: They're in the green trunk in the other room.

GIULIANO: Francesco! *(Enter Francesco, the hired boy.)* Go into the other room and see if there is a pair of patent leather boots in the green trunk. *(Exit Francesco.)* Ah, by Jove, I knew I had forgotten something!

LUISA: Good gracious! What else?

GIULIANO: Why, of course, my other pair of trousers.

LUISA: They're right here at the bottom of the box.

GIULIANO: Oh, well how was I to know? I hope you didn't expect me to go in these, did you? Say, that reminds me of a funny story! A fellow was caught by an irate husband in his wife's bedroom, and the fellow didn't have his trousers on, so . . .

LUISA *(interrupting):* Never mind, never mind! I would not like that story any better now than the first time you told it to me.
(Enter Francesco without the boots.)

GIULIANO: What about my boots?

FRANCESCO: They're in the green trunk.

GIULIANO: Haven't you brought them?

FRANCESCO: You told me to see if they were there, sir. You didn't say anything about bringing them.

GIULIANO: I must say you're wonderfully intelligent for your age. *(With ironic amiability.)* Go back again, my dearest boy, open the trunk, and take out that pair of varnished boots. Do you know, by the way, what varnished means? It means that they have never been polished by you, despite all my entreaties that you do so. It is a new pair that has not been worn yet. Take them in your hands, lift them out of the trunk, turn around, and bring those boots here to me.

FRANCESCO: Do you want me to bring the green trunk, too?

GIULIANO: Tell me, Francesco, what did your mother say when she saw you were such an idiot?

FRANCESCO: She said nothing, sir. She cried.

GIULIANO: I don't doubt it. Well, you can leave the trunk in the other room. *(Walking up and down, while Luisa and Lauretta are unpacking. He is talking, as if to himself.)* Oh well, this situation does have its good side. After two years of marriage, it will be nice to go out by myself.

LAURETTA *(aside to Luisa):* Oh-oh, so that's why he's getting so dressed up! If I were you, Mistress, I wouldn't let him go by himself.

LUISA: Oh, he's only joking, Lauretta. If I didn't have so many things to unpack . . .

GIULIANO: Let me see . . . to whom should I devote my attention more particularly? Hmmm, there's no one better than the doctor's wife with her two nice . . .

LUISA *(breaking in):* Lauretta, where did you put my light silk dress?

LAURETTA: In the other trunk, on the top.

GIULIANO *(still walking up and down and talking aloud to himself):* Yes, yes; that's it! The doctor's wife. After the dance I'll see her home. Who knows? Maybe . . .

LUISA *(aside to Lauretta):* Hurry; just open the other trunk and take out my blue dress. *(Aloud, to Giuliano.)* Listen, Giuliano, I've been thinking it over, and, well, I think I'll come too.

GIULIANO: But just think, dear; you'll have to turn everything upside down and undo all the boxes you've packed.

LUISA: Never mind.

GIULIANO: But don't you see? You have your dresses in this trunk, your tulle and flowers and lace in that box, your jewelry in . . .

LUISA: All right, you wretch, stop! You needn't try to have revenge on me. It isn't necessary. I tell you, I don't mind. I'll unpack everything and come to your party; that is, if you *want* me!

GIULIANO: Want you? How can you doubt it? But you'll have to be quick. Anyway, you have everything the doctor's wife has, and yours is far more available.

LUISA *(running to Lauretta):* Oh I'll be ready soon, never fear. Quick, Lauretta, just throw the things anywhere; never mind where, as long as you can get at my dress.

GIULIANO: Let us be clear about things, dear wife. "Soon" is a relative term, and when it relates to a woman's preparations it is difficult to find a fixed standard by which a man can judge. Well then—*(watch in hand)*—how much time will you require?

LUISA: Oh for heaven's sake! A quarter of an hour—a half hour at the most. I'm sure it won't take more than three quarters—maybe a little more.

GIULIANO: You're worse than a Sicilian lawyer. Well, at least try to make an effort.

LUISA: Don't worry. I told you, I won't be a minute.

GIULIANO: I tell you what I'll do: while you're dressing I'm going to lie down a while and rest. When you're ready, just let me know—I won't be a minute dressing—and I *do* mean a minute! *(Exit, but goes on speaking behind the scenes.)* Remember, I want you to look your best. What dress are you going to put on?

LUISA: My blue silk.

GIULIANO: Fine! It matches your lips—I mean eyes!

FRANCESCO *(returning with the boots):* Where's the master?

LAURETTA: In the bedroom. *(Exit Francesco.)*

FRANCESCO *(behind the scenes):* Sir.

GIULIANO *(in a sleepy voice):* Let me alone.

FRANCESCO: The boots are here, sir.

GIULIANO: Are you deaf? Go away!

FRANCESCO: But you told me . . . *(Comes out on stage, followed by a pillow thrown by Giuliano. Mutters to himself:)* The proverb is right, after all. "Let sleeping dogs lie."

LUISA: Really, in this house we are not likely to die of melancholy. Come, Lauretta, and help me get my dress on. *(Exit Luisa and Lauretta.)*

FRANCESCO: As long as I've nothing to do, I might as well go to my room and sleep awhile. By Jove, I think it's raining! *(Goes to look out of window.)* Yes, indeed! I wonder how the mistress will manage to go to that dance.

LUISA *(within):* Francesco!

FRANCESCO: Yes, ma'am.

LUISA: Is it raining?

FRANCESCO: I'm afraid so. If you'll allow me, ma'am, I'll go to my room: you can give me a call whenever you want me.

LUISA: Yes, of course. You may go. (*Exit Francesco.*)

———

(*Enter Cavalotto, the coachman.*)

CAVALOTTO: What's this? (*Looks all around at open trunks and boxes, with their contents strewn about.*) Everything was ready, and now ... *Mama mia!* What does all this mean?

LUISA (*within, with Lauretta*): You needn't bring your mother into this, my good man. We are going to a dance.

CAVALOTTO: And when will you start?

LUISA: We'll start later.

CAVALOTTO: But that doesn't suit me at all, madam! Do you realize we have forty miles to go? And I don't want to find myself on the road after dark.

GIULIANO (*within, awakening*): What's going on out there?

LUISA: Oh, we don't mind the dark. Giuliano, would you mind speaking to Cavalotto?

GIULIANO (*still off stage*): Oh, it's you, Cavalotto. What do you want? We'll start later.

CAVALOTTO: But, I repeat, I don't ...

GIULIANO (*half asleep*): Don't bother me now. I'll pay you extra. We'll make two days' journey of it, all right? Anything you like, as long as you just go away.

CAVALOTTO: Well, if you're willing to do that, stopping halfway, I have no more to say. In fact, I'm glad of it, because one of my horses has a pain—

GIULIANO: By God, you scoundrel, *go away!* (*Exit Cavalotto, shrugging his shoulders.*)

(*Enter Luisa, in evening dress, arranging her costume jewelry.*)

LUISA: My good Cavalotto ...! Why, he's gone. So much the better. Now I must call Giuliano and find out what he wants to do if it keeps on raining.

LAURETTA (*entering*): After all, it is only a few steps to the Manfredi Palace.

LUISA: I know, but it's time to call him. Giuliano!

GIULIANO: What is it this time?

LUISA: It's time to get up.

GIULIANO: What the hell for? Oh yes, the dance. Damn! I was sleeping so comfortably.

LUISA: Come on, then. Be quick!

GIULIANO: Tell me, Luisa, have you really set your heart on going to this damn dance?

LUISA: My God, Giuliano, if you're not enough to provoke a saint!

GIULIANO: Don't get excited, dear; I'm coming. (*Enters in his dressing gown. He sits down near the front of the stage.*) Look here, Luisa; while I was in there on the bed, I was reflecting seriously. . . .

LUISA: Just tell the truth, dear, and say you were sleeping.

GIULIANO: Maybe, but even in sleep the mind continues its intellectual processes, and, as I said, I thought over those fine objections you made.

LUISA (*angered*): Really, this is too much! First you nearly drove me out of my senses, till I made up my mind to come with you to the dance; then, when I unpacked all my boxes and took all the trouble to dress, and am all ready, you want. . . . *Will* you be kind enough not to carry the joke too far!

GIULIANO: All right! *All right!* I have never seen such an unreasonable woman! Let us perform this heroic action of yours and attend the confounded dance. Francesco!

FRANCESCO (*within*): Sir?

GIULIANO: Come here, right now. (*Enter Francesco.*) Take my things and come help me dress. (*Exit into his bedroom, followed by Francesco.*)

LUISA: Oh, these men! All tyrants and bullies—even the best of them. Come! Where are my bracelets?

LAURETTA: This time, at least, it went off all right.

LUISA: Oh, it's not ended yet. If you knew . . . I'm afraid I made an awful blunder.

LAURETTA: What kind of blunder?

LUISA: I'm afraid I gave Giuliano the wrong pair of trousers: those that didn't fit, and made him so angry.

LAURETTA: Those that he threw at the tailor's head after the first time he tried them on?

LUISA: Yes, those.

GIULIANO (*from within*): LUISA!!

LUISA (*aside to Lauretta*): Oh-oh! Didn't I say so? (*Aloud.*) What is it?

GIULIANO: Which trousers did you give me?

LUISA: I—I—don't know what you mean.

GIULIANO: I'll tell you what I mean! They are those that ass of a tailor made. I kept the damn things out for charity, but I never meant to wear them—*never!*

LUISA: Oh, they can't be those.

(Enter Giuliano from the bedroom.)

GIULIANO: Can't they? I'm telling you it's the very same pair. And I'll tell you something more: I won't wear them. And if you don't give me another pair I won't come to your party.

LUISA: *My* party! That dance was certainly not. . . . Well, it doesn't matter now. I just don't feel like pulling all those things out of another trunk. Anyway, it's nothing but an excuse to make me stay home. But anyway. . . .

GIULIANO: Good God, another sermon! Never mind; just be quiet. I'll resign myself and try to endure. Francesco, my boots! *(He puts them on at the back of the stage, turning his back to the audience.)* Ow-wow, how tight they are! Damn that shoemaker! How can I hold out with my feet in these things? *(Rises and walks about stiffly and clumsily.)*

LUISA: Another excuse!

GIULIANO: What do you mean, *excuse!* I swear, it feels as though I had my feet in a vice. I can't move.

LUISA: After all, you're not going to play tennis.

GIULIANO: So what? If a man doesn't feel like playing tennis, is he supposed to be laced up so he can't move?

LUISA *(angrily)*: Very well—I understand. Do you want me to stay at home? Why not come right out with it and say so? Perhaps it bores you, taking me to the dance. Would you rather go to bed? Then we'll stay home—we won't go to the dance. We *will* go to bed. You don't need your trousers or boots for that!

GIULIANO: Be careful I don't take you at your word.

LUISA: Much it matters to me if you do. And don't think for a moment you'd profit by it. I'm certainly not in *that* mood. Come, Lauretta, help me off with these things.

GIULIANO: It's impossible to get along with you, no matter how hard I try. Francesco, get over here and help me get these boots off. *(Exit.)* *(Luisa sits down with signs of great annoyance, and Lauretta begins to undo her headdress.)*

FRANCESCO (following Giuliano): I'm really beginning to get tired of this business.

LUISA *(rises and walks to the door of Giuliano's room, Lauretta following her and taking off her ornamental jewelry)*: Giuliano, I tell you all the same, sir, that this is not the way to treat me. Definitely it is not the way to my womanly heart. If you play that sort of trick again, I know very well what I will do. *(Returns to the front of the stage and sits down, still followed by Lauretta.)* *(Enter Giuliano, followed by Francesco.)*

GIULIANO: And what, if you please, do you expect me to do? This is a fine mess! Is it my fault if my clothes and boots are too tight? Am I to be condemned to walk about like a wooden doll—like an elephant—for a whole night, just to please you? Your pretensions are too much to believe! *(Exit.)*

MARCO *(behind the scenes):* Is Giuliano here? May I come in?

LUISA: Come in.

(Enter Marco, with an umbrella, in a black, full-dress suit.)

MARCO: Madam—

(Enter Giuliano, in dressing gown and slippers.)

GIULIANO: Marco, my dear fellow, are you looking for me?

MARCO: Indeed I am.

LUISA: With your permission. . . . *(Exit with Lauretta.)*

MARCO: Ah, you are just dressing.

GIULIANO: Exactly: we were just dressing. What's the news?

MARCO: The news is, it's raining, and in this weather, none of the ladies wanted to come to our improvised party. So we thought of sending a carriage for them.

GIULIANO: Well?

MARCO: It's not so well. It isn't easy to find a carriage in our village. But there are two cabdrivers in the place, and we've made arrangements with them to fetch the ladies in their cabs.

GIULIANO: Fine!

MARCO: So I came to give you notice that in a little while they'll be here for your wife and you; and do try to be ready.

GIULIANO: But really. . . .

MARCO: There's no "really" about it, my friend. If you don't come in the cab, we'll come to get you with a stick.

GIULIANO: No, not that! Bruises for bruises; I'll take my chances with those of the cab. I'll come.

MARCO: With your wife, you hear?

GIULIANO: I hear. With my wife.

MARCO: Goodbye till then. *(Exit.)*

(Enter Luisa, still in evening dress, followed by Lauretta.)

GIULIANO: Well, that's what Marco told me. So, you understand, you must absolutely go.

LUISA *(laughing aloud):* Now isn't that too bad! No doubt you want me to be quick about it.

GIULIANO: Go ahead and laugh. See if I care. Francesco!

FRANCESCO: Here I am.

GIULIANO: Hurry, I want to dress! *(Exit.)*

FRANCESCO: Now I really am disgusted! *(Exit.)*

GIULIANO *(within):* Luisa, pity me! I am putting my feet back into the vice!

LUISA: One can suffer anything for so sweet a cause!

GIULIANO: Ah. . . ! May you be bitten by a hyena!

LUISA: What's the matter this time?

GIULIANO: That idiot of a Francesco just stepped on my foot with one of his iron-heeled boots.

FRANCESCO *(within):* I beg your pardon, sir, but would you please remember that it was you who put your foot under my heel?

GIULIANO: And hurt your heel, eh?

LAURETTA *(laughing):* I think, ma'am, the scenes that take place in this house, especially this evening—I must say it's a pity people can't see them in a theater.
(Enter Giuliano in his shirtsleeves, followed by Francesco.)

GIULIANO: Where's my necktie? *(Francesco hands it to him and he puts it on. Luisa looks on, laughing.)* You laugh because you simply cannot understand the seriousness of your husband's position. . . . My waistcoat! *(Francesco hands it.)* My dress coat! *(Francesco hands it, as before.)* Give me a pin for my necktie! *(Luisa brings him one.)* Do me a favor and put it on for me, will you? *Ouch!* I didn't ask you to make a hole in me, madam!

LUISA: Now, let the cab come when it likes. We're ready.

GIULIANO: Yes, the victim is prepared for the sacrifice. Just imagine it! My feet are so numb I could pass for a Chinese; or a remnant of the Russian army after a hard winter in the snow. And then you expect me to finish the evening dancing with you or doing a mazurka with the mayor's daughter!
(Enter Marco.)

MARCO: May I come in?

GIULIANO: Oh, it's you? Here we are, all ready.
(Luisa puts on her shawl and hood, helped by Lauretta. Giuliano takes his hat and gloves.)

MARCO: I came here myself because . . .

GIULIANO: Thanks for taking the trouble, my dear fellow. Come along, Luisa. *(Gives her his arm.)*

MARCO: Please! One moment!

LUISA: What is it?

MARCO: I hate to tell you this, but I must.

GIULIANO: What is this all about?

MARCO: One of our two cabdrivers we were counting on is away. The other. . . .

LUISA: That's our Cavalotto. I know *he's* not away. He was here earlier this evening.

MARCO: One of his horses is sick, and can't be harnessed. The rain is still coming down in torrents, so we just had to give up the whole idea of a dance. We'll have one another time.

LUISA: Are you saying the dance is canceled?

GIULIANO: No dance?

MARCO: None. I came to make my apologies to you, and now I must run along home to change my clothes—I'm wet as a drowned chicken. Madam, Giuliano old fellow, I wish you good night and a pleasant journey. *(Exit.)*

(Giuliano and Luisa stand arm-in-arm, looking at each each other comically.)

LAURETTA *(aside to Francesco)*: Go tell the cook to bring in supper.

FRANCESCO: A good idea. *(Exit.)*

GIULIANO *(looking around)*: A magnificent room, isn't it?

LUISA *(who has laid aside her wraps, imitating him)*: Splendidly illuminated.

GIULIANO: Ladies in great numbers.

LUISA: Plenty of gentlemen.

GIULIANO *(looking at Luisa)*: I think I may be a bit jealous. See how gracious my wife is to the mayor!

LUISA *(looking at Giuliano)*: And look at my husband being so charming to the doctor's wife!

GIULIANO: Madam, will you kindly favor me with this polka?

LUISA: With great pleasure, sir.

GIULIANO *(to Lauretta and Francesco, who are standing at the back of the stage, laughing)*: Orchestra! A polka!

(Lauretta sings a polka, Francesco taking the bass. Giuliano and Luisa take a few steps together.)

(Enter the cook, in white cap and apron.)

COOK: Sorry, madam—sir. You weren't supposed to dine at home this evening. There was nothing here to cook. Can I fix you some scrambled eggs?

LUISA: Ah, what a grand finale to a perfect evening.

GIULIANO *(putting his arm around Luisa's waist)*: Now, shall we attend our banquet?

—Paolo Ferrari

PULCINELLA'S DUEL*

COLBRAND (*muttering to himself*): We shall soon see if it is possible or not for that idot, Pulcinella, to take Nanon away from me. I'll ornament his face for him! If he is a man of his word and keeps his appointment, too bad for him!

PULCINELLA: You are here! I thought, perhaps you might not. . . ."

COLBRAND: Oh! Bravo! You kept your word this time. You came.

PULCINELLA: Listen, Colbrand, if you want to fight, I'm quite ready. But tell me, first, how long it has been since you learned fencing?

COLBRAND: Why? What does that matter?

PULCINELLA: It matters to me.

COLBRAND: Five years.

PULCINELLA: I've been learning for ten. I don't want to take advantage of you. Go home and take lessons for five more years, and then I'll give you satisfaction.

COLBRAND: Oh, you coward! You won't get away. You're caught! Only one of us will remain here on the field of honor.

PULCINELLA: Very well. You remain and I'll leave.

COLBRAND: You needn't pretend you don't understand me. I mean that one of us has to remain here dead.

PULCINELLA: Dead? Is that what you said? *Dead?*

COLBRAND: That is precisely what I said. Dead!

PULCINELLA: Well, have it your way. You remain here dead, and everything will be all right.

COLBRAND: And who will kill me, may I ask!

PULCINELLA: I will, if you wish.

COLBRAND: I wish nothing of the kind. I intend to defend myself to the utmost.

PULCINELLA: Now look here, let's say no more about it. Is it reasonable to kill a man for the sake of a woman?

COLBRAND: Draw your sword, coward, or I will strike!

PULCINELLA (*under his breath*): Oh, I'm dead! (*Aloud*): Listen to me. The first time I ever wore my sword I made a vow that it would never be stained with blood.

COLBRAND: You ass in clothes! You will either give up Nanon, or I'll rid the world of you.

PULCINELLA: Now look here! You have a quarrel with *me* out of jealousy, because I took your sweetheart from you. But, on the other hand, I have no quarrel with *you*. You didn't take *my* sweetheart from *me*. I would really regret killing you when I'm not even mad at you.

---

*The actor portraying Pulcinella wears a comic mask, in the tradition of this type of farce.

COLBRAND: I'm not listening. This blade will be your answer. Get ready for some cold steel. Defend yourself!

PULCINELLA: No! I have no quarrel with you. How many times must I repeat that, my good man?

COLBRAND: What must a man do to make you fight?

PULCINELLA: Let's see now. How about calling me some vile names? Then I'll get angry and draw my sword against you. After all, a man must defend his honor.

COLBRAND: An excellent idea! Very well; you are a scoundrel, a ruffian, a cowardly knave.

PULCINELLA: Supposing what you say is the truth. What reason would I have to be angry?

COLBRAND: You are a dissolute wretch, a bastard, a son of a bitch!

PULCINELLA: You must be a gypsy fortune-teller to know that. You are saying nothing but the truth.

COLBRAND: We'll never get around to fighting this way. Coward! You deliberately misled me.

PULCINELLA: Coward, am I? You just try telling me things about myself that are *not* true. *Then,* by God, you'll set me afire. I know my nature.

COLBRAND: Very well. You are a gentleman.

PULCINELLA: A gentleman! I? When was I ever that?

COLBRAND: Always. Yes, a valiant and honorable gentleman.

PULCINELLA: And do you expect a valiant and honorable gentleman like me to fight with a dirty blackguard of a pig like you?

COLBRAND: What! You say this to *me*? By the powers that be, draw your sword this moment, or I'll strike!

PULCINELLA: Steady now, steady. Whoa! Wait a minute! Can't you see I haven't got it drawn?

COLBRAND: Well, go ahead then. I'm waiting. If you don't draw, I can't strike.

PULCINELLA: Pardon me, but did I understand you to say that you won't strike unless I draw?

COLBRAND: You understand correctly. Draw!

PULCINELLA: My dear fellow, I am not going to draw for at least ten years. Oh, very well, if you insist. (*Draws his sword.*) Here, I'm ready. (*He strikes at Colbrand, standing as far away from him as he can, meanwhile shouting at the top of his voice.*)

COLBRAND: Hold on, Pulcinella. Stop! Now see here; how can a man fight a respectable duel with all that noise? Be quiet, will you! You'll only attract someone's attention and our fight will be interrupted.

Pulcinella, seeing Mastro *Logman approaching, makes more noise than ever. When Logman arrives on the scene, he demands an explanation of the quarrel. The*

presence of a third party revives Pulcinella's courage,
and he loudly declares his intention of running Colbrand
through and through till his person is like a sieve. He then
starts to scold Colbrand who loses his temper and finally
walks away. Pulcinella, leaving the stage, asks:

"You think I am leaving because I'm afraid, don't you? Well, I'll have you know that you are right—I *am* afraid!"

(Colbrand, seeing that he is now out of harm's
reach, remarks to Logman:)

"For your sake, and your sake alone, I won't attack. But, another time. . . ." He leaves the terrible threat incompleted.

—Francesco Cerlone (1750-1800)

CONTRADICTING, ALWAYS CONTRADICTING!

PANDOLFO: It's intolerable! They do it on purpose to drive me out of my mind.

PAOLO GALANTI: Who has made you so angry, *Signor* Pandolfo?

PANDOLFO: Who? Need anyone ask? My wife and daughter; that's who! Wait a minute! Is that Benini I see coming over here? You, Benini!

BENINI: So you recognized me at once? I thought you'd forgotten me altogether.

PANDOLFO: No, sir, I hadn't forgotten you. Am I the kind of man to forget old friends? And we certainly are old friends.
(They shake hands cordially.)

BENINI: We are indeed! Twenty years—

PANDOLFO: No, not twenty years; eighteen or nineteen. We used to see a great deal of each other. Remember.

BENINI: Well, I—I—

PANDOLFO: We often argued. You had a very contradictory nature.

BENINI: I?

PANDOLFO: Are you denying it, sir?

BENINI: Well, I suppose not. I was young and impetuous in those days, and hadn't much sense—or perhaps none at all.

PANDOLFO: That's just not the case: you were not altogether without sense. It's true you had your little eccentricities, but after all. . . !

BENINI: Anyway, you never paid too much attention to my words.

PANDOLFO: That's not so! I always paid the closest attention to you. I always had the greatest consideration for your views, such as they were. And I assure you, it gives me more pleasure than I can express to find you here again.

(They shake hands once more.)

GALANTI *(aside to Benini): Madre mia!* I have never yet seen him get along with anyone as well as he has with you!

PANDOLFO: You must come to see my wife.

BENINI: I don't know whether *Signora* Angelica will feel like welcoming me after all these years.

PANDOLFO: Of course she will! I'll answer for that! Yet she does everything she possibly can to contradict and oppose me, that woman! She doesn't have a bad disposition—I'm not saying that; but you might call it a perversity of character. Just imagine! At this very moment, when all the visitors are about to assemble in this place, she can find no better time to go for a long walk on the beach. Never lets herself be seen: persists in withdrawing from society. Sheer madness, I call it. We have a daughter, and if this sort of thing keeps up, how will we ever get her settled in life?

GALANTI: Oh, come now, the young lady can't fail to find . . .

PANDOLFO: What? Are you contradicting me, too?

GALANTI: No, certainly not! Only, since the ladies are going out, if you will permit me, I'd like to accompany them for part of the way.

PANDOLFO: Hmmm.

GALANTI: I'll go get my hat and umbrella.

PANDOLFO*(aside):* What a bore he is! Always in the way!

GALANTI *(aside to Benini): Signor* Pandolfo appears to have a great regard for you.

BENINI *(aside to Galanti):* Yes, it's true. There was a time when I could get him to do anything I wanted.

GALANTI *(as before):* Really? Look, would you do me a favor? Put in a good word or two for me. You know, about his daughter.

BENINI: A few words on your behalf? All right. I don't mind at all.

GALANTI: Thanks, very much! I'll be back soon. *(Exit.)*

BENINI *(aside):* I might just as well take care of that little favor right now. *(To Pandolfo):* I understand why you gave permission to that young man to escort your wife and daughter.

PANDOLFO: I never gave him permission. And what did you understand?

BENINI: Galanti is a pleasant fellow.

PANDOLFO: He is nothing of the sort!

BENINI: And witty.

PANDOLFO: Do you see a grain of wit in *him?*

BENINI: Good looking.

PANDOLFO: A dandified fool!

BENINI: Courteous.

PANDOLFO: Too much so. The fellow agrees with everyone.

BENINI: He would be a son-in-law after your own heart.

PANDOLFO: Son-in-law be hanged! If you continue like this you will make me use language I'll regret.

BENINI: Come now, Pandolfo. Everyone believes he's going to marry your daughter.

PANDOLFO: Then he'll wait till Judgment Day. My Elisa's husband ought to be a young man with brains. This Galanti of yours is a fool.

BENINI: Well, not quite that.

PANDOLFO: He is! I want a man of character: a man who will stand up for what he believes in; a man who won't always be contradicting me!
                                    —Vittorio Bersezio (1830-1914)

POSTMORTEM CONCERN FOR A LOST EXPLORER*

(Bertrando, the editor of the Demos, and Serpilli, the publisher, have just received word of the death of their friend Arganti, who had gone on an exploring expedition into the Sudan.)

BERTRANDO: Ah, this is sad news! Poor Arganti! The sudden loss has just about paralyzed me. It is all very well to make a parade of one's lack of feeling and pretend to be a cynic, but when the thunderbolt falls at your very feet. . . .

SERPILLI: Yes, I understand. But what *I* say is: what crazy notion was it that made him go and get himself killed out there? At fifty, too! Weren't there enough harebrained young fellows eager to discover new outlets, new resources for commerce and industry, for African humanity, which, by the way, loves us about as well as people love smoke in their eyes? Wasn't he comfortable here, in this charming house, with the best of wives? No, sir! He must be off poking his nose into other people's affairs!

BERTRANDO: You forget how many years he traveled, his love of science, his discoveries.

SERPILLI: I could overlook it if the misfortune had been confined to the late lamented Arganti, or *poor* Arganti as you so sorrowfully referred to him, but his misfortune touches not only the dead but the living.

BERTRANDO: Serpilli!

SERPILLI: My dear fellow, it is all very well for you to talk, but I have already arranged to publish a complete illustrated edition of all his travels. Sixty thousand francs, do you understand? I'm ruined!

BERTRANDO: Do you think this is the time. . . ?

---

*From the comedy *Corvi* (*The Crows*).

SERPILLI: Yes, certainly! I mourn for him—I'm deeply grieved; but who will give me back my sixty thousand francs? It's ruin—bankruptcy! Oh, who would have thought this could happen to me, of all the men in the world!

BERTRANDO: Come now, enough of this! Who prevents your continuing the issue? Surely Arganti's writings have not lost their value through his death.

SERPILLI: Who would be interested in his expedition to Palestine, undertaken twenty years ago, now that people can make a holiday excursion of it and travel by rail? It needs something else to tickle the public's palate. And I might add that the public, nowadays, is perfectly familiar with Afghanistan, Zululand, and Basutoland; not to mention journeys to the center of the earth, to the bottom of the sea, and the moon itself, being written by insane writers and read by lunatic people. Oh, my poor sixty thousand francs! If he had lived it wouldn't have been so bad. With a mutual admiration society such as the fashionable papers know how to create, something might have been done. But now that Arganti is dead, who is going to waste his time in praising him? You'll have your time fully occupied with bringing out some new genius: one of those startling and powerful ones who open new horizons to the heart and mind, to science, and their country every quarter of an hour! And I'll be sacrificed!

BERTRANDO: You are both ungrateful and mistaken. You made quite a nice little sum out of our poor friend's works, which, I might add, we advertised for you at reduced prices and reviewed in special feature articles.

SERPILLI: Look here, Bertrando, I spent my whole advertising budget on the new edition, and now, just as I am about to reap the fruits of all that judicious spending, everything is upset by death—the one thing I hadn't figured on.

BERTRANDO: Serpilli! Serpilli!

SERPILLI: It's enough to bring on an attack of the jaundice! If Arganti had at least confined himself to writing a couple of volumes, it wouldn't be so bad. But, no sir! Twenty-seven!

BERTRANDO: Would you want the scientific and literary heritage of Italy to be diminished because of sordid self-interest?

SERPILLO: Aha! You're laughing at me. You are quite right, I've been an idiot. Let's not deprive our dear country from its heritage . . . especially since the advertising is all paid for.

BERTRANDO: I respect everyone's convictions.

————

(Serpilli and Geronte, an embalmer. Enter Francesco.)

FRANCESCO: The telegraph messenger has just brought these six telegrams.
SERPILLI: Give them to me.
(Francesco gives them, and exits.)

SERPILLI *(opening the telegrams and reading):* The Independent Liberal Democratic Association—the syndic—the Association of Watchmakers' Apprentices—the tribunal—the prefect. . . . "Unspeakable grief"—"sorrow of the human race"—"words fail." *(Throws the telegrams on the table.)* "In great misfortunes vibrates the heart of great nations."
(Enter Peralti, the sculptor.)

PERALTI: Yes, the heart of great nations—and of great artists.
GERONTE: Ah, Peralti, a dear friend and one of our associates.
SERPILLI *(to Peralti):* Have you heard, too?
PERALTI: I have read some twenty or thirty telegrams posted up at the street corners, and hastened here to present to the widow this design for a monument to be erected to her husband.
SERPILLI: You mean you had it ready?
PERALTI: An artist never lets himself be taken unawares.
GERONTE: You have the instinct of a genius!
PERALTI *(unrolling a sheet of paper which he holds in his hand, and giving it to Geronte):* You see, a large pedestal with three steps—two sleeping lions, in Canova's manner—a cubic block of granite, which has a philosophic significance. The statue is seated on a curule chair.* Just look at the subtlety, the diapson, the *tonality*, the depth of the *tout ensemble!*
SERPILLI: But surely this is the drawing you made for Professor Giulini!
GERONTE *(handing the paper to Serpilli):* I thought I'd seen it exhibited as a design for a monument to General Quebrantador.
SERPILLI *(handing it to Peralti):* Not at all. I tell you it was Giulini.
GERONTE: And I maintain. . . .
PERALTI: Calm yourselves, gentlemen. The artist of any *elan* dashes off his ideas just as genius inspires him. It then serves its purpose when a purpose is made apparent. *(Rolls up the drawing.)*
GERONTE: Bravo! I hold exactly the same theory with regard to my own science. I prepare the embalming acids. . . .
(Enter Francesco.)

---

*In ancient Rome, a folding seat with curved legs and no back, often ornamented with ivory; used only by certain officials.

FRANCESCO: What in the world is all this, *Signor* Serpilli? Just look, what a bundle of telegrams!

SERPILLI: Excellent! Go tell *Signor* Bertrando.

FRANCESCO *(laying the telegrams on the table):* Oh, by the way, I almost forgot! What's become of my head? There's a photographer outside who insists on seeing *Signora* Arganti.

SERPILLI: Show him in. *(Exit Francesco.)*

PERALTI: Just give me fifty thousand francs and Arganti will have the most characteristic monument of the age.
(Enter photographer, with his camera.)

SERPILLI: What is it, sir?

PHOTOGRAPHER: I saw all the telegrams posted up. Everyone was in a state of consternation, asking who Arganti was. I made some inquiries on the subject and then hurried over here. I now request the favor of taking a picture of the illustrious Arganti's portrait. . . . Begging your pardon, sir, but what was his Christian name?

SERPILLI: Ettore.

PHOTOGRAPHER: Ah, poor Ettore! I will guarantee a work of art that will be a tremendous success! I will also take photographs of his bedroom, his study, his inkstand, the front of the house—everything! And I'll advertise them in all the papers.

SERPILLI *(shaking him by the hand):* I thank you in the name of the family. To honor the noble dead is not only a work of merit, it is a duty, a duty which we are here to carry out.

GERONTE: I alone can do nothing! Ah, *Signor* Serpilli, why did our explorer have to lose his body in the untracked jungles!

SERPILLI: Since common feelings of delicacy have assembled us here, let us take steps for transferring to the public this great sorrow at our loss.

PHOTOGRAPHER: Poor Ettore!

PERALTI: Poor, dear fellow!

GERONTE: My poor friend!

SERPILLI: Well . . . *(after a pause, rubbing his hands):* we are all mortal. Now then, *Signor*, how many photographs did you say you can sell? And you, my dear Peralti, that monument of yours . . . fifty thousand francs, you say? I realize it was inadvertent, but you neglected to mention the small matter of a discount or commission. . . .

—Carlo Lotti (1832-1915)

PAOLO PUNCTURES A PROUD
MOTHER'S PRIDE

[PAOLO SEVERI IS IN LOVE WITH HIS COUSIN, EVELINA, WHO, UNKNOWN TO

HIM, IS BEING COURTED BY HIS OLD SCHOOLMATE, ADOLFO BRIGA. ADOLFO
PURPOSELY ENCOURAGES HIS RIVAL, WHO IS FROM THE COUNTRY AND UNUSED TO
SOCIETY, THINKING HE WILL BE SURE TO MAKE HIMSELF RIDICULOUS, AND
THEREFORE FAIL. IN ORDER TO BETTER CARRY OUT THIS PLAN HE PRETENDS TO
DEVOTE HIMSELF TO GRAZIOSA, THE DAUGHTER OF PRESIDENT MANLIO, WHO IS
VISITING AT THE HOUSE OF EVELINA'S PARENTS. PAOLO, IN HIS SIMPLICITY, DOES
HIS BEST TO FURTHER ADOLFO'S SUIT BY PLEADING HIS CAUSE WITH SIGNORA
VERECONDA, GRAZIOSA'S MOTHER, A LADY WHOSE LOVE OF ADMIRATION HAS
SURVIVED HER YOUTH, AND WHO HAS TAKEN ADOLFO'S ATTENTIONS AS AN
HOMAGE TO HERSELF.]

> SCENE: *A drawing room in the house of Advocate Scipioni, with
> a door opening on the garden. Adolfo and Vereconda
> are seated, and conversing. Enter Paolo from the garden
> just as Adolfo kisses Vereconda's hand.*

PAOLO *(aside):* If you want canes, you must go to the canebrake; if you
  want the daughter, you must make yourself agreeable to the moth-
  er.*
VERECONDA *(aside to Adolfo):* Don't be nervous. He could not possibly
  have seen.
PAOLO: Am I intruding?
VERECONDA: Sir! Do you think for one moment that. . . ?
PAOLO: I've just come in to get a volume of my aunt's poetry. Here it is.
  I'm very sorry that my aunt should expose herself to ridicule by
  publishing verses like these. Even the syntax and spelling are wrong!
  I have a good mind to tell her so myself.
ADOLFO *(aside to Paolo):* So you've left Evelina? Well done!
PAOLO *(aside):* Well done, indeed! It wasn't *my* choice!
ADOLFO *(aside):* My friend, it's nothing more than a female maneuver of
  war. A woman entreated denies; a woman denied entreats. Why
  don't you remain here, instead of me?
PAOLO *(aside):* Indeed *not!*
ADOLFO *(aside):* Indeed *yes!* I'll go and speak up in your behalf and set
  things right in no time.
PAOLO *(aside):* But. . . .
ADOLFO *(aside):* I'll beat the big drums for you, you'll see! Let me go!
PAOLO *(aside):* All right, go ahead.
ADOLFO *(aside to Vereconda):* I've removed all suspicion on his part.
  Now, I'm leaving to make things quite safe. *(Aloud):* Will you excuse
  me, *Signora* Vereconda?
VERECONDA: Do as you think best.

---

*An ancient Italian proverb.

PAOLO: And, in my place, take these—well—let's call them verses. Don Vincenzo, rest his soul, would have called them uncultivated, rugged songs which would have brought a blush to the revered countenances of Apollo and the Muses.

VERECONDA (*aside to Adolfo*): Who in the world was this Don Vincenzo?

ADOLFO (*aside to Vereconda*): Who knows? Ah, I have it: the schoolmaster at Borgo di Castello! (*Exit.*)

VERECONDA (*aside*): How easy it is to recognize the country lout at once!

PAOLO (*aside*): What a first-rate friend Adolfo is! And now that I am with his Graziosa's mother, I can do him a service. I'd be ungrateful if I didn't try. But I, too, am a real friend.

VERECONDA (*aside*): He looks as though he had just come in from the plow trail.

PAOLO: Madam.

VERECONDA: Sir?

PAOLO: With your kind permission, may I stay and talk to you a little?

VERECONDA: Yes, of course. Please sit down.

PAOLO: It isn't easy to take the place of my friend.

VERECONDA (*aside*): How crudely he expresses himself!

PAOLO: There are very few like him. He's a fellow who is liked by everyone—particularly by girls' mothers.

VERECONDA (*aside*): Oh my! Could he have noticed something after all?

PAOLO: He is very fortunate. But he deserves his luck.

VERECONDA (*aside*): Yes, he *must* have noticed. (*Aloud*): I don't understand.

PAOLO: Look, dear madam, Adolfo has no secrets from me. How could he? We've been friends from childhood.

VERECONDA: What is all this leading up to?

PAOLO: This—that the poor fellow has opened his whole heart to me, and told me in particular that you are inclined to look on him with favor.

VERECONDA: Incredible! To go and tell anyone!

PAOLO: And he hopes—yes, I say hopes—that you will grant his request.

VERECONDA (*rising*): What does he want of me? Suppose my husband....

PAOLO: He wants what any other young man would want from a mother as affectionate as you—your daughter's hand.

VERECONDA: What are you saying!

PAOLO: Believe me, there is no one more worthy to marry her. He loves her, loves her devotedly. But the poor fellow needs some encouragement—some protection. Won't you, dear madam, take him under your broad and protecting wings?

VERECONDA (*choking with suppressed vexation*): Ah! Under my wings? My *broad* wings?

PAOLO: I have already given him a hint as to his right course of action: "If you want canes, you must go to the canebrake."

VERECONDA *(aside):* You and your canebrakes!

PAOLO: Anyway, a mother who has attained a certain age. . . .

VERECONDA *(aside):* A certain age!

PAOLO: Such a mother, I say, should have no other thought than that of settling her daughter comfortably before she dies. . . .

VERECONDA *(aside):* Before she dies!!!

PAOLO: Particularly a good mother like yourself. What do you say, eh? Will you be on his side?

VERECONDA: I'll—I'll—well, I will be on whatever side my conscience dictates. *(Aside):* Adolfo, you traitor! In love with Graziosa, are you? So that was the reason for your attentions to me!

PAOLO: Will I be able to give my friend some hope?

VERECONDA: Sir, you may give him whatever you think best. *(Aside):* At a certain age! . . . Before she dies! . . . *(Aloud):* Excuse me, please. I must go. *(Aside):* Only wait till I get at you! . . . *(Aloud):* Perhaps I'll see you later. *(Exit.)*

PAOLO: Well now, if Adolfo is a real friend, then so am I. He may have been beating the big drum for me, but I've certainly been blowing the trumpet for him with all my might. Let us hope that he has done as well for me as I have for him!

—Achille Torelli (1844-1917)

5

Pasquin—and the Saga
of the Scathing Epigram

One species of wit and humor in which Italians have always excelled is the impromptu epigram—the stinging comment in verse on passing events. The language abounds in rhymes, and easily lends itself to meter. Indeed, it is rare to meet an Italian, however uneducated, who cannot string together a few lines of at least passable quality. Any family event— a marriage, a baptism, or a death—is sure to call forth a shower of sonnets from friends and acquaintances; and on a few special occasions these contributions are published in volume form. Most of these, however, are dull reading, but the satirical comments suggested by public, rather than private or family events, are often amusing, though sometimes so local in their application as to have little meaning or interest to outsiders.

Many of those epigrams translated in the following pages are in Latin, but the knowledge of this language was common enough in Rome to make them almost as popular as verses in the "vulgar"[1] or people's tongue. It must be remembered that any Italian with the smallest pretension to culture can turn out a few Latin elegiacs fairly well. At least, to go back in time, this was the case under the *ancien régime*[2] when such education as was to be had was almost exclusively classical, and therefore thoroughly laced with Latin.

This tendency to satiric comment was curbed, but never quite re-

---

[1]It is interesting as well as enlightening to recall the historical evolution of the word, "vulgar." It was originally used to describe the language of the common folk of Rome and its colonies *(vulgatus)*—a kind of patois which differed markedly from the highly-structured Roman Latin. By the fourth century, Saint Jerome had produced, for the benefit of the great number of people who had lost touch with imperial Latin, a common-language version of the Scriptures, the *Vulgate*. It is also interesting to note the totally unreligious connotation the word "vulgar" carries today, sixteen centuries later.

[2]"Old regime," designating the order of things in France before the social and political changes of the French Revolution in 1789.

pressed, by the censorship of the ancien regime. In Papal Rome it found an outlet in Pasquin, from which the word *pasquinade* has passed into most of the languages of Europe.[1] A detailed dissertation concerning Pasquin and the epigrams for which he became responsible, will be found in Story's *Roba di Roma*.[2]

It is believed by some scholars that the only type of true Roman humor which now remains is that of Pasquino. He is the public satirist who lances his pointed jokes against every absurdity and abuse. There he sits on his pedestal behind the Palazzo Braschi—a mutilated torso which, in the days of its glory, was part of a noble group of statues, representing, it is believed, Menelaus dragging the dead body of Patroclus from the fight, according to Greek mythology. Whatever may have been the subject of this once beautiful and now ruined work, it grew, in time, no less famous under its modern name. Pasquino became the mouthpiece for the most pungent Italian wit.

We first meet Pasquin as an abandoned, limbless fragment of an antique statue, which serves as a target for boys to throw stones at, as well as for other slings and arrows of outrageous fortune. Nearby this remnant of a statue lives a tailor named Pasquino, skillful in his trade and still more skillful in his epigrams. At his shop, many of the literati, prelates, courtiers, and wits of the town meet to order their robes and dresses, report scandal, to anatomize reputations and to kill time.

Pasquino's humor was contagious, and so many sharp epigrams were made in his shop that it grew to be famous. After Pasquino's death, in mending the street, it became necessary to remove the old statue embedded in the ground. It was set up at the side of his shop to clear the roadway. People jokingly said that Pasquino had come back, and so the statue acquired its nickname, which stuck. That, at least, is the account published by Castelvetro in 1553. In any case, it became the custom to attribute to the statue any lampoon, epigram, or satiric verse which the author preferred to leave anonymous, and to pretend that it was a pasquinade.

From that time onward, Pasquino became a name and a power. His tongue could never be ruled. He had his bitter saying for everything. Vainly, Government and Church strove to suppress him. At one time he

---

[1] The word *pasquinade* has several meanings and nuances. As a noun, it denotes a satire or lampoon, especially one posted in a public place. As a verb, it also means "to assail in a *pasquinade*." The word is derived from *Pasquino*, the name given an antique Roman statue, unearthed in 1501, which was actually decorated and posted with verses. The final consonant has been dropped in the Anglicized *Pasquin*.

[2] "Roman Stuff," Vol. 1, pp. 254-93. Although very rare in the United States, a few copies may be found in the libraries of England.

narrowly escaped being thrown into the Tiber by Adrian VI, who was deeply offended by some of his sarcasms. But he was saved from that fate by the wisdom of the Spanish Legate, who gravely counseled the pope to avoid any such act lest he teach all the frogs in the river to croak pasquinades.

Pope Paul III was among those who made various attempts to silence him. In an epigram addressed to him, "Pasquin" said:

> "Great were the sums once paid to poets for singing;
> How much will you, O Paul, give me to be silent?"

Finally, his popularity became so great that all epigrams, good or bad, were attributed to him. Against this, he remonstrated, crying:

> "Alas! the veriest copyist sticks upon me his verses;
> Everyone now on me his wretched trifles bestows."

That protest seems to have had good results, for shortly after, he said:

> "No man in Rome is better than I; I seek nothing from any.
> I am never verbose; here I sit, and am silent—for now!"

In the past two or three hundred years no collection has been made (as far as this author knows) of Pasquin's sayings. It is only here and there that they can be found recorded in books or in the hidden tablets of the brain, passed down orally from one generation to the next as part of the people's folklore. But in 1544 a volume of 637 pages was printed, with the title, *Pasquillorum Tomi Duo*, in which, among a mass of epigrams and satires from various sources, a considerable number of real pasquinades were preserved. That volume is now quite rare and costly, since most of the copies were burned because of the many satires it contained against the Church. So rare, indeed, is the volume, that the celebrated Dutch scholar Daniel Heinsius (1580-1655) thought his copy to be unique, as he stated in the flyleaf inscription (as though Pasquin himself were speaking):

> "Rome to the fire gave my brothers—I, the single phoenix
> Live—by Heinsius bought for a hundred pieces of gold."

In this, however, Heinsius was mistaken. There are a few other copies known to be in existence, but probably none in the United States.

That collection, the aforementioned *Pasquillorum Tomi Duo*, was edited by a reformer, *Caelius Secundus Curio*, a free-thinking Piedmontese who had suffered persecution, confiscation, exile, and imprisonment in the Inquisition. He escaped to Switzerland where, in exile, he published the volume of pasquinades, and sent it forth to harass his enemies and bigoted opponents.

The chief aim of the collection was to attack the Church, and it is small wonder that the satires were put to the torch whenever found. Indeed, it was worth a man's life to be caught with a copy of the book. Regrettably, no other collections exist, and, since the voluminous collections of popular songs, proverbs, and sayings of Tuscany have been so successful, it is to be hoped that an Italian scholar will be found with the determination and patience to collect the pasquinades of more modern days.

The earliest pasquinades were directed against the Borgian Pope, Alexander VI (Sextus), who led a rather infamous life. Of him, Pasquin said:

> *"Sextus Tarquinus. Sextus Nero—Sextus et iste;*
> *Semper sub Sextus perdita Roma fuit."*

Again, alluding to the charge that he obtained his election by the grossest bribery, and, as Guicciardini expressed it, "infected the whole world by selling without distinction holy and profane things," Pasquin says:

> "Alexander sells the keys, the altar, Christ:
> He who bought them first has a good right to sell."

Here, too, is another savage epigram on the Borgian Pope, referring to the murder of his son, Giovanni, Duca di Gandia. Giovanni's brother, Cesare, Duca di Valentino, slew him at night and threw his body into the Tiber, from which it was fished out next morning:

> "Lest we should think you not a fisher of men, O Sextus,
> Lo, for your very son with nets you fish!"

Pasquin was at his most scathing to the licentious and venal Leo X, who raised money for his vices by the sale of cardinals' hats and indulgences. Many of the epigrams are too coarse for translation in this volume, but here is one which, while decent, is also less bitter than most:

> "Bring me gifts, spectators! Bring me not verses.
> Divine money alone rules the ethereal gods."

Here is another, referring to the story, then current in Rome, that Leo's death was occasioned by poison, and because of its suddenness there was no time to administer the last sacraments:

> "At the last hour of life, if, perchance, you ask why Leo
> Could not the sacraments take—'tis plain he had sold them all!"

Under Clement VII, Rome was besieged, taken and sacked by the

---

*"Always under the Sextuses Rome has been ruined."

Constable de Bourbon, and through the horrors of those days Pasquin's voice was seldom heard. One saying of his which was uttered during the period of the Pope's imprisonment in the Castle Saint Angelo has been preserved. With a sneer at the Pope's infallibility and his imprisonment, Pasquin declared: *"Papa non potest errare."* (The pope cannot err or wander.)—*errare* having both meanings. Pasquin cast no flowers in the Pope's path during the latter's lifetime, but at the pontiff's death he threw a handful of epigrams on his coffin. One of them referred to the physician, Matteo Curzio, or Curtius, to whose ignorance Clement's death was attributed:

"Curtius has killed our Clement—let gold then be given
To Curtius for thus securing the public health."

On Paul III, the Farnese Pope, Pasquin frequently exercised his wit, but not always successfully. This Pope was celebrated for his nepotism, and the high-handed manner in which he enriched his "house" and the members of his family, of whose extravagances the Pope complained that he was becoming pauperized. Pasquin jibed:

"Let us pray for Pope Paul, for his zeal,
For his house is eating him up."

With Pope Paul III, the record ceases; the 1544 publication of *Pasquillorum Tomi Duo* comes to an end, and only rarely do we now find an authentic pasquinade of that day and age. Not all of the barbs were directed against the Roman Catholic Church, however. They lasted only through that period from the Middle Ages to the Renaissance, when the succession of poorly qualified popes was a scandal to Christianity.

In 1798, when the French occupied Rome under Napoleon Bonaparte, "Pasquin arose to utter some bitter epigrams, among them—

"I Francesi son tutti ladri—
Non tutti—ma Buona parte."*

Here is one, admirable in wit, referring to the institution of the Cross of the Legion of Honor in France:

"In times less pleasant and more fierce, of old,
The thieves were hung on crosses, so we're told;
In times less fierce, more pleasant, like today,
Crosses are hung upon the thieves, they say."

---

*"The French are all thieves—nay, not all, but a *good part*"—(or, in the original, *Buonaparte*").

When the Emperor Francis of Austria visited Rome, Pasquin called him *"Gaudium urbis—Fletus provinciorum—Rises mundi."*[1]

A clever epigram was also made on Canova's draped statue of Italy:

"For once Canova has surely tripped:
Italy is not draped but stripped."

The wit of Pasquin, as of all Romans, is seldom purely verbal; for the pun, simply as a pun, is little relished in Italy. Ordinarily the wit lies in the thought and image, though sometimes it is expressed by a play upon words as well, as in the epigram on Buonaparte. The ingenious method adopted by the Italians to express their political sympathies with Victor Emmanuele was thoroughly characteristic of Italian humor. Forbidden by the police to make any public demonstration in his favor, government officials were astonished by the constant shouts of "Viva Verdi! Viva Verdi!" in theaters and in all public places, as well as finding those words scrawled on all the walls of the city. But they soon discovered that the cries for Verdi were through no enthusiasm for the composer, but only because his name was an acrostic signifying Vittorio Emmanuele, Re D'Italia![2]

Of a similar character was a satire in dialogue, which appeared in 1859, when almost everyone in Rome was waiting and doubtlessly hoping for the death of King Bomba, a hated despot. Pasquin imagines a traveler just returned from Naples, and inquires what he has seen there:

TRAVELER: *Ho visto un tumore.* (I have seen a tumor.)

PASQUIN: *Un tumore? Ma che cosa e un tumore?* (A tumor? But what is a tumor?)

TRAVELER: *Leva il "t" per risposta.* (Take away the "t" for the answer.)

PASQUIN: *Ah! Un umore! Ma questo umore porta danno?* (Ah! A humor![3] But is this humor dangerous?)

TRAVELER: *Leva l'"u" per risposta.* (Take away the "u.")

PASQUIN: *More! Che peccato! Ma quando? Fra breve?* (He dies [*more*]! What a pity! But when? Shortly?)

TRAVELER: *Leva l "m."* (Take away the "m.")

PASQUIN: *Ore! Fra ore! Ma chi dunque ha quest' umore?* (Hours! [*ore*] In a few hours! But who then has this humor?)

---

[1]"The joy of the city—the tears of the provinces—the laughter [or perhaps "laughing stock"] of the world."

[2]"Victor Emmanuele, King of Italy!"

[3]Used in the same sense (i.e., a "vapor") as by our sixteenth and seventeenth century writers. The old medical terminology still survives to a small extent in the rural areas of Italy, or did until recently, although the ancient practice of medicine which consisted chiefly in bloodletting, has disappeared.

TRAVELER: *Leva l'"o."* (Take away the "o.")
PASQUIN: *Re! Il Re! Ho piacere davvero! Ma poi, dove andra?*
   (King! [*Re*] The king! I am delighted! But then where will he go?)
TRAVELER: *Leva l' "r."* (Take away the "r.")
PASQUIN: *E-eh! e-e-e-h! . . .*
said with a shrug and a prolonged tone peculiarly Roman: indicative of
an immense doubt as to Paradise, and little question as to the other place.

Another specimen of pure Roman wit was the epigram made upon the
movement of the Piedmontese and Garibaldians on Naples and Sicily:

*Tutti stanno in viaggio—soldati vanno per terra—marinari vanno per
mare, e preti vanno in aria.* (Everybody is in movement—the soldiers go
by land, the sailors by sea, and the priests vanish into air.)

Here is a last one, full of barb and spirit.

When the conference of Zurich was proposed, it was rumored that
Cardinal Antonelli was to go as the representative of the Roman States,
and to be accompanied by Monsignor Barile. Commented Pasquin:

"*Il Cardinale di Stato va via con Barile, ma tornera con fiasco*"—which
is untranslatable.*

Let us add *fine* to this chapter with one last pasquinade—short and, as
usual, not so sweet:

   I do not please all my readers? But see—
   Is it every reader that pleases me?

---

*The meaning is, "The cardinal is going away with the cask [*Barile*], but he will
come back with the flask"—the word *fiasco* also has the sense of failure or
disaster. Needless to add, the above was written before the establishment of the
Regno in 1870, when Rome joined the unification of Italian states to form a united
Italy under King Victor Emmanuele.

6

Nineteenth and Twentieth Century Italian Newspaper Humor

INTRODUCTION

The close of the nineteenth century and the dawn of the twentieth witnessed a period of journalistic freedom that was a natural consequence of the period of Enlightenment in Italy. But political and social forces that would soon shake and almost destroy the nation were at work. And as the freedom of the press slowly eroded, humor declined, for no despotic government can tolerate the scorn of a people when it is made the butt of a joke.

It was during the period from 1925 to 1930 that the Italian free press was nearly bludgeoned to death by the fascist government. Prior to that, the factions representing the various political parties made full use of the press to deride their opponents and exchange the usual insults. The result was not only a cornucopia of incisive and very funny humor, but a standard of journalistic excellence that was the envy of all Europe.

On the left of the political spectrum were the Socialists who boasted such respected newspapers as the *Critica Sociale*, the *Lotta di Classe* (Class Struggle), and *Avanti!* (Forward!). All of these publications rivaled the best metropolitan dailies in quality of reportage, and often surpassed them in literary quality and topical interest.

To the extreme right of the political center were a number of ultranationalistic newspapers as *Idea Nazionale,* whose editor, Enrico Corradini, made a career of fulminating against democratic institutions, and of pleading for passionate devotion to the destiny and renewed glory of the nation as it was under the Roman Empire. There was also Giovanni Papini (now remembered, strangely enough, for his later *Life of Christ),* editor of the nationalistic *Voce,* of Florence, who urged that "Italy, without unity to its vision, needs someone to beat it, so that it may awaken, and someone to incite it so that it may act." Mussolini, for one, took the admonition to heart.

The large metropolitan papers were indeed sensitive to the inherent threat to their journalistic freedom and opposed any such notions. Benedetto Croce, among many others, quickly pointed out, in *La Critica,*

189

the dangers of superstate and super-race doctrines. But such efforts were too few to stop, or even to impede effectively, a movement which rested on such deep human emotions as pride, self-esteem, and the conviction of one's natural superiority. The traditional Italian patriotism was to be transformed into nationalism. It wasn't long before the liberals, socialists, and even the lesser dignitaries of the Church were tainted with the new militant doctrines.

As long as the country's newspaper editors and writers were free to defend their cause and criticize the opposition in a free press, satire, ridicule, irony—all the many facets of humor—grew and flourished. But the end was predictable when, beginning in 1925, the weight of the absolutist fascist control of the state inevitably broke down Italy's internal freedom; for absolutism, by its very nature, requires the destruction of all opposition. Accordingly, beginning in 1925 with the legislation against freedom of the press, fascist control of the communication media grew until, by 1930, the government was issuing detailed instructions to all publications, not only regarding the news it was allowed to print, but also concerning such things as the relative importance to be attached to each newsworthy item, *and* the place on the page that the item was to occupy! Any editor or journalist who could not bring himself to agree with the state on these matters was visited by Mussolini's *Opera Volontaria Repressione Antifascista,* or O.V.R.A.—the inevitable secret police.

With the overthrow of Mussolini and his dictatorship, Italian newspapers again reverted to their rightful independence. And with the return of freedom came the resurgence of published native humor. Much of this post-World War II humor has been printed in the Italian-American press, but little of it can be compared with the delightful gems that were published in the latter part of the 1800s and in the beginning of this century—until the fateful 1925 legislation that denied freedom of expression to the Italian people.

The collection in this chapter is a small representation of the wide variety of bubbling mirth that filled the pages of Italian newspapers and magazines prior to Mussolini's control of the press. Some of the anecdotes are old; quite ancient, in fact. But there is always a new generation to whom the jokes are brand new. Here, then, are the comic notices that brought laughter to a people who often had little else to laugh about.

—H.D.S.

"UNLIBERATE ME, FOUL LIBERATOR!"*

During the recent elections there was a large popular demonstration at Bergamo, where the police were gathered in great force to prevent a disturbance. A fiery-spirited youth, seeing a gentleman in civilian clothes escorted by two burly uniformed policemen, made a sudden rush to free him from his captors. In vain the supposed victim protested that his generous effort to liberate him was not needed.

"Ah, *Signore*, I would not for a moment think of leaving you alone with these minions of injustice!" insisted the young man.

"Please—just calm yourself!" urged the "victim."

"Calm myself? We are not Moderates, we're Progressists!"

"I don't doubt it, but I'll thank you just the same to let me alone."

"No, I intend to rescue you. Come on!"

The young fellow dragged the gentleman along in spite of his protests. At last, in order to escape from his inexorable liberator, he was compelled to inform him that he was Rizzi, the superintendent of police himself.

What the two uniformed policemen were doing all this time has not been reported to us, but we do know that our young hero was let off with a gentle admonition.

—Fanfulla

WINE IN THE HEAD— FEET IN THE BED

A gentleman and his long-time valet, who was more like a friend than a servant, went to a party where both of them indulged a little too freely in the cup that leers. Returning home, and well in their cups, the valet staggered into his employer's bed, mistaking it for his own, while the gentleman, also not knowing what he was doing, lay down with his feet on the pillow and his head at the foot of the same bed. In the middle of the night, one of them began to kick and awoke the other.

"*Signor* Padrone," exclaimed the valet, "there's a robber hiding in my bed!"

"You don't say!" gasped the gentleman, awakening, and just as befuddled with wine as his valet. "In that case there must be two of them. I've got one on my bed, too. You try and get rid of yours—I'll make short work of mine."

They went at it with a vengeance, each grabbing the other by the feet,

---

*English translation by *Signora* Pasqualina Sanchetti, Rome, 1915.

and wildly thrashing about. Inevitably, they rolled out of bed and fell to the floor, where they again closed their eyes in sodden slumber. They awoke the next morning with throbbing heads.

"What are you doing in my bedroom when you have a perfectly good room of your own to sleep in?" asked the gentleman.

"I don't know," replied the valet. "But what are you doing on the floor when you have a perfectly good bed to sleep in?"

Gazetta di Malta

AMBITION OF YOUTH

An old beggar, sitting near a church door, had a sign suspended from his neck, inscribed: BLIND FROM BIRTH.

Two other beggars, passing by, noted the pitiful announcement.

"*Ebbene!*"* remarked one. "Now there's a man who started young in the business!"

Il Mondo Umoristico

END OF A BUDDING CAREER

Alberto Gelsomini, an aspiring actor, joined an amateur dramatic group, where he found a small part in a play. He was given only one line, but he rehearsed it diligently in his room: "*Signore*, a gentleman of about fifty years has been waiting for some time in the outer room. Shall I show him in?" Hour after hour he repeated the line, until the very day of the performance, his first acting attempt in public.

The big moment was now at hand. Behind the curtain, Gelsomini, just to be doubly sure, murmured the line to himself: "*Signore*, a gentleman of about fifty years has been waiting for some time in the outer room. Shall I show him in?"

The director gave him his cue, and Gelsomini rushed onstage in a blur of feverish excitement.

"*Signore*," he blurted out, "a gentleman has been waiting fifty years in the outer room. Shall I show him in after all this time?"

Il Cittadino

ALL OR NOTHING

CUSTOMER: Do you have any piano pieces?
NEW APPRENTICE: No, madam. What do you think this is—a junk shop? We sell only *whole* pianos!

Don Chisciotte

---

*Very good! Fine!

DIGNITY OF A HAT

A beggar, indescribably filthy and dressed in tattered rags, was plying his trade in a prosperous section of the city where it was unlawful to beg. He accosted a handsomely attired gentleman.

"Very well, here are two *soldi*," snapped the aristocratic-looking man, "but you might at least have the manners to take off your hat when you beg."

"I don't dare," replied the shabby bum. "That policeman watching us across the street might become suspicious and I'd be arrested for begging in a restricted area. But if I keep my hat on, he'll just think we're a couple of friends."

Fanfalla

FAIR EXCHANGE

A young dramatic author took his new play to the manager of a popular theater. Months passed without a reply. At last, overcoming his natural shyness, he called for his precious manuscript. The impressario looked but was unable to find it.

"I'm sorry, young fellow, but it seems that your play is lost," he said at length. "But I'll tell you what. See that pile of manuscripts on the desk over there? Well, you pick one out—any one at all. They're guaranteed to be every bit as good as yours, and what's more, the quality of the paper is better!"

Il Mondo Umoristico

A RELUCTANT DUELIST
OFFERS
CLEANING INSTRUCTIONS

Spippoletti had been threatened with a duel. He explained the confrontation to our editor, thus:

"I was trying to persuade him to forget the matter, when he threw one of his gloves in my face, saying he was going to wash that glove in my blood."

"Good heavens! What did you do?"

"I stood right up to the brute and told him that if he did, the best way to clean kid gloves was with benzine!"

Il Progresso

Quid Pro Quo

Fasollacci is an elegant youth, with an elegant style of living, but with a rather inelegant purse to match his needs. With that description of his character and financial situation out of the way, let us proceed to the story.

For the past several months he had been spending right and left, so that he found himself unable to pay the bill at the hotel where he had been staying.

Taking his courage in both hands and laying it before him on his desk, he determined to apply to his uncle for help,—the well-known avarice of his father precluding all hope of assistance from *that* miser. Diligently, he began his letter:

> Dear Uncle,
> If you could only see how I blush with shame while I write to you, I know you would pity me. Do you know why? Because I must ask you for a hundred francs, and do not know how to express my humble request.
> No! It is impossible for me to tell you. I prefer to die!
> I am sending this to you by a messenger, who will await your answer.
> Your most obedient and affectionate nephew,
>
> *Fasollacci*

> P.S. Overcome with shame for what I have written, I have been running after the messenger to take the letter back, but I could not catch up with him. Heaven grant that something may happen to stop him, or that this letter gets lost.

The uncle, naturally, was touched. He considered the matter fully, and then replied:

> My beloved nephew,
> Console yourself, and blush no longer.
> Providence has heard your prayers,
> The messenger lost your letter.
> Goodbye.
> Your affectionate uncle,
>
> *Aristippo**

---

*Other variants of this tale are found in the folk cultures of Ireland, England, and among the Jewish people of Eastern Europe. (See *The Lilt of the Irish*, 1978, and *Encyclopedia of Jewish Humor*, 1969, by the present author. New York: Jonathan David Publishers, Inc.)

Why Book Collectors Go Mad

A book collector had just purchased a rare volume at an exorbitant price. Entitled *Migratory Habits of the Bastusi Poopoo Bug*, the edition had no value whatever except for its rarity.

"It's very expensive," commented a friend.

"I know, but it's the only copy in existence."

"Yes, but suppose some publisher decides to reprint it?"

"Are you crazy? Who'd be stupid enough to buy it?"

Il Progresso

Aroma in a Roman Restaurant

Mario and Rosalinda Luisa decided to celebrate their first wedding anniversay in a romantic little restaurant that had been recommended to them. Mario, a fat little man who was nicknamed *polpette** by his friends, a reference to his bulging cheeks and billowing buttocks, sank down into a chair while the waiter solicitously held a chair for Rosalinda.

"Bring me an order of fish," said Mario to the waiter.

"And I'll have the veal cutlet," ordered Rosalinda.

The waiter soon returned with the orders and grandly set the plates before them. He then stood back, waiting for the usual compliments for food and service. Besides, it always helped increase the amount of the tip that would come later.

Mario picked up a fork and was about to taste his food when he stopped, fork in mid-air, and sniffed suspiciously. He sniffed again, this time wrinkling his nose in disgust.

"*Persicomele!*"** he literally snarled. "This fish positively stinks!"

"I'm afraid you're mistaken, *Signor*," countered the waiter gravely.

"But smell it yourself. I tell you, it stinks!"

"And I tell you, *Signor*, you are mistaken. It isn't your fish; it's your wife's veal cutlet that stinks!"

La Nazione (Florence)

Nothing Could Be Worse

Last month a young poet, still attending the university here, brought two sample poems to our offices, hoping for publication.

---

*Dumplings, sometimes made of meat. Meatballs.

**"Peaches and apples!" A mild oath popular in nineteenth-century Italy.

Vittorino, our editor, read the first poem, scowled, and then handed it back to the aspiring poet.

"Young man," he said tersely, "burn this one, and then do some extensive rewriting on the other."

"But you haven't even looked at the other one," protested the young fellow.

"I don't need to," snapped Vittorino. "Just revise it!"

L'Osservatore (Venice)

A Negative Affirmative

Spippoletti's son, having reached that age when the heart is susceptible, fell in love with a pretty little milliner, and wrote to her declaring his eternal devotion. After filling four pages with passionate phrases and noble words he scarcely understood, he concluded—

"I hope that my confession of true love and proposal of marriage will be acceptable to you, and that I may expect from you shortly an *affirmative* reply in which you will say either *yes* or *no*."

Il Progresso

Mother's Little Secret

The mother of a seminary student sent her son a new black soutane (an ecclesiastical robe), and inserted a letter in the pocket:

"Dear Gigetto—look in the pocket of this soutane and you will find Mama's letter."

La Stampa (Venice)

Irrefutable Logic

At the busy railway terminal in Torino, a traveler approached the vendor at the station's newsstand and asked for a copy of the *Daily*.

"Does it appear everyday?" asked the traveler.

"Certainly," replied the news vendor with some irritation. "You can tell that yourself, by the very name of the paper. What else would "Daily" mean?"

"It could mean anything," maintained the traveler stoutly. "After all, does the *Century* come out every hundred years?"

Il Mondo Umoristico

I Know That You Know That I Know

Spippoletti awoke early one morning to find that someone had slipped a postcard under his door. The card informed him that he was an imbecile, a fool, and a senile old idiot.

The evaluation did not agree with Spippoletti's opinion of himself. Thinking that he recognized the handwriting of Vincenzino, a friend who enjoyed a practical joke, he confronted the man that very afternoon.

"Did you send me this infamous libel?" demanded Spippoletti.

"No, I didn't," replied Vincenzino.

"But who else could it be?"

"Now look here," replied Vincenzino, "I'm not the only one who knows you!"

Il Progresso

Local Pride

A Neapolitan, paying a visit to Milan, told his host how pleased he was with the city and all the nice people he had met. He was particularly pleased with the artistic temperament of the inhabitants. "In fact," he added, "before leaving for home, I would like to have your portrait done in oil."

"In *oil?*" gasped the host. "Where do you think you are, in Naples?" Here in Milan we do everything in *butter!*"

Corriere delle Sera (Milan)

Mistaken Identity

Franco Satrielli, in mourning for the recent death of his mother, was riding one day on a horse with a crimson saddle. On the way he met Priest Pettegolo.

"*Signor* Satrielli," commented the priest reprovingly, "that bright red saddle doesn't look much like mourning to me."

"Father Pettegolo, you seem to have forgotten," replied Satrielli coolly, "it was *my* mother who died, not the horse's!"

La Rassegna Settimanale

Epitaph for an Absent Body

Signor Merbi, who had served for many years as the mayor of Ronciglione, found it necessary to journey to Rome on matters of business. While there, he suddenly became ill and within a few days he breathed his last and died.

His friends and neighbors, grieving for this good man who had governed their town so lovingly and well, erected a headstone in his memory. The inscription is still legible for all to see, in the cemetery of Ronciglione:

Here lies

MARCO BENEDETTO GIULIO MERBI

Who died in Rome and was buried there.

Il Pappagallo

OBSESSIVE RESCUER

There are some people with a mania for suicide, and others with one for saving lives. Neither all the angels in heaven nor all the demons in the other place can change them.

Within the last few days a brickmason at Rovigo threw himself under the wheels of a train. Death was imminent, when a passerby, Ranchetti by name, sprang in front of the onrushing train and, at the risk of his own life, saved the unfortunate workman.

The brickmason hurried home, shut the door of his house, locked all the windows, and proceeded to hang himself. But he had reckoned without his unknown rescuer. Ranchetti, guessing the man's intentions, had followed him. Peering through a window, and perceiving the scene inside, he broke the glass, entered the room, cut the rope, called for help, and saved the would-be suicide a second time.

"If this sort of thing keeps up," observed a doctor who had been summoned to the house, "Ranchetti will have plenty to do. One can only hope that his obsession for rescuing people will not interfere with his civic, social, and marital duties."

La Nazione

THE UNQUALIFIED CARRIAGE

A well-known lawyer of Naples, as a result of various political changes and his own merits, obtained the title of Count, and assumed a high post in the government.

"I'm curious about something," commented a friend one day. "Why don't you have your coat-of-arms painted on your carriage?"

"Because my carriage is not only older than my title," replied the Count, "but it has done nothing to be entitled to a title."

Il Mondo Umoristico

MILITARY MATHEMATICIANS

A soldier in the Naples militia asked his captain for permission to leave the military base for a half hour so that he might conduct some private business. The captain refused. A little later he renewed his request for a half-hour's leave, with the same result. After waiting some time he made a third appeal, and that, too, was denied. At last, for the fourth time, he asked for thirty-minutes' leave, but finally the captain granted the request. However, he did not return for two hours.

"What's the meaning of this?" demanded the captain. "You asked for only a half-hour leave of absence."

"That's all I took," protested the soldier. "But I asked four times. Four half-hours make two full hours—right?"

"Right!" agreed the captain. "And I sentence you to the stockade for two days. I sentence you for two days. For two days. Two days. Four times two days is eight days. Right?"

"Er—uh—I think so. But it's really not fair. You went to college."

Italia Militare

POETIC REMORSE

It is said of Mario Lessona, brother of the distinguished writer, Michele, that he fought fourteen duels in order to maintain that Dante was a greater poet than Ariosto. The last of his encounters was fatal to Mario.

"And to think," he moaned on his deathbed, "I never read either of them!"

Fanfalla

MISTAKEN IDENTITY

Angelo Mattarazzo, an actor appearing in Torelli's *Triste Realta,* had received no payment for several weeks. Summoning up his courage, he approached the theater manager—a man well known for his sharp tongue—and asked for his arrears in wages.

"I'm in danger of dying of starvation," Angelo concluded dolefully.

"That's hard to believe," observed the manager, scrutinizing the actor's plump and ruddy features. "Not with those fat cheeks."

"Don't let yourself be misled by that," insisted Angelo. "This face isn't mine; it belongs to my landlady. She's been letting me live on credit for the last six months!"

La Stampa

Man of Honor

Gennaro, of Naples, received an anonymous letter that was, as might be expected, highly uncomplimentary. But he simply tossed it into a wastebasket and went about his business, apparently unconcerned.

"You don't seem to be bothered by that poison-pen note," observed his friend.

"It doesn't annoy me at all," affirmed Gennaro. "I have too much contempt for anyone who'd write an anonymous communication of any kind. I consider myself an honorable gentleman. When *I* write anonymous letters, I *always* make it a point to sign them!"

Gazetta di Malta

Limpid Landmark Decisions

Francesco Gallina, the Florentine lawyer, was disputing a legal point on civil rights with his colleague, Giacomo Sanciotti, who practiced law in Sicily.

"I tell you," insisted Gallina, "that citizens of Florence have broader rights in Italy than Sicilians have."

"Just how do you support that foolish line of reasoning?" demanded Sanciotti.

Gallina, a quick thinker, immediately improvised a law that would reinforce his argument. "The Immigration Act of 1881," he said boldly.

"That law was superseded by the Federal Citizens Act of 1889," said Sanciotti, perceiving his companion's strategy and inventing a law of his own.

"I never heard of such a law," grumbled Gallina. "Can you give me a reference?"

"Sure," replied Sanciotti agreeably. "You'll find it on the same page as the Act you just quoted!"

La Stampa

None of His Business

A farmer, attending church at a distance from his own village, was listening to a fiery sermon on the consequences of doing evil. Suddenly, as if the inspired priest had beseeched Heaven for a demonstration, the sky darkened, thunder crashed, a lightning bolt hit the church, and a mighty voice from Somewhere Above boomed down: "So be it to all who disobey My commands!"

Children screamed, strong men shook, women fainted. The priest, raised to the pinnacle of grace, feverishly went through every applicable ritual he could think of in those frenzied minutes. Finally, when all the commotion and near hysteria had abated, he fixed a pious though indignant eye on the farmer who had sat unmoved throughout the miracle.

"What's the matter with you?" called the good father from his pulpit. "Didn't you see anything? Didn't you hear anything? How could you sit there like that, silent and unshaken?"

"Sir," replied the farmer, "I don't belong to this parish!"*

Il Cittadino

CHECKMATE!

A young man with literary aspirations, applied to the editor of an important newspaper and asked for employment.

"What kind of work did you have in mind?" asked the understanding editor.

"I would like to write your front page articles and perhaps write all your editorials."

"Hmmm, that requires some experience," commented the editor, suppressing an urge to laugh. "Before you can be given such assignments you would have to be known to the public."

"And how do I become known?"

"To become known you must publish."

The youth rushed home and retrieved a novel he had hastily written the year before and which he hoped to "polish" some day. He then hurried with his precious manuscript to a publisher and asked him to print it.

"My dear young fellow," advised the publisher, "if you want to publish, you must first become known."

"*Mama mia!*" groaned the crestfallen youth, "No wonder the Italians lost an empire. They just can't make up their damn minds!"**

Fanfulla

CANDID CONFESSION

Our Paris correspondent, reporting a socialist meeting, wrote:

"The orator made use of a set of commonplace catchwords, cliches,

---

*Several other versions of this tale will be found in the folk literature of the Irish, English, and in nearly all Latin American cultures. The origin of the anecdote is lost in antiquity.

**This anecdote was brought to the United States in the 1920s, where, in the burgeoning motion picture industry, it was revised by the acting fraternity. (An actor needs experience to get a part, but cannot get experience until he gets the part.)

and high-sounding phrases, calculated to make a profound impression on the fools who attended the gathering.

"I was present. . . ."

La Nazione

ITALIAN MEDICAL SCIENCE

Several of our readers commented to us about the peculiar advertisement which appeared on the last page of this newspaper last week.

Our editor, his sense of curiosity aroused, decided to investigate. Perhaps—who knows?—it might alleviate his own affliction. He answered the announcement, which read: "RED NOSES—INSTANT CURE!" There followed detailed instructions for enclosing payment, to be sent to a *Signor* Dulcamara.

A few days later, our intrepid editor received a postcard: "Continue drinking until your nose turns blue!"

Il Progresso

CONCERNED WAITER

DINER: Waiter, this minestrone is cold.

WAITER: Cold? But, *Signor,* you must be mistaken. I just tried it myself before I brought it to you. It was steaming hot.

DINER: What! You dared to taste . . .

WAITER: Oh no, *Signor!* What kind of pig do you think I am? I only dipped my finger in it!

Perseveranza

COURTROOM DRAMA— ITALIAN STYLE

JUDGE: What! You here again? You are absolutely incorrigible! Perhaps you can now see what bad company leads to.

PRISONER: Your Honor, how can you say that? Bad company? Why, I never see anyone but policemen and judges!

Perseveranza

PRETENTIOUS PARVENUE

Nouveau riche Agnese Mondella, in her new villa on the Mediterranean seashore, decided that her recently acquired wealth entitled her to a place in "high society." Accordingly, she sent out engraved invitations to several hundred of Italy's aristocracy to visit as guests at her housewarming. To provide the entertainment, she approached the eminent violinist, Edmondo Bugliosi.

"What is your usual fee, my good man?" she asked, unable to forget her life of economy.

"I am not your 'good man,'" snapped *Signor* Bugliosi, and, aware that she had inherited her money from a distant relative in the United States, he added, "My fee will be one thousand dollars—American!"

Agnese was about to refuse what she considered an exorbitant demand, but remembering that he was the darling of the society set, she reluctantly agreed. "However," she told the famous man, "I must remind you that you are an entertainer, so you must not mingle with my guests."

"In that case," he growled, "my fee will be only five hundred dollars."

"You needn't be sarcastic," retorted Agnese. "Just bring your violin in time so that you can play before dinner is served."

"*Signora* Mondella," exploded Bugliosi, unable to endure this imperious woman a moment longer, "my violin never plays before dinner, and in any case, it refuses to dine out. I suggest that you employ an organ grinder and a monkey!"*

Corriere Italiano

Always the Star

The manager of *La Scala* was interviewing an applicant who claimed to be very famous, but whose operatic career, if any, was completely unknown to him.

"Now look here," said the tenor, "I have sung in all the operas, and have always taken the principal part. In *Robert le Diable* I was Robert. In *Hernani*, I was Hernani."

"Did you perform in the *Siege of Corinth?*"

"Of course," cried the applicant. "I played Corinth."

Corriere Italiano

Definition of a Secret Society

A secret society is a group of people who meet from time to time in the

---

*This nineteenth-century anecdote was also popular in the Slavic and American nations at about the same time. Outside Italy, however, the tale was told as two separate jokes: the line, "My fee will be only five hundred dollars" told as one story, and "my violin never dines out" told as another. Curiously enough, the joke does not appear to have been introduced to the United States by the Italians, but by Russian, Polish, and Yugoslav immigrants in the 1880s.

most secret way possible, to shout their secrets in each other s ears at the top of their lungs.

HIGHER EDUCATION

During dinner at the castle, the tutor was being questioned about the progress made by the young heir-presumptive to the coronet.[1]

"At the moment," said the tutor, "we are studying algebra. I might also add that our noble pupil is doing very well in chemistry."

"Chemistry?" asked the Marchioness[2] quickly. "Is he learning about dynamite?"

"Not yet, madam," explained the tutor. "Dynamite comes under the heading of political science."

Corriere Italiano

IT TAKES ONE TO KNOW ONE

An old lawyer, originally from Sicily but lately proclaiming Rome as his birthplace, arrived a little early at the opera house with his wife. They passed the time engaging in small talk.

"I'm curious about something," said the wife. "Just who is the Fra Diavolo[3] of this opera?"

"Oh, him!" replied the lawyer. "If I remember correctly, he was one of those Sicilian lawyers!"

Fanfulla

MIRACLE WORKER

An elderly schemer, formerly a pickpocket who abandoned his life-long profession when arthritis lessened his manual dexterity, now wandered the country as a self-professed pilgrim. To support himself he sold little one-inch squares of cloth which he swore came from the robe of Saint Martin.

---

[1] A small crown; a crown worn by noblemen, sometimes of gold and jewels.

[2] An Italian noblewoman, usually the wife or widow of a marquis.

[3] Fra Diavolo (friar devil) (1771-1806) was a bandit and soldier whose real name was Michele Pezza. He entered the service of the king of Naples in 1798 and with Cardinal Ruffo resisted the French invasion (1799) of the kingdom. He was captured in 1806 and hanged by the French. The plot of Auber's opera, Fra Diavolo (*libretto* by Scribe), is in no respect historical.

In a remote village, one day, he came upon a prosperous-looking house where a farmer and his wife resided. They appeared to be good candidates for a sale, and he quickly spread his little "miracle cloths" on a paper before him.

"But what are they good for?" asked the farmer's wife, a fat woman with a strong sense of practicality.

"Well, er—they'll keep out of the cold," replied the pilgrim.

The woman eyed him stonily.

"That is," he added hastily, "if you wear them in large quantities!"

Il Cittadino

Why Judges Go Mad

In the Naples police court, just two weeks, ago, a witness was asked where he lived.

"With Gennaro."

"And where does Gennaro live?"

"With me."

"But where do you and Gennaro live?"

"Together."

Fanfulla

Open-minded Editor

Some time ago, the government decided, in its wisdom, to have the *Official Gazette* printed by convicts, in order to keep out the writings of radical elements.

Now that the secret has been made public, the decision has been rescinded, and the convicts will no longer do the printing.

This second resolution has been explained by saying that the government wishes to give no cause for accusations of family favoritism.

We are quite willing to accept both excuses.

La Stampa

How To Stop a Pestilence

A telegram received from Lisbon informs us that "a terrible hurricane has literally wiped Manila off the face of the earth."

A few hours later another cable arrived: "The cholera epidemic has entirely ceased."

We have no hesitation in believing it. Surely, if Manila no longer exists, everything, including cholera, undoubtedly ceased.

La Stampa

7

Traditional Folktales

INTRODUCTION

Folktales are an integral part of the body of folklore, which also includes folk music, folk dances, folk medicine, and proverbs. They revolve around social, environmental, philosophical, and religious factors, unlike orthodox history which is primarily concerned with the political, military, and economic events of the past.

As a general rule, folktales are transmitted orally from one generation to the next; in many cases it is the only means of preserving a local culture where educational facilities are lacking and written literature impossible.

Not all folktales are humorous, of course. Those dealing with demons stem from ancient myths: in Italy they come from the ancient Roman mythology, originally told in Latin, often dealing with Roman gods. Other examples revolve around folk medicine, with a good deal of attendant wisdom. Still other folk stories follow the pattern of the old exemplum, which was a tale with a moral lesson, although it may have included some humor in the telling.

The folktales in this chapter were selected for their humor alone, each representing a different era in Italian history with its own point of view. They are authentically Italian, but it should be pointed out that some of the stories are universal, and found in the folktales of other cultures. Perhaps it is because poverty, oppression, and our innermost emotional drives combine to stimulate anecdotes that appeal to common folks everywhere. But other stories which do not seem to have any profound thoughts between the lines have also appeared in remote areas of widely separated countries, no doubt carried by wayfaring travelers and later adapted to local mores and attitudes. These latter anecdotes usually had little more to offer the listener than amusement, and, like any good tale, were repeated down through the years until the original foreign qualities were completely eliminated and the finely honed variant reflected the customs and characteristics of the local denizens.

Those folktales with universal histories are so designated in the footnotes. But, for the most part, the anecdotes selected for this chapter are native to Italy, primarily its southern region. Some are fairly new; that is, they seem to have originated within the past two hundred years or so—which means "recent" in the annals of folklore. Most of these offerings, however, are quite ancient, their origins long since lost in the dim recesses of time. Among those which are very old, and probably have their roots in the ninth through the twelfth centuries, are *The Beggar and His Brother—the King; Ever the Fool; Punishment for a Naughty Horse; Once a Fool, Always a Fool; Giucca and the Hollow Statue; The Hermit and the Thieves; The Old Lady and the Devil;* and *Howl of the Owl.*

Published here together for the first time in the United States, the stories merit retelling so that they may not be lost to future generations.

—H. D. S.

The Beggar and His Brother—the King

A shabby beggar somehow managed to present himself before the king of Naples, and asked for alms.

"I am your brother," said the beggar boldly. "Would you refuse me your charity?"

"My brother?" answered the surprised king. "How do you claim kindred to me?"

"We are all descended from Adam and Eve, our common father and mother."

"Yes, you are right," agreed the king. "Here is a coin."

But when the beggar saw that the coin was but a small copper piece of money, he was offended.

"Is it possible," he moaned, "that your Majesty would give no more than this to your brother?"

"Away with you," roared the monarch. "If all the brothers you have in the world were to give you as much as I have, you'd be richer than I!"

Proof of a Fool

A certain man, although not old, had a luxuriant growth of whiskers. By chance, he happened to read a book dealing with the secrets of nature, in which it was said that a young man who has a long beard wears the badge of a fool. He immediately lit a candle, as the day had turned to evening, and viewed himself in the mirror. But so careless was he that the candle came too close to his face and he accidentally burned more than half his beard.

Sighing deeply, he returned to the book, and in the margin he wrote:
Probatum est—I *know* he is a fool.

He who cannot learn, except through bitter experience, remains a fool forever.

RATHER A LIVE COWARD THAN A DEAD HERO

An obnoxious man insulted another person without cause, and was immediately challenged to fight a duel. The obnoxious one, knowing that his antagonist was not only a braver man but a better swordsman than he, sped off as fast as possible.

A few days later, as he was regaling some companions with an account of the near-duel, they reproached him for having fled in so scandalous a manner.

"Pooh!" replied the ever-obnoxious one. "I would much rather that the world say a coward was put to flight, than a brave man had been killed!"*

OLD-AGE EXPECTATIONS

Signor Corradi, a prosperous merchant who owed much of his wealth to his monumental greed, had only one annoying and continuing problem in his life. His father, a very old man, required some attention everyday because he was now too feeble to attend to his own needs. The ancient one was kept in a dark room behind the kitchen. Why spend good money for candles when the old man could no longer see well enough to read or even to look out of a window? So he just sat there, day after day, in a shabby, threadbare robe that had been patched and re-patched until the original material could hardly be seen.

At last the old man died. *Signor* Corradi made preparations to bury his father in the tattered old robe, and to clean out the dark little room where the old one had spent his last years. Watching him was his own son, Antonio, nine years of age.

"Papa," said the little boy suddenly, "we must save the robe and keep the room as it is."

"Why?" asked the father.

"I'll need them for you," replied Antonio, "when *you* are old!"

---

*This folktale has been told for centuries throughout Europe and in the English-speaking world everywhere. It appears to have originated somewhere in the area of Trieste, during the Middle Ages.

CLASS DISTINCTION

Tesetto was having a heated argument with Zerbo the physician. As usual, the slower-thinking Zerbo could not keep pace with his glib-tongued opponent.

Finally, in the heat of the controversy, the physician blurted, "I refuse to argue with you another minute. After all, your father was only a bricklayer."

"No one could have told you that but your own father," retorted Tesetto without hesitation. "Your father carried the cement to mine!"

PRENATAL EDUCATION

For several years, Giuseppe had insisted that he was thirty years old. His friend. Tesetto, who had gone to school with him when they were boys, grew tired of hearing Giuseppe's repeated references to his falsified age.

"My friend," interrupted Tesetto when Giuseppe again mentioned his thirty years, "if I remember correctly, you were not even born when we studied logic together!"

BELATED GRIEF

Alfonso the thief, hurrying away from a house that he had just burglarized, was confronted by a policeman.

"Where are you taking that trunk?" asked the man of the law. "And what is in it?"

"A man just died in that house over there," replied Alfonso quickly, pointing to the residence, "and his family asked me to take his personal belongings to my house."

"But if that man just died," insisted the policeman, "why aren't they weeping and mourning his death?"

"Oh, I assure you, sir," said Alfonso, "you'll hear plenty weeping very shortly."

MISDIRECTED BLESSING

A farmer was bitterly complaining to the parish priest of his bad luck.

"If it doesn't rain soon," bemoaned the farmer, "I will not only lose my corn crop, but even the beasts will die."

"Oh, heaven preserve you!" exclaimed the priest.

Doctor's Golden Rule

A physician who had his married son under treatment, gave him no remedy, and prescribed nothing except that he was to observe a regular diet. His daughter-in-law complained.

"Why don't you treat him like other sick people?" she demanded.

"Daughter, we physicians know enough about medicine to abide by the Doctor's Golden Rule," he replied solemnly: "Never treat your loved ones or yourself as you would treat others."

Ever the Fool

A rich man of Florence had a son who possessed little sense, and, anxious to get him a wife, found a suitable girl. Her parents, willing to overlook the defects of the intended groom for the sake of his father's wealth, agreed to the marriage.

Immediately thereafter, when they were alone, the father cautioned his son to remain as silent as possible so that his near-idiocy might not be discovered. The son readily agreed.

But, at the wedding feast, it so happened that not only the foolish son remained silent, but everyone else held their tongues. At last a lady with more courage than the rest spoke up.

"Surely there must be a fool at this table," she said, "since no one ventures to speak a word."

The bridegroom immediately turned to his father.

"Papa," he said happily, "now that they have found me out, may I have permission to talk?"

Punishment for
a Naughty Horse

A simple farmer had a horse named Niccolo. One summer morning, as he was leading Niccolo along a country road, he grew tired from so much walking. Tying the horse to a small tree, he lay down in a shady place for a nap.

A short while later, two thieves appeared, and seeing the farmer sound asleep, and Niccolo unattended nearby, they decided to steal the horse.

"But the farmer is on his way to the same town where we will be," said one. "He will surely report the loss to the authorities."

"Just leave everything to me," said the first thief confidently. "I will take the horse's place, while you take the animal to town and sell him as soon as you can."

"What will you tell the farmer when he wakes up?"

"I have a plan," said the other.

Stealthily creeping up to Niccolo, they freed him. The first thief then slipped the bridle over his own head while the second led the horse away with a halter.

When the farmer awoke from his nap, his eye fell on his horse, or what used to be his horse. His amazement quickly turned to terror, however, when "Niccolo" spoke to him.

"Have no fear, my master," said the thief who was now wearing the bridle and was tied to the tree.

"Who are you?" cried the farmer.

"I was your horse for many years," replied the thief. "But before that I was a man, as I am now, once again. Because of my evil ways, the Lord condemned me to lead the life of a horse, as penance."

"Oh, how terrible. What awful things did you do that the Almighty would change you into an animal?"

"I was once a priest. But my heart was not pure. I drank to excess, I gambled, stole money from the poor, and lusted after women."

"No wonder the Lord condemned you," snapped the horrified farmer. "You deserved the punishment."

"Yes, but He has forgiven me for my sins," replied the thief. "Surely, you, a mere mortal, can find it in your heart to forgive me, too."

"Yes, I can do no less," agreed the farmer. "You are free. Go!"

The thief thanked him with appropriate humility and then scurried off to join his companion in town, where he had already sold the horse.

When the farmer arrived in town an hour or two later, he went to a stable to buy another horse. There, the stableman brought out his own stolen animal. No question about it—the poor thing had been changed back into a horse!

"Niccolo!" shouted the outraged farmer, recognizing him at once. "So you were up to your old tricks again! And so soon!"*

ONCE A FOOL, ALWAYS A FOOL

There was once a husband and wife who lived on a remote farm. Both were deaf mutes. They had three sons, but never having heard spoken language, they were unable to talk, although they could hear perfectly well. The time came when their parents died, and when they had been buried, the children held a conference, communicating with each other through hand signs.

---

*This story, almost identical in its variations, is found in the folk literature of early Americana, and the peoples of most Mediterranean countries. It is also well established in Jewish folklore.

"We must now go out into the world," said the eldest boy, "so that we can hear people talk, and learn to talk ourselves."

All three then set out on their travels until they came to a place where the road divided into three separate ways.

"Let each of us go in a different direction," said the eldest, "and as soon as we have learned anything, we will return here to the crossroads. Then we will seek service at some nobleman's palace."

The eldest took the middle road, and soon came to a churchyard where he saw two men talking together. As he passed close by, he heard one of them say, "Yes."

"Ah! I have learned enough. Now I can talk. It is time for me to go back to the crossroads."

When he returned, he found no one there, so he sat down to wait for his brothers.

The second brother went on till he came to two peasants carrying a bundle of hay. He listened to their idle talk, and heard one say, "It is true."

"I have learned enough," said the second son happily. "I will go back."

Before long, he arrived at the crossroads where he met his brother.

The youngest went on till evening, when he saw a shepherdess and her little sister as they were tending their flock. Distinctly, he heard the older girl say, "That's right."

"That is all the learning I need," he said. "I'm going back."

He came to the crossroads and found his brothers there.

"What have you learned?"

"I learned 'yes.'"

"And you?"

"That's right."

"And you?"

"It is true."

"Now that we know so many words," said the eldest brother, "we can go to the king's palace and enter his service."

As they proceeded along the road they came upon a man lying dead in the dust.

"Oh, look at this poor fellow!" exclaimed one, in his hand signs. "We must take his body to the city, and let the police know."

When they arrived at the nearby town, the police began their questioning.

"Who did it? Did you kill him?"

The eldest, who could say nothing else, answered, "Yes."

"It is true," said the second.

"Then you must be sent to prison until your trial," said a police officer.

"That's right," said the youngest.

The three were arrested and taken away to jail. Meanwhile, news of the crime passed swiftly from one townsman to another, and they soon gathered around the jail, crying, "They should be torn to pieces! They confessed to everything, the villains! So cold-blooded, too. All they would answer is 'yes,' 'it is true,' and 'that's right.'"

But, inside the prison, after long questioning, and receiving the same answers to whatever was asked, the police realized that the three prisoners were only fools. They were released, and told to leave the city at once.

So the brothers went home, resolving not to seek out the king's service until they had mastered the Italian language by learning at least three more words.

GIUCCA AND THE HOLLOW STATUE

One day Giucca's mother said to him, "I want this cloth sold, but if I let you take it to the market you will be up to your old tricks again."

"No, mother, you'll see; just tell me how much you want for it. I'll do it right this time."

"I want ten crowns, and be sure you sell it to a person who does not talk much. You know what happens when a buyer starts arguing with you. Soon he has the goods and you have no money."

Giucca took the cloth and went out to sell it. Before long he met a peasant.

"Giucca, is that cloth for sale?" asked the peasant. "How much do you want for it?"

"Ten crowns."

"That's too much."

"Well, now I can't let you have it at any price, because you talk too much. Sorry."

"What has my talking to do with buying the cloth?"

"There you go again. Mother was right. Goodbye!"

Giucca continued on his way. When he had gone a little further, he came to a statue.

"Oh, good woman," asked Giucca, "do you want to buy some cloth?" The statue, of course, said nothing.

"This is perfect. Mother told me to sell the cloth to someone who does not talk. I couldn't do better than this. Madam," Giucca said loudly, "I want ten crowns for it." He threw the cloth at the feet of the statue, and added, "I will return tomorrow for the money."

"Giucca," asked his mother when he arrived home, "did you sell the cloth?"

"Yes, I sold it," answered her son. "I will be paid tomorrow."

"But, tell me, did you give it to a trustworthy person?"

"Certainly. She never said a word, either—just as you wanted."

Let us leave Giucca, and go back to the statue. This statue was hollow, and served as a hiding place where a band of robbers hid their stolen money and jewels. That evening, they came with some more money and gems to put inside the statue.

"Look," exclaimed one of the thieves, "someone has left a fine cloth here! Let's keep it. They then busied themselves with hiding the money, and then left, carrying the cloth with them.

In the morning, Giucca arose early and prepared to leave and collect the money due him.

"Be sure you get the whole ten crowns," warned his mother.

"Of course," replied her son cheerfully. "She had a very honest face."

Giucca arrived at the statue a half hour later. "Good morning, madam," he said politely. "I've come for the money."

There was no reply.

"Now look here, madam. I see you've used the cloth. Either pay me for the goods or return it."

The statue said nothing.

Enraged, Giucca picked up a large stone and threw it at her. The force of the blow broke the statue, and all the stolen money and gems spilled out onto the ground. Giucca, delighted, gathered up the robbers' loot and went home.

"Look, mother, how much money and jewels I've brought you! I told you she was a good woman with an honest face. At first she wasn't going to pay me, but when I threw a rock at her she gave me all this."

"Giucca," shrieked the mother, "you hit a woman with a rock and made her give you this fortune? Who is this woman?"

"You know her—the one who has been standing upright at the edge of town in the little park. She's been standing there for years."

"Oh, you fool! You fool! Do you realize what you have done? Dear me, with all this money I had better find you a wife to look after you. Some day I'll be gone, and you are simply too foolish to be entrusted with this vast fortune."

"But, mother, you know very well, from past experience, that no decent girl would marry a fool like me."

"The situation has now changed," replied the mother reassuringly. "A fool without money can never find a truly worthy wife. But a fool with a fat purse can have his choice of the finest women in all of Italy."

THE HERMIT AND THE THIEVES

A long, long time ago, there was a hermit, a poor sort of priest, who lived alone, with no company but his pig, with whom he used to eat at the same table as a kind of penance for his sins. In addition to his pig, he also owned a box of money which he had collected in small sums given to him as charity over the years. The box of money, which now amounted to a large sum, was kept hidden under his bed.

It happened that there were two evil men, both of them robbers, who heard of the box, and made up their minds to steal it. After much planning, they contrived a scheme to deceive the poor old hermit. One night, they went to his house and quietly climbed upon the roof. From there, they stealthily let down a strong rope to which they had tied a large basket. When the basket reached the windowsill, near where the hermit was sleeping, both of them sang—

> "Arise, arise, O hermit,
> And come up in the basket, O;
> The saints in glory ask it, O,
>   Waiting in Paradise!"

The poor hermit, hearing the call, was convinced that the angels had descended from Heaven to bring him his reward. He jumped from his bed and opened the window. There, before his very eyes, was the basket! Needless to say, the pious man's joy was great in expectation of journeying in it all the way up to heaven. He crossed himself devoutly and leaped in, murmuring—

> "Lord, Lord! I am not so good
> That I should get into this basket of wood."*

Before he could even utter a word of apology to the Creator for his poor poetry, the robbers yanked him upward until he was halfway to the roof. They fastened the rope around the chimney, climbed down on the other side of the house, entered his room, stole the box of money and, still unseen, made their escape.

Meanwhile, the hermit hung there in mid-air, waiting and wondering why he had stopped rising Heavenward, and praying with tightly shut eyes. But at last he grew impatient. Hearing nothing more of the mysterious voices, he wriggled about so much that the rope broke, and down he came to the ground, not without several bruises.

But what was his indignation, upon dragging himself to his room, to find that his money box had vanished! Now he was left with only his pig. However, he accepted his loss philosophically, muttered *"Pazienza!"*** and prayed again, but a little more earnestly.

Some distance away, in their hideout, the two robbers began to think about what fools they had been to leave the pig, which they could easily

---

*The original is a ludicrous mixture of Latin and Italian which, in itself, was intended to amuse.

**Patience.

have sold for a good price at the fair. After a few long drinks of wine, they decided to try the same trick again, and then take possession of the pig. Once more they climbed to the roof and sang the same "Heavenly" song: "Arise, O hermit," and so forth and so on.

But this time the hermit was not to be taken in, even though he still believed them to be angels. Poking his head through the open window, he lifted his face toward the sky and answered the robbers with a song of his own—

> "Go back, you blessed angels,
> And let the good saints know
> That once they've put one over me,
> A second time's no go!"[1]

THE OLD LADY
AND THE DEVIL[2]

A certain aged lady, *Signora* Vecchia[3] by name, was seized with a sudden desire to eat some figs. She went into her garden, intending to knock down a few with a long pole. But, finding herself unable to do this, she started to climb the tree despite her infirmities, not even bothering to remove her slippers.

As she was scrambling up to the lowest of the large branches, the devil, in human form, happened to pass by.

"My good woman," he said to her, thinking she might fall, "If you must climb a tree to gather figs at your age, you should at least remove your slippers; otherwise you will surely fall and break your bones."

"My dear sir," snapped *Signora* Vecchia angrily, "it is none of your affair whether I climb the tree with slippers or without them. Do me the big favor of going about your own business, or to perdition, for all I care!

The old lady proceeded with her climbing, but just as she was about to seize the branch that was most heavily laden with figs, one of her slippers came off and she fell to the ground. Lying there, enraged, she screeched at the top of her brittle voice until her family came running to see what was the matter.

---

[1]The age of this folktale is unknown, but believed to stem from the eleventh or twelfth centuries. It appears to be among the earliest enunciations of the popular phrase, "Fool me once and it's *your* fault: fool me twice and it's *my* fault."

[2]In medieval times, this ancient tale was always introduced with the adage, in Latin, "The most perverse creature in the world is an obstinate old woman." It is still quoted as an old Italian proverb.

[3]A play on words, *vecchia* meaning "Old crone" in Italian.

"The devil did it!" she screamed. "He chased me up into the tree and tried to touch my breasts!"

The devil, who was not far off, heard the statement. His face darkened in anger at the falsehood, and he strode back to the scene of the accident.

"Madam," he said in a low, ominous voice, "I warned you, and asked you not to climb the tree in slippers, and in return you gave me a very rude answer. And now, instead of saying, 'If I had listened to that wayfarer I would not have fallen,' you say, 'The devil tried to touch my breasts.' Well, let me enlighten you, madam. It so happens that I *am* the devil, but you were only half right. I did not touch your breasts. But since you are so fond of figs, I touch them now, so that you may carry your figs with you for as long as you live."

The devil then pronounced the terrible words, "Shrivel and shrink! Shrink and shrivel!" He touched the old crone on each side of her chest and vanished in a wisp of smoke.

And that is why all Italian *vecchie*, no matter how abundantly endowed in their youth, now end their days with fig-size *mammelle*.*

ROMOLO'S UNSAINTLY LAWYER

Romolo, a man of Celento, journeyed to Naples to attend to a lawsuit. There, in order to be near the *Vicaria*,** he rented a house close to the Convent of San Giovanni a Carbonara. Among the several portraits in this house, he found an old picture hanging on the wall, all black and grimed with smoke. Romolo, a pious man, was sure that it represented some saint, and he beseeched its kind favor, praying fervently that he might be preserved from every misfortune, find a good lawyer, and win his case.

But the first time he said his prayers before the picture, he was attacked and beaten by thieves as he was returning home that night. The next day he fell down the stairs and bruised himself all over; and on the third he was arrested and imprisoned for a crime which had been committed near his house.

Upon his release from prison, he once more addressed his prayers to the unknown image for a good lawyer. But this petition, too, was granted the wrong way. He fell into the clutches of a lawyer who was the greatest scoundrel and blunderer that could be imagined. The poor man of Celento, quite broken down by his troubles, redoubled his prayers to the

---

*Breasts.

**The prison and court of justice.

smoky picture, hoping that at least he would win his lawsuit. But the court ruled against him, and Romolo returned home in a fury.

"Now," he snarled, "I want to see what that picture is, which has gained me so many benefits from Heaven and worked so many miracles in my behalf!"

He tore the picture from the wall, carefully cleaned it, and then stood back in horror. There before him was the picture of an attorney in his robes.

"A lawyer!" he howled, beside himself with rage. "A fine saint I chose as my protector! O, thou accursed race! No other could have worked such miracles!" Romolo's voice rose to an almost incoherent shriek. "May the bird of paradise fly up your *culo!* May your sex life be as good as your miracles!"

He raised his fist to strike the picture, but suddenly stayed his hand. "No," he said. "A man should never hit a lawyer in anger. It is better to wait until one is calm and more accurate!"

HOWL OF THE OWL

A peasant of Chiaramonte,[1] returning home by moonlight on his donkey, with two baskets of fresh-plucked grapes, passed by a cypress tree on which an owl was roosting. The owl began to hoot in so piteous a manner that it seemed he would moan out his very heart. Poor Vito (every Chiaramonte man is called Vito) was a fool, but he had a kind heart. He stopped, saddened by the pathetic sound.

"Are you hungry, old owl?" he called out, overcome by compassion. "Would you like a nice bunch of grapes?"

"*Cciu,*"[2] hooted the owl once again.

"What? Is one bunch not enough? Do you want two?"

"*Cciu.*"

"Oh, you poor creature! How hungry you must be. Do you want two bunches—perhaps three?"

"*Cciu.*"

"What's that you say? *Maledizione!*[3]—is there no satisfying you? No doubt you would like all of my two baskets!"

---

[1] A town in the south of Sicily.

[2] This (pronounced *chew* in English) is the local rendering of the owl's *tu-whoo*, and also the Sicilian and Calabrian dialectical form of *piu*, meaning *more*. The same joke was told, in a different part of Sicily, where an old church was haunted by owls. A countryman, taking their lamentable cries for those of souls in Purgatory, asked how many Masses were required to set them free, and got the answer, "*More*" to every number he suggested. This variant and the above version are probably more than a thousand years old.

[3] "Dammit all!"

"Cciu!"

The peasant's face turned red; then it turned blue; then a ghastly white; and then back to red again.

"Mannaggia,* what a greedy *bastardo* you are!" he yelled in high anger. "Go to hell! You'll get more there than you expected!"

"Cciu!" replied the owl mournfully.

---

*An expression of angry annoyance. Also used in the shortened form, *mannagg'*.

8

The Italians Said It First

INTRODUCTION

A great number of familiar sayings have become so much a part of the English language that, upon hearing or even thinking of an oft-used expression, we almost automatically attribute it to the Bible, or to Shakespeare, or perhaps to an American innovator such as Benjamin Franklin—if we think of it at all. But a surprisingly large number of quotations used in our daily conversation originated in Italy, some as long ago as five hundred years before the birth of Christ.

The selections offered in the following pages do not presume to be exhaustive: no writer would dare such an impertinence. The renderings are representative of their times. Part One of this chapter offers the wisdom of ancient Rome, uttered by such titans as Cicero, Caesar, Virgil, Ovid, Seneca, Pliny the Elder and Pliny the Younger, Marcus Antonius, and others of equal stature. Not everything they said was witty; some of their brief statements were quite profound. Credit, therefore, is finally given where credit is due, and many readers may be astonished to learn that the familiar sayings they have been using and hearing throughout their lives emanated from the statesmen and poets of the Roman Empire at the height of its glory.

Quotable Notables, comprising Part Two of this chapter, spans a seven hundred-year period, beginning with Dante Alighieri, the magnificent pre-Renaissance poet, and ending with today's eminently likable Dean Martin. Few of the quotations originally voiced by the early sages are witty, but all are thought-provoking; and once again we are reminded that they were first uttered by Italians. It will be noticed that as the quotations approach modern times they become progressively funnier. Perhaps the appeal lies in the difference between the portrayals of conscious wit and unconscious humor. Dean Martin, for example, acknowledges that Frank Sinatra, when he was unmarried, played around with girls. "What did you expect him to do?" demands Martin, "play with knives and maybe cut himself?"

Compare that gem of conscious wit with the unconscious humor of little Yolanda Luisi, pupil at Saint John's Catholic School in New York. "Yolanda," asked the Sister, "do you say your prayers before you eat?" Yolanda shook her head. "No, Sister, we don't have to. My mother is a good cook!"

Most of the sayings and comments are memorable because of the profundity in their message, but those that have been included for their entertainment value reveal the exquisite Italian sense of humor as it is seldom presented in the American press or on television.

Part Three of this chapter is devoted to Italian proverbs. The proverb is a minor expression of folklore, but used in contemporary life to a greater extent than any other of the folk arts. Originally the proverb was a means of preserving a people's experiences, passing them along in the oral tradition, from one generation to the next. They were confined to the material aspects of life. Gradually, over the ages, the proverb changed from a materialistic expression to a philosophical one; from attempts to understand the unknown and the mystifying, to explanations of reality. Some of the proverbs may evoke laughter, but all share a common characteristic: they seek to enlighten, to educate, to inform. Frequently the message is indirectly stated, but the underlying idea remains clear: to help ease such problems as how to live and behave.

The proverbs in Part Three have been classified into 18 categories. All but the last four are devoted to those that are known to have existed from the days of ancient Rome to, and including, the period known as the Renaissance. The latter four sections comprise those sayings that appear to have been created as recently as the nineteenth century. Many of the newer ones are quite funny, but, on reflection, they will be found to possess as much wisdom as their predecessors. Italian philosophy, after all, has not changed too radically in the last thousand years.

—H.D.S

PART ONE

Wit and Wisdom of Ancient Rome

PLAUTUS (Titus Maccius
Plautus, 254-184 B.C.)

No one can be so welcome a guest that he will not annoy his host after three days.

Miles Gloriosus (205 B.C.)

He whom the gods favor dies in youth.

Bacchides, Act IV, Scene 7, Line 18

Not by years but by disposition is wisdom acquired.

Trinummus, Act II, Scene 2, Line 88

In the one hand he is carrying a stone, while he shows the bread in the other.

Aulularia, Act II, Scene 3, Line 18

There are occasions when it is undoubtedly better to incur loss than to make gain.

Captivi, Act 2, Line 77

Patience is the best remedy for every trouble.

Rudens, Act 2, Line 71

Consider the little mouse, how sagacious it is to never entrust its life to only one hole.

Truculentus, Act IV, Scene 4, Line 15

Nothing is more friendly to a man than a friend in need.

Epidicus, Act III, Scene 3, Line 44

To blow and swallow at the same time is not easy.

Mostellaria, Act III, Scene 2, Line 104

QUINTUS ENNIUS
(239-169 B.C.)

No sooner said than done—so acts your man of worth.

Annals, Book 9 (Quoted by Priscianus)

I never indulge in poetics
Unless I am down with rheumatics.

> *Fragment of a satire* (Quoted by Priscianus)

The ape, vilest of beasts; how like us!

> *De Natura Deorum*, Book I, Chap. 35
> (Quoted by Cicero)

No one regards what is before his feet; we all gaze at the stars.

> *Iphigenia* (Quoted by Cicero in *De*
> *Divinatione*, Book II, Chap. 13)

Whom they fear they hate.

> *Thyestes* (Quoted by Cicero in *De*
> *Officiis*, II, Book II, Chap. 7)

CAECILIUS STATIUS
(220-168 B.C.)

Let him draw out his old age to dotage, drop by drop.

> *Hymnis* (Quoted by Festus)

He plants trees to benefit another generation.

> *Synephebi* (Quoted by Cicero in *De*
> *Senectute*, Book VII)

POLYBIUS
(second century, B.C.)

Peace, with justice and honor, is the fairest and most profitable of possessions, but with disgrace and shameful cowardice it is the most infamous and harmful of all.

> *Histories*, Book IV, Chap. 31

Those who know how to win are more numerous than those who know how to make proper use of their victories.

> *Ibid.*, Book X, Chap. 31

There is no witness so dreadful, no accuser so terrible as the conscience that dwells in the heart of every man.

> *Ibid.*, Book XVIII, Chap. 43

TERENCE (Publius Terentius
Afer, 185-159 B.C.)

In fine, nothing is said now that has not been said before
Eunuchus, The Prologue, Line 41

There is a true proverb which is commonly quoted: all had rather it were well for themselves than for another.
Andria, Act II

The quarrels of lovers are the renewal of love.
Ibid., Act III, Scene 3, Line 23

Immortal gods! how much does one man excel another! What a difference between a wise person and a fool!
Ibid., Act II, Scene 2, Line 1

I have everything, yet have nothing; and although I possess nothing, still of nothing am I in want.
Ibid., Act II, Scene 2, Line 1

I did not care one straw.
Ibid., Act III, Scene 1, Line 21

I know the disposition of women: when you will, they won't; when you won't, they set their hearts upon you of their own inclination.
Ibid., Line 42

I took to my heels as fast as I could.
Ibid., Act 5, Scene 2, Line 5

I only wish that I may see your head stroked down with a slipper.*
Ibid., Scene 8, Line 1

I am a man, and nothing that concerns a man do I deem a matter of indifference to me.
Heauton Timorumenos, Act I, Scene I,
Line 25 (Quoted by Cicero in De
Officiis, Book I, Chap. 30)

Rigorous law is often rigorous injustice.
Ibid., Scene 4, Line 48

---

*According to Lucian, there was a story that Omphale used to beat Hercules with her slipper or sandal.

There is nothing so easy but that it becomes difficult when you do it with reluctance.

Ibid., Scene 5, Line 1

Fortune helps the brave.*

Phormio, Act I, Scene 4, Line 26

Marcus Tullius Cicero
(106-43 B.C.)

If you aspire to the highest place it is no disgrace to stop at the second, or even the third.

De Oratore, 1

. . . the freer utterances of poetic license.

Ibid., 38

The mind of each man is the man himself.

Ibid. 78

He was never less at leisure than when at leisure.

De Officiis (Quoted by Scipio Africanus)

What a time! What a civilization! *(O tempora! O mores!)*

Catiline, 1

[For] how many things, which for our own sake we should never do, do we perform for the sake of our friends?

*De Amicitia,*** Book XVI

Nothing can be more disgraceful than to be at war with him with whom you have lived on terms of friendship.

Ibid., Book XXI

He removes the greatest ornament of friendship, who takes away from it respect.

Ibid., Book XXII

---

*Pliny the Younger stated (Book 6, Letter 16) that Pliny the Elder said this during the eruption of Vesuvius: "Fortune favors the brave."

**Translated by Cyrus R. Edmonds.

There is no greater bane to friendship than adulation, fawning, and flattery.

Ibid., Book XXV

Laws are dumb in the midst of arms *(Silent enim leges inter arma).*
Pro Milone, Book IV, Chap. 32

Who stood to gain?

Ibid., Book XII, Chap. 32

The good of the people is the chief law *(Salus populi suprema est lex).*
De Legibus, Book III, Chap. 3

Crimes are not to be measured by the issue of events, but from the bad intentions of men.

Paradox, Book III

There is no place more delightful than home.
Epistolae, Book IV, Chap. 8

While the sick man has life there is hope.
Ibid., Book IX, Chap. 10

Old age is by nature rather talkative.
De Senectute, Book XVI

Intelligence, and reflection, and judgment, reside in old men, and if there had been none of them, no states could exist at all.
Ibid., Book XIX

The short period of life is long enough for living honorably.
Ibid.

Old age is the consummation of life, just as of a play.
Ibid.

JULIUS CAESAR (Caius Julius
Caesar, 102?-44 B.C.)

All Gaul is divided into three parts.

Men freely believe that which they desire.

I wished my wife to be not so much as suspected.*

I came, I saw, I conquered (*Veni, vidi, vici*).

LUCRETIUS (Titus Lucretius Carus, 95-55? B.C.)

Continual dropping wears away a stone.

De Rerum Natura, Book I, Chap. 314

Pleasant it is, when the winds disturb the surface of the vast sea, to watch from land another's mighty struggle.

Ibid., Book I, Chap. II

Why do you not withdraw from life like some sated banqueter and, with calm spirit, seek untroubled rest?

Ibid.

What is food to one man may be fierce poison to another.

Ibid., IV, 637, Chap. 637

In the midst of the fountain of wit there arises something bitter, which stings in the very flowers.

Ibid., IV, Chap. 1133

VIRGIL (Publius Vergilius Maro, 70-19 B.C.)

Love conquers all (*Omnia amor vincit*).

Eclogues, X, Line 69

Be favorable to bold beginnings.**

Georgics, I, Line 40

I fear Greeks, even when bringing gifts.

Aeneid, Book II, Line 49

I shudder at the word.

Ibid., Line 204

---

*Caesar's wife should be above suspicion.

**Virgil's line appears on the reverse side of the Great Seal of the United States, but adapted to read: He smiles on our beginnings (*Annuit coeptis*). Virgil wrote it, *Audacibus annue coeptis*.

A fickle and changeful thing is woman ever *(Varium et mutabile semper femina).*

Ibid., Book IV, Line 569

Each of us suffers his own hell.

Ibid., Book VI, Line 743

HORACE (Quintas Horatius Flaccus, 65-8 B.C.)

Pale Death, with impartial step, knocks at the poor man's cottage and at the palaces of kings.

Odes, Book I, i, Chap. III, Line 13

The brief span of life forbids us to cherish long hope.

Ibid., Book IV, Line 15

Seize now and here the hour that is, nor trust some later day. *(Carpe diem, quam minimum credula postero).*

Ibid., Book I, xi, last line

Thrice happy they, and more, whom an unbroken bond unites and whom love, unsevered by bitter quarrels, shall not release until the last day of all.

Ibid., xiii, Line 20

O fairer daughter of a fair mother *(O matre pulchra filia pulchrior).*

Ibid., xvi, Line 1

What cannot be removed becomes lighter through patience.

Ibid., xxiv, Line 19

Now's the time for drinking! *(Nunc est bibendum!)*

Ibid., xxxvii, Line 1

Whoever cultivates the golden mean avoids both the poverty of a hovel and the envy of a palace.

Ibid., Book II, x, Line 5

Force without wisdom falls of its own weight.

Ibid., Book III, iv, Line 65

I would not have borne this in my flaming youth while Plancus was consul.

Odes, xiv, Line 27

Summer treads
On heels of Spring.

Ibid., Book IV, vii, Line 9

We are dust and a shadow.

Ibid., Line 16

We rarely find a man who can say he has lived happy, and, content with life, he can retire from the world like a satisfied guest.

*Satires,** Book I, i, Line 117

This is a fault common to all singers: that among their friends they never are inclined to sing when they are asked: unasked they never desist.

Ibid., Book III, Line 1

Ridicule often decides matters of importance more effectually, and in a better manner, than severity.

Ibid., Book X, Line 14

In peace, as a wise man, he should make preparation for war.

Ibid., Line 110

At Rome, you long for the country; when you are in the country, fickle you, you extol the absent city to the skies.

Ibid., Book II, vii, Line 28

Get place and wealth, if possible with grace;
If not, by any means get wealth and place.****

Epistles, Book I, 1, Line 53

He has half the deed done, who has made a beginning.

Ibid., 11, Line 40

In the midst of hope and care, in the midst of fears and disquietudes, think every day that shines upon you is the last. Thus the hour, which shall not be expected, will come upon you as an agreeable addition.

Ibid., iv, Line 12

---

*Translated by Christopher Smart (1722-70).

**Translated by Alexander Pope (1688-1744).

You may drive out nature with a fork, yet still will she return.

Ibid., x, Line 24

Whatever prosperous hour Providence bestows upon you, receive it with a thankful hand; and defer not the enjoyment of the comforts of life.

Ibid., xi, Line 22

They change their climate, not their disposition, who run beyond the sea.

Ibid., Line 27

A word once sent abroad flies irrevocably.

Ibid., xvii

For nature forms, and softens us within,
And writes our fortune's changes in our face.

Ars Poetica,* Line 130

The lab'ring mountain scarce brings forth a mouse (*Parturient montes nascetur ridiculus mus*).

Ibid., Line 168

Old men are only walking hospitals.

Ibid., Line 202

[But] words once spoken can never be recalled.

Ibid., Line 438

PROPERTIUS* (Sextus Propertius, 50? B.C.-2? A.D.)

Never change when love has found its home.

Elegy, Book I, i, Line 36

Scandal has ever been the doom of beauty.

Ibid., Book II, 32, Line 26

---

*Translated (1680) by Wentworth Dillon, Earl of Roscommon (1633?-85).

Ovid (Publius Ovidius Naso, 43 B.C.-18 A.D.)

They come to see; they come that they themselves may be seen (*Spectatum veniunt, veniunt spectentur ut ipsae*).

The Art of Love, Book I, Line 99

It is expedient that there be gods, and, as it's expedient, let us believe there are.

Ibid., Line 637

To be loved, be lovable.

Ibid., Book II, Line 107

You will go most safely in the middle.

Ibid., Line 137

I see and approve better things, but follow worse.

Ibid., Book VII, Line 20

While fortune smiles you'll have a host of friends,
But they'll desert you when the storm descends.

Tristia, Book I, Chap. 9, Line 5

It is annoying to be honest to no purpose.

Epistolae ex Ponto, Book II, Chap. 3, Line 14

A faithful study of the liberal arts humanizes character and permits it not to be cruel.

Ibid., Chap. 9, Line 47

Grateful must we be that the heart may go wherever it will.

Ibid., Book III, Chap. 5, Line 48

How little you know about the age you live in if you fancy that honey is sweeter than cash in hand.

Fasti, Book I, Line 191

Publilius Syrus* (42? B.C.-?)

We are all equal in the presence of death.

Maxim 1

---

*Commonly called Publius, but spelled Publilius by Pliny in his *Natural History*, Chapter 35, section 109.

To do two things at once is to do neither.

Maxim 7

We are interested in others when they are interested in us.

Maxim 16

Everyone excels in something in which another fails.

Maxim 17

A good reputation is more valuable than money.

Maxim 108

Many receive advice; few profit by it.

Maxim 149

While we stop to think, we often lose our opportunity.

Maxim 185

Even a single hair casts its shadow.

Maxim 228

Crime is honest for a good cause *(Honesta turpitudo est pro causa bona).*

Maxim 244

Hammer your iron when it is glowing hot.

Maxim 262

Fortune is like glass—the brighter the glitter, the more easily broken.

Maxim 280

There are some remedies worse than the disease.

Maxim 301

It is easy for men to talk one thing and think another.

Maxim 322

Anyone can hold the helm when the sea is calm.

Maxim 358

The judge is condemned when the criminal is absolved *(Judex damnatur cum nocens absolvitur).*

Maxim 407

Practice is the best of all instructors.

Maxim 439

It is a bad plan that admits of no modification.

Maxim 469

It is better to have a little than nothing.

Maxim 484

The fear of death is more to be dreaded than death itself.

Maxim 511

A rolling stone gathers no moss.

Maxim 524

Never promise more than you can perform.

Maxim 528

It is only the ignorant who despise education.

Maxim 557

Not every question deserves an answer.

Maxim 581

You cannot put the same shoe on every foot.

Maxim 596

Go to the pear tree for pears, not to an elm.

Maxim 674

It is a very hard undertaking to try to please
everybody.

Maxim 675

Pardon one offense and you encourage the commission of many.

Maxim 750

He gets through too late who goes too fast.

Maxim 767

No one knows what he can do till he tries.

Maxim 786

It matters not how long you live, but how well.

Maxim 829

It is better to learn late than never.

Maxim 864

Better be ignorant of a matter than half know it.

Maxim 865

Better use medicines at the outset than at the last
moment.

Maxim 866

Prosperity makes friends, adversity tries them.

Maxim 872

Let a fool hold his tongue and he will pass for a sage.

Maxim 914

It is a consolation to the wretched to have companions in misery.

Maxim 995

I have often regretted my speech, never my silence.

Maxim 1070

Speech is a mirror of the soul: as a man speaks, so
is he.

Maxim 1073

SENECA (Lucius Annaeus
Seneca, 3? B.C.-65 A.D.)

What fools these mortals be *(Tanta stultitia mortalium est)*.

Epistles 1, 3

Love of bustle is not industry.

Ibid., 3, 5

Men do not care how nobly they live, but only how long, although it is within the reach of every man to live nobly, but within no man's power to live long.

Ibid., 22, 17

Man is a reasoning animal.

Ibid., 41, 8

It is quality rather than quantity that matters.

Ibid., 45, 1

All art is but an imitation of nature.

Ibid., 65, 3

It is a rough road that leads to the heights of greatness.

Ibid., 84, 13

It is better to know useless things than to know nothing.

Ibid., 88, 45

We are mad, not only individually, but nationally. We check manslaughter and isolated murders; but what of war and the much-vaunted crime of slaughtering whole peoples?

Ibid., 95, 30

I do not distinguish by the eye, but by the mind, which is the proper judge of the man.

Moral Essays, On the Happy Life, 2, 2

Whom they have injured, they also hate.

Ibid., On Anger, 2, 33

There is no great genius without some touch of madness.*

Ibid., On Tranquility of the Mind, 17, 10

---

*Seneca, in his *Epistles*, states that this saying was enunciated by Aristotle. It was also quoted by Plato.

You roll my log and I'll roll yours.

Apocolocyntosis, Chap. 9

Successful and fortunate crime is called virtue.

Hercules Furens, 1, 1, 84

Light griefs are loquacious, but the great are dumb.

Hippolytus, II, 3, 607

PHAEDRUS (8? A.D.-?)

It is unwise to be heedless ourselves while we are giving advice to others.

Book I, Fable 9

Whoever has even once become notorious by base fraud, even if he speaks the truth, gains no belief.

Ibid., Fable 10

No one returns with good-will to the place which has done him a mischief.

Ibid., Fable 18

Everyone is bound to bear patiently the results of his own example.

Ibid., Fable 26

Things are not always what they seem (*Non semper ea sunt quae videntur*).

Book IV, Fable 2

"I knew that before you were born." Let him who would instruct a wiser man consider this as said to himself.

Book V, Fable 9

PLINY THE ELDER (Caius Plinius Secundus, 23-79 A.D.)

It is ridiculous to suppose that the Great Head of Things, whatever it be, pays any regard to human affairs.

Natural History, Book II, Section 20

It is far from easy to determine whether Nature has proved to be a kind parent or a merciless stepmother.

Ibid., Book VII, Section 1

Man alone at the very moment of his birth, cast naked upon the naked earth, does Nature abandon to cries and lamentations.[1]

Ibid., Section 2

To laugh, if but for an instant only, has never been granted to man before the fortieth day from his birth, and then it is looked upon as a miracle of precocity.[2]

Ibid.

With man, most of his misfortunes are occasioned by man.

Ibid., Section 5

The human features and countenance, although composed of but ten parts or little more, are so fashioned that among so many thousands of men there are no two in existence who cannot be distinguished from one another.

Ibid., Book VII, Section 8

When a building is about to fall down, all the mice desert it.[3]

Ibid., Book VIII, Section 103

The agricultural population produces the bravest men, the most valiant soldiers, and a class of citizens the least given to evil design.[4]

Ibid., Section 26

It was a custom with Apelles [the artist] to exhibit his completed pictures to the view of the passersby in his studio, while he, himself, was concealed behind the picture where he would listen to criticisms.

Under these circumstances, they say, he heard himself censured by a shoemaker for having painted the subject's shoes with one latchet too few.

The next day, the shoemaker, quite proud of seeing the former error corrected, thanks to his advice, began to criticize the leg.

This was too much for Appelles. Full of indignation, he popped his head out and reminded him that a shoemaker should give no opinion

---

[1] It was the custom among the ancients to place the newborn infant upon the ground immediately after birth.

[2] The term of forty days is mentioned by Aristotle in his *Natural History*.

[3] Also mentioned by Cicero in his letters to Atticus. Compare the modern proverb, "Rats desert a sinking ship."

[4] Pliny attributed this saying to Cato.

beyond the shoes—a piece of advice which has passed into a proverbial saying.*

> *Ibid.*, Book XXXV, Section 84

PETRONIUS (Petronius Arbiter, ?-66 A.D.)

Beware of the dog.

> *Satyricon*, Section 29

Without why or wherefor.

> *Ibid.*, Section 37

A man who is always ready to believe what is told to him will never do well.

> *Ibid.*, 43

One good turn deserves another.

> *Ibid.*, Section 45

Every man has his faults.

> *Ibid.*

Not worth his salt.

> *Ibid.*, Section 57

My heart was in my mouth.

> *Ibid.*, Section 62

Beauty and wisdom are rarely conjoined.

> *Ibid.*, Section 118

QUINTILIAN (Marcus Fabian Quintilianus, 35?-95? A.D.)

We give to necessity the praise of virtue.

> *Institutiones Oratoriae*, Book I, Chap. 8

A liar should have a good memory.

> *Ibid.*, Book IV, Chap. 2

Vain hopes are often like the dreams of those who wake.

> *Ibid.*, Book VI, Chap. 2

Ne supra crepidam sutor judicrat (Let not a shoemaker judge above his shoe; or, Let the cobbler stick to his last).

Those who wish to appear wise among fools, among the wise seem foolish.

Ibid., Book X, Chap. 7

JUVENAL (Decimus Junius Juvenalis, 47-138 A.D.)

Honesty is praised and starved.

Satire I, Line 47

He pardons the ravens and censures the doves.

Satire II, Line 63

No man ever became extremely wicked all at once (*Nemo repente fit turpissimus*).

Ibid., Line 83

Unhappy poverty has no worse trait than that it makes men ridiculous (*Nil habet infelix paupertas durius in se quam quod ridiculos homines facit*).

Satire III, Line 152

We all live in a state of ambitious poverty.

Ibid., Line 182

But who would guard the guards themselves?

Satire VI, Line 347

Two things only the people anxiously desire—bread and circuses (*Duas tantum res anxius optat*).

Satire X, Line 80

We should pray for a sane mind in a sound body (*Orandum est ut sit mens sana in corpore sano*).

Ibid., Line 356

TACITUS (Cornelius Tacitus, 54-119 A.D.)

. . . the desire of glory clings even to the best men longer than any other passion.

History, Book IV, Chap. 6

Whatever is unknown is magnified.

Agricola, Section 30

To plunder, to slaughter, to steal, these things they misname empire; and where they make a desert, they call it peace.

Ibid.

It is characteristic of human nature to hate the man whom you have wronged.

Ibid., Section 42

PLINY THE YOUNGER (Caius Plinius Caecilius Secundus, 62?-113? A.D.)

. . . the biggest rascal that walks upon two legs.

Letters, Book I, Letter 5

There is nothing to write about, you say. Well, then, write and let me know just this—that there is nothing to write about; or tell me in the good old style, if you are well, if you *are* well. That's right! I am quite well.

Ibid., Letter 11

An object in possession seldom retains the same charm that it had in pursuit.

Ibid., Book II, Letter 15

He [Pliny the Elder] used to say that no book was so bad but some good might be gotten out of it."

Ibid., Book III, Letter 9

. . . that indolent but agreeable condition of doing nothing.

Ibid., Book VIII, Letter 9

His only fault is that he has no fault.

Ibid., Book IX, Letter 26

MARCUS AURELIUS ANTONINUS (121-180 A.D.)

This being of mine, whatever it really is, consists of a little flesh, a little breath, and the part which governs.

———

Live every day of your life as though it were your last.

———

A man should *be* upright, not *kept* upright.

———

Never esteem anything of advantage that will make you break your word or lose your self-respect.

———

The universe is change; our life is what our thoughts make it.

———

Nothing can come out of nothing, any more than a thing can go back to nothing.

———

Whatever happens at all happens as it should.

———

How much time he gains who does not look to see what his neighbor says or does or thinks, but only at what he does himself, to make it just and holy.

———

Whatever is in any way beautiful has its source of beauty in itself, and is complete in itself; praise forms no part of it. So it is none the worse nor the better for being praised.

———

Life is a battle and a sojourning in a strange land.

———

Remember this: there is a proper dignity and proportion to be observed in the performance of every act of life.

———

All is ephemeral—fame and the famous as well.

———

Deem not life a thing of consequence, for look at the yawning void of the future, and at that other limitless space, the past.

———

The controlling Intelligence understands its own nature, and what it does, and how it works.

———

What is not good for the swarm is not good for the bee.

——

It is man's peculiar duty to love even those who wrong him.

——

Remember this—very little is needed to make a happy life.

——

Think not disdainfully of death, but look on it with favor; for even death is one of the things that Nature wills.

——

A wrongdoer is often a man that has left something undone, not always he that has done something.

Saint Jerome (Sophronius Eusebius Hieronymus, 347-420 a.d.)*

Avoid as you would the plague, a clergyman who is also a man of business.

——

A fat paunch never breeds fine thoughts.

——

It is not the fault of Christianity if a hypocrite falls into sin.

---

*Although he bore a Roman name and attained fame as a pagan scholar, Jerome later became a Father and Doctor of the Church.

PART TWO

Quotable Notables

Dante Alighieri (1265-1321)

If thou follow thy star, thou canst not fail of glorious haven.
Divine Comedy. Inferno,
Canto X, Line 34 (circa 1300)

He listens well who notes it.
Ibid., Canto XV, Line 99

Consider your origin; ye were not formed to live like brutes, but to follow virtue and knowledge.
Ibid., Canto XXVI, Line 119

O conscience, upright and stainless, how bitter a sting to thee is a little fault!
Ibid., Purgatorio, Canto III, Line 8

The Infinite Goodness has such wide arms that it takes whatever turns to it.
Ibid., Line 121

O human race, born to fly upward, wherefore at a little wind dost thou so fall!
Ibid., Canto XII, 95

To a greater force and to a better nature, ye, free, are subject; and that creates the mind in you which the heavens have not in their charge. Therefore, if the present world go astray, the cause is in you: in you it is to be sought.
Ibid., Canto XVI, Line 79

Love kindled by virtue always kindles another, provided that its flame appears outwardly.
Ibid., Canto XXII, Line 10

The greatest gift which God in His bounty bestowed in creating, and the most conformed to His own goodness, and that which He prizes the most, was the freedom of the will, with which creatures that have intelligence, they all and they alone, were and are endowed.
Ibid., Paradisio, Canto V, Line 19

Vanquishing me with the light of a smile, she said to me, "Turn thee, and listen, for not only in my eyes is Paradise."

Ibid., Canto XVIII, Line 3

PETRARCH (Francesco Petrarca, 1304-74)

The end of doubt is the beginning of repose.

———

Love is the crowning grace of humanity, the holiest rite of the soul, the golden link that binds us to duty and truth, the redeeming principle that chiefly reconciles the heart of life, and a prophetic of eternal good.

———

Five great enemies to peace inhabit with us: avarice, ambition, envy, anger, and pride. If those enemies were to be banished, we would infallibly enjoy perpetual peace.

———

Where you are is of no moment, but only what you are doing there. It is not the *place* that ennobles you, but *you* the place; and this only by doing that which is great and noble.

DONATELLO (Donato di Niccolo di Betto Bardi, 1386-1466)

I smiled at him, and he smiled at me.*

LEONARDO DA VINCI (1450-1519)

Whoever in discussion cites authority uses not intellect but memory.

Note-Books

No counsel is more trustworthy than that which is given upon ships that are in peril.

Ibid.

Intellectual passion drives out sensuality.

Ibid.

---

*For the anecdote behind this saying, see p. 56.

Let the street be as wide as the houses.

Ibid.

No member [of the human anatomy] needs so great a number of muscles as the tongue; this exceeds all the rest in the number of its movements.

Ibid.

It is of no small benefit on finding oneself in bed in the dark to go over again in the imagination the main outlines of the forms previously studied, or of other noteworthy things conceived by ingenious speculation.

Ibid.

As a well-spent day brings happy sleep, so life well-used brings happy death.

Ibid.

A bird is an instrument working according to mathematical law, which instrument it is within the capacity of man to reproduce with all its movements.

Ibid.

NICCOLO MACHIAVELLI
(1469-1527)

There is nothing more difficult to take in hand, more perilous to conduct, or more uncertain in its success, than to take the lead in the introduction of a new order of things.

The Prince, Chap. 6

The chief foundation of all states, new as well as old, are good laws and good arms. As there cannot be good laws where the state is not well-armed, it follows that where they are well-armed they have good laws.

Ibid., Chap. 12

A prince should have no other aim or thought, nor take up any other thing for his study, but war and its organization and discipline, for that is the only art that is necessary to one who commands.

Ibid., Chap. 14

Among other evils which being unarmed brings you, it causes you to be despised.

Ibid.

When neither their property nor their honor is touched, the majority of men live content.

Ibid., Chap. 19

There are three classes of intellects: one which comprehends by itself; another which appreciates what others comprehend; and a third which neither comprehends by itself nor by the showing of others. The first is the most excellent, the second is good, the third is useless.

Ibid., Chap. 22

Where the willingness is great, the difficulties cannot be great.

Ibid., Chap. 26

God is not willing to do everything, and thus take away our free will and that share of glory which belongs to us.

Ibid.

The prince must be a lion, but he must also know how to play the fox.

Ibid.

Ambition is so powerful a passion in the human breast, that however high we reach we are never satisfied.

Various writings

If the course of human affairs be considered, it will be seen that many things arise against which heaven does not always allow us to guard.

Ibid.

It is not titles that reflect honor on men, but men on their titles.

Ibid.

Who makes war his profession cannot be otherwise than vicious—war makes thieves, and peace brings them to the gallows.

Ibid.

Michelangelo Buonarroti
(1474-1564)

The more the marble wastes, the more the statue grows.

Sonnet

If it be true that any beautiful thing raises the pure and just desire of man from earth to God, the eternal fount of all, such I believe my love.

Ibid.

I live and love in God's peculiar light.

Ibid.

Francesco Guicciardini
(1483-1540)

He who imitates evil always goes beyond the example that is set; he who imitates what is good always falls short.

———

To rule self and subdue our passions is the more praiseworthy because so few know how to do it.

Lodovico Ariosto
(1474-1533)

Nature made him, then broke the mould (*Natura lo fece, e poi ruppe la stampa*).

Orlando Furioso, Canto X, Stanza 84

Torquato Tasso
(1544-1595)

How much better it is that he should speak ill of me and to all the world, than all the world speak ill of me to him.

———

The guard of virtue is labor, and ease her sleep.

Pietro Metastasio
(1696-1782)

Every noble acquisition is attended with its risks; he who fears to encounter the one must not expect to obtain the other.

———

He who despairs wants love and faith; for faith, hope, and love are three torches which blend their light together, nor does the one shine without the other.

———

If the internal griefs of every man could be read, written on his forehead, how many who now excite envy, would appear to be objects of pity?

Iolanda Riccobini
(1713-92)

Fortune does not change men; it only unmasks them.

Cesare Bonensano Beccaria
(1735-94)

The ambitious man grasps at opinion as necessary to his designs; the vain man sues for it as testimony to his merit; the honest man demands it as his due; and most men consider it as necessary to their existence.

Johann Pestalozzi
(1746-1827)

There is no happiness for him who oppresses and persecutes; there can be no repose for him. For the sighs of the unfortunate cry for vengeance to Heaven.

———

Thinking leads man to knowledge. He may see and hear, and read and learn whatever he pleases; he will never know anything of it, except that which he has thought over, that which by thinking he has made the property of his own mind. Is it then saying too much if I say that man, by thinking only, becomes truly man? Take away thought from man's life, and what remains?

Vittorio Alfieri
(1749-1803)

Society prepares the crime; the criminal commits it.

———

Disgrace is not in the punishment, but in the crime.

———

Almost all my tragedies were sketched in my mind, either in the act of hearing music, or a few hours after.

———

Deep vengeance is the daughter of deep silence.

GIUSEPPE MAZZINI
(1805-72)

Nations, like individuals, live or die, but civilizations cannot perish.

———

Constancy is the complement of all other human virtues.

———

By the law of God, given them by humanity, all men are free, are brothers, and are equals.

———

Slumber not in the tents of your fathers. The world is advancing. Advance with it.

———

Music is the harmonious voice of creation; an echo of the invisible world; one note of the divine concord which the entire universe is destined one day to sound.

———

Pardon is the virtue of victory.

———

The moral law of the universe is progress. Every generation that passes idly over the earth without adding to that progress remains uninscribed upon the register of humanity, and the succeeding generation tramples its ashes to dust.

———

Men of great genius and large heart sow the seeds of a new degree of progress in the world, but they bear fruit only after many years.

———

The obscurist sayings of the truly great are often those which contain the germ of the profoundest and most useful truths.

———

Great revolutions are the work rather of principles than of bayonets, and are achieved first in the moral, and afterward in the material sphere.

Giovanni Ruffini
(1807-81)

If country life be healthful to the body, it is no less so to the mind.

———

Stories first heard at a mother's knee are never wholly forgotten—a little spring that never quite dries up in our journey through scorching years.

———

Rank and riches are chains of gold, but still chains.

Giuseppe Garibaldi
(1807-82)

It [poetry] is forged slowly and patiently, link by link, with sweat and blood and tears.

———

This [the Bible] is the cannon that will make Italy free.

Dante Gabriele Rosetti
(1828-82)

Was it friend or foe that spread these lies?
Nay, who but infants question in such wise.
'Twas one of my most intimate enemies.

Fragment (1881)

———

Look in my face: my name is Might-have-been;
I am also called No-more, Too-late, Farewell.

The House of Life

Christina Georgina Rosetti
(1830-94)

Does the road wind up-hill all the way? Yes, to the very end.

Up-Hill (1861), Stanza 1

———

My heart is like a singing bird.

A Birthday, Stanza 1

—

When I am dead, my dearest,
　Sing no sad songs for me;
Plant thou no roses at my head,
　Nor shady cypress tree.

Song (1862), Stanza 1

—

Better by far you should forget and smile,
Than that you should remember and be sad.

Ibid.

—

One day in the country
Is worth a month in town.

Summer

—

Silence more musical than any song.

Rest (1862)

CESARE LOMBROSO
(1836-1909)

Good sense travels on the well-worn paths; genius, never. And that is why the crowd, not altogether without reason, is so ready to treat great men as lunatics.

The Man of Genius, Preface

—

A patient one day presented himself to Abernethy; after careful examination the celebrated practitioner said, "You need amusement; go and hear Grimaldi; he will make you laugh, and that will be better for you than any drugs."

"My God," exclaimed the invalid, "I *am* Grimaldi!"*

Ibid., Part 1, Chap. 2

Kloptock was questioned regarding the meaning of a passage in his

---

*This anecdote also appears in Irish-American folk literature. See *The Lilt of the Irish op. cit.*

poem. He replied, "God and I both knew what it meant once; now God alone knows."

———

The appearance of a single great genius is more than equivalent to the birth of a hundred mediocrities.

———

"Lawsuit mania" . . . a continual craving to go to law against others, while considering themselves the injured party.

GABRIELE D'ANNUNZIO
(1863-1938)

It is not necessary to live, but to carve our names beyond that point, this is necessary.

RAFAEL SABATINI
(1875-1950)

Born with the gift of laughter and the sense that the world was mad. . . .*

Scaramouche, Chap. 1

FIORELLO H. LAGUARDIA
(1882-1948)

Ticker tape ain't spaghetti.

Speech to the United Nations, March 29, 1946

BENITO MUSSOLINI
(1883-1945)

Fortunately the Italian people are not yet accustomed to eating several times a day.

Written for *the Italian Encyclopedia*

---

*Inscribed over a door in the Hall of Graduate Studies, Yale University. The architect, John Donald Tuttle, in a letter to *The New Yorker* (December 8, 1943), explained that he could not bring himself to enthuse over the collegiate Gothic, "a type of architecture that has been designed expressly to enable yeomen to pour molten lead through slots on their enemies below. As a propitiary gift to my gods . . . and to make them forget by appealing to their senses of humor, I carved the inscription over the door."

We have buried the putrid corpse of liberty.

> *Speech*, Quoted by Maurice
> Parmelee, in *Fascism and the
> Liberal-Democratic State* (1934).

—

The Italian race is a race of sheep. Eighteen years are not enough to change them. It takes a hundred and eighty, and maybe a hundred and eighty centuries.

> Quoted in *The Ciano Diaries* (January 29, 1940)

—

It is humiliating to remain with our hands folded while others write history. It matters little who wins. To make a people great it is necessary to send them into battle even if you have to kick them in the pants. This is what I shall do.

> *Ibid.* (April 11, 1940)

—

The youth of Italy shall be trained so that in this country there shall be a place for every person and every person shall be in that place. I am here today and gone tomorrow; but let no one think that Fascism goes with me.

> *Ibid.*

BARTOLOMEO VANZETTI
(1888-1927)

I found myself compelled to fight back from my eyes the tears, and quanch my heart trobling* to my throat to not weep before him. But Sacco's name will live in the hearts of the people when your name, your laws, institutions and your false god are but a dim rememoring of a cursed past in which man was wolf to man.

> *Last speech to the Court***

---

*"Quench" and "troubling."

**Vanzetti and Nicolo Sacco, Italian anarchists, were executed August 23, 1927, by the Commonwealth of Massachusetts on charges, never conclusively proved, of murder and robbery.

ALFONSO CAPONE ("Scarface" Al Capone, 1899-1947)

I'm just a businessman who supplies people with what they want to buy, in the good old American way.

Complaint to U.S. agent, Elliot Ness, (June, 1928)

——

Well, my mother loved me.

Chicago Tribune (March 14, 1929)

——

I don't tell you how to run your game; stop telling me how to run my racket.

Ibid. (To reporters)

——

If I wanted [J. Edgar] Hoover's advice, I'd ask for it.

Chicago Daily News (December 8, 1929)

——

Why is everybody always picking on me?

Ibid.

DEAN MARTIN

Sure, Frank Sinatra plays around with girls. What else should he do— play with knives and maybe cut himself?

Dean Martin Celebrity Roast

PART THREE

A PLEASURY OF PITHY PROVERBS

BEAUTY

- A homely wench becomes lovely by lamplight.
- The devil himself was handsome as a youth.
- A handsome man is never really poor.
- One puts a chicken in the pot, never a peacock.
- The loveliest rose loses its fragrance.

HONESTY

- For the buyer, a hundred eyes are too few; for the seller, one is not enough.
- A clear conscience makes the most comfortable bed.
- The butcher is honest who has hair on his teeth.
- Ask the price at three shops before you buy, and you will not be cheated.
- When a man boasts of his honesty, hold on to your teeth.
- The poorhouse is filled with honest people.
- It is more honorable to cheat than to steal, but expect no applause for either.
- Drunken lips disclose the heart's secrets.
- A clear conscience protects the honest man, but it is best to have a witness.
- An open countenance can conceal closed thoughts.
- An honest man needs but half his brains; the scoundrel needs all of them.
- The thief's worst punishment is to be known by all for what he is.
- If you would steal, first learn to conceal.
- There are more thieves outside than inside the jails.

FOOD AND DRINK

- Do not ask the host whether his wine is good.
- Drink wine and let water drive the mill.
- Peel the fig for your enemy and the peach for your friend.*

---

*The skin of the fig was supposed to be injurious, that of the peach wholesome.

- The best advice one can give to the hungry is bread.
- A full belly makes for an empty head.
- The best sermons on the benefits of fasting are preached by full stomachs.
- Wisdom is neither present nor desired at a feast.
- The language of hunger is more persuasive than even love.
- However neat and handsome, judge the house by the kitchen.
- Alas, if it doesn't poison, it fattens.
- Nothing improves the taste of pasta more than a good appetite.
- Think not of the cost lest you destroy the taste.
- A fish should swim twice: in water and in wine.
- Talk will not cook the *brodo di pollo.**

SICKNESS AND HEALTH

- The healthy man invents maladies.
- Today's illness is not cured by tomorrow's remedy.
- Sit with your back to a draft and you face your coffin.
- The thinner the patient the fatter the doctor.

TRUTH AND FALSITY

- Women always tell the truth, but never the whole truth.
- Lies have short legs.
- Truth is sometimes blind, but it always recovers its eyesight.
- The occasional lie is a sign of good breeding.
- Eyes believe themselves, ears other people.
- Better a fool who speaks the truth than a hundred liars.
- More people are convinced by a good lie than a bad truth.
- Disregard the cry of "wolf" at your peril: the wolf is somewhere about.
- A beautiful woman's tears denotes a purse in tears.
- If you would know yourself, listen at the keyhole.
- To these three only, you must always confess the truth: your priest, your doctor, and your lawyer.
- Even when he speaks the truth, the liar is not believed.
- Truth hurts—and angers.
- Talk much, lie much.
- Better to tell an innocent lie than a hurtful truth.
- Deny all, and you confess all.
- Doubt nothing, know nothing.

---

*Chicken soup.

- He who serves two masters must lie to one; he who serves two sweethearts must lie to both.

FRIENDSHIP

- A mile walked with a friend has only one hundred steps.
- The flatterer brings water in one hand and fire in the other.
- He has no enemy who has no friend.
- The eye of a needle provides enough room for two friends, but the entire earth is too small to contain two enemies.
- Reveal no secret to a friend that you would not disclose to an enemy.
- Better a close friend than a distant relative.
- Proclaim that you have two hundred friends, but know that you have but two.
- Life without a friend is death without a witness.
- Money and friendship belittle true justice.

LOVE AND MARRIAGE

- When buying a horse or taking a wife, shut your eyes and trust God for your life.
- Italian girls dream of marriage; when married they dream of love.
- Jealousy is an ax at the tree of love.
- Women are saints in church, angels in the street, devils in the marketplace, owls (*civette, i.e. coquettes*) at the window, and whores in the bedroom.
- He who wants canes should go to the canebrake; and he who would court the daughter should be polite to the mother.
- When two have set their minds on each other, a hundred cannot keep them apart.
- A man's self-esteem is no greater than the esteem he accords his wife.
- Virginity is noted only in its absence.
- It may be quieter to sleep alone, but not warmer.
- Feed your wife vinegar, and you will gather no honey from her lips.
- An Italian woman, like a mule, does all that is expected of her—until she marries.
- An Italian man makes a servant of his first wife, a lady of his second.
- Love is not measured by passion alone, for when passion is fulfilled, love often dies.
- A bad wife is like a wolf that changes its coat with the seasons, but not always its nature.
- No man is a hero to his wife or servant.

- She who marries a handsome man marries trouble; he who marries an ugly woman marries contentment.
- The wise hen does not cackle in the presence of the cock.
- Love makes time fly; time makes love fly.
- If you would conquer love, flee.
- Speak well of marriage, but remain a bachelor.
- Love, if you would be loved in return.
- Love needs no sword to rule its kingdom.
- The first wife is marriage; the second company; the third foolishness.
- Remain a bachelor and you will have good days and bad nights; marry and you will have good nights and bad days.
- Eve's legacy: if a woman takes, she sells herself; if she gives, she surrenders; if she neither takes nor gives, she is cold and unfeeling.
- Women dislike each other because of men.
- Never advise a man to go to war or marry.
- Only a fool asks "What do you want with my wife?"
- A daughter married is a daughter lost; a son married is a daughter gained.
- The expert dancer goes from one wedding to another, but never his own.
- The wife's face is a mirror of her husband's character.
- Love, sorrow, and money are not easily concealed.
- Travel far to marry and you are either a deceiver or about to be deceived.
- The husband who will not stoop to pick up a pin does not love his wife.
- A beard well-lathered is half-shaved; a woman well-flattered is half-won.

FORTUNE AND MISFORTUNE

- Tie up the mule where the owner tells you, and if he breaks his neck, the blame is not yours.
- You cannot drink and whistle at the same time; you cannot both carry the cross and sing with the choir.
- Three are powerful: the Pope, the king, and the man who has nothing.
- The diamond is not polished without friction, nor man perfected without adversity.
- Make me your steward for one year, and I will be a rich man.
- Never give a woman as much as she wants—unless it be flax to spin.
- The poor man's commandments are these: Thou shalt not eat meat on Friday, nor on Saturday, nor yet on Sunday.

- The successful man hides his ambition under the cloak of humanity.
- Know where your fortune lies: you will not find ivory in a rat's mouth.
- If you would view the plains and valleys, you must first climb the mountain.
- Bad luck comes by the pound and leaves by the ounce.
- The boiling pot attracts no flies.
- Lady Luck smiles on those who court her.
- Minor misfortune frightens, but great tragedy tames.
- He is luckiest who believes he is.

WEALTH AND POVERTY

- He who accepts a lofty position, knowing he has not the capability, embarks on the road to humiliation and failure.
- To the rich, poverty is the one great and unforgivable sin.
- Hunger teaches young women to be whores and old women to work.
- Every kernel in an ear of corn was matured by the sweat of someone's labor.
- A wagonload of sympathy is not worth one crust of bread.
- He is the richest man on earth who is content with the worldly goods allotted him by his Creator.
- The ladder to success begins with the bottom rung.
- Many heirs make small portions.
- Little and often fills the purse.
- The rich man pays with his purse, the poor man with his hide.
- It is no shame to be poor, but neither is it a virtue.
- If cursing helped, we would all be rich.
- If you were wealthy, you would not recognize yourself; if poor, nobody would recognize you.
- Spend too little and you will spend too much.
- Good character is not destroyed by poverty nor conferred by wealth.
- A tattered sack is not chosen to hold grain; a poor man is not consulted.
- The poor pay for the sins of the mighty.
- It is easier to find beauty in poverty than to endure it.
- Failures are but mileposts on the road to success.
- You need only to turn away from God to attain wealth—if you don't mind the consequences in the next world.
- Build on another man's ground and lose your stone and mortar.
- An egg today is worth two hens tomorrow.
- A wagonful of regrets will not pay a handful of debts.

- Divide honey with a bear and you will get the smaller portion.
- ... always generous with another's money.
- The rich preach to the poor; the poor aid each other.
- The worms make no distinction between the rich and the poor.
- Every new debt is another strand in the noose around your neck.

Fools

- He who seeks better bread than is made of wheat must be either a fool or a knave.
- On a fool's beard the barber learns to shave.
- Give a fool a knife and you become a murderer.
- We can occasionally learn from a fool: even the most foolish will sometimes utter a word of wisdom.
- If foolishness were a disease, the world would be one great hospital.
- Weep for the wise man who is forced to bow to the judgment of fools.
- It is easier to endure a total fool than half a fool.
- Gold casts its sheen upon the fool, but only for as long as he possesses it.
- Let the jackass hide its ears; its voice will still betray him.
- Dress a monkey in the finest silks and it still remains a monkey.
- Wait for the horse without fault and you will walk.
- Only a fool argues with a fool.
- He who makes the doctor his heir heads the list of fools.
- Silly men create new fashions; sillier women follow them.
- One does not point out the way to a blind man, or dispute with a foolish one.
- Follow your own counsel, and take the consequences.
- Only a foolish mouse is caught twice by the same cat.
- Trust the prophecies of children and fools.
- Creative artists are a rarity, but every ignoramus is a critic.
- A fool's spark glows in all men.

Greed

- Let us have florins, and we will find cousins.
- The smaller the landlord, the bigger the rent.
- Beware those who take by the bushel and give by the spoon.
- Invite a beggar in for one glass of wine and he becomes your heir.
- There has never been a war in which land was not an issue.
- The greater the wealth, the greater the avarice.

Goodness and Evil

- Pride went out on horseback and came home afoot.
- When God gives flour, the devil takes away the sack.
- Have nothing to do with an innkeeper's daughter or a miller's horse.
- God keep thee from the fury of the wind, from a monk outside his monastery, from a man who cannot hold up his head, and from a woman who can speak Latin.
- All the seven deadly sins are feminine.
- Beware of fire, of water, of dogs, and of the man who speaks under his breath.
- He who sleeps with dogs will get up with fleas.
- Bread and kicks will get no thanks, even from a dog.
- As long as war is a game, peace can never be serious.
- Fear the devil when he comes as a roaring lion, but doubly so when he comes as a wagging dog.
- Deal with dogs and you will soon learn to bark.
- It is useless to scold the man who lacks inborn morality.
- The narrower the mind the broader the tongue.
- The wrongdoer is always frightened when a policeman stops at his door.
- When God says today, the devil says tomorrow.
- He who hangs himself in the chimney has no right to complain of the smoke.
- Expect the devil to leap over the lowest hedge.
- One must make himself despicable before he is despised by others.
- Where God gives no sons, the devil gives nephews.
- One vice leads to a greater.
- Trust the reformed thief.
- An insignificant enemy, like a small scratch, can kill.
- Let the devil sneak into church and he will mount the altar.
- Hell and the police station are always open.
- The cautious man remembers that enemies never sleep.
- For good or evil, everything tires, everything passes, everything breaks.
- To the fox, everyone acquires chickens the way he does.
- Only he who practices virtue in youth can defy sin in old age.
- A good broom sweeps clean for three days.
- It is useless to discuss the cross with the devil.
- The less heart, the more tongue.
- Make too much honey of yourself and the flies will consume you.
- Make a dove of yourself and the hawks will devour you.
- Fire, water, and politicians quickly make room for themselves.
- The sun passes over filth and is not defiled.
- Applaud the man who cheats a cheater.

- Run with jackals and learn to howl.
- The good and dedicated man or woman is the jackass of the people.
- The public servant has a scurvy master.

JUSTICE AND INJUSTICE

- Paradise will remain empty of lawyers until hell is full.
- He wastes his tears who weeps before a judge.
- A stout stick makes the best argument.
- Fear the judge, not the law.
- Who holds the ladder is as guilty as the thief.
- The crime that goes unpunished is followed by others.
- The more laws, the less justice.
- Where might is master, justice is servant.
- The law governs people; money governs the law.

THE HUMAN CONDITION

- Heaven keep you from a bad neighbor and from a man who is learning the violin.
- If I sleep, I sleep for myself; if I work, I don't know whom I work for.
- If you want to have your hands full, buy a watch, beat a friar, or take a wife.
- He carries both yes and no in his pocket.
- Who has been bitten by an alligator will fear lizards.
- You call on Saint Paul without having seen the viper.*
- Great sorrow brings tears from the heart, not from the eye.
- The farmer values manure more than he does ancestors.
- The crow thinks its song is sweetest.
- Joy and sorrow are closely related.
- You are the servant of words uttered, the master of those suppressed.
- Beware the man who is too polite.
- The point of a needle will not fit between a woman's "yes" and "no."
- There never was, nor will there ever be, an Italian woman who sleeps so soundly that the twang of a guitar will not bring her to the window.
- The worst children always live next door.
- Every man credits himself with more brains and less money than he possesses.

---

*You cry out before you are hurt.

- A good reputation is like a cypress: once cut it never sprouts again.
- The closed mouth catches no flies.
- She who exercises the most caution will be thought most chaste.

RELIGION

- Old maids weep with one eye, wives with two, and nuns with eight.*
- Italians always think of God as a fellow-countryman.
- God never accuses Italians. He punishes.
- God has never asked for our certificate of baptism.
- Let a pretty whore walk naked in the street, and the Pope would turn his head.
- We are not as close to God as He is to us.
- No man grows so tall he can touch Heaven.
- God will not be bribed.
- Poverty produces one pious man to every hundred thieves.
- Good example is half the sermon.
- Had God wanted us on our knees, He would have endowed us with knee pads.
- He who has the Pope for a cousin, soon becomes a Cardinal.
- The truly pious man avoids those acts in privacy which he would not do in public.
- A defrocked priest never speaks well of the Church.
- Nearer the Church does not necessarily mean nearer to God.
- If you would unlock the gate to Paradise, be sure you forged the right key.
- Converts flock to convenient religions.
- Even the devil was once an angel.
- The devil himself will swear on a stack of Bibles.
- There are three sexes: men, women, and priests.
- Do as the priest says, not as he does.

OLD AGE

- Old mice like young corn, even when they lack the teeth to eat it.
- An old man shortens his life when he takes a young woman, but an old woman lengthens her life when she takes a young man.
- Borrowers and old people forget easily.
- A hundred years from now we'll all be bald.

---

*Their own two eyes, and those of the Father, the Son, and the Holy Ghost.

- A fat, elderly widow should either get married, buried, or hidden in a convent.
- There can be no lasting bond between red lip and gray beard.
- Foolishness and old age make sad companions.
- Alas, the old man forgets what the young man has yet to know.
- An old man's body is his almanac.
- The old cow thinks she never was a calf.
- The old man who leaves his young wife at home deserves the consequences.
- Man finally knows what life is all about when he is ready to leave it.
- Fools and whores can expect little in their old age.

Death

- He who yearns for a lasting peace will find it in the cemetery.
- Better a hard bed than a soft coffin.
- Italy lives on when the king dies.
- Wait for the dead man's cloak and you may freeze.
- The widow buys a young husband with the old one's bones.
- The miser and the pig benefit no one till dead.
- When they are dead and buried, the angel and the scoundrel are equally honored.
- However tall the tree, its leaves will return to earth.

Post-Renaissance Sayings

- Pay beforehand and be served behindhand.
- Never overwork a willing horse.
- Should the king declare himself a Negro, his courtiers would paint themselves black.
- Don't lend your knife in pumpkin-time.
- Better to be a lizard's head than a dragon's tail.
- All the brains are not in one head.
- Don't sew the bridal gown before you find the bridegroom.
- Everything has its purpose: a horse does not lift its tail without reason.
- Never disclose the contents of your purse—or your mind.
- A man's three faithful friends: an old dog, an old wife, and money.
- Beware the tattletale: he not only brings gossip, he starts it.
- Don't cook the *minestra di verdure** till you've gathered the ingredients.

---

*Vegetable soup.

- We cannot be aware of the mistakes of our teachers until we have heard their doctrines challenged.
- Big ships have been sunk by small holes.
- We are born with wisdom; stupidity is acquired.
- The wise man has long ears, big eyes, and a short tongue.
- Burn your mouth once and you will always blow your soup.
- Question a wise man and you have taken your first step to wisdom.
- Kings judge the world, but the wise judge the kings.
- Birds of a feather flock together—except birds of prey.
- There is no greater enmity than the enmity of brothers.
- The man who cannot mind his own business should never be trusted with yours.
- The cow must lose her tail before she realizes its value.
- When in a hurry, dress slowly.
- Fear, Avarice, and Laziness, in that order, are the greatest of all inventors.
- Love the oceans but stay on land.
- Keep a man waiting and he'll tally all your vices.
- Compliments are free, but we sometimes pay dearly for them.
- The eagle flies alone.
- Half the world laughs at the other half.
- If you will not ask for a bargain, don't expect one.
- The smallest blade of grass casts a shadow.
- He who disparages wants to buy.
- Great promises, no performance; modest promises, great performance.
- A hundred-year-old revenge still has its baby teeth.
- There are many roads to Rome.
- Better weak wine than grape juice.

9

Paisani in America

INTRODUCTION

In the year 1860 there were only 10,000 Italian-born residents and their children in the entire United States, a tiny minority in a population of 28 million. Nearly all had emigrated from the north of Italy, and represented the middle to upper classes. They had little in common with the few poor who had begun to seek America's shores as early as 1832.

The annual rate of Italian immigration began to swell until the year 1900, when over 100,000 immigrants were admitted. There was a buoyant hope in the breasts of these *contadini* (peasants, farmers) and *pescatori* (fishermen) who had left their native *Mezzogiorno* for a better life in America. And there was a degree of nervousness, too, as they recalled the familiar admonition: *Chi lascia la via vecchia per la nuova, sa quel' che perde ma non sa quel' che trova* (Whoever forsakes the old way for the new, knows what he is losing but not what he will find). They were aware that the New World also meant new ways.

Thousands of Italian immigrants flocked to such neighborhoods as the Mulberry Street area in downtown Manhattan, "a street that crooks itself like an elbow," to use a phrase by Jacob Riis. More familiarly known as Mulberry Bend, it was only one of many such enclaves, called "Little Italies," in other major port cities such as Boston and Philadelphia. Spreading out to upstate New York, throughout New England, and then southward to New Orleans and westward to California, they settled in whatever towns and cities that offered work—often the most menial jobs that were scorned by native Americans. Wages ranged from $10 to $15 per six-day week, for ten-hour days or longer. But it must be remembered that 80 percent of the Italian immigrants were males, men who could not afford to bring their women with them. So it was that they eagerly accepted any employment that paid even the lowest of slave wages: it gave them the opportunity to scrimp and save their pennies, nickels, and dimes until they had accumulated ship's passage fare for their wives, children, mothers, and other family members. Yes, family ties were strong indeed.

Italians did not easily enter the "melting pot" that was America. They clung together, not only because of their inability to speak fluent English, but also because of their rigid family customs, the system known as *l'ordine della famiglia*. Having been forced to leave their homeland by the specter of starvation, their strict adherence to family tradition was an important means of continuing their familiar and respected culture, and helped them to resist the encroachment of *la via nuova*, the new way, which they felt would destroy what they held most dear.

But it was anti-Italian prejudice, born of ignorant fear, that reinforced their clannishness. In many areas they dared not step outside their own neighborhoods. This prejudice reached its peak in the first decade of the twentieth century when 2,045,877 Italians entered the United States. By 1921, when Congress passed the first Quota Act, the Italians had become the most numerous foreign stock, second only to the German-Americans, in the United States.

The depth and extent of the prejudice against Italians has been, for the most part, forgotten by today's Americans of Italian extraction. Some will smile indulgently when reminded of their "quaint" grandparents and great-grandparents. They would do well to remember that thirty-nine Italians were lynched or shot by vigilantes just before and immediately after the turn of the century. Those hard-working immigrants who sought only to feed their families and give them a decent, secure life, were openly termed "dagoes," "guineas," and "wops" in the nation's press. The *New York Times* referred to *all* Italians as "these sneaking and cowardly Sicilians, the descendants of bandits and assassins, who have transported to this country the lawless passions, the cutthroat practices of their native country, are to us a pest without mitigation." And just what had the Italian community done to deserve that diatribe? They had protested the lynching of ten Sicilians in New Orleans. Nothing more. All ten, incidentally, had been acquitted by a jury after their arrest on a clearly trumped-up charge of murder.

Prejudice against Italians began with native American fear of competition for jobs—the newcomers from the south of Italy and Sicily were nearly all poor and desperately in need of employment. This fear mounted as labor agitators and others were referred to as "Italian Anarchists," although 90 percent of them would not have known an anarchist from a horticulturist. And then, of course, there was the Mafia (in those days, The Black Hand). No one pretends that the Mafia does not exist, but the average Italian-American knows as much about them as he does about the German-American Bund. All of these factors seemed to coalesce into a general notion that Italians were criminally inclined and dangerous political radicals, when, in fact, they were politically among the most conservative in the United States.

It has been a long struggle for Italian immigrants to gain a respected place in American society, but gain it they have. Today, their descendants are represented in every profession: medicine, law, government, and education. They serve as judges, congressmen, and sports heroes; as laborers, merchants, teachers, and artists. They are, in short, Americans.

Through all its bitter trials and tribulations, however, the sunny nature of the Italian-American was never stilled. Perhaps it is true that adversity will often heighten our sense of humor, but the sons and daughters of Italy seem particularly able and willing to laugh at themselves—surely the true definition of humor. However, the *contadini* who first came to America would be horrified at the outrageous distance their descendants have strayed from the old ways; especially as it concerns the humor of their grandchildren.

There is little to be found in Italian-American humor that pays "honor" to *l'ordine della famiglia,* to the *capo di famiglia* (head of the family), or even to *la via vecchia*—the old way, which, perhaps more than any other factor, had preserved family life for generations, through every calamity and sorrow; yes, and through the happy times, too.

Authentic Italian-American humor, technically, is that which is told by one Italian to another, and which revolves around a subject of particular interest to Italians in general. Technically! But that definition seldom applies to the humor of today. Yet, somehow, it has retained its own unique character, described elsewhere in this volume as the flavor of *pasta,* of fresh green vegetables—peppers and tomatoes and garlic and onions and olive oil—of ages-old native expressions. The humor of modern Italian-Americans may have strayed from the narrow paths trod by their ancestors, but it remains distinctively Italian.

The selections in this chapter represent the different facets of Italian-American life, thought, and attitudes. All were created by Italians, and if the anecdotes, quips, and poems seems intrinsically similar (as some are) to those of other ethnic groups, Italians will nonetheless recognize in them that elusive quality that makes them their own.

—H.D.S.

Romeos and Juliets—American Style

VICTORIAN PRUDERY

Whatever may be said of the philandering nature attributed to Italian men, the women have a well-merited reputation for circumspect conduct. True enough, the present generation of American girls of Italian extraction, emulating their sisters of other nationalities, include some who are amenable to a proposition rather than a proposal. On the whole, however, most retain the strict moral codes of their forebears, or a reasonable facsimile thereof.

Take the case of nineteen-year-old Paolina Fraschetti, of Schenectady, New York, as reported by the late Robert De Cicco, of that State's Circuit Court. Judge De Cicco may have been joking, but the anecdote proves our point.

Paolina was walking home from the library where she worked, when, in the gathering twilight, she was seized by a would-be rapist and dragged into some nearby bushes. The attacker started to disrobe her.

"Sir," admonished Paolina sternly, "if you are going to do this sort of thing we might as well get married!"

PITH AND VINEGAR

Fiorello LaGuardia, yesteryear's popular mayor of New York City, was fond of his long-time secretary, Estrella, but he did not approve of her fiance, a vain and arrogant young fellow. When asked the reason for his dislike, LaGuardia told it all in one vinegary, pithy sentence: "He's the kind of guy who'd like to die in his own arms!"

LUIGI'S DOWNFALL

"Papa," stormed the college-educated daughter, "I know you like Luigi, and that he makes a good living, but I just can't marry him."

"Why not-a?" asked Papa.

"Because he's plain stupid, that's why not. Last night I asked him if he ever heard of the fall of Rome. You know what he answered? 'No, but I remember hearing something drop.'"

"You right—he's a stupid," agreed Papa. "I'm-a heard it fall, too, back in Italia, but-a before he was born."

TENDER REFUSAL

"Darling," pleaded the young swain, "will you marry me?"

"No." replied the girl sweetly, "but I will always admire your taste."

Adagio, Act I. Ernesto Bonetta

DOUBLE TROUBLE

Carlo had been "cruising" in his new car, hoping to meet a lonely girl. He soon spotted a likely looking candidate, pulled over to the curb, and parked. When she came near, he got out of the car and approached her.

"Pardon me," he murmured, "but you look like Helen Green."

"So what?" snapped the young lady. "I look worse in red!"

Ibid.

INVITATION

They had only met a few days ago, and now the shy young man was seated with the girl in a cozy, quaint little restaurant, illuminated only by candlelight. It was all very romantic.

"Honey," he said falteringly, a few glasses of wine lending him courage, "I've been thinking how nice it would be to kiss you."

"Well," she said, leaning forward and pursing her lips, "think fast— while I'm still young!"

Il Progresso, N.Y.

JOB ORIENTED

Tomas, the young tailor, was doing better than even he had anticipated. It was only his second date with the girl, but she was clearly taken with him.

"Take me in your arms, Tomas, and press my lips," she whispered feverishly.

"Why?" he asked nervously, drawing back. "Are they wrinkled?"

Ibid.

ON THE FIRING LINE

The newly engaged couple were on the verge of their first argument. "Why are you so quiet?" he asked. "You look mad as hell."

"I have every right to be," she replied, her voice rising with indignation. "I saw you with that blonde last night at Ciro's. You were both drinking wine and holding hands. I want an explanation—and I want the truth!"

"Make up your mind," he growled. "You can't have both!"

Ibid.

FORGETFUL FRANKIE

Frankie Largo, the hockey player, has been described by sportswriters as having the mind of a computer—at least on the hockey field. But, according to his teammates, his memory, otherwise, leaves much to be desired. This little anecdote was told by his brother and, we might add, with unrestrained glee.

Frankie accepted a blind date, arranged by his sister, and was introduced to a very attractive young lady. He was absolutely smitten with her. She was not only lovely but intelligent and charming as well. The nicest part was that she clearly liked him too. As the evening drew to a close, he took her in his arms.

"Baby," he murmured caressingly, "it will take me a long time to forget you."

"How long?" she asked coyly.

"Beg pardon," he replied, staring at her, "have we met?"

Alberto Largo, *Sports World*

SHORT FUSE

Italians, with some justification, are well known for their explosive tempers. Luigi Roma, proprietor of Boston's *Pizza Palace*, tells about one such type in this droll gem.

A day or two earlier, Luigi's headwaiter had become interested in the new waitress just hired by Luigi. The waiter, inspired by the girl's visible charms and intrigued by her invisible ones, decided to ask her for a date.

"How about having dinner with me tonight, at my apartment?" he asked, with as much innocence in his voice as he could muster.

"Sorry," she answered curtly, "you're not my type."

"F'r chrissake!" he exploded. "What d'ya mean, *type*? All I want is a date, not a blood transfusion."

DAINTY CANNIBALS

Grandpa, the old soldier, met Grandma when she was a nurse, both serving in Ethiopia during Mussolini's invasion of that country. In their early years of marriage Grandpa loved to tell romantic stories about his courtship, but as he grew older his tales gradually lost their romantic flavor and grew increasingly far-fetched, until his exaggerations lost whatever truth and glimmer of realism they may have once possessed.

One evening, when little Eleanora, his granddaughter, was in his lap, and listening attentively to one of his tall stories, she asked: "Grandpa, weren't you afraid that you and Grandma would be eaten up by cannibals?"

"Well, it almost did happen once," the old-timer admitted, a wild gleam in his eye. "Grandma and I were smooching in the Ethiopian jungle, one day . . . "

"Rodolfo!" gasped Grandma indignantly.

" . . . when suddenly a bunch of ferocious cannibals sprang out of the bushes and grabbed us."

"Ooh!" exclaimed Eleanora excitedly, while Grandma listened aghast at the outrageous fib. "How did you escape?"

"We didn't have to," said Grandpa, his voice as serious as though he were in a confessional. "Luckily for us, those cannibals were on a diet. They only ate midgets!"

WHERE THERE'S A WILL, THERE'S A WIFE

"Liliana," said the young woman's father gently, "I realize that your job as a kindergarten teacher doesn't give you much opportunity to meet eligible young men. But you don't seem to be making an effort to find suitable fellows."

"You brought me up to be a good Italian girl, and to choose my future husband carefully," replied Liliana.

"Well, it really is time you married. You're not getting any younger," he argued.

"Yes, I know. But I'm looking for a very special man."

"How special?"

"For one thing, and most importantly, he should have a very strong will—made out to me!"

SWEET REVENGE

This anecdote goes back to 1921, and illustrates one of those extemporaneous remarks that merits repeating.

As youths in their early twenties, Evandro Petrosino and Guglielmo de Palma emigrated from Palermo and arrived in the United States together. Both were bakers' apprentices at the time, and each worked for rival bakeries in Rochester. In time, they established their own businesses, always competing for customers. They had never been close as boys, although they were neighbors, and as they grew older their mutual dislike grew in intensity. Evandro married and fathered ten children. Guglielmo remained a bachelor.

One day, according to legend, Evandro's daughter told him that Guglielmo, now in his sixties, had finally married.

"That's-a good!" replied Evandro spitefully. "I'm-a never like that guy. Eet serva him right!"

DATE BAIT

In her book, *Little Italy*, authoress Valentina Pagano tells of the time her teen-aged daughter went out on her first real date.

"It isn't easy to bring up a daughter in the traditional old ways," wrote Mrs. Pagano. "A girl, today, would be shocked and outraged at the mere suggestion that a chaperone be present on a date. But I had a mother's feeling that my daughter was mature enough to take care of herself.

"Returning home from her evening out with a young man she had met a few weeks earlier, I saw at once that she was disenchanted.

"'What happened?' I asked.

"'I never want to see that fellow again,' she replied indignantly. 'He talked me into going to his apartment to listen to his new stereo set.'

"'How did it turn out?' I asked, with some apprehension.

"'It turned out,' she snapped, 'that he had an eight-track stereo and a one-track mind!'"

Il Progresso Italo-Americano

INDIAN LOVE CALL

Twelve-year-old Bennie Adamo had only been in the United States for a year or so when his parents announced that they were moving from their cramped apartment in the Bronx to the wide open spaces of New Mexico. There, in a small town, the boy's father had been offered a good job by a relative.

Little Bennie was delighted. He not only acclimated himself to living among the cowboys he had admired so much on television, but he promptly experienced the pangs of romance. Yes, Bennie fell in love—with a pretty Indian maiden. She was a year or two older (and wiser) than he, but what does age matter to a descendant of hot-blooded Sicilians whose passions were kindled under an Italian sun by day and Mediterranean zephyrs by night?

Bennie's parents were amused when, one Sunday, he strolled over to the Indian reservation to be with his lovely maiden. But they were surprised when he returned shortly, leading a pony.

"Where did you get that pony?" asked the boy's father, in Italian.

"From Running Deer, the Indian girl," replied Bennie, also in the native tongue.

"But why?"

"Well, Papa, it was like this," explained Bennie. "She rode this pony to the place in the woods where we were supposed to meet. When she got off, the first thing she said was, 'Kiss me.'

"I said, 'No; nice Italian boys don't kiss girls.'

"So she opened up her blouse and showed me those things hanging on her chest. And she said, 'You can touch them, if you like.'

"But I said, 'No; nice Italian boys don't touch those things.'

"Then, Papa, she started breathing real hard and got close to me, and she said, 'You can have anything I've got.'

"So I took her pony!"

Ibid.

Mangled Matrimony

Rich, Handsome, and Absent

Adriana, who weighed 150 pounds and was scarcely five feet in height, was on her way to the corner grocer's to buy some provolone—a hard, round cheese from southern Italy. With her chubby face, plain features, and slight waddle, it is fair to say that she caused no men to turn their heads for a second look. In any event, romance was not on Adriana's mind, nor had she given it any thought for years.

She had not walked halfway to her destination when she noticed a new sign in a storefront window: FORTUNES TOLD. An impish and unusual impulse seized her, and she entered. Inside the dimly lit "parlor," she was seated by a mysteriously-veiled gypsy woman. A crystal ball was placed on the table, and after Adriana had made a "good-will offering," the prophecies began.

"You will soon meet a tall, dark, and handsome man," predicted the gypsy. "He will fall madly in love with you."

"How I'm a-gonna know him?" gasped Adriana.

"He will step out of his limousine and sweep you off your feet. You won't have to recognize him. He will realize, the minute he sees you, that you are the one woman in the world for him."

"He's a-rich?"

"A multimillionaire. He owns gold mines, ships, and a chain of hotels."

"*Mama mia!*" gasped Adriana. "An'a he's gonna love *me*?"

"Absolutely. He will shower you with gifts: diamonds, flowers, candy, new cars, beautiful gowns. . . ."

Adriana's face turned pale. "Gonna be plenty trouble," she moaned. "How I explain-a that to Joe, my husband, an'a my five-a kids?"

Truthful Hubby

Settled comfortably in front of his television set, and sipping a glass of wine, Lorenzo—or "Larry," as he was usually called—was absorbed in the program and quite content with life. Suddenly his tranquility was shattered by the snappish voice of his wife, a shrew whose tongue could clip a hedge.

"I just found over a dozen empty wine bottles in the basement," she screeched, "and they're all your brand, too. I demand to know how they got there."

"How would I know?" he replied genially. "I never bought an empty wine bottle in my life!"

ALESSI'S ENDURING HUMOR

Vittorio Alessi, owner of a fishing fleet in San Diego during the 1930s, was a happily married man, devoted to his wife and six children. But despite his obvious contentment, his humor on the state of matrimony could be devastating. A number of his observations are still recalled by southern Californians, although Alessi has long since gone to his reward.

"You seem to have a well-ordered household," a neighbor once commented.

"Well, I like to run my home like a ship, with me as the captain," said Alessi. "The trouble is," he added with a merry twinkle in his eye, "I married an admiral!"

——

"There's a great deal to be said about marriage," Alessi once told his younger brother, Carlo, "but I just don't have the nerve."

——

At a party celebrating his twentieth wedding anniversary, Alessi said to his assembled children, "Your Mama and I were engaged for two beautiful years. Our romance didn't end until we got married."

Maria, the oldest daughter protested: "Oh, Papa, you and Mama are very happy together."

"Perhaps," he replied, nodding his head, "and I guess there's still some romance left, too. Every time I leave the house to begin another fishing trip, your Mama and I always shake hands."

——

At dinner, one evening, Vittorio Alessi and his wife Bettina were reminiscing about their courting and honeymoon days.

"The only thing that worried me in those days," declared Vittorio, "was that these May-December affairs never work out—or so I thought."

"May and December!" exclaimed Bettina. "What are you talking about? You're only a year older than I."

"I wasn't referring to age," he said, grinning. "What I meant was that you wanted to get married in May and I wanted to call it off in December!"

——

Perhaps it was due to a kind of intellectual osmosis, but occasionally Bettina Alessi would surprise her husband with a quip of her own.

Whether her humorous comments could be ascribed to conscious wit or unconscious humor is not known, but here is a sample:

Bettina and Vittorio were discussing a movie star of Italian extraction.

"She doesn't act like a decent Italian girl," said Vittorio disapprovingly. "I hear that she's getting ready for her fourth husband."

"Yes, and I think it's awful," remarked Bettina. "She's so busy planning her fourth wedding, she doesn't even have time to cook for her third husband!"

———

One day, during a fishing voyage, Vittorio's first mate commented in an off-handed way, "My wife tells me that your best friend just married your sister."

"Yeah," replied Vittorio, "and now he hates me like a brother!"

———

Vittorio and his brother, Carlo, were sharing a bottle of wine after dinner, while their wives were in the kitchen, washing the dinner dishes.

"We have fine wives," said Carlo. "How long have you been married: eight years or so?"

"Ten," corrected Vittorio. I was married on August 5th, in Palermo."

"You have a good memory."

"Not really," Vittorio sighed. "I remember where and when I got married, but what escapes me is *why*!"

———

"You shouldn't make fun of marriage," scolded Bettina after one of Vittorio's numerous and usually disparaging jokes. "Marriages are made in Heaven."

"I know " he replied somberly, "but so is thunder and lightning!"

DISDAINFUL JIBES FROM THE DISTAFF SIDE

"My husband is so considerate: he never forgets to start the lawn-mower for me before he goes out to play golf."

———

"Husbands are like cars. Take care of them and you won't have to get a new one every few years."

———

"The trouble with a husband who works like a horse is that all he wants to do evenings is to hit the hay."

—

"My husband doesn't know the meaning of fear. But, then, there are many things he doesn't know."

Gemma Silvio, Giornale Nazionale

LOYALTY

It was vacation time at the steel mill, and the workers were discussing their plans.

"I'm gonna visit Yellowstone Park," averred Gaetano, the straw boss at the plant.

"Hey, that's terrific!" enthused his fellow worker. "Don't forget Old Faithful."

"Of course not," replied Gaetano mournfully. "I'm taking her with me!"

Paul Gallico

VOICES FROM APARTMENT 3-B

For the economy-minded reader, here are two quips in one exchange of caustic comments:

"You have no idea how nervous I was when I proposed to you," said Olivio, the olive-stuffer.

"And you have no idea how nervous I was until you did," replied Paula, the pimento pusher.

He regarded her thoughtfully. "Sometimes I think you married me for my money."

"Well," she retorted, "I couldn't get it any other way."

Alfredo Rizzo, Literary Digest, April 1939

MARCELLA'S MADCAP
MARRIEDS AND ABOUT-TO-BE'S

Rocco was in love with Gretchen Schmidt, a German girl. He was a romanticist of the old school; she a practical young woman. They were seated before a glowing fireplace, sharing a bottle of wine. A Sinatra record played a soft ballad on the stereo.

"*Innamorata*,"* he whispered hoarsely, overcome with sweet passion, "I would get down on my knees and die for you."

"That's very sweet of you," said Gretchen in an even voice. "But the question is, would you stand up and work for me?"

---

*Sweetheart.

——

Papa: Tell me, Vito, when you gonna get married an' make-a some *bambini?"*

Vito: I haven't found the girl I'd want to marry.

Papa: What-a kind girl you want?

Vito: Papa, I'm looking for a girl who doesn't smoke, drink, or fool around.

Papa: Why?

——

Joe loved his wife, but it seemed to him that she was always asking for something new. She never appeared to be satisfied. His irritation boiled over one day, when she said, "I wish I had a grand piano instead of this old upright."

"For heaven's sake," he snapped, "you're always wishing for something you haven't got."

She gave him a look of complete surprise. "Why, Joe, what else is there to wish for?"

——

Bianca, a muscular but attractive young woman, was the physical education instructor at the local high school; Jimmie, an Irish-American, was a math teacher, and in love with her. The lady, however, clearly did not return his affection.

"I'm sorry," she said, after he proposed to her, "but I don't think I could ever be happy with a man who was not Italian." It was a rather lame excuse in today's society, she realized, but it was the only one that came readily to her mind.

"Italian men aren't any better lovers than we Irishmen," he retorted, misinterpreting her rejection. "I could make you melt in my arms."

"Jimmie," she replied carefully, "I'm not that soft and you're not that hot!"

——

"Oh, Grandpa," gushed the old-timer's granddaughter, "just think, you'll be celebrating your golden wedding anniversary tomorrow. Fifty years! How romantic!"

"Yeah," said Grandpa matter-of-factly, "seems like Grandma and me got married only yesterday . . . and you know what a lousy day it was yesterday!"

——

---

*Little boys.

"Do you still love me as much as you did when we were first married?" asked the insistent wife for the third time that week.

"Yes," the husband replied wearily. "I'd grant your smallest wish."

"Do you really mean that?"

"Of course, honey," he replied smoothly, "if it was small enough!"

———

It was three o'clock in the morning when Mrs. Ponzi shook her husband awake.

"Mike," she whispered urgently, "I hear a mouse squeaking in the kitchen."

"Well, whaddya want me to do about it?" he grumped. "Oil it?"

———

Don't think for a moment that a Sicilian has to come to the United States to be insulted. We brought this one to America from Rome.

A Roman fellow who had recently married a girl from Palermo visited his parents' home one Sunday while his wife was in church.

"Are you happy, my son?" asked the young man's father.

"Oh, yes," replied the son, "but I'm afraid my wife is sad. I believe she was crying yesterday."

"You believe? If you actually didn't see her crying, then how do you know?"

"Because," explained the groom, "her face was clean!"

Marcella Lolli, *Buono Come il Pane* (As Good as Bread)

Ragazzi e Ragazze[1]

La Via Nuova[2] of
Literature

Bernardo Toledano, *il capo di famiglia*,[3] had just returned from an afternoon's walk along Arthur Street, in the "Little Italy" of the Bronx. He sank into a chair, lit a *Di Nobili*[4] and spoke to his wife amid clouds of appallingly acrid smoke.

---

[1]Boys and girls.

[2]The new way . . .

[3]The head of the family.

[4]A wrinkled, black, slender cigar that produces dense smoke, and considered to be less than fragrant by those who are not accustomed to the strong aroma. Known in less elegant circles as a "Guinea stinker."

"I don't know what our children are coming to in America," he sighed in Italian. "That son of ours goes to a fine public school like we never had in the *Mezzogiorno*,* yet he doesn't seem to know as much as we do."

"He's a smart boy," said the wife defensively. "Why do you say such things?"

"While I was taking a walk today I found a fine-looking book, and I gave it to him," explained Bernardo. "But he gave it back to me. Why? He complained that he didn't know what to do with it—there was no place to put the batteries!"

ARE THESE OUR CHILDREN?

La via nuova has taken a firm hold in many Italian-American families, especially those of the second and third generations. This "new way" has even penetrated such stalwart areas of old world *ordine della famiglia******* as Mulberry Street in downtown New York's "Little Italy." As witness thereto, we introduce Tony and Arturo, eleven-year-old twins, and their long-suffering parents, the DePaolas.

Bob and Mary DePaola were both born on Mulberry Street, and like other second generation residents of the neighborhood, had no intention of leaving. "Little Italy" was *home* to them: they would have been uncomfortable without the familiar sights, sounds, and smells to which they had been accustomed all their lives.

Tonight they were seated at the table, having supper (dinner was eaten at "lunch" time). Tony and Arturo were carrying on an animated conversation.

"I knew our stickball team would win," ventured Tony.

"Yeah," agreed Arturo, "us mountain guineas can beat them valley wops any time."

"Arturo," shrieked the boys' mother, "don't ever let me hear those words in this house again, you hear?"

"Them spaghetti-benders oughtta go back to sellin' bananas," ven-

---

*Refers to the areas south and east of Rome, comprising the six provinces of Abruzzi, Campania, Apulia, Luciana (also known as Basilicata), Calabria, and Sicily. The *Mezzogiorno,* also called *Meridione* by Italians, is loosely interpreted as "the land that time forgot."

**The phrase pertains to the comprehensive, though unwritten, system of laws which establish the conduct of a person to other members of his family, his or her responsibilities to the family, and his attitude to those outside the family. *L'ordine della famiglia* is observed in many areas of northern Italy, and especially in the southern part (the *Mezzogiorno*), where all institutions outside the family are regarded with indifference and even contempt.

tured Tony, no doubt thinking his mother's rebuke was intended for his brother alone, but not for him.

The boys' father rose from the table, incensed. "Didn't you just hear your mother tell you to watch your language?" he barked.

"She told Arturo, not me," Tony answered, his face a picture of innocence.

"Well, now *I'm* telling you! Furthermore, we happen to be Americans of Italian descent. We are not wops and we're not guineas. And another thing, we don't eat spaghetti any more often than any other family. As for selling bananas, there is nothing wrong with earning a living, but in any case, no one in our family sells bananas, nor do any of our neighbors. So let's not hear any more of *that!*"

Arturo and Tony realized they had gone too far, and remained silent. After a few moments of peace at the table, the father asked, "Where did you boys hear all that anti-Italian junk?"

"We heard it yestiddy," explained Arturo, "at the Sons of Italy party."

POWER OF THE SUBCONSCIOUS

It was a balmy afternoon in June, and a father and his small son were settled comfortably on the banks of a pond, fishing. The older man was Amadeo Peter Giannini, son of Genoese immigrants and founder of the Bank of America. The little boy was Mario, who was later to succeed his father as head of the huge banking institution, until his own untimely death. At the moment, however, they were happily occupied with the day's sport.

"Papa, how will I know when I've got a bite?" asked Mario, who had never been fishing before.

"The line goes down a little," explained the elder Giannini.

"How much?"

"Oh, I don't know," replied Papa abstractedly. "About one-and-a-half percent."

LA PICCOLA PRIGIONIERA*

When Galeazzo Alfieri was appointed Cultural Attache to the Italian Embassy in Washington, D.C., during the 1950s, he brought his wife and all seven children with him, as a good husband and father might be expected to do. In their new home, in nearby Arlington, the family was well-liked by its neighbors and made new friends quickly.

One evening, Galeazzo's wife was called to the home of another

---

*The little prisoner.

diplomat at the embassy where the lady of the house had just given birth and needed a little help. Galeazzo was left to babysit for his brood, ages ranging from two to ten.

All went well. The children amused themselves at play, ate their dinner dutifully, and at bedtime they were sent upstairs. Now seated peacefully at his desk, Galeazzo immersed himself in some official papers he had brought home. All at once he heard a noise at the top of the stairs leading to the childrens' bedrooms. He glanced up, and, in the dimly lit passageway, he discerned the figure of one of the youngsters.

"Back to bed!" he ordered sternly, sending the child scuttling to her bedroom.

An hour or so later, the little girl again appeared at the top of the stairs.

"Piccola Americana!"[1] Galeazzo snapped. "Didn't I tell you to go to bed? Now be off with you!"

But a half hour later, there was the girl again, silhouetted at the top of the stairs.

"Basta!"[2] he roared. "This is the last straw. You either go back to bed and stay there, or you'll get a spanking!"

The child beat a hasty retreat, and Galeazzo, feeling that the warning would end the problem, settled back to his papers. He was lost in his work when, at ten o'clock, a loud and insistent ringing of the doorbell brought him to his feet. He opened the door, and there in the entranceway was his next-door neighbor, frantic with worry.

"My little girl has been missing all evening," she said tearfully. "Is she here?"

"Why, no," said Galeazzo.

"Yes I am, Mama," piped a little voice at the top of the stairs, "but he won't let me go home!"

Those New Car Names

Little Ernesto was very happy. His Daddy had agreed to take him for a ride in his new car this very Sunday. While Mama was visiting her sister, the boy climbed into the car and he and his father set off for the countryside.

They returned late in the afternoon. Mama had already returned home and was busily preparing dinner. Ernesto, bubbling over with excitement, rushed into the kitchen to tell his mother all about the day's happenings.

---

[1] Little American: used as a term of reproach for acting contrary to the *via vecchia* (the old way).

[2] Enough!

"We saw lots and lots of brand new cars," he cried happily, his words gushing forth like a fountain.

"And did Daddy tell you the names of all those cars?" she asked, smiling at her son's exuberance.

"Oh, yes, Mama," said Ernesto. "We saw ten Pintos, fifteen Chevvies, three Mercurys, two Thunderbirds, one Cadillac, four Chryslers, and fifty-six *stupidi bastardi!*"

LITTLE ENRICO GREETS THE NEW NEIGHBOR

"*Buon giorno,* I'm Enrico. Are you the *cafone** from Abruzzi who just moved next door?"

BLACK DAY FOR BERNARDO

Bernardo, age seventeen, was a rotten kid—and that was the good part of him. He was a born loser who just couldn't do anything right, even on those occasions when he wanted to. It wasn't because he was stupid, you understand, but rather that he just didn't give a damn.

But his worst day occurred when his world collapsed about his head. On that day he failed his driver's test, his intelligence test, his college entrance test, and his Wasserman test.

Emigrants and Immigrants

IT ALL STARTED WITH COLUMBUS

Except for the fact that Cristoforo Colombo discovered the New World on October 12, 1492, the day was like any other in the twilight of feudal Europe—lousy. Serfs continued to live in fiefs instead of apartments. Lords and ladies lived in Manors Born. Military officers were quartered in High Dudgeons, while privates and noncoms were drawn and quartered in Low Dudgeons. Kings lived in Walt Disney castles and dreamt they sat in marble halls; tiled bathrooms with appropriate fixtures having not yet occurred to them.

Seven years earlier, Cristoforo had approached the ruling monarchs of Italy for a loan so that he could prove the earth was round—and make a

---

*Simpleton.

few *lire* in the process. But you know how Italians are about laying out cold cash for round worlds and islands that aren't there.

Legend has it that Colombo then went to the King of Poland, Wladimir Kowalski, to plead his case. King Wladimir, who didn't even *have* a seacoast, let alone free ships, was nevertheless intrigued with the idea. Personally, he had never believed the earth was flat. He held to the opinion that it was concave, like a deep bowl, and anyone who sailed to the edge would forever remain there, the sides being too steep to climb out. Unfortunately (for Colombo), King Wladimir, who was visiting a French health resort in Beanveaux, suffered a severe attack of escaping borborygmi after consuming six bowls of *fagioli*,* and was killed in the resultant cannonade.

It was at this point that the future discoverer of America appealed to Ferdinand and Isabella of Spain. Cristoforo explained that he was seeking a shortcut to the Far East, but when he stated that he intended to sail due West to find it, Ferdinand demanded prior proof that the earth was round, and not oblong as he believed. Cristoforo, to demonstrate his theory, tapped a hardboiled egg on one end, causing it to stand upright on the table. What this proved has not been handed down to us by the historians, except that Cristoforo was one of those characters who liked to carry numerous hardboiled eggs around in his pockets. There's one in every crowd.

Then Lady Luck, or a close relative thereof, smiled on the explorer. Queen Isabella, who had been experiencing some personal problems with Ferdie, perceived Colombo's eggs as sexual symbols, and, in a process of thinking not readily understood, she swung over to the round earth point of view. She urged the king to bankroll the expedition, and when he refused, she sold her jewels to Enrico, a courtier, otherwise known as "Hockshop Henry." Actually, Isabella didn't do too badly on the deal, considering her successful claim on the insurance company for the "lost" jewels.

Colombo was elated. At last he had his ships! There were three of them: the Nina, the Pinta, and the Santa Fe. Eagerly he set sail across the uncharted Atlantic Ocean, sailing West to the East. After a mutiny or two (he had informed his crew they were headed for Paris and the Follies Bergeres), he finally discovered America.** At least, he almost discovered America. On his first trip he landed in the Bahamas. Well, he was

---

*Beans.

**Actually, Leif Ericson, a Norseman, discovered America in the year 1000. His public relations man, regrettably, left his pencil home in his other pants, and as a result, the historic event was never recorded. Perhaps it was just as well. Ericson was the son of Eric the Red, a known communist. Had either Leif or Eric been successful in colonizing this country, the United States might today be under the domination of the Soviet Union instead of the Democratic Party.

new to the business and had never been there before: better luck next time. He tried again, and on this second voyage he brought his keel to rest on the shores of Cuba. But this was hardly New York. "If I'da known Vespucci was tail-gatin' me, I'da sailed East," he complained. "I just know that guy will get all the credit!"[1]

Let's face it, the man was looking for China, and two slack seasons in a row are pretty hard to take. Small wonder, then, that Columbus[2] was discouraged. *"Madonn',"* he muttered disconsolately, "I could-a swore Hong Kong was around here someplace!"

Somehow, Columbus found his way back to Spain, via Oslo, where Queen Isabella, her visions of cheap chop suey and exotic spices now gone, dubbed him Public Enema No. One, and inconvenienced him by insisting upon his lodgement, at government expense, in Low Dudgeon.

His parting words, when finally released, were: *"I marinai vecchii non mai muoiono; ma solo puzzano cosi."*[3]

H.D.S.

Nonna[4] Assists Her Sister

Elderly *Signora* Sicca, now a widow, decided to visit her children and grandchildren in Los Angeles. But first there were the preparations: she had never been outside her little town near Boston since she emigrated to this country, some sixty years ago. How to get across the continent safely! Using her good judgment, Grandma Sicca went to the local train depot and, in her flowing, liquid accent, she asked the information clerk to guide her.

He nodded agreeably and consulted a sheaf of schedules, making notes as he went along, and explaining in detail the three connections she would have to make.

Grandma thanked him and went on her way, but an hour later she was back.

"Is anything wrong, ma'm?" he asked courteously.

"No, everyting she's-a all right," replied Mrs. Sicca. "I'm-a joost-a need wan more paper weeth all-a da writing."

---

[1]America was named after Amerigo Vespucci, an Italian navigator. He evolved a system for computing nearly exact longitudes and discovered the Amazon River in 1499. According to his new system, he was 123 knots south of Boston. Amerigo was the child of a singularly unhappy marriage which was never consummated.

[2]Cristoforo Colombo, at this time, anglicized his name to Christopher Columbus, so the natives wouldn't think he was some foreigner just off the boat.

[3]"Old sailors never die; they just smell that way."

[4]Grandmother.

"Did you lose the one I prepared for you?"

"Oh, no, I'm-a still got it," explained the old lady, smiling. "But now my seester, she's-a wanna come, too!"

SHOES OF THE FISHERMAN

Old Arturo Pagano, the fisherman of Messina, had hoarded his meager supply of money most of his life to achieve his lifelong ambition to emigrate to America. Now he had enough, and he, his wife and three teen-age children soon found themselves in the United States.

In Syracuse, New York, they prospered from the very beginning, although the parents experienced some difficulty adjusting to the unfamiliar ways of the New World.

Not so the oldest son, Angelo, however. The eighteen-year-old youth entered the mainstream with a verve and enthusiasm that surprised his family. He quickly located a job and when he had accumulated enough for a down payment, he bought a jalopy. He then proceeded to dress it up with a fancy new paint job in violet and red, installed green and orange seat covers, and hung a pair of baby shoes from his rear view mirror, as he had seen in the cars of his contemporaries in the neighborhood. Now he was ready to display his ornate vehicle to the American public.

As Angelo proudly backed his car out of the driveway, he hit something in the rear of the vehicle. He jumped out and was immediately confronted by his angry neighbor, also recently arrived from the old country.

"Angelo, you backed into my truck," the neighbor wailed in Italian.

"Sorry, I didn't know it was there," explained Angelo. "I guess I just wasn't looking."

"Sorry?" grated the neighbor. He pointed to the baby shoes dangling against the boy's windshield. "This wouldn't have happened if you had your shoes on!"

MAN OF FEW WORDS

Upon leaving the ship that brought him to America from Calabria, Raimondo managed to find his way to a hotel near Court Street, in Brooklyn's Little Italy. He had been told that all the guests as well as the management spoke Italian, and he wasn't disappointed. He explained to the desk clerk that he had had a long, tiresome journey, that he had been unable to sleep well on the high seas and that he was very weary. All he wanted was a good night's rest. It was probably the longest speech he had ever made. He was a man of very few words.

But five minutes later, Raimondo came down to the desk, his suitcase in hand. "Checking out," he said tersely in Italian.

"What's the trouble?" asked the puzzled desk clerk in the same tongue. "Something wrong with the room?"

"No," replied Raimondo.

"Was it the bed?"

"No."

"Well, maybe the room was too small, or too drafty?"

"No."

"Then why are you checking out so soon?"

"*La maledetta camera e in fiamme!*"[1]

TONY THE LINGUIST

Marco was homesick. Far from the province of Campania whose towns and villages he had not seen for three months and which he knew he would never see again, he would eat his supper at the boarding house he had found soon after arriving in Brooklyn and take his evening walk along Union Street. Especially did he love to see the little food stores that reminded him so much of home. He would gaze with rapture through the plate glass windows at all that he saw within as though he were admiring floral displays. And indeed they were colorful. There were gaudy cans of imported olive oil stacked in pyramids, sausages and cheeses hanging in profusion, baskets of onions and garlic, pungent herbs, and big, firm sacks of rice from the Po Valley.

Marco soon struck up a friendship with Tony, proprietor of a little fruit store, and many an evening did they spend together, talking about old times in the *Mezzogiorno*. Tony understood Marco—after all, he had gone through the same period of homesickness himself.

"You no gotta no worries," Tony admonished him. "You gotta good-a job and you gotta fine-a girl. So what-a da hell you makin' da complaint?"

Marco started to answer in Italian.

"Hey, spikk-a da inglese!" Tony interrupted. "How you gonna learn-a eef you spikk-a *italiano* all-a da time?"

"*Non capisco l'inglese,*"[2] said the poor fellow helplessly.

"You gotta notting to worry about-a," said Tony, slapping his palm on the table for emphasis. "When you here in dis-a country tree-four-five-a year, you gonna spikk-a inglese like-a da *professore*.[3] In-a fact-a, you gonna spikk-a as good-a as me!"

---

[1] The goddam room's on fire!

[2] I do not understand English.

[3] Professor.

An Immigrant Learns About Italian-American Justice

Abraham Goldberg, an immigrant from Russia who had been in the United States for less than a year, was unjustly accused of a misdemeanor. He appeared in court at the time set, quaking with fear that he would not be able to explain his plight because of his inexperience with the English language. Compounding his anxiety was his knowledge of how courts operated back in the Soviet Union. There, he knew, there were only two verdicts: "guilty" and "guilty as charged."

Goldberg approached the bench, where Judge Michael Rossi presided.

"Please, your honor, mine English is not so good," explained Goldberg falteringly. "Dis crime I'm not committing, I'm swearing to you. Oy, meester Jodge, how I'm givink mine side wid sotch a bed eccent?"

Judge Rossi, his face softened with compassion, leaned forward and replied, slowly and with deep understanding.

"Listen to me," he said, his words dripping with sympathy, "joost-a because you no spikk-a da good *inglese,* dat no mean-a you can't-a get joostice in-a dis court-a!"

Diabolical Hot Dogs

Two young emigrants from Abruzzi, Carlo and Domenico, through the efforts of a cousin who had arrived in America the year before, found jobs across the city, and in the same company. Each bought a box lunch and boarded a train to the other side of town for their first day of work. It was also their first ride on a train in their new homeland, and they watched the passing scenes with high interest. Knowing little of the English language, their conversation was in Italian.

"Did you ever taste one of these American hot dogs?" asked Carlo, just as the train went into a tunnel.

"No," came Domenico's answer in the dark, "why?"

"Then don't touch it, whatever you do," hissed Carlo in an agitated voice. "I took one bite and went blind!"

Buon Appetito!

Perspective

A new resident of New York's Mulberry Bend entered a small, family-owned restaurant and ordered a meal. The proprietor, noting the patron's distinguished appearance, personally brought the food to the table. When the diner had finished eating, he called the restauranteur to his side.

"Sir," he began with reserved but apparent enthusiasm, "I must compliment you on this food. Your veal parmigiana is better than I ever tasted, better even than I had in Italy "

"Of course it's better," replied the proprietor. "It should be. In Italy they use domestic cheese. Here we use only imported cheese."

Oh, That Italian Coffee!

If you are even remotely acquainted with espresso, the mighty concoction Italians call coffee, you will appreciate this trio of observations by Carlo Crespi, the Count of Court Street.

"The trouble with drinking a cup of Italian coffee in the evening," observed Carlo, "is that a week later you're sleepy again."

——

"You gotta be careful when you drink espresso," warned Carlo. "My grandma went blind drinking just one cup of Italian coffee. She left the spoon in the cup."

——

"I hate to talk like this about my own people, but too much Italian coffee actually killed my father," said Carlo. "A hundred-pound sack fell on his head."

Inflation

From Elena, the poetess of Elizabeth Street, comes this roster of witticisms:

"Italian restaurants always use short waiters and tiny tables, so the plates will look bigger."

——

"Eating Italian food used to be a necessity for Italian-Americans; then it became a luxury; and now it's an investment. We no longer consult a menu to determine the price of a meal: we have it appraised by a jeweler."

"There was a time, not too long ago, when we put fifty dollars worth of groceries into the trunk of our car. Now we put it in the glove compartment. Prices have gotten so ridiculous, we eat three square meals a day and pay for six."

"So eat, drink, and be merry, for tomorrow it will cost you more."

American Restaurant Blues

Italian-Americans, especially those who have spent most of their lives in one of New York's "Little Italies," find little to be enthusiastic about in the average non-Italian restaurant. The food in those "alien" eateries is so bad, according to knowledgeable Italians, they serve Pepto-Bismol for dessert. In the more expensive restaurants, they have so many French dishes, you have to eat with an interpretor.

"You can always tell an American restaurant," averred writer Emilio Pitre of New York University. "The food is frozen and the waitress is fresh. In Italian restaurants, it's just the opposite.

"American restaurants offer more services than do Italian ones," Emilio continued. "They honor all cards—even Blue Cross.

"I don't know why it is, but American restaurants are always so brightly lit," Emilio Pitre observed. "I like the dimly lit Italian places. By the time the waiter finds the twenty-cent tip, you're gone."

Appetite Stifler

"Say, honey," enthused the young husband, "this *stufato di manzo** is delicious! What's in it?"

"Don't ask that question," said the wife. "It's best you don't know."

He stared at a piece of beef suspiciously. "This meat tastes okay," he ventured, "but it looks funny. What kind is it?"

"I don't know," she confessed.

"Didn't the butcher tell you, when you bought it?"

"I didn't buy the meat," she finally confessed. "I found it."

Ancient Wisdom

An old Italian proverb tells us that if you eat green vegetables regularly for at least eighty years, you'll never die young.

---

*Beef stew.

Famous Last Words

"Okay! Okay! I'm sorry! This tasteless, dry, awful-looking *polpettone*[1] is delicious!"

Placing the Blame

Luisa, the new bride, strode into the corner grocery store and shook a paper bag in the proprietor's face.

"*Al ladro!*[2] *Mascalzone!*[3] *Briccone!*"[4] she shrieked. "Give me back my money!"

"*Signora,*" replied the storekeeper soothingly, "control yourself. What have I done?"

"What did you do? I'll tell you what you did! You sold me a bag of flour that was too old and tough to cook with!"

"Tough flour?" the grocer asked, bewildered. "I don't know what you're talking about."

"You don't?" snapped Luisa. "Well, listen to this: I used some of that tough flour to make *cannelloni*[5] for my husband, and they were so hard he broke a tooth trying to eat them!"

Eating Can Be Hazardous
to Your Health

The following dialogue between a young husband and his bride of two months could never have taken place in the old country—especially in southern Italy—where *la via vecchia* is strictly observed, even today. There, a girl is taught the fundamentals of proper housekeeping and culinary skills by her mother. By the time she marries, she is usually well able to assume her wifely household duties.

Not so in the United States, however, where so many Italian-American girls have strayed from the system of social attitudes known as *l'ordine della famiglia.* Let us evesdrop on one such newly-married young woman and her hubby.

"You think I have it easy, don't you?" complained Christina. "You forget that I have to sweat over a hot stove all day long, cooking for you."

"I hate to say this, honey," said her husband, Rocco, "but you're

---

[1]Meatloaf.
[2]Thief.
[3]Rascal.
[4]Crook (or scoundrel).
[5]Large, round envelopes of flaky pastry dough stuffed with minced meat or fish.

forgetting something. "Actually, you do have it easy. All you have to do is cook the meals, but I have to eat them!"

Christina glared at him. "I didn't hear any complaints about that fancy breakfast I cooked for you this morning."

He nodded agreeably, which only increased her anger. "I must say, you boil the softest hardboiled eggs ever seen," he admitted. "I just didn't like it when you asked if I wanted my eggs without ham or without bacon. By the way, what was that stuff you served with the eggs?"

"*Salsicce.*"[1]

"And what was it before you cooked it?"

"All right, that does it!" she said in a tight voice. "You like to criticize, but I never hear a word of praise. You didn't say one nice word about that dessert I prepared for you last night, even though I fixed it nice and crisp."

"But, honey," he protested, "tapioca isn't supposed to be nice and crisp!"

"Well, if that's the way you feel about it, cook your own meals from now on," she snapped.

"Aw, Chris, I'm sorry," he apologized. "I was just joking. Actually, I thought the *manzo arrosto*[2] you cooked last Sunday was excellent."

"Then why didn't you say so?"

"I couldn't talk," he explained. "I broke a tooth on the gravy!"

Wits and Wags in the Workaday World

SUPREME INSULT

Nonno[3] Corresca liked to reminisce about his younger years when he was a well-known concert violinist, back in Livorno. In America he had found immediate employment with the New York Philharmonic and other prestigious orchestras, and was understandably proud of his long carreer. Now retired, he was especially fond of teen-aged Rocco, whom he called *nipotino*,[4] hoping the youth would follow in his footsteps.

But *Nonno* Corresca's faith in the fun-loving boy was badly shaken when he happened to overhear his *nipotino* in the midst of a tall story:

"My grandfather had a three-piece combo when he came to this country," boasted young Rocco—"an organ, a cup, and a monkey."

[1]Highly spiced pork sausage.
[2]Roast beef.
[3]Grandfather.
[4]Fine little grandson.

"Rocco," the old-timer roared, forgetting the *"nipotino"* he usually used, "shall I tell your friends about your own progress as a violinist? You've been practicing for six years, and you can finally play the violin just like me—under your chin. Why don't you play for your friends like you've never played before?—in tune! And you might also explain to your friends why it is that you always look so sharp and play so flat. Away with you, *idiota!"**

Rocco fled in terror.

Double Trouble

"Boy, am I in trouble," moaned the young journalist. "My editor told me to put more life in my stories, and I write the obituaries!"

"You think you got troubles?" sneered his companion. "My brother has *real* problems. He's a deep-sea diver. Last week he was coming up, and passed his ship going down!"

Il Progresso Italo-Americano

Lift Up Thine Eyes

One of the most successful real estate salesmen in Brooklyn, in the 1940s, was Robert Celebrezze. Robert was not always scrupulous in his descriptions of property, as this little anecdote will attest.

A client, who was seeking a house for himself and his family, made it clear to Celebrezze that he wanted "a home with a nice view."

"I have just what you want," said the salesman immediately. "This house has a magnificent view."

"Fine," replied the client. "Let's go see it."

But when they arrived at the site, the client was flabbergasted. On both sides of the property the view was hidden by a high wooden fence. In the back was a tall brick building. In front, a tall, uncared-for hedge grew to a scraggly height of twelve feet.

"I thought you said this place had a magnificent view," protested the client indignantly.

"It does," said Celebrezze evenly—"if you look straight up!"

Who Said This Was
a Free Country?

Teen-aged Giuseppe, recently arrived from Spoleto, shared the belief

---

**Idiot.

of most Italian immigrants that America was truly the land of the free. Giuseppe's Americanization began immediately. He acquired a collection of rock recordings, picked up the street jargon of his contemporaries, aped their dress and mannerisms, and settled down to the good life, as he perceived it.

Unfortunately, it had never occurred to Giuseppe that one also had to work for a living in the United States; until, that is, he was reminded of that distressing fact by his uncle, who had sponsored him. The youth was sternly ordered to report for duty at the offices of an olive oil importing company, owned by another relative. As in most closely-knit Italian families, the job was assured.

Giuseppe confronted his uncle the next day, clean-shaven for a change, but a picture of dejection.

"Why do you look so sad?" asked the uncle. "Didn't you get the job?"

"No, I didn't," replied Giuseppe hollowly. "And don't ever tell me again that this is a free country."

"What are you talking about? What happened?"

"*Caro mio zio*,"* cried the nephew, his voice strained as though his very heart were breaking, "they told me that if I wanted the job I'd have to shave off my sideburns, my mustache, and my beard. Then, when they got a look at my face, they wouldn't hire me!"

GIANNINI'S HATCHET MAN

This anecdote goes back a half century or more, but is as witty today as when it was first told. The scene is a wooded area of some ten acres, near San Francisco, which had just been purchased by the estimable A. P. Giannini, founder of the Bank of America. Mr. Giannini wanted the property cleared of trees so that he could build homes. He approached his new gardner, an old Italian gentleman he had hired only a few days earlier. The old-timer spoke very little English, so their discussion was conducted in Italian.

"Do you think you can cut down all these trees in a week?" asked the bank president.

"I'll have the job finished by tomorrow," said the gardener matter-of-factly.

"What!" exclaimed Giannini. "Just one day? But that's impossible! We don't have any power tools."

"I have a small hatchet," said the gardener. "It will be enough."

The next day Giannini returned to the property, and there, lo and

---

*My dear uncle.

behold, every single tree had been chopped down! The gardener was sitting on a fallen log, calmly smoking his pipe. Alongside him was his little hatchet.

"I can't believe my eyes!" cried Giannini, his voice incredulous. "Where in the world did you ever learn to chop down trees like this?"

"In the Sahara Desert, when I was with Mussolini's army in Africa," explained the old-timer.

"But, my dear man, there are no trees in the Sahara."

"No," agreed the old one, "not now!"

MAN OF THE HOUSE

The Italian-American community, like its counterparts in Italy, has always been considered a patriarchal society: the man is in charge of his household. But reports of recent changes are enough to make older-generation Italian males weep. One such incident added still another nail in the coffin of masculine domination when a reader, in a letter to the editor of an English language Italian magazine, stated:

"No wife of *mine* is going to work. I'm afraid to stay home alone!"

DISILLUSIONED

An immigrant, who had always believed those old stories that the streets of America were paved with gold, learned the awful truth when he reached New York. In a plaintive letter to his wife who had remained in Taranto until he could send for her, he wrote: "The only thing you can get in the United States without working is hungry!"

SHIRTSLEEVE PHILOSOPHY

Salvatore, the straw boss of Syracuse Cement Company, was a born philosopher. He said things that must be said, but he did it with a touch of humor. Of course, it may not be so funny if you happened to be one of those working under him.

"Your new job," Salvatore told a group of new employees, 'will just about kill you until you get used to it. It's hard, back-breaking work, day after day. Breathing all the dust can give you lung cancer. But there's one bright spot you can be happy about: the job is permanent."

On another occasion, he told his work gang, "I understand your problems, fellas. It takes some of you an hour to get to work—after you get here."

During a lunch break, Salvatore offered this sage observation:"The reason worry kills more people than work is because more people worry than work."

And to his own son, Salvatore advised:

"It's always a good idea to learn a trade. Then you'll always know what kind of work you're out of!"

Those Affluent *Compares*

A TEXAN MEETS HIS
MATCH IN FLORENCE

During the latter part of the nineteenth century, the name of Luigi Procacci was one to be reckoned with in west Texas. Luigi, who was born in Florence, came to the United States in 1851 as a penniless immigrant. Somehow, he managed to save enough for ship's passage money to New Orleans, and from there worked his way westward into Texas. How he managed it is not known, but before long he was the owner of a small cattle "spread." An astute, though uneducated man, he built his spread into a large cattle-raising and shipping company until, years later, it was absorbed by the giant King Ranch. Yes, Luigi Procacci was a real, live person who helped build the West.

Many stories, now folk legends, have been told about Luigi. One of them, in admiration of his cattle-shipping prowess and perhaps his other obvious qualities, referred to him as "the biggest bull-shipper in Texas."

He was a fast talker, this Luigi. But there was one time that his glib tongue was frozen to his palate when he met his match in an old man who had never been more than thirty miles from his home. In 1881, by that time a wealthy man, "Bronco" Procacci, as he was now called, decided to celebrate his thirtieth year as an American by visiting his place of birth and perhaps to do a little boasting to those relatives he had left behind.

To his surprise, his maternal grandfather was still alive. The man must have been over a hundred. He agreed to show Luigi, or "Bronco," the sights he knew as a boy. Astride a mule, the old-timer soon came to the magnificent Medici Villa, outside Florence.

"Isn't that absolutely marvelous?" asked the grandfather.

"Oh, I don't know," replied "Bronco," the Texan. "I've got an outhouse bigger that."

The old man looked him over. His eyes traveled from Luigi's feet, to his large rump, his flabby breasts, and his thick neck, finally meeting his grandson's eyes with his own.

"Your outhouse is bigger than this villa?" he echoed.

"Sure!"

"You need it!" he snapped.

EQUAL FOR YOU—
EQUALLER FOR US

In California, early in 1979, the Department of Water and Power increased its rates far in excess of a level most people thought fair. "Scandalous" was the word most often used by consumers to describe the inordinate increase in the price of electricity.

Like many public announcements made by large corporations in similar circumstances, the "explanation" advertised in local newspapers subtly insulted the reader's intelligence. In this instance, even the corporate chiefs of the utility company must have been aware of their lame excuses. As though to soften the blow, the bottom of the printed announcement carried the legend, in large, bold type: "*An Equal Opportunity Employer.*"

"Yeah," wrote one outraged citizen, Salvatore Mangione, in an indignant letter to the editor, "they screw everybody alike!"

UPS AND DOWNS
OF WALL STREET

Victor Selveggio, the stockbroker, tells this one on himself.

"Having suffered a slight nervous problem which I feared might lead to a breakdown from the constant pressure of a fluctuating stock market, I fled to the sanctuary of a hospital for a rest.

"My nurse was handing my chart to the doctor when I heard her say, 'Temperature today 102.'

"I was in something of a daze, but I weakly raised my head and said, 'When it reaches 102½, *sell!*'

"Then I wearily fell back against my pillow."

BORN LOSER

In his "autobiography," a book the author claims to be a true account of his experiences, Silvano Sturzo recounts some of the funniest antics imaginable as he aspires to become a millionaire. But whether they are true or not, some of the anecdotes merit repeating.

"I started the first Italian-American Bank in New York," wrote Silvano. "Everyone in my family—aunts, uncles, cousins—chipped in a few hundred each so I could get started. But the bank failed: I had more vice presidents than I had depositors."

"My nephew, Domenico, deposited $300 in my bank. It was supposed to be a savings account, but I guess Dom wasn't the saving kind. Each week he would drop in and take out his "interest" at the rate of $50 per visit. So, in six weeks, when he came for his money, I had to tell him the awful truth:

"'Dom, I'm afraid that the interest ate up all your principle.'"

"After the bank failed, I tried the magazine business, but I failed in that, too. I just wasn't cut out to be a publisher. The magazine I started was the *Friday Evening Post*. My biggest problem was insufficient money. You just can't put over a vast idea with a half-vast bank account."

"The IRS didn't make a single important change in the income-tax blanks for 1974. Apparently they had already simplified it beyond all understanding. I'll never forget that year. I spent all of 1974 complaining about my income, only to discover that I had made more money than I could afford."

Appreciation

For this whimsical contribution we go back to October 17, 1904, when Andrew Sbarboro opened his new Banca d'Italia in North Beach, California, on the former site of a saloon.

Other established banks contemptuously referred to the new enterprise as "that little dago bank," but the established bankers were to see their institutions completely obliterated by the great earthquake in San Francisco, and their depositors flocking to Sbarboro's "little dago bank" in North Beach.

It was on that first day of banking business when a newly-arrived immigrant entered the establishment. Speaking no English, he asked, in Italian, for a loan.

"Sure," agreed Sbarboro, and then proceeded to help the man fill out the financial form.

"*Oh, grazie, signore,*" cried the applicant when the details were completed, "*saro sempre nel vostro debito!*"*

To the Point

Catherine Pagano, librarian at Columbia University, once owned a bookstore—at least for a few months. But business was so bad she was forced to close.

In her window she placed this pithy sign:

WORDS FAILED US!

Close Enough

We have already mentioned Andrew Sbarboro: this one is about his

---

*"Oh, thank you, sir . . . I shall be eternally in your debt!"

wife, described by her contemporaries as an arrogant, haughty woman who demanded the utmost respect as a bank president's wife. In her twenty-room mansion overlooking the Pacific Ocean, the formal gardens, the stables, and the servant's quarters, she was, as she described herself at every opportunity, "the mistress of all I survey."

One day in 1908, Madame Sbarboro was informed by an agitated servant that her new gardener, a young fellow named Antonio, had been kicked by a horse and was in the local hospital. She attempted to visit the patient on the following day.

"He's very sick and really shouldn't have any visitors today, except members of his family," said the head nurse. "Are you his wife?"

The bejeweled lady drew herself up haughtily. "Certainly not," she declared, her imperious voice now indignant with outrage. "I happen to be his mistress!"

TRAVELER'S LAMENT

A businessman arrived in New York from Italy, and checked into the swankiest, plushiest hotel in town, *Casa Gyp-Artiste*. It wasn't long before he realized he had entered a place that apparently was run by Ali Baba and the forty thieves. When he returned to Italy, the size of his expense account stunned his boss. "How can this be?" he asked.

"That American hotel was so exclusive—and in New York 'exclusive' means expensive—it cost me 35 cents to change a quarter," explained the traveler. "Even if you pay cash for everything, they demand to see your bank references."

"That must have been a fancy hotel," observed the boss.

"The fanciest in New York," affirmed the traveler. "Even the guests have to use the service elevator. In the dining room they butter your toast on both sides—at a dollar a side. Then they have the nerve to demand that you wash your hands before they let you use the fingerbowl.

"But when they insisted that I wear a tie to the swimming pool, that's when I got the hell out. The only thing I liked about that place was that they showed movies in the elevators."

AMONG THE NEWLY-RICH

Mike and Alicia Franconi were ecstatic. An uncle, whom they scarcely knew, had died and left them his entire estate—a total of half a million dollars. They spent all that day planning on the worldly goods they would acquire: a new house, furniture, fancy cars, and so forth. Mike, the cultural one in the family, went downtown to make the banking arrangements.

That afternoon, the phone rang, and Alicia picked up the receiver. "Honey," came Mike's excited voice, "I just bought a Rembrandt." "Oh, I'm so happy!" she gushed. "How many cylinders?"

Proverb from the Prophet of Palermo

It makes no difference if you're rich or poor—if your nose runs and your feet smell, you're built upside down.

Religious Matters and Don't Matters

A Girl Named Joe

Italian-Americans are becoming resigned, if not accustomed, to modern women who assert their so-called civil rights by joining "liberation" groups, as if they were not overly liberated already. But when an otherwise decent Italian lady expresses such departures from *la via vecchia,* it makes strong men weep.

As a sad example, we here introduce a pious young woman named Josephina, who decided that the Church was remiss in not allowing females to enter the priesthood. She fought her battle all the way up to Cardinal Vitelli. That dignitary, unable to dodge her any longer, finally granted her an interview.

"I realize, Your Eminence," she began without further preamble, "that this is a complex problem, and to solve the issue of female priests will take the wisdom of a Sheba."

"Well, Josephina . . ."

"Call me Joe."

"Ah—er—*Signorina* Joe," he said falteringly, "you must understand the position of the Church. Women were meant to be nuns, not priests. We must obey God's command."

"Don't tell me God commanded that only men could become priests!"

"Yes, he did," corrected Cardinal Vitelli. "He commanded, indirectly of course, that nuns and priests are to be distinguished by their bodily differences. Now, if you are prepared to prove to me that you are more qualified to be a priest than a nun, I will be happy to ordain you."

"But, Your Eminence," she protested, "a person's intimate parts have nothing to do with higher feelings."

"Is that so?" he exclaimed in great surprise. "The hell you say!"

Vincenzo Capini, *Corriere Italiano*

Pious Poultry Pun

A monk who tends to the poultry at a Benedictine monastery speaks of his hens as "lay sisters."

Brother Maurus Wolf (quoted in the *Washington Star*)

Baptist Morality

Pasquale Malatesta, the turn-of-the-century writer, stands sponsor for this one.

The way Pasquale told it, his cousin, Vito, had struck up a friendship with a co-worker at the trucking company where they both worked. Vito's friend, a Baptist, talked him into attending Protestant services at his Four-Square Gospel Temple. "At least you'll hear our point of view," argued the Baptist.

In church, that Sunday, Vito listened with keen interest as the minister delivered his sermon. But he sat bolt upright and broke his silence when the preacher concluded earnestly:

"Ask yourself this vital question: Would you rather walk in the light with the ten wise virgins, or in the dark with the foolish virgins?"

Vito leaned aside toward his friend in the next seat, and, hand over mouth, whispered fiercely:

"Jimmy, that guy's gotta be kiddin'!"

All in the Family

Missionary recruitment ad: "Ever think of going into your Father's business?"

Al Marchi, *Il Progresso,* New York

Setting the Record Straight

Cardinal Vitelli was not always the forceful speaker he became in his later years. He recalled, with a chuckle, his first sermon. He had stammered and stuttered, forgot several of his most important points, and finished lamely, unable to assemble his thoughts in a concluding sentence or two. He poured out his lamentations to his bishop.

"I'm afraid I'll never be a good preacher," he mourned.

"Father," the bishop said evenly, "just remember this: there are not many good anything!"

Vincenzo Capini

INTERFAITH ECUMANIA

A Catholic priest and a Protestant minister were discussing their respective viewpoints. The minister was an evangelist who preached hell's fire and brimstone retribution for earthly sins, and the imminent end of the world.   .

"Tell me something," asked the priest, "aren't you a little embarrassed, preaching the imminent end of the world for over twenty years?"

"No indeed, Father," said the preacher abruptly. "I have never given up hope that it will happen sooner or later!"

LONG AND SHORT OF IT

Joseph Califano, then chief of Health, Education, and Welfare, once reminded Federal employees at a communications workshop, how words can run away with the speaker. Here is his example, illustrating one government-sponsored memo that ran frighteningly amok:

"We respectfully petition, request, and entreat that due and adequate provision be made, this day and the date hereinafter subscribed, for the satisfying of this petitioner's nutritional requirements and for the organizing of such methods as may be deemed necessary and proper to assure the reception by and for said petitioner of such quantities of baked cereal products as shall, in the judgment of the aforesaid petitioners, constitute a sufficient supply thereof.

"That," explained Califano, "is 'long' for 'Give us our daily bread!'"

INFLATION HITS THE CHURCH

Father Ruffo was reading the announcements for the week.

"Next Sunday, at Crotona Park, Saint Thomas Aquinas Church will hold its annual Strawberry Festival. However, because of the poor collection these past few weeks," he concluded, "stewed prunes will be served."

SURPRISE

The third- and fourth-grade teachers at Saint Vincent Elementary School in Philadelphia decided to have a picnic out in the country. Few of them had room enough in their cars for the children, so they used the regular schoolbus.

The aisle was already full of milling people by the time Joey, age seven, clambered aboard with his picnic basket. Soon all were seated their boxes and baskets of pickles, jams, and jellies set in place. There seemed to be no room for the youngster.

Father Trozzolo, in charge of the outing, beckoned to the boy. "Over here, Joey," he called. "Come sit beside me."

Joey hurried over to the empty seat and the priest helpfully took the youngster's basket and placed it on the rack over their heads.

A few minutes later Father Trozzolo felt something wet trickling down on his head and neck. He looked up.

"Joey," he exclaimed, "your pickles are leaking out of your basket!"

"Them ain't no pickles," corrected Joey. "Them's puppies!"

The Skeptic

Cynical Sal, the Sicilian scoffer, attended the funeral of a neighbor. As he was sauntering through the cemetery after the services, he came upon a headstone with the epitaph NOT DEAD—JUST SLEEPING.

Sal contemplated the inscription for several moments and then walked on, muttering, "Dat-a guy he no fool-a nobody but-a hisself!"

Political Big Shots and Little Shots

Longo's Logic

Many of the pompous, often exaggerated, and self-serving statements offered by political figures, government officials, their underlings and overlings, literally cry out for the devastating retort. As a rule, the President's annual State of the Union message to Congress may be considered worthy of a Fiction-of-the-Year award.

———

A few years ago, the White House outdid itself when the Press Secretary issued a public statement revealing that President Carter "has been sleeping with the annual budget for three months."

"Surely," sighed White House correspondant Gina Rossi, "the President's wife must have objected."

———

It is claimed that Senator Wilbur Mills posted a warning sign in his office, cautioning against the use of alcoholic beverages. But a wag changed the word "drinking" to more accurately portray the intellectual state of Congressional activity. The altered sign now read: "NO THINKING DURING WORKING HOURS!"

———

We hate to say it, but the women's liberation movement has even penetrated the hallowed halls of the Senate Office Building. A sign in one of the washrooms proclaimed, "THIS MEN'S ROOM DISCRIMINATES AGAINST WOMEN!"

At that, it was an improvement over the sign posted on the door inside the toilet cubicle—at sitting height, no less—"SMILE! YOU'RE ON CANDID CAMERA!"

———

Congressman Vito Marcantonio employed an opening line that was not only entertaining but a real attention-getter. When campaigning, he would approach a voter, extend his hand, and, with a grin, he would say: "If you have an hour or so to spare, I'd like to talk to you for a minute!"

———

Mayor Fiorello LaGuardia knew his politicians. On his desk was this credo:

"When in charge: ponder. When in trouble: holler. When in doubt: mumble."

———

But don't get me wrong—I love politicians. Just remember that half the people in Washington are hoping to be discovered, and the other half are afraid they will be!

Louis Longo, from *The Voice of Elizabeth Street*

APOLOGIES TO SHAKESPEARE

Republican State Senator from Staten Island, John Marchi, was once asked, "Do you think you'll still be a senator when the campaign is over?"

"Will I still be a senator?" echoed Marchi. "To be or not to be, that is the question: now all I need is the answer!"

WE HATE TO SAY IT, BUT . . .

When Evandro Bandelari, the New York obstetrician, won his election to the House of Representatives during the 1940s, Congress, for the first time, finally got a friend of labor.

Pietro Bacigalupi, *Il Progresso, N.Y.*

LONESOMEST MAN IN TOWN

Show me a politician who enrolls in a class in ethics and I'll show you a man who's in a class by himself.

Pietro Bacigalupi

QUESTION OF SANITY

Congressman Mario Biaggi, of New York, wasn't troubled one bit when he learned that his political opponent, an Irishman named O'Tool, would be a sure winner because he had kissed the Blarney Stone.

"He hasn't got a chance," snapped Baggio—"not with that kind of sex problem!"

WORDS FAILED HIM

Domenic Volpe, the volatile Washington correspondent, quit his job in disgust during the aftermath of the Watergate scandals.

"It's impossible for a political reporter to operate in Washington, D.C. anymore," he explained to his sympathetic readers. "All my unimpeachable sources have been impeached!"

FIORELLO'S SHORT FUSE

The fact that Fiorello LaGuardia's temper could be directed against a fellow Italian whom he believed to be unworthy is a matter of record. Indeed, he could sometimes be more severe with other politicians who shared his national ancestry because he fervently desired them to set a good example: one which would instill a sense of pride throughout the Italian-American community.

Old-timers will recall that, back in 1935, Willie Ruotolo was running for the New York State Legislature; and, to put it kindly, the man was the greatest bore ever to hit the huskings in local politics. His campaign rhetoric consisted of one theme: "Crack the Government-Industry conspiracy." Willie Ruotolo, in short, had a one-crack mind.

In October of that turbulent campaign year of 1935, Willie approached the colorful and recently elected Mayor Fiorello H. LaGuardia, seeking his support, even though he knew that the mayor had little liking for him.

"Willie," growled LaGuardia, "why don't you go someplace where it would cost me a dollar to send you a postcard?"

"All right, be a comedian," said politician Ruotolo, shrugging off the insult. "I'm throwing a big birthday party a week before the elections."

"Who are you kidding?" exploded LaGuardia. "You just had a birthday party a few months ago."

"Yeah, but this one will give me some public exposure when I need it most. I'd like you to show up."

"Like hell I will."

"Well, I'll come back tomorrow when you're in a better mood."

"Look, Willie, why is it that you never seem to have a previous engagement before you visit me?" snapped the mayor. "Birthday party? You could invite every friend you have and hold your big party in a telephone booth—with elbowroom to spare."

"Fiorello, what the hell have you got against me?" asked Ruotolo plaintively.

"Just this one thing, Willie," replied LaGuardia in Italian. "Your supply of talk greatly exceeds the demand!"

NOT THE WORDS BUT THE FEELING

The role played by the Italian-American community in the Civil War was a noble one. Scarcely a family did not have one or more sons or a father serving in the armed forces. In the Union Army, where they fought for the preservation of the nation, Americans of Italian ancestry boasted more heroes, in proportion to their numbers in the general population, than any other group in the United States—and more medal winners. Union forces included every rank from buck private to brigadier general.

Among the higher Union officers was the dashing and eloquent Brigadier General Francis Spinola,* who had been a New York State Senator at the outbreak of the war between the states. Twice wounded while leading a bayonet charge at the Battle of Wapping Heights, Spinola became a celebrated hero and was later elected to Congress.

During his tenure in Washington, D.C., Spinola was an enthusiastic supporter of Abraham Lincoln, and after the President's assassination, he lost few opportunities to pay tribute to his memory. As usual, his oratory would capture the rapt attention of his audiences. For example, speaking at the unveiling of a monument to the fallen martyr, he uttered the phrase:

"Abraham Lincoln—that mystic symbiosis of stone and star: that man of peace with sword of gentle diadem." The comment was loudly applauded.

Later, a fellow congressman approached him.

"Frank, what in the name of heaven does that mean?"

"I don't know," admitted Spinola, "but it gets 'em every time!"

---

*Two other Italian-Americans were promoted to the rank of brigadier general in the Union army: Enrico Fardella and Eduardo Ferrero.

Prodigal Son

Ben Biaggi enjoyed telling his few friends that he was an important man in Frank Costello's organization. The truth is that he hovered around the fringes, running errands for a few hirelings, and booked a few numbers when the regular runners were sick or on other business. A sniveling little man with a perpetually runny nose, he was hardly the man Costello would have selected for "important work."

The inevitable day came when Biaggi realized that he would never find the pot of gold in the American rainbow. Reluctantly, he decided to return to his place of birth in Sicily.

"That jerk left his hometown as a barefoot boy," commented Costello when informed of the departure, "and now he's returned for his shoes."

Italo-Americana Poetica

Mia Carlotta

Giuseppe, da barber, ees greata for m'ash,*
He gotta da bigga, da blacka moustache,
Good clo's an' good styla an' playnta good cash.

W'enevra Giuseppe ees walk on da street,
Da people dey talka, "How han'some! How neat!
How softa da handa, how smalla da feet!"

He leefta hees hat an' he shaka hees curls,
An' smila' weeth teetha so shiny like pearls;
Oh, manny da heart of da seely young girls
         He gotta.
      Yes, playnta he gotta—
        But notta
        Carlotta!

Giuseppe, da barber, he maka da eye,
An' lika da steam engine puffa an' sigh,
For catcha Carlotta w'en she ees go by.

Carlotta she walka weeth nose in da air,
An' look through Giuseppe weeth faraway stare,
As eef she no see dere ees somebody dere.

---

*From "masher"—one who flirts.

Giuseppe, da barber, he gotta da cash,
He gotta da clo's an' da bigga moustache,
He gotta da seely young girls for da mash,
But notta—
You bat my life, notta—
Carlotta.
I gotta!

—Thomas A. Daly (1871-1948)

Fleas Without End

Great fleas have little fleas upon their back to bite 'em.
And little fleas have lesser fleas, and so *ad infinitum*.
The great fleas themselves in turn have greater fleas to go on.
While these again have greater still, and greater still, and so on.

—*Rudolph Altrocchi* (1882-1955)

Viva the Insect Wives

I'm told that certain insect wives, as soon
As they've enjoyed their buzzing honeymoon,
Not merely fire their hubbies from the hive
Or nest or hole, but eat them up alive.

He never has a chance to criticize her,
For she'll soon snack him as an appetizer;
He cannot bore for long, his wedded kin—
She'll pack him, with the wedding cake, within.

Her widowhood advanced with every crunch,
She takes her bliss companionate with lunch;
While he, now freed from feminine abuses,
Devotes himself to draw her gastric juices.

No sexy problems fret this wifely bug;
She solves them all with her initial hug.
All wives will welcome such a dainty system
Of shaking mates as soon as they have kissed 'em!

—Rudolph Altrocchi

GENESIS

The cheese-mites asked how the cheese got there
    And warmly debated the matter;   '
The Catholics said it came from the air,
    The Protestants said from the platter.

                    —Rudolph Altrocchi

LIQUOR AND LONGEVITY

The horse and mule live 30 years
And nothing know of wines and beers.
The goat and sheep at 20 die
And never taste of Scotch or Rye.
The cow drinks water by the ton
And at 18 is mostly done.
The dog at 15 cashes in
Without the aid of rum or gin.
The cat in milk and water soaks
And then in 12 short years it croaks.
The modest, sober, bone-dry hen
Lays eggs for nogs, then dies at ten.
All animals are strictly dry:
They sinless live and swiftly die;
But sinful, ginful, rum-soaked men
Survive for three score years and ten.
And some of them, a very few,
Stay pickled till they're 92.

                    —Bianca Galelli (1838-1919)

DA BABY SHOW

Giovanni ees conceited man.
    He t'rowa heem out he'sa chest.
He'sa tink heemself an' all he own
    Eesa better dan da rest.

He'sa make beeg money in da mine,
    And buy greata house and lot;
And den dosa friends he used to know
    He'sa very quick forgot.

He'sa car eet ees a Rollsa Royce,
    And everywhere he go

Dat-a car do seexty mile an hour
    Joosta for make a show.

One day he stoppa my wife and say:
    "Eesa dat you leetle lad?"
She'sa answer, "*Si*," and den he'sa laugh.
"He'sa homely, dat'sa too bad.

"He'sa look like he'sa ol' man," he say.
    "He'sa gotta no shape, and fat."
And den he looka at me and smile:
    "Don'ta blame da keed for dat."

I'ma so mad I no can speak:
    I swallow me my tongue.
I weesh Giovanni heema dead:
    I'ma like to see heema hung

Now once a year in Villa Maria
    Dey'sa hol' a Baby Show.
Dey'sa gotta da band an'a everyteeng,
    An'a everybody go.

Giovanni senta hees baby dere,
    All-a perfume' up like a rose;
An' nurse-a maid by heem all-a da time
    To keepa heem clean da nose.

Mio bambino he'sa enter too:
    He have-a sooch pretty eyes;
But da joodges dey no see dat, an'a geev
    Giovanni's keed firsta prize.

But joosta when dey go to geev
    Dat baby boy da cup,
He'sa yell heem "Whoop!" an' keeck heesa toes,
    An' trow heesa breakfus' up.

I'ma say to Giovanni: "My *bambino*'s looks
    May not be besta in town;
But-a when he go to Baby Show
    He'sa keep hees breakfus' down."
               —Giorgio Manzoni (1901-75)

The Wreck of the Julie Plante

(A legend, recounted by an Italian sailor aboard the ill-fated French-Canadian vessel.)

Wan darka nighta on-a Lake St. Pierre,
　　Da win' she'sa blow, blow, blow,
An' da crew of da wooda scow *Giulia Planta*
　　Gotta scairt an-a run below—
For da win' she'sa blow like da hurricane
　　An' soon she'sa blow some more,
An' da scow bust-a up on Lake St. Pierre,
　　Wan mile-a from da shore.

Da *capitano*[1] he'sa walk on da fronta deck,
　　An'a walk on da hin' deck too—
He'sa call da crew from up-a da hole,
　　He'sa call da cook also.
Da cook she'sa name was Rosa,
　　She'sa come-a from Montreal,
Was-a chambermaid on a *legname*[2] barge,
　　On-a da Granda Lachine Canal.

Da win' she'sa blow froma nor'-eas'-wes'
　　Da sout'a win' she'sa blow too,
W'en Rosa cry, "*Caro mio capitano!*[3]
　　W'at I'ma gonna do?"
Da *capitano* he'sa t'row da beeg *ancora*,[4]
　　But stilla da scow she'sa dreef,
Da crew he no can pass to da shore-a,
　　Because he'sa lose heesa skeef.

Da night she'sa dark like'a wan black cat,
　　Da wave she'sa run high an'a fast,
W'en da *capitano* take-a da Rosa girl
　　An' he'sa tie her to da mast.
Den he'sa also take da life-a preserve,
　　An' he'sa joomp off on-a da lake,

[1]Captain.
[2]Lumber.
[3]My dear captain.
[4]Anchor.

An' he'sa say, "*Addio*,[1] mia Rosa dear,
　　I'ma gonna drown for you-a sake."

Nexta *giorno*,[2] w'en stilla early,
　　'Bout-a half-a past two-t'ree-four,
Da *capitano*, crew, an' da poor Rosie
　　Was-a corpses on-a da shore.
　　　For da win' she'sa blow lika da hurricane
An' da scow boosta op on-a Lake St. Pierre,
　　Wan mile-a from da shore.

Moral
Now all good wooda-scow sailorman
　　Take-a da warning from dat-a storm,
An'a marry some nice Italiana girl
　　An'a leev on wan beega farm.
For da win' can-a blow like-a da hurricane,
　　An'a eef she'sa blow some more,
You no gonna drown on Lake St. Pierre
　　So longa you stay on-a shore.

　　　　　　　　　　　　　—Giorgio Manzoni

Ballad of a Loving Man

Bruno Santini he'sa easy-mark,
　　Mosta ever'body know.
He'sa never lose he'sa temper wance:
　　He'sa too beeg an' slow.

Da leetle boys dey'sa come at-a night
　　An' steal-a hees eggs an' hen;
An' den come-a back w'en he'sa no look,
　　An' steal-a some more again.

Da keeds dey see he'sa no gonna run,
　　He'sa too slow an' beeg;
An' so wan keed he'sa steal hees cow,
　　Anodder steal-a hees peeg.

Bruno gotta heem pretty wife;

---

[1]Goodbye.
[2]Morning.

Her tongue eet ron heem wild.
She'sa no stop her talk-a wance,
  Seence she'sa small-a child.

Wan day a handsome-a neighbor-man
  He'sa steal dat-a wife away,
He'sa take her to United-a State
  An' keep-a her dere to stay.

But Bruno he no getta mad;
  He'sa smile an' say to me:
"Last-a Sonday, at-a da church, da priest
  Preach 'Love-a you enemy'

"An' so I'ma love dat man what-a steal
  My rake an' hoe an' plow.
I'ma even-a love a leetle beet
  Dat-a man what-a steal my cow.

"I'ma love dat man what-a steal my pipe:
  For heem my love eesa small.
But dat good-a man who'sa steal my wife,
  I'ma love heem best of all."

—Giorgio Manzoni

LAY OF ANCIENT ROME

Oh, the Roman was a rogue,
He erat, was, you bettum,
He ran his automobilis
And smoked his cigarettum,
He wore a diamond studibus,
An elegant cravattum,
A maxima-cum-laude shirt
And *such* a stylish hattum!

He loved the luscious hic-haec-hock
And bet on games and equi;
At times he won—at others, though
He got it in the nequi.
He winked (quo usque tandem?)
At puellas on the Forum
And sometimes even made
Those goo-goo oculorum!

He frequently was seen
At combats gladiatorial
And ate enough to feed
Ten boarders at Memorial;
He often went on sprees
And said, on starting homus:
"Hic labor—opus est,
Oh, where's my hic—hic—domus?"

Although he lived in Rome,
Of all the arts the middle,
He was (excuse the phrase),
A horrid individ'l—
Oh, what a diff'rent thing
Was the homo (dative, hominy),
Of faraway B.C.
From us of Anno Domini!

—T. R. Ybarra (1880-1959)

PASQUINADE—AMERICAN
STYLE

Soldiers who wish to be a hero
Are practically zero,
But those who wish to be civilians,
Madonn', they run into the millions!

Army latrine inscription found in
Palermo, Italy, during World War II

PETRILLO*

What musical numbers float over the breeze,
    Singing Trillo, Petrillo, Petrillo!
The sweet little woodwinds, in several keys,
    Play Trillo, Petrillo, Petrillo.

---

*James Caesar Petrillo, Chicago musician and bandleader. In 1915, he became president of the American Musicians Union (an independent union in Chicago). In 1940 he was elected president of the American Federation of Musicians, and held that post until 1958. He was known for his very tough bargaining efforts on behalf of his membership, often in defiance of public opinion. He is credited with advancing the cause of musicians more than any other single individual in the United States

But where are the rest of the musical crew,
And what shall the listening multitudes do
Who crave something more than the metrical coo
 Of Trillo,Petrillo, Petrillo?

Now I feel just as sure as I'm sure that my name
 Isn't Trillo, Petrillo, Petrillo,
That sweetness and light are not quite the whole game
 Of Trillo, Petrillo, Petrillo,
For still there are spaces in music for which
Some others than Trillo can set the right pitch,
Though I doubt if they ever can grow quite so rich
 As Trillo, Petrillo, Petrillo.

But as to the name that so limpidly flows
 In Trillo, Petrillo, Petrillo,
Now take it in full, and observe how it goes—
 It's Caesar, James Caesar Petrillo.
And Caesar, remember, is nothing but Czar,
And Czars, on the market, have dropped below par—
They drop very fast, and they drop very far,
 O Trillo, James Caesar Petrillo!

        —Gilbertulus (1865-?)

Biographical Index of Authors

ARIENTI, GIOVANNI SABADINO DEGLI (*c.* 1450-1500). A Bolognese, he was the author of the *Porretane,* one of those collections of short stories so numerous in Italian literature, which often furnished subjects to England's Elizabethan playwrights. In addition to the *Porretane* (so called because the stories were supposedly told by a holiday party at the baths of Porretta), Arienti wrote poems, treatises, and biographies. Very little is known about him, although he was quite popular during his lifetime.

ARIOSTO, LUDOVICO (1474-1533) He was born in Regio, near Modena (not to be confused with the Reggio in Calabria). An epic and lyric poet of acclaimed talent among his contemporaries, Ariosto studied law at Padua, but never had any taste for that profession and never practiced it. In 1503 he entered the service of Ippolito I, Cardinal d'Este, who employed him on various diplomatic missions, but left him enough leisure time to continue his studies. In 1516 he published his great poem, the *Orlando Furioso,* which had taken him ten years to write. This epic treatment of the Roland story, theoretically a sequel to the unfinished masterpiece of Boiardo, greatly influenced Shakespeare, Milton, and Byron. After the death of his patron in 1520, Ariosto transferred his services to the Cardinal's brother, Alfonso, Duke of Ferrara, who, in 1522, appointed him governor of the mountainous district of Garfagnana, near Lucca—a post he humorously described in his autobiography, *Satires.*

Never properly rewarded by his patrons, Ariosto returned to Ferrara in 1525, where he spent his time writing until his death at age fifty-nine.

ARLOTTO, PIOVANO (*See* Mainardi, Arlotto.)

BERNI, FRANCESCO (1490-1536) A humorous poet and priest, Berni was noted for his burlesque *capitoli,*—light, often ribald verses in

315

terza rima. He revised Boiardo's *Orlando Innamorato,* adding humorous and what he considered stylistic improvements. For many years, his rendering of Boiardo was the standard version, but has been generally discarded.

Berni spent the greater part of his life at the court of Rome, in the service of various cardinals and prelates. He was a principal writer of Italian humorous poetry, which has since retained the name of *Poesia Bernesca.* This style was introduced before him (*see* Pucci, Antonio), but Berni carried it to a degree of perfection which has rarely been equalled since. His satire was generally of the milder sort, but at times it rose to a bitter strain of invective.

"Berni's humor may be said to be untranslatable," wrote one observer, "for it depends on the genius of the Italian language, the constitution of the Italian mind, and the habits and associations of the Italian people."

Berni's language was choice Tuscan. One of the features of his humorous poems was his frequent licentious allusions and equivocations, though clothed in acceptable language, and well understood by his readers. However, he was not the only priest to employ what modern critics might term "immoral" references in jocular writings; Casti, among other clerics, used them liberally.

Three volumes of Berni's *Poesie Burlesche* were collected and published after his death. (His works were not called "Bernesca" during his lifetime.) He also wrote *La Catrina* and *Il Migliazzo,* once very popular plays written in the rustic dialect of Tuscany.

BOCCACCIO, GIOVANNI (1313-75) The Italian poet and storyteller was born in Paris, the illegitimate son of a Tuscan merchant and a French woman. His father, a native of Certaldo, brought him to that city as a child, and then to Naples, where he received his education in commerce and law. He escaped from that life at the age of twenty by promising his father to study canonical law. But that proved as uninteresting to him as business. His main pursuits at the University of Naples were Greek (then beginning to be studied in Italy), Latin, and mathematics. In 1336, at Naples, he fell in love with the Princess Maria d'Aquino, illegitimate daughter of King Robert, whom he was to immortalize in prose and verse as Fiametta. She is believed to have introduced him at court and to have urged him to write his early *Filocole,* a long vernacular prose romance.

In 1350, Boccaccio returned to Florence and there he met the illustrious poet Petrarch, who became a lifelong friend. Eleven years later, forsaking his old and roistering ways, he became a priest. He was commissioned by the Florentine Republic, in 1773, to give public readings, with comments, of his beloved Dante, but these lectures were often interrupted by illness. His later years were troubled by poor health and poverty, but he remained active until his death.

Boccaccio's *Decameron* was one of the earliest prose works written in Italian (rather than Latin), and is esteemed for its stylistic mastery. Written in his middle years (1348-53), the great secular classic is a collection of one hundred witty and occasionally licentious tales. It was with the introduction of this work that the courtly themes of medieval literature began to give way to the voice and mores of early modern society. Included in this present volume is one of the tales, "Calendrino and the Heliotrope," an innocuous but funny story that portrays the author's enjoyment of the practical joke.

Boccaccio's *Decameron,* which includes his more earthy anecdotes, may be found in most public libraries.

BRACCIOLINI, POGGIO (1380-1459) The noted Florentine humanist was born in Terranuova d'Arezzo. After serving eight successive Popes as apostolic secretary, he was appointed secretary and historian of the Republic of Florence in 1452. He died there, seven years later, and was laid to rest in the church of Santa Croce, burial place for many distinguished Italians.

A scholar of wide repute, Bracciolini wrote a number of serious books, all in Latin, including his *History of Florence.* But he is best remembered for his *Liber facetarium** (Book of Pleasantries), also written in Latin. The collection represents the waggish tales told by himself and his friends of the Roman Curia, related over a span of years covering his entire adult life. Although not as sophisticated or explicit as Boccaccio's *Decameron,* his *Liber facetarium* had wide appeal among the reading public, no doubt because the anecdotes were shorter, more to the point, and with a recognizable "punch line."

Bracciolini's style, which extracted the humor of an anecdote and discarded the moralizing, was sometimes bawdy by today's standards, but served to influence countless writers of the fifteenth and sixteenth centuries throughout Europe.

BUCINE, NICCOLO ANGELI DAL (*c.* 1450-1530) Born in Florence, he

---

*It was Cicero who gave the name *facetia* to the humorous anecdote, which differed from the exemplum of the day in that it did not pretend to illustrate a moral or religious point, but sought only to amuse. From *facetia,* we have the Italian noun *facezia,* and the English adjective "facetious."

was appointed professor of humanities in 1497. Very little else is known about him. However, he must have been a man of distinction to have occupied the same chair previously filled by the noted Angelo Poliziano, whose work is also represented in this volume.

Bucine's work was not published until almost 350 years after his death, when, in 1874, the manuscript was discovered by a researcher, Giovanni Papanti, in a Florentine library. Papanti subsequently published the work, titled, *Facezie e motti dei secoli XV e XVI* (Pleasantries and Witticisms of the XV and XVI Centuries).

Although Bucine seems to have been strongly influenced by Poliziano, his own style is pervasive and his collection of entertaining anecdotes is an excellent representation of what made the Renaissance man laugh.

CAPUANA, LUIGI (1839-1915) The Sicilian novelist and critic was born in Mineo, in the province of Catania. After writing a number of poems, he went to Florence in 1864, where, for two years, he was the drama critic for *La Nazione*. The best of his articles for that paper he later published under the title, *Teatro Italiano Contemporaneo*. In 1877, after an eight-year return to Mineo, he moved to Milan and resumed his literary labors, writing critical articles in the *Corriere delle Sera*, and also a number of sketches, afterward collected in volume form, under the title, *Profili di donne*.

Capuana's activities included teaching, scientific study, and politics. He wrote in almost every genre, but his reputation rests upon his naturalistic novels and criticisms. Among his best works are the short stories in *Paesane* (Peasant Women), the novel *Il marchese di Roccaverdina*, and his *Studi della letteratura contemporanea*. His stories for children include a charming collection of popular fairy tales, retold for youngsters under the title *C'era una volta* (Once upon a time). The specimens in this present volume are taken from a collection titled *Fumando*.

CASTELNUOVO, ENRICO (1839-1909) He was born in Florence and passed the greater part of his life in Venice. From 1853 to 1870 he was engaged in business, but in the latter year became editor of a political paper, *La Stampa*. He thereafter published several novels and collections of short stories, some of which appeared in *Perseveranza*. Some of the best known of them are: *La Casa Bianca*, *Vittorina*, *Lauretta*, *Il Professor Romualdo*, *Nuovi Racconti*, *Alla Finestra*, and *Sorrisi e Lacrime*, from which the sketch in this present volume was taken.

CASTI, GIOVANNI BATTISTA (1721-1803) Casti was an ecclesiastic and the author of many satirical works, of which the best known is

Gli Animali Parlanti (The Speaking Animals). He also wrote a sequence of a hundred amusing sonnets entitled, *I Tre Giuli*. But a much greater contribution to the humor of nations is his "opera buffa" of *Il Re Teodoro,* for which Paisiello wrote the music, and from which we have given an extract.

Casti wrote other comic operas, one of the best of which is *Catiline's Conspiracy,* in which the famous exordium of Cicero's oration, *Quousque tandem,* is rendered (and quite closely, too) into funny burlesque verse. Cicero is shown in his study, preparing his oration with infinite pains. When at length it is delivered, the interruptions by Catiline and others are faithfully reported:

> CICERO: *Fin a quando, o Catiline*
> *L'esterminio e la rovina*
> *Contro a noi meditarai?*
> *Fina a quando abuserai*
> *Con contesta impertinenza*
> *Della nostra pazienza?*
> *Va, rubello, evadi,espatria,*
> *Traditore, della patria,*
> *Conciofossecosache . . .*
> CATILINE: *Traditor rubello a me?*
> CICERO: *Conciofossecosache.*
> PEOPLE: *Si ch e' ver . . .*
> OTHERS: *No che non e!*
> CICERO: *Conciofossechosache. . . .*

This, in the vernacular, is pretty good fooling around, and the compound conjunction (a sort of double-barreled "forasmuch as" or "inasmuch as" so dear to the hearts of lawyers), to which the orator clings desperately when so rudely thrown off balance in his speech, comes off with the happiest effect. But that effect of the rapid rush of the double-rhymed octo-syllables would be quite lost in a translation. They have somewhat the same character as the clever and fluent verse of W. S. Gilbert's operettas.

In addition to his verse, Casti wrote prose novellas. It is said of him that he once boasted he could make anyone laugh with his prose. When a Corsican accepted the challenge, and could not even be made to smile, let alone laugh, Casti beat him with a stick, all the while yelling, *"Stupido bastardo!"*

CASTIGLIONE, BALDASSARE (1478-1529) He is considered a titan of the Italian Renaissance. Born in the province of Mantua, of a noble family, he was attached first to the court of Lodovico the Moor, in

Milan; afterward, in succession, at the courts of Francesco Gonzaga (Marquis of Mantua) and Guidobaldo (Duke of Urbino). He was a polished gentleman and brilliant scholar, "a perfect knight, second to none, either in intellect or culture." Charles V pronounced him "one of the best knights in the world."

The court of Urbino, at that time "a school of courtesy and valor, as well as learning," was a fitting home for such a man. But, for all his scholastic excellence, he took part in more than one military campaign, and was sent as ambassador to England, Milan, and Rome. He died in Toledo while on a diplomatic mission to the Emperor Charles V, it is said, of grief at the sack of Rome by the Spaniards under the Constable de Bourbon. Raphael painted his portrait in life; Guido Romano designed his tomb after his death; and Pietro Bembo wrote his epitaph.

Castiglione wrote many elegant and scholarly poems, both in Latin and Italian, but his fame as an author rests entirely on the book, *Il Cortigiano* (The Courtier). It consists of a series of dialogues in which the qualities necessary to the character of a perfect courtier are discussed. It seems to have been written in Mantua, during the short period of his happy wedded life. His wife, Ippolita Torelli, whom he married in 1516, died three years later.

The style of *Il Cortigiano* is courtly and polished, with a charming but deceptive simplicity in its stateliness. The subjects in his dialogues often relieve their grave philosophy with humorous anecdotes, a comparatively large number of which are given in this text. Some respected scholars state that Castiglione possessed a greater insight into the psychology of humor, a term not then known, of course, than any other person in history. Extravagant as the claim may be, it merits consideration.

CERLONE, FRANCESCO (1750-1800) He wrote a great many plays of the Commedia dell'Arte type (*see* Preface, page xi), but, surprisingly for so prolific an author, little seems to be known about him. His works were published in a collected form at Bologna in 1787, and again (in 22 volumes) at Naples, in 1825-29. Cerlone had a keen sense of humor and a rare gift for communicating his ideas. But, for reasons not readily apparent, a sample of his work had not been previously published in the United States until its inclusion in this present anthology.

COLLODI, CARLO (1826-90) The pseudonym of a brilliant Tuscan writer named Carlo Lorenzini, he is best known as the author of *Pinocchio*. First written in 1880 for the *Giornale dei bambini*, the story appeared in book form in 1883 and soon became one of the most widely read juvenile classics. It was first translated into English in 1882, and in 1940 *Pinocchio* was made into an animated film by Walt Disney.

Although a prolific journalist, Collodi was unable to save enough money for a comfortable retirement. He received only a few dollars for *Pinocchio*, and died in near poverty ten years after he created the puppet character.

CORAZZINI, NAPOLEONE (1840-1909) He was born in Tuscany, and early in life displayed a natural proclivity for humorous writing. Circumstances, however, prevented him from following it through, although one of his parodies, *The Duel*, was published and also performed on the stage. The play has been included in this present text.

Corazzini spent some time in the former Republic of Bosnia (now Yugoslavia) as a newspaper correspondent, but he was vastly underpaid for his efforts, and was forced to return to Italy. Forsaking literature for business, his writing career regrettably came to an end.

DA VINCI, LEONARDO (1452-1519) Painter, sculptor, architect, musician, engineer, and scientist, Leonardo was born near Vinci, a hill village in Tuscany. He was the illegitimate son of Ser Pietro d'Antonio, a Florentine notary public, and a peasant girl. In 1466 he moved to Florence where he became an apprentice in the workshop of Andrea del Verrocchio, and first met such artists as Botticelli, Ghirlandaio, and Lorenzo de' Credi.

In 1482 he went to Milan where he remained at the court of Lodovico Sforza for the next sixteen years. It was during this period that he composed the greater part of his *Trattato della pittura* and the extensive notebooks which attest the marvelous versatility and penetration of his genius. As court artist he also organized elaborate decorations and background sets for the frequent festivals of the court.

After the fall of Lodovico Sforza in 1499, Leonardo left Milan and, following brief sojourns in Mantua and Venice, he returned to Florence in 1500. Here he pursued his studies in theoretical mathematics and continued his anatomical studies at the hospital of Santa Maria Nuova. In 1502 he entered the service of Cesare Borgia as a military engineer. His commission took him to central Italy to study swamp reclamation projects in Piombino and to tour the cities of Romagna. At Urbino he met Niccolo Machiavelli, who was to become his close friend. During the following year, while back in Florence, he was commissioned to execute the fresco of the Battle of Anghiari. This work, like its companion piece assigned to Michelangelo, was never completed, and the cartoons were subsequently destroyed.

In 1513 Leonardo went to Rome, attracted by the patronage of the newly elected Medici Pope, Leo X, and his brother Giuliano. At a meeting between Pope Leo and Francis I, King of France, which Leonardo attended, the king invited him to his country. In any case, the great painter had been planning a move. In the service of the Pope, he had quickly perceived that the field was dominated by Michelangelo and Raphael. So, in 1516, following the death of Giuliano de' Medici, he left Rome and settled in France, at the castle of Cloux, near Amboise, where, three years later, he died at the age of sixty-seven.

Space does not permit a detailed acknowledgment of his numerous accomplishments. Most standard encyclopedias, and the many biographies written about him, accord him the recognition he so well merits. Leonardo da Vinci was a true Renaissance genius, as borne out by his tangible successes and his voluminous notebooks.

He was no collector of humorous anecdotes, but, interspersed among his notes were a number of amusing stories, some of which were original, and others which he retold in his own concise, witty style. Nearly all were "salacious," in keeping with the mores of that Renaissance period.

DE AMICIS, EDMONDO (1846-1908) Novelist and essayist, he was born in Oneglia (on the Genoa coast), and educated at Cuneo, Turin, and the Military College of Modena, which he left in 1865 with the rank of sub-lieutenant. In 1866 he participated in the Battle of Custozza, and in 1867 he edited a military periodical in Florence. After the Italian occupation of Rome in 1870 he left the army and devoted himself entirely to literature.

De Amicis seems to have been influenced by Manzoni (also represented in the present text), who encouraged and directed his early efforts. His "Sketches of Military Life," one of which is translated in this volume, first saw light in the pages of the *Italia Militare,* and were followed by a collection of short stories and novels, all sentimental but occasionally quite moving. *Cuore: an Italian Schoolboy's Journal,* which he wrote in 1886, was for many years one of the most widely read of all Italian books.

DOMENICHI, LUDOVICO (1515-64) Proofreader and historian, he is remembered as the chronicler of the largest collection of humorous anecdotes of the sixteenth century, and is still considered by scholars to be one of the most entertaining writers of the Italian Renaissance. True enough, he created few, if any, of the jokes and witticisms, but his stylistic editing and rewriting earned his works immense popularity in Italy and throughout Europe.

Born in Piacenza, Domenichi majored in law at the University of Pavia, but soon found the practice of that profession not to his liking. He thereafter devoted himself to a literary career. His first humorous work was inspired by a *"Bel Libretto"* (as he himself described it)—"a beautiful little book." The witty tales so captivated him that most of them were included in his *Facetie et motti*, published in Florence in 1548. The work also contained a section of jokes titled *Facetie raccolte per M. Ludovico Domenichi* (Pleasantries Collected by Messer Ludovico Domenichi). The book was poorly received.

Sixteen years later, however, in 1564, he published his great collection of anecdotes, comprising seven books. The edition, his third and last, was titled *Facetie, motti et burle di diversi signori et persone private* (Pleasantries, Witticisms and Jests of Several Gentlemen and Private Persons).

Domenichi, who had been imprisoned by the Inquisition for repeating a joke about the Church, was careful to censor or delete those stories which might again call the attention of Church officials to his writings. Nevertheless, his remarkably well-written works offer today's readers a keen insight as to what made the Renaissance man laugh. Ludovico Domenichi died a few months after his prodigious last volume was published.

FERRARI, PAOLO (1822-1901?) Ferrari was born in Modena. His father was an official in the service of the duke, and young Ferrari's liberal sentiments were a great disadvantage to him at the outset of his career. It is even said (with what truth we do not know) that certain influential friends and politicians induced the duke to interfere with the granting of his university degree, which, as a consequence was long delayed. But Ferrari's legal studies had been pursued with so little ardor as to suggest another reason for the action of the university authorities.

His first comedy was written in 1847 and was called *Bartolomeo the Shoemaker*, a title later changed to *Uncle Venanzio's Codicil*. After contending with many difficulties, he wrote his *Goldoni* in 1852 but had to wait two years before it was produced, when it became a signal success. Thereafter, and for as long as he lived, Ferrari gave to the world a long series of admirable works, chiefly comedies, and was considered by many Italians as their first comic dramatist. Some of his greatest successes were dramas drawn from Italian history, in which the characters—unlike those in the ordinary historical dramas—were literary rather than political. These would include *Dante a Verona, Parini e la Satıra,* and the above-mentioned *Goldoni e le sue Sedici Commedie.* He wrote either in prose or in a kind of rhymed alexandrines (a verse or line of poetry of twelve syllables) called *Versi Martelliani.*

Of his other dramas, the greatest are *Il Duello, Il Suicidio, Gli Uomini Serii, Cause ed effetti, Gli amici rivali, Il Ridicolo.* Nearly all of Ferrari's plays, some of which are still on the stage, received the government prize offered in Italy for dramatic excellence.

FERRIGNI, PIERO FRANCISCO LEOPOLDO COCCOLUTO (1836-1917) Better known as "Yorick," he was a Tuscan writer who was born in Leghorn, though of Neapolitan descent. He began his literary career in 1854 by contributing correspondence (or "letters to the editor") to some of the Florentine papers. In 1856, for the first time, he adopted the pseudonym which became so famous— from Hamlet, not from Sterne. Indeed, when he became acquainted with the latter's works, he felt as if he had been guilty of presumption, and thereafter signed his articles, "Yorick, son of Yorick."

A brilliant student, he earned his law degree at Siena in 1857, and made his mark as an attorney, though his reputation is principally journalistic and literary. Florentine newsboys could be heard crying his name to enhance the attractions of their wares. *"C'é l'articolo di Yorick!"* they would call to passersby; or more briefly, *"C'é Yorick!"* (There's Yorick in it!)

As with many other Italian writers of the day, he bore his part in the War of Liberation. He volunteered in 1859 when, for some time, he acted as Garibaldi's private secretary. In 1860 he was wounded at Milazzo. He was a writer of great ease and fluency, and not only in his own language: he also sent contributions in French to the *Indépendance Italienne,* and in German to the *Neue Freie Presse.*

Ferigni appears to be one of the few Italians who found literature profitable. Many of his newspaper articles have been collected in volume form and may be found in some Italian libraries, but most are, today, sold by dealers in out-of-print books. The specimens quoted in this volume are excerpted from *Cronache dei Bagni di Mare* and *Sue e giù per Firenze.*

GALELLI, BIANCA (1838-1919) A person of mystery, she was born in Palermo and brought to the United States by her parents when she was six years old. The family first settled in Troy, New York, then in Boston, and finally in New York City, where they remained.

Whether Bianca Galelli was a man or woman has not definitely been ascertained. She described herself as a "true hermaphrodite," and declared that she possessed the genital structures of *both* sexes. However, she considered herself to be predominatly female, probably because of her breast development, small though it was; but, on occasion, she assumed the dress and mannersisms of a male. In any event, her writings were masculine and she is believed to have had several female lovers.

Bianca Calelli is believed to have been a teacher in New York's public school system employed under the name Blanche Gales. She wrote only in English, although she was fluent in her Sicilian-accented Italian. Her sense of humor was chiefly directed to the foibles and weaknesses of humankind, but was never malicious, moralistic, or vulgar. She ceased writing for publication at about age sixty, and for the next twenty-one years until her death, she lived quietly on Elizabeth Street, in downtown New York's "Little Italy."

The data contained in this brief biographical sketch is based upon a poorly-printed paper, unearthed from the dusty bins of a rare-book dealer in Los Angeles. No other information pertaining to this obscure but talented writer has been found.

GHISLANZONI, ANTONIO (1824-91) He was the son of a doctor in Lecco, on the Lake of Como. His father first wished him to become a priest, and then sent him to study medicine at Pavia. The youth, however, had a fine baritone voice, and decided to study singing instead. He soon attracted the attention of several impressarios, and in 1846 obtained an engagement at the Lodi Theater.

In 1848 he embarked on a career in journalism, and published two papers in Milan. But the extreme political opinions he advocated quickly landed him in prison. After the return of the Austrians he was exiled, and after another imprisonment in Corsica, he continued his musical career there, and later in Paris, till he lost his voice in 1854, as the result of an attack of bronchitis. He then returned to Italy and literature. Ghislanzoni edited various papers, wrote a variety of articles, mostly of a comic character, and composed the *libretti* to several operas, of which the best known is Verdi's *Aida*.

He spent the rest of his life in a little house of his own in Lecco, where he edited, and in great part wrote, the *Revista Minima,* which afterward passed into the hands of his friend, Salvatore Farina.

GIUSTI, GIUSEPPE (1809-50) He was born at Monsummano, in Val di Nievole, Tuscany. He received his early education, between the ages of seven and twelve, from a priest; its results being, to use his own words, "sundry canings, not a shadow of Latin, a few glimmerings of history, discouragement, irritation, weariness, and an inward conviction that I was good for nothing." He then attended a school in Florence where he came under the care of more intelligent and sympathetic teachers, and began to awaken to the love of knowledge. He later went to the University of Pisa, but his untiring quest for wine, women, and song in the countryside about, and his resultant sleepiness during classes, did not make him the greatest scholar at the university.

In later life he lamented the idleness, womanizing, and desultory habits of his youthful years. Nevertheless, it is probable that in following his inclinations, during which time he picked up the songs and racy idioms of the Tuscan hills, he was laying the best possible foundation for his future career as a poet.

His health was never good, and he died at a comparatively young age, thus disappointing the brilliant expectations his friends had formed. What he did accomplish, however, is sufficient to secure him a place in the front rank of Italian literature. Besides his *Poems,* of which several collected editions have been published, his principal works are a collection of Tuscan proverbs and a *Discourse on the Life and Works of Giuseppe Parini,* the satirist.

Giusti's poems are peculiarly difficult to translate, because of their exceedingly idiomatic character, as well as, in many cases, their personal and political bearing. They have a directness, vigor, and pungency rare in the literature of Italy during the first half of the nineteenth century. His political satire sometimes rose to noble indignation, as in his fine poem, *A noi, larve d'Italia,* which has been translated into the English language at least twice.

As to Giusti's nonpolitical satire, it was always kindly and good-humored. That same spirit, coupled with an irrepressible cheerfulness and boyish love of fun, comes out in his letters—especially those to his intimate friend, Manzoni, who is also represented in this text.

GOZZI, COUNT GASPARO (1713-86) Elder brother of Carlo Gozzi, the dramatist, he was a Venetian and a member of a family that might be described as "a penniless laird wi' a lang pedigree." The *Memoirs of Count Carlo* contain a vivid account of the straits and turns (usually for the worse) to which they were put. Gasparo hoped to retrieve the family circumstances by his marriage with a learned lady given to poetry, Luisa Bergalli or Bargagli (who rejoiced in the academic title of Irminda Partenide). But her extravagance and shiftlessness only made matters worse, and he was forced to do anonymous hack work—translations from the French, and the like, for a living; or, as he called it, to wear himself out "in unknown writings with the daily sweat of one s brow, and drag works—either insignificant or vile—out of the Gallic idiom into the Italian language."

Notwithstanding his circumstances, he contrived to do a moderate amount of work which has lasted. His style is clear and pure, with the quality of coupling fancy with observation and wit with feeling. Gozzi published a paper called *L'Osservatore* on the plan of Addison's *Spectator*. He also wrote sonnets, satirical pieces and a great many "Bernesque" poems (*see* Francesco Berni).

GUICCIARDINI, LUDOVICO (1521-89) He was born in Florence, but spent most of his adult life in other European countries. Nephew of the eminent statesman and historian, Francesco Guicciardini, he was, however, quite unlike his uncle. He did write one historical book titled *Commentari (Commentaries)*, in the wake of his illustrious uncle's exhaustive *Storia d'Italia (History of Italy)*.

Ludovico Guicciardini is best known for his *Le ore di ricreatione (The Hours of Recreation)*, although much of it seems to be rewritten versions of the tales told by Castiglione and Domenichi (see those entries). However, he also recounted the stories of several lesser known humorists, written in his own terse but highly entertaining style. This innate ability to communicate his ideas in so vivid and understandable a manner, along with his carefully deleted references to the Church and political establishment which might cause them offense, made his book immediately acceptable and popular, unopposed as it was by the censors of either faction.

Hours of Recreation has been reprinted many times in the original Italian and in several other Western languages, the foreign translations occurring during Guicciardini's lifetime. He died in Antwerp at the age of sixty-eight, a wealthy and honored man.

LEOPARDI, GIACOMO (1798-1837) Born in Recanti, in the Duchy of Urbino, Leopardi suffered all his life from poor health and real or fancied uncongenial surroundings. He was heavily handicapped in the race of life, being hunchbacked as well as constitutionally diseased. Thus, the pessimistic doctrines which he imbibed from Pietro Giordani fell on fertile soil. His father was rich and possessed an excellent library, and though he refused to allow Giacomo to go to school, the boy threw himself into his studies at home with so much ardor that at fifteen he was a brilliant classical scholar, and wrote an ode in Greek which competent critics believed to be ancient. Yet he remained unknown, thwarted by his father's harshness in all his efforts to obtain a wider culture and more literary opportunities.

At last he was able to escape from his hated home to Rome,

where he enjoyed the society of literary men, but could not succeed, as he had hoped, in obtaining a professorship. Embittered and disgusted with the world, he then retired to Milan where he lived in the house of a publisher and prepared his poems for the press. Here, again, he was unable to escape from the misery which pursued him, and his health became progressively worse. At last, in the autumn of 1831, he took his last journey—to Naples, where Antonio Ranieri, his devoted and long-time friend, received him into his house. There, worn out by dropsy and tuberculosis, he died.

Of his philosophical works, and his gloomy though splendid verse, it is not the place or time to speak. I have included him in this collection because of some of his dialogues, which are masterpieces of a subtle irony which has the air of simplicity and bites to the bone. One cannot imagine that Leopardi ever laughed, but no one could read the "First Hour and the Sun," and think him lacking in humor.

LOTTI, CARLO (1832-1915?) An obscure but very talented playwright and poet, Lotti was born in Sicily, but was brought to Rome as a boy and attended school there. Lotti studied medicine and might have lived a life of moderate comfort had he practiced that profession; but for him there was only one outlet for his creative gift—writing. His failure to earn a living from his literary output does not, however, detract from his ability, which was indeed noteworthy. Later, his frustrations could be easily detected in his satirical and often ironic essays, plays, and anecdotes dealing with publishers, as in "Postmortem Concern for a Lost Explorer," excerpted in this book from the play, *Corvi*.

Surprisingly enough, Carlo Lotti was not a man given to verbal jokes. Friends have described him as a rather dour person, often unsmiling and taciturn. But when he put his thoughts to paper, his humor, to quote one critic of the day, "shone like polished silver."

MACHIAVELLI, NICCOLO (1469-1527) He is included in this volume because of his comedy of *La Mandragola*, of which a scene is given, and a few brief anecdotes told about him by contemporaries. But these, of course, are not the works by which he is best known in history. Macaulay's well-known essay gives a very good summary of his political and literary labors.

Machiavelli first participated in public affairs in 1494. In 1498 he was elected Secretary to the Florentine Republic, an office from which he resigned in 1512, after the return of the Medici. Some time later, being suspected of a conspiracy against the Medici, he was imprisoned and put to the torture, under which he nearly died. He was included in the amnesty proclaimed by Giovanni de Medici, when raised to the Papacy under the title of Leo X.

Although restored to liberty, he could take no part in politics, and finding himself unable to serve Florence, and condemned to a hateful inaction, he retired to his country house, where he wrote the greater part of his works. The last of these was the *History of Florence*, written at the request of Pope Clement VII, and completed in 1525. In 1519 Leo X consulted him about reforming the government of Florence, but his advice was not followed. In 1526, when the Constable Bourbon began to threaten Tuscany and Rome, Clement VII again consulted Machiavelli and entrusted him with the fortification of Florence and with the precautions to be taken for the safety of Rome. But these precautions came too late. The Pope was taken prisoner, and the Medici once more were driven from Florence. Machiavelli, now considered to be a partisan of that family, became something of a recluse, and, in the colorful literature of earlier times, is said to have "died shortly thereafter of grief and disappointment."

Machiavelli, who has often been maligned for his realistic outlook on various aspects of life, numbered among his chief works, besides the *History*, such books as *The Prince, Art of War*, and the *Discourses on the First Decade of Livy*. Moreover, he wrote two or three comedies and a witty novella titled *Belphegor*. It relates how one of the devils, taking the form of a man, came to earth in order to try the experiment of matrimony, but was so wretched in his married life that, after a short trial, he preferred returning to hell. It is said that Machiavelli's experiences in his own home gave point to his descriptions of Madonna Onesta's folly and extravagance.

The *Mandragola*, in spite of Macaulay's high praise, offers scarcely anything adapted for quotation in this text. The play is admirably constructed, but the story is one which is simply not suited to our needs. We have been forced to confine ourselves to a soliloquy of Fra Timoteo's and one of the lyrical interludes between the acts which has the merit of brevity in addition to its humor. A few random sayings of Machiavelli's are also included.

MAINARDI, ARLOTTO (1396-1484) A Florentine, he was born in nearby San Cresci a Maciuoli, where he became a parish priest. Mainardi, usually referred to as *Piovano* (Priest) Arlotto, was one of the few actual creators of most of the humor attributed to him, although some of his witty tales also appeared in the folk humor of medieval Italy.

Piovano Arlotto, a wise and compassionate man, was held in high esteem and affection by all who knew him, from the local peasants and craftsmen who attended his church, to the powerful Medici family and the artistic and intellectual colony who comprised the Medici's intimates and peers. Indeed, because of his several voyages as ship chaplain to western European ports and a number of cities along the Italian peninsula, his fame as a man of wisdom as well as wit went far beyond the confines ordinarily associated with that of a simple parish priest. He was welcomed at many Italian courts, but it seems that he never lost his appeal among the common people—the villagers and farmers whom he apparently loved in return.

Arlotto did not write down the jokes, witty sayings, and humorous anecdotes which won him such renown. Just as Johnson had his Boswell, so Arlotto had his own biographer—a dedicated man whose name, unfortunately, has not been handed down to us. This anonymous disciple carefully noted Arlotto's comments during the priest's lifetime, and continued to add to his manuscript after Arlotto died. The results were published thirty years after *Piovano* Arlotto's death, and titled *Motti e facezie del Piovano Arlotto*. The first edition was published around 1515, and reveals a fun-loving but highly intelligent man of good will who spoke in the Tuscan dialect of the day.

MANZONI, ALESSANDRO (1784-1873) Born in Milan, he was one of the leaders of the Romantic Movement in Italy, and the founder, in that country, of the historical novel in the style of Scott. The *Promessi Sposi*, published in 1827 (from which we have quoted a scene or two), has probably been translated into every European language. Less widely known are his dramas, *Adelchi* and *Il Conte di Carmagnola*, and his *Odes* (1815)—the most famous of which is that of the death of Napoleon, *Il Cinque Maggio*.

Manzoni was followed in the department of historical fiction by his son-in-law, d'Azeglio, and by Grossi, Guerrazzi, Rosini, Ademollo, and others. Though at first sight *I Promessi Sposi* might seem anything but a humorous work, there are scenes equal in this respect to some of the best in Scott's novels. That of the attempted irregular marriage (which we have chosen for quotation) is especially good, and the character of Don Abbondio is comically conceived throughout.

PARABOSCO, GIROLAMO (1507-57) Born in Piacenza, he was a writer of rhyme and prose comedies. Moreover, he was esteemed as one of the best musicians of his time. For a number of years Parabosco served as organist and choirmaster at Saint Mark's, in Venice. But he is best known for his *I Diporti*, a collection of stories after the model of Boccaccio's *Decameron*, supposedly told by a hunting party weatherbound on an island in the Venetian lagoon.

PENANTI, FILIPPO (1776-1837) Born in Ronta, district of Mugello, Tuscany, he studied law at Pisa, but afterward devoted himself entirely to literature. Penanti went abroad in 1799, and after visiting France, Spain, and Holland, obtained a position as librettist with the Italian Opera Company in London. When returning to Italy by sea, he was taken prisoner by Algerian pirates, but liberated through the intervention of the English consul.

Penanti then went to Florence, and published his works: *Il Poeta di Teatro, Prose e Versi, Viaggio in Algeria,* in which it may be said that although he made unnecessarily excessive use of foreign (non-Italian) expressions, his work was widely acclaimed. This acceptance was undoubtedly due to his ease and fluency, and his vivid and racy way of expressing himself.

His *Il Poeta di Teatro* is a lively and amusing poem descriptive of the miseries endured by a poet of small means. It is thoroughly good-humored, and has no "Grub Street bitterness" about it. We have selected a few passages for this text.

POLIZIANO, ANGELO (1454-94) Poet and humanist, his surname derives from his birthplace, Montepulciano, or *Mons Politianus,* in Latin. At the age of ten, his widowed mother sent him to a relative in Florence where he was given a classical education, completed under the patronage of Lorenzo de' Medici.

Although of middle-class origin, he became the close companion of Lorenzo, and was entrusted with the tutoring of Lorenzo's son, Piero. For Lorenzo he translated much of the *Iliad* into Latin, and also taught classics at the Medici's school, or university.

Poliziano was one of the most learned scholars of his century, and became a leader, with Lorenzo, in the use of the Tuscan vernacular in poetry. His verse, tranquil and beautiful, shows the growing emphasis on style and form. Among his poetic works are the charming *Stanze per la giostra,* celebrating the jousting prowess of Lorenzo's brother, Giuliano; *Orfeo,* a captivating poetical version of the legend of Orpheus and Eurydice, one of the earliest plays in the Italian language, and many lyrics in both Latin and Italian.

A creative writer rather than a collector, Poliziano was the author of an unpublished book of humorous anecdotes, comprising more than four hundred of the stories he had heard while in the employ of the Medici household. It was later titled *Bel Libretto (Beautiful Little Book)* by Ludovico Domenichi (see separate entry), who published it, or a close version, under his own name.

Poliziano continued as a teacher of Latin and Greek letters at the Medici university until his death at the early age of forty.

PRATESI, MARIO (1842-1915?) He was born in Santafiora, in the district ot Monte Amiata. At eighteen he became a clerk in a government office and remained at this distasteful (to him) employment till 1864, when he returned to his studies. In 1872 he obtained an appointment as lecturer on Italian literature at the Pavia Technical Institute, then a similar post at Viterbo, and from there to Terni.

Most of his stories, since collected in volume form, first appeared in the *Nuova Antologia*. He also wrote excellent poetry. Many of his short works were contributed to the *Diritto*, the *Rassegna Settimanale*, and the *Nazione* (Florence).

Pratesi was clearly at his best when describing the scenery of his native mountains. Monte Amiata, during Pratesi's day, was the locale of the strange religious revival led by the insane peasant-preacher, David Lazzaretti, who was shot down by the police in August 1878. It was a wild, lonely region, lying between the river Ombrone and the Roman border—a land of craggy peaks and dark glens, inhabited by simple, serious-minded people with a touch of gloomy mysticism in their character, perhaps due to their Etruscan ancestry. The immediate neighborhood of the district where the tragedy occurred is admirably described in *Sovana*.

Pratesi was intensely sympathetic in his manner of depicting life. He did not aim at an "objectivity" which seems to glory in appearing cold and heartless; but neither did he dwell unnecessarily on his pathetic scenes. He related them with grim brevity, leaving them to produce their own effect. Despite his somber outlook on life, he did have an eye for the ludicrous, although it did not predominate in his view of existence. He never laughed, according to one biographer, but he would often smile quietly, and sometimes grimly. His forte was irony, at which he excelled.

PUCCI, ANTONIO (1312-75) The son of a bell-founder, Pucci was a poet, although he kept a shop. He wrote in that easy, sparkling vein which, a century later, was so abundant in Francesco Berni (see entry), as to make Berni seem like the creator of a new style of poetry.

Pucci's date of death is usually given as 1375. However, according to Ambrosoli's *Manual of Italian Literature*, a nineteenth-century publication, Pucci died in Florence, his native city, "some time after 1375."

The sonnet, *A Poet Complains of Unreasonable Friends*, which introduces this volume, is a good example of his humor. Here he describes the indignities to which a poet is subject at the hands of his friends—a specimen of what the Italians call *poesia bernesca*, after Berni. This kind of sonnet is known as a *sonetto a coda*, or "with a tail." It is much used in humorous and satirical writing, as a kind of style in which more license is allowed metrically, when the idea cannot be brought within the limits of the strict sonnet form. The "tail" may be lengthened at the writer's pleasure, but always in sets of three lines—one short and two long—and sometimes attains a greater length than the original sonnet.

REDI, FRANCESCO (1626-98) Born in Arezzo, Tuscany, Redi was a jovial physician, no less famed for his wit than for his learning and medical skill. He studied philosophy and medicine at the University of Pisa, and was then invited to Rome by the princes of the House of Colonna, in whose palace he lectured in rhetoric. He later became court physician to the Grand Dukes of Tuscany. During the last years of his life he was afflicted with epilepsy, and retired to Pisa, which he believed was a healthier place than Florence.

Redi's published works consist of poems, scientific treatises, and a large collection of letters which show his wide learning, his shrewd sense, and the merry, genial spirit which could see the funny side of his own troubles.

SACCHETTI, FRANCO (c. 1335- c. 1400) He was a Florentine, about contemporary with Chaucer. He was brought up to engage in commerce, but later devoted himself to literature, and took a considerable part in politics, being sent on several ambassadorial missions by the Florentine Republic. On one of those missions he was plundered at sea by Pisan warships, and, a short time later, his property near Florence was laid waste in the war with Gian Galeazzo Visconte. The date of his death is uncertain, but it probably occurred during the first few years of the fifteenth century.

Sacchetti wrote sonnets, *canzoni*, madrigals, and other poetry, but his best known works are his *novelle* or short stories. There were originally 300 of them, but we only possess 258, the remainder having long since been lost. They are not fitted into any framework, like that of Boccaccio's *Decameron*. The best of them are of a humorous character; and the style is simpler and more colloquial than Boccaccio's.

TASSONI, ALESSANDRO (1565-1635) He was a member of a noble family, but early in his youth was left an orphan, and his very moderate patrimony was further diminished by lawsuits and by the dishonesty of his guardians. Born in Modena, the greater part of his life was spent at court, beginning his career by entering the service of Cardinal Ascanio Colonna in Rome, and ending it at the Ducal Court of Modena. He was, like so many Italians of that period, a skilled politician as well as a finished scholar.

His principle works belong to the departments of reflective philosophy and literary criticism. For a number of years he was engaged in an acrimonious controversy in which the chief bones of contention were the poetry of Petrarch and the philosophy of Aristotle. He attacked both these idols of the age unsparingly.

Tassoni is best known to posterity for his heroico-comic poem of *La Secchia Rapita (The Stolen Bucket)*, said to have been written in 1611. It is based on the tradition that, during a war between Modena and Bologna, the Modenese forces (in 1325) carried off a wooden bucket from a public well in the hostile city. The trophy was hung in the Cathedral of Modena, and remained there as a witness to the truth of the story—which, as a matter of history is somewhat doubtful. In any case, it is genuine burlesque, and very good burlesque, too; the absurdity being heightened by Tassoni's high sense of humor.

Tassoni was, according to an Italian biographer, "of a lively and grotesque fancy, of a cheerful disposition, and fond of jesting, so much so that he could not refrain from jokes even in his will."

TORELLI, ACHILLE (1844-1917) A dramatic author, he was born in Naples although he is said to have been of Albanian descent. His first success was the comedy, *After Death*, written when he was only seventeen years old. It was acted in Naples and then at Turin. This was followed by several comedies, most of which were successful. *La Verita*, from which the scene given in this volume is extracted, was also acted in Naples, and, further, in Milan and Turin in 1865.

Torelli volunteered in the Italian army in the campaign of 1866, and was out of action for several months as the result of a fall from his horse at Custozza. Upon his release from military service, he resumed writing, and produced a long list of plays, both dramas and comedies, of which perhaps the best is *Triste Realta* (1871), which won the applause of the veteran Manzoni (see entry).

VASARI, GIORGIO (1512-74) Writer, goldsmith, and painter, Vasari was born in Arezzo, and studied drawing under Michelangelo, Andrea del Sarto, and others. Between 1527 and 1529, driven by necessity and having several relations in need of help, he worked as a goldsmith in Florence, but later returned to painting. However, he was rather a writer on art than an artist.

Vasari was the author of several works on painting and architecture, of an autobiography, and, above all, of the celebrated *Lives of Famous Painters*. The anecdotes quoted in that volume were traditionally current in Vasari's time, and most had already been recorded by Franco Sacchetti (see entry).

VERGA, GIOVANNI (1840-1922) Born in Catania, Sicily, he wrote *Storia d'una Capinera, Eva, Nedda, Eros, Togre Reale, Primavera.* He also produced two masterly collections of stories and sketches from Sicilian life titled, *Vita dei Campi* and *Novelle Rusticane,* and a continued story, *I Malavoglia.*

A Neapolitan journal described him as "thin and pale . . . with iron-gray hair and moustache. His lips are thin, chin somewhat too long, the mouth retreating, the nose straight, the forehead spacious. He is not handsome, but has a noble face, a little like that of Dante. His appearance is that of a man of cold temperament. Some of his speeches—some pages in his books—are those of a cold skeptic. . . . He is not by any means a sentimental man. Sentimentalism in others always contracts his lips in a fleeting, ironical smile."

It is strange that a man of that description could write with such high, sometimes outlandish humor as he did in his *War of the Saints,* selected for inclusion in this volume. Yet, this dour, aloof writer possessed a deep reservoir of ironic wit that was also manifest in his other writings.

YORICK Pseudonym for Piero F. L. C. Ferrigni. (See entry.)

General Index